Putting Psychology in its Place

The second edition of *Putting Psychology in its Place* builds on the first to introduce the history of psychology and place the discipline within a historical context. It aims to answer questions about the role of psychology in modern society, by critically examining issues such as how psychology developed, why psychoanalysis had such an impact and how the discipline has changed to deal with contemporary social issues such as religion, race and gender.

In this second edition, the text has been restructured and contains additional chapters on memory, personality, religion, language and applied psychology. The book has a new user-friendly format with chapter summaries, further reading sections and glossary definitions.

Putting Psychology in its Place is imaginatively written and accessible to all. It will be an invaluable introductory text for students of the history of psychology and of interest to all studying psychology or the history of science.

Putting Psychology in its Place

A Critical Historical Overview

Second edition

Graham Richards

Routledge
Taylor & Francis Group

LONDON AND NEW YORK

First published 2002
by Psychology Press
27 Church Rd, E. Sussex
Hove, BN3 2FA

Simultaneously published
in the USA and Canada
by Taylor & Francis Inc
270 Madison Avenue, New York
NY 10016

Reprinted 2004 and 2007

*Routledge is an imprint of the
Taylor & Francis Group
an informa business
Psychology Press is part of the
Taylor & Francis Group
an informa business*

© 2002 Psychology Press

Typeset in Century Old Style by
Graphicraft Limited, Hong Kong
Printed and bound in Great
Britain by TJ International Ltd,
Padstow, Cornwall

This publication has been produced with paper manufactured to
strict environmental standards and
with pulp derived from sustainable forests.

*British Library Cataloguing in
Publication Data*
A catalogue record for this book
is available from the British
Library

ISBN 978-1-84169-233-3 (hbk)
      978-1-84169-234-0 (pbk)

Paperback cover design by
Lisa Dynan.

... every human being is making history all the time. We live in history as we live in air and we cannot escape it.

C.V. Wedgwood

And if the world were black or white entirely
And all the charts were plain
Instead of a mad weir of tigerish waters,
A prism of delight and pain,
We might be surer where we wished to go
Or again we might be merely
Bored but in brute reality there is no
Road that is right entirely.

Louis MacNeice

This is still just for Maura

Contents

CONTENTS

Illustrations

Figures

Tables

ILLUSTRATIONS

Preface to Second Edition

This second edition differs from the first primarily in being somewhat longer. It still does not purport to offer a comprehensive history of Psychology and large swathes of Psychological work have perforce gone unmentioned. The aim of the book, as before, is to help readers explore and think about Psychology's place (or places) within its host societies, adopting a broadly critical approach. The added chapters on Applied Psychology, Psychology and Religion, Language, Memory, and Personality all have direct bearings on this. I have also tinkered with and updated much of the previous text, even if only slightly in many cases, as well as correcting errors. The chapters have now been thematically grouped in order to impose some overall structure. Each group may be seen as representing a different angle from which Psychology can be viewed in order to triangulate its 'place'. Thus we can consider Psychological theories themselves (Part One, in which I have also placed an Introduction and some basic history on Psychology's founding phase), specific topics which Psychologists have tackled (Part Two), how it has related to particular categories of 'subjects' (Part Three), and the nature of its engagements with wider cultural and social issues (Part Five). Part Four looks at two underlying, pervasive topics that cannot be neatly categorised under these: measurement and language. Each of these perspectives raises its own kinds of question, and draws our attention to matters which the others can overlook.

As well as expanding the content I have tried to render the book more accessible to students who are new to Psychology by adding a glossary, a timeline and chapter summaries plus some illustrations and tables. It should nonetheless be stressed that the underlying object of the exercise is to provoke readers, especially beginning students, into thinking about the nature of Psychology rather than to provide them with a neatly packaged, cut-and-dried account of what that nature is (although some provisional conclusions are drawn in the Epilogue). It might be argued that this task is best left for the more advanced levels of study. The present author begs to differ, believing that some kind of critical overview and an awareness of basic theoretical and conceptual problems cannot be acquired too early if the student is to engage with Psychology intelligently, proactively and creatively. Hopefully this text will aid them in doing so.

Some brief further comment on the general orientation of this book is necessary. There is, I must concede, an underlying tension between what may be called 'revolutionary' and 'conciliatory' objectives. The more passionately radical may feel I am offering only a harmless, low-fat version of the critical approach, the more passionately orthodox that I am disingenuously presenting a Trojan horse. The tension is in fact quite genuine: I have no wish to play alpha-male stag horn-locking games and am happy to concede that – barring evidence to the contrary – colleagues of most persuasions are acting in good faith (although a few persuasions are themselves sufficient evidence that they are not). Manichean confrontations no longer interest me. Nonetheless I do believe that Psychology needs to confront the growing volume of historical-cum-philosophical critiques of its character. These concern such things as its status as an orthodox scientific project, its power allegiances, and its own psychological roles vis-à-vis the populations among, and upon, whom it has been practised. The book is meant as a starting point for considering such matters, not an end point. Nonetheless, the tension remains unresolved. Whether that is a virtue or weakness, stimulating or ennervating, others must judge. In further mitigation, however, it might be pleaded that these issues have been receiving serious scholarly attention for barely two decades, and initially only fitfully. We thus have a considerable way to go before genuine historical scholarship is of sufficient depth and weight to permit an entirely confident resolution of the tension. In that sense this work can only represent 'critical history of Psychology in progress'.

Since the early 1990s numerous sophisticated historical treatments of various topics have appeared, indeed History of Psychology scholarship is currently enjoying a highly creative phase. The 2001 centenary of the British Psychological Society has also improved the British academic climate. The next tasks are to establish a regular place for History of Psychology in the undergraduate curriculum, and a clearer consensus on its agenda as an active and autonomous sub-discipline. The somewhat downbeat undertone of the original Preface is thus no longer entirely operative.

To those whose support was previously acknowledged I must add Jacob Belzen, Geoff Bunn, John Burnham, Alan Collins, Judy David, Pippa Dell, Maarten Derksen, Trudy DeHue, Douwe Draaisma, Rob Farr, Mike Sokal, Hendrika Vande Kemp, Paul Whittle and Andrew Winston. I am also grateful to Staffordshire University for enabling me to establish the Centre for the History of Psychology there in 1998, and for the support of the British Psychological Society in that endeavour. Thanks also to George Singer who took many of the book-illustration photographs (as credited).

Lastly, without doing the equivalent of an Oscar speech, love and thanks to all my friends, who made their feelings so clear at my 60th birthday party – and again, of course, to Maura.

Tunbridge Wells, October 2001

Preface

The nature and aims of this book require a brief explanation. It is intended as a critical introductory overview of Psychology from a historical perspective. Some such overview is, I believe, necessary for anybody venturing into the discipline, particularly as A-level or undergraduate students. As numerous histories of Psychology are available, some statement of how this differs is in order. First, it seeks to use history as a basis for understanding the nature of Psychology as a cultural and intellectual phenomenon characteristic of late nineteenth and twentieth century western cultures. Second, it attempts to incorporate some insights and approaches of recent history of science which have radically altered how the tasks and issues facing historians of science are conceptualised. In both respects it differs in orientation from histories published prior to the mid-1980s (see Chapter 1).

In a relatively brief text of this kind one difficulty is striking a balance between the conflicting needs to provide both factual information and broad interpretation of what this historical data mean. I have striven to do so, although perhaps more by see-sawing than stasis.

A statement of my general theoretical position was published in 1989 as *On Psychological Language and the Physiomorphic Basis of Human Nature*. While I would now couch some of this differently, my position is essentially unchanged. I have, however, become increasingly aware of the centrality of the 'reflexivity issue', of which more in due course.

This book largely derives from undergraduate courses on the history of Psychology which I have taught for many years. The approach taken evolved considerably over time. A major influence was through personal contacts made during the 1980s with those in the wider history of science field to whom I am particularly indebted. My three years as Chair of the British Psychological Society's History and Philosophy Section (1991–1994) were invaluable in numerous respects, including the moral support and intellectual stimulation of such stalwarts as Alan Costall, Clare Crellin, Jim Good, Sandie Lovie, Ullin Place, Carol Sherrard, John Soyland, Arthur Still, Elizabeth Valentine and Norman Wetherick. Also within the history of Psychology field my exchanges with Kurt Danziger, David Leary, Jill Morawski, Roger Smith and Robert Wozniak have been helpful in numerous ways. Mary and Geoff Midgley, my undergraduate mentors in the lamentably deceased Philosophy department of the University of Newcastle upon Tyne, have continued

to provide moral support and an example of intellectual integrity of more importance to me than they probably appreciate. Special thanks is due to the constant
backing of John Radford, who first set me to teaching in this field, as well as
to Marian Pitts and David Jary (Staffordshire University), John Hodge and Geoff
Cantor (Leeds University) and Keith Sumner (Guildhall University), who have
enabled me to continue pursuing my career in this field following early retirement
from what was, from my standpoint, fast becoming an academic sinking ship. My
many students over the years have also played their part in helping me hone my
ideas and I am ever-grateful to them.

Finally, any credit must be shared with Maura whose loving support has
never flagged.

Everything wrong with this book is my own fault – well almost.

Part one

ORIGINS AND THEORIES

In this Part we will first consider the nature of the sub-discipline of History of Psychology and why it is important. Chapters 2–4 then provide an introductory sketch of how and why Psychology emerged as a discipline in the late nineteenth century. Chapters 5–7 look at three major Psychological theories (or theoretical orientations); the approach adopted in these is not to provide detailed expositions of the doctrines but rather, in a critical fashion, to indicate their distinctive features and character, why they arose when they did and the factors affecting their fates. In this way we begin to see how Psychological theories, while striving to be orthodox scientific theories, are also products of specific cultural contexts and bear the hallmarks of the settings in which they originated.

Chapter 1

Introduction: Psychology and History

- Psychology and history
- The nature of history of Psychology
- The reflexive character of Psychology
- The need for history of Psychology
- The problem of psychological language

The first thing likely to strike any new student of Psychology is probably its sheer diversity. Its sub-disciplines range from Physiological Psychology to Social Psychology, and the approaches adopted from experimental to philosophical. Also puzzling is that apparently near-synonymous titles are given to different subjects, such as 'learning' and 'memory', 'reasoning' and 'intelligence'. Nor are the discipline's boundaries very rational: the dances of honey bees belong in Comparative Psychology, but what about human dancing? That is the business of anthropologists – who also study kinship while psychologists study parenting. More disturbingly, this diversity extends to the very goals and 'projects' of the discipline. Psychologists are far from agreed that their task is 'to predict and control behaviour'; many see it in rather opposite terms as enabling people to understand themselves sufficiently well that they can, among other things, resist attempts to predict and control them. And pondering on how this chaotic situation arose are historians of Psychology.

These latter are in an unusual situation. Most historians of science see themselves as belonging to a discipline called History of Science, and would not claim to be contributing directly to the disciplines they study; many of Psychology's historians, by contrast, see themselves as also being psychologists. Prior to about 1980 they rarely had close dealings with other historians of science, though nowadays they tend to have a foot in each camp. Historians of Psychology adopt this position because they believe their work bears directly on current disciplinary concerns, shedding light on a variety of crucial theoretical issues pertaining to that diversity mentioned at the outset, to the status of the discipline itself and to its relationship with its subject matter – referred to throughout this work as 'psychology' (and 'psychological') with a lower-case 'p', reserving 'Psychology' (and 'Psychological') for the discipline itself.

Historians of Psychology thus see themselves as representing a self-reflecting facet of Psychology, as the discipline's introspectors, doing what is sometimes referred to as 'metapsychology'. Students often find it hard to grasp the point of this or see its relevance to their aspirations to become clinical, educational or industrial psychologists. It is therefore necessary to justify the claim that it *is* highly relevant for anyone wishing to understand Psychology (the discipline) and also sheds light on psychology (the subject matter).

We did not cast ourselves in this role until fairly recently. Until the 1970s most histories of Psychology, of which there are many, were written with rather different intentions. (Such histories in fact began appearing soon after Psychology acquired a formal academic identity in the 1880s and 1890s.) One major reason for this is that Psychology long felt pressurised, especially in English-speaking countries, to prove its scientific credentials (an anxiety less acute than once it was). Psychologists interested in history therefore used history of Psychology as a way of furthering this cause, providing simple story-lines that unfolded Psychology's increasing commitment to scientific methods, and what it has accomplished by so doing. These invariably centred on a series of 'Great Men' and their theories or methodological innovations. By the 1940s most such histories were being written for the undergraduate market in the United States. These acquired a further role; in addition to proving Psychology's scientific credentials they also suggested to students that they were the direct intellectual heirs of Aristotle and Plato. A phrase, now become a cliché, coined by the German psychologist Herman Ebbinghaus, 'Psychology has a short history but a long past', was often invoked. Anybody who had ever written anything about psychological matters for whatever reason, and however they went about it, was retrospectively baptised as a psychologist before the fact. Ever since ancient Greece, it was stated, the questions had remained constant, only the methods of answering them had changed. While rhetorically appealing, this does not actually bear close examination (see Chapter 2). Not all earlier histories of Psychology were of exactly these kinds, some; like D.B. Klein (1970) sought in a scholarly way to elucidate how western concepts of human nature had evolved, others, such as J.R. Kantor (1963, 1964) strove to show how the author's particular theoretical school was the true and logical culmination of this process.

Few contemporary historians of Psychology endorse these older approaches, but it would be quite wrong to dismiss all the earlier works. Many are of exemplary scholarship, some still essential for the working historian. Nor are they devoid of valuable insights. What has happened is that history of Psychology belatedly caught up with developments in mainstream history of science during the 1960s, which involved rejecting such approaches in regard to the physical sciences and medicine. Several more-or-less denigratory terms are often used in this context and it will be helpful to identify them here. One is 'Whiggish', coined with a more specific meaning by the political historian J.H. Plumb but which came to be used to refer to the general assumption that history is necessarily progressive ('progressivist' being a frequent synonym). It is now recognised that even in history of science this simple plot cannot do justice to the real complexities, that failures are as interesting and illuminating as successes. Our current global predicament renders it difficult in any case still to see science as an ever-progressing, unalloyed benefit to humanity. Closely linked with this are the self-explanatory terms 'celebratory' and 'heroic'.

Another common term is 'internalist', introduced by the sociologist Robert Merton in the late 1930s. As the limitations of heroic history began to be appreciated, it was felt that two possible tacks could be taken: to concentrate purely on the development of a discipline's research, theories and discoveries in its own terms, or to look at how its fortunes were determined by economic and cultural factors. These were called 'internalist' and 'externalist' respectively. In the 1970s it was realised that these were not always separable, but sometimes interpenetrated in a thoroughgoing fashion. 'Internalist' has remained in use, however, both as a pejorative term for those who think that focusing exclusively on the internal history of a discipline is sufficient, and more neutrally for internally directed research undertaken within broader frameworks making no such claims.

Histories 'proving' that their author's theoretical position is the valid one are termed 'presentist'. It is never possible, of course, to write history from anything other than the 'present'; the interests, priorities and questions directing historical research inevitably arise within present cultural and intellectual climates. The 'presentist' error is in imagining today's perspective on the past to be the final one, enabling us to see the past 'objectively' and adjudicate with certainty on the merits and demerits of all past science. If we believe our presently favoured theory has arrived at the truth, history becomes the heroic saga of how that truth was realised.

But we can never transcend time in this way. What we can do is try to be open about how present interests are shaping our historical agenda.

The 'heroic' and 'great man' approaches to history see historical events as resulting primarily from the efforts of a succession of great men (and a few women), the rare benign or malevolent geniuses whose periodic appearance determines humanity's fate. While appealing to the school-child, this grossly distorts how history, including history of science, actually happens and is quite incompatible with taking 'external' or 'contextual' factors into account. That there are and have been people whom we might legitimately call 'great' is undeniable, but they are not the only players and do not succeed single-handed. Explaining history in terms of the efforts of a handful of autonomous geniuses is tantamount to not explaining it at all, and in science conveys the erroneous impression of a simple yet mysterious division between these geniuses – apparently dwelling on a higher plane – and the rank and file labouring in their wake. Their sheer impact renders it all the more important to scrutinise how such figures achieved their successes, and demystify, though not deny or denigrate, their accomplishments. For psychologists particularly it is surely of paramount interest to understand them as human beings rather than stay forever spellbound.

From what was said about earlier history of Psychology, it was (if not quite always) clearly guilty of most of these errors. But as already stated, history of Psychology is unlike most other areas of history of science in that its practitioners usually picture themselves as contributing to the very discipline they are chronicling – and in the very act of doing so. To understand this claim we must say a little more regarding developments in history of science, philosophy of science and sociology of knowledge since the 1960s. One underlying trend in all these fields (the boundaries between which have become extremely blurred) has been towards the detailed examination of scientific practice. In pursuing this, in a variety of ways and at various levels of analysis, many have concluded that we can only understand the nature of science if we view it as the product of complex social processes. This has some serious implications when explored further because it means that no 'knowledge', not even scientific 'knowledge', has any final absolutely 'objective' status but is the product and expression of a specific cultural and historical context. Science too is embedded in the present. Without going further into this knotty issue, one spin-off has been that these fields have themselves acquired an increasingly 'Psychological' character. Understanding 'scientific behaviour' raises issues of perception (e.g. how one makes sense of what one is seeing when nobody has seen it before), cognition (e.g. how scientists really create their theories and decide what their results mean), personality (e.g. what motivates a scientist to devote their life to a particular topic), communication (e.g. how scientists succeed or fail in getting their work accepted as valid and how controversies are resolved) and group dynamics (e.g. how scientific disciplines are organised and managed). Of course there are sociological and economic level issues as well, but such psychological questions have become part and parcel of the current agenda.

What does this mean for Psychology? For a start it places it in a rather odd position in relation to the other sciences because, as the science of human behaviour, its subject matter logically includes scientific behaviour. The numerous paradoxes arising from this cannot be addressed here, but it is important to appreciate that it casts Psychology in a quite ambiguous position *vis-à-vis* the natural sciences, for while trying to operate as a normal science, it is also on the outside looking in. Psychology as a discipline is perhaps in a similar self-reflecting relation to the rest of science as historians and philosophers of Psychology are to Psychology. The old question 'Is Psychology a science?' thus evades any easy answer, it is not even entirely clear any more quite what it means. This issue will keep recurring in the ensuing chapters.

This view of science as a product and expression of specific social contexts has, moreover, been developed into a way of looking at human behaviour and ideas in general, merging into the approach, adopted by many social psychologists over the last thirty years, known as 'social constructionism' – and thus represents a Psychological, or 'metapsychological', thesis in its own right. And now we at last get to the nub of the issue. Psychology itself must be one of the routes by which this process of 'social construction' operates. The history of Psychology thereby becomes one aspect of the history of its own subject-matter, 'psychology'. The historian of Psychology is not only looking at the history of a particular discipline, but also at the history of what that discipline purports to be studying. Whereas in orthodox sciences there is always some external object of enquiry – rocks, electrons, DNA, stars – existing essentially unchanging in the non-human world (even if never finally knowable 'as it really is' beyond human conceptions), this is not so for Psychology. 'Doing Psychology' is the human activity of studying human activity, it is human psychology examining itself – and what it produces by way of new theories, ideas and beliefs about itself is also part of our psychology! This self-referring relationship is known technically as 'reflexivity'.

For the historian of Psychology who is also a psychologist, the discipline's history is therefore in itself a psychological phenomenon. More specifically, we are looking at Psychology's role in the dynamic psychological process by which human nature constantly recreates, re-forms, and regenerates itself, primarily in western cultures. This sounds very grandiose, of course, and I would immediately concede that not all my colleagues see things in these terms. Nevertheless, I believe it is logically necessary to acknowledge that Psychology has the complex reflexive character being outlined here. To put it bluntly, Psychology is produced by, produces, and is an instance of, its own subject matter. More debatable is how seriously we should take this, whether it has genuinely important implications. One bottom-line lesson which I feel to be important is really a moral one: the psychologist is not outside the things which he or she studies, not an external 'objective' observer of the human psyche, but an active participant in the collective psychological life of their community, culture and, ultimately, species. This means that what psychologists say and do, the theories, images and models of the psychological they devise and promote, have, as we will be seeing throughout this book, real consequences for everybody else. They are in an even weaker position than physical scientists to disclaim responsibility for what society does with what they produce, for even in producing it they are participating in this collective social psychological process.

Stated in these terms the case may sound rather abstract and nebulous. This is why we need history of Psychology – to flesh out this situation in a visible, concrete fashion. In what follows I hope to provide a more comprehensive picture of the enterprise Psychology is engaged in than is usually given, one which takes account of its perplexing reflexivity and identifies more clearly its places in modernist culture. This clearly has implications for how the discipline should view itself in the rapidly evolving 'post-modernist' era.

There are easier justifications for the history of Psychology. One is simply that we cannot understand the present situation without knowing something about how and why it arose. Another is that it provides some check on needlessly repeating work that has been forgotten – something psychologists are curiously prone to do. In this sense it might be seen as serving to maintain access to the discipline's long-term memory, preventing present-day psychologists from re-inventing the wheel. A third would be that it extends our sampling, enabling us to track changes over time in how people perform on, say, a particular Psychological test. Each of these has some merit, but they all cast history in a sort of service role in relation to the rest of the discipline, failing to acknowledge that history has its own autonomous agendas which historians naturally see as being as important as anybody else's. In fact the incompatibility of the first and third of these with the approach espoused here is more apparent than real. Showing how and why the present situation arose is an intrinsic part of the present enterprise as is the identification of psychological change over time. The second 'memory' role can, though, only be considered a subsidiary aspect of the historian's job, to be under-taken on a one-off basis with colleagues who have specific questions or concerns. This might well have incidental pay-offs – as well as averting total academic isolation! But just to make things a bit more complicated, it should be noted that the newer approaches to history may themselves be crudely differentiated into 'revisionist' and 'critical' – the former tending to provide alternative 'mirror image' readings of traditional narratives debunking heroes, redeeming failures and recasting triumphs as betrayals, etc., the latter producing narratives of a funda-mentally different kind. The present work is an attempt of this latter sort, but the boundary is not, one must admit, entirely clear.

Finally we need to turn to the linguistic dimension mentioned earlier. This arises directly from the reflexivity issue in the following way. Let us begin with the question, 'how are we able to talk about psychological phenomena?' The answer is not straightforward for we cannot actually define the words and expressions we use in our 'psychological language' by pointing to the phenomena to which they refer. If language is to remain meaningful there must be public criteria for deciding whether it is being used correctly, yet psychological phenomena (and the psychological meanings of behavioural phenomena) are by definition private – you cannot directly observe my experiences of pain, hate, bewilderment, colour, anxiety, etc. When we examine the words and expressions actually used in psy-chological discourse, however, we find that they nearly all appear to be metaphorical – and the exceptions (like *sad, happy*, etc.) are those with a large number of figurative synonyms (like *depressed* or *delighted* respectively). We are in effect saying 'I am like that' where 'that' refers to some public phenomenon or property. Moreover, we can go further, for what this in turn amounts to is that we structure and explain our private psychological experience in terms of how the public world is structured and explained in our culture. Insofar as we can actually communicate about the psychological it is therefore as a sort of internal reflection of the outside world. But is there anything *beyond* this reflection – something that is *really* going on independently of our efforts to verbally describe it? Well, there might be, and not all psychological communication is verbal anyway, but the point is that whatever *cannot* be communicated about (e.g. those fleeting moments when a taste sensation triggers an undefinable emotion-cum-memory) is something we cannot really be said to know about. We can only talk about that which we have a language for talking about – and as far as the psychological is concerned we have no way of knowing what psychological phenomena are, no way of giving them meaning, except in terms of that language.

If this is so, then we are bound to accept (with whatever degrees of reluctance or glee) that *changes in psychological language signify psychological change in their own right*. This is clearly important for history of Psychology. At one level what we are studying is, quite literally, language – for it is only in this form that previous accounts of the psychological are available. When psychologists introduce a new concept or theory about the psychological they are therefore directly engaged in *changing* it. It is at this linguistic level that the reflexive loops mentioned earlier, notably 'Psychology produces its own subject matter', are most tangibly manifested. To classify and explain the psychological in a new way is to be involved in changing the psychological itself. To think about oneself differently is to change oneself.

Contrary to some contemporary psychologists (such as Paul and Patricia Churchland), I do not believe there is some independent psychological 'reality' beyond the language to which it refers with greater or lesser 'accuracy' – and which Psychology may eventually succeed in 'scientifically' capturing in a new technical vocabulary. This is not to be understood as saying that language is all there is but that psychological language is itself a psychological phenomenon – a psychological technique for both talking about other psychological phenomena *and* for giving them form and meaning. Furthermore, psychological language facilitates and structures psychological practices – compare for example the consequences of calling a child with literacy problems 'lazy' and calling it 'dyslexic'. We all have innumerable private, 'psychological' experiences which we find it impossible to 'put into words', but this very fact makes us say things like 'I don't know what it meant' etc. – we never know what to actually *do* with such experiences. We may try communicating them via another medium, like music or painting, but even then we cannot, by definition, say *what* has been communicated or know that we have succeeded.

Students often have great difficulty in grasping the consequences of this – that nobody prior to Freud had an Oedipus Complex, that nobody before Pavlov and Watson was ever 'conditioned' and that nobody before about 1914 had a 'high IQ'. What this means is that however similar to such phenomena previous ones retrospectively appear to be, they were not terms in which the psychology of people prior to their introduction was actually structured. They had no psychological *reality*. The very act of introducing such concepts changed the situation by providing people with new terms in which to experience themselves – and only *then* can they be properly said to refer to really occurring psychological phenomena. The same point holds true for much of everyday psychological language ('folk psychology' as it is somewhat patronisingly called) – nobody 'went off the rails' before the advent of railways, nobody was 'on the same wavelength' before radio was invented, and further back, nobody could 'spell things out' before the invention of alphabetic writing. Identifying the psychological impacts of new Psychological ideas as linguistically encoded should then occupy a high place in our priorities, for it promises further insights into the discipline's roles in modern cultures over the last century and a half.

The purpose of this book is therefore to 'put Psychology in its place', to provide readers, especially those new to the discipline, with an, albeit provisional, overall picture of what kind of an enterprise it is and how it acquired its present cultural functions. But in keeping with my guiding philosophy I should stress that this is, in the end, my own particular view of it. Other historians and philosophers of Psychology, if undertaking a similar task, would undoubtedly produce accounts differing from it to a greater or lesser degree. While my own position might be read as a variety of social constructionism I am happy to concede that critical realism and even internalism have their own insights to offer. It is not presented as the final word on the matter but, like all other Psychological work, as a contribution to an on-going process of dialogue and debate, and its merits and flaws are matters for readers and critics to sort out.

Further reading

Danziger, K. (1990) *Constructing the Subject: Historical Origins of Psychological Research*. Cambridge: Cambridge University Press. Highly acclaimed study of the reflexive nature of experimental Psychology.

Danziger, K. (1997) *Naming the Mind. How Psychology Discovered Its Language*. London: Sage. A quite invaluable investigation into how and why much of Psychology's technical vocabulary (e.g. 'motivation', 'personality', 'attitude') was generated and adopted.

Latour, B. (1987) *Science in Action. How to Follow Scientists and Engineers Through Society*. Milton Keynes: Open University Press. Perhaps the best starting point for an understanding of the orientation of current history and philosophy of science, although only one version among several of the 'constructionist' approach (a label Latour himself has since vehemently rejected).

Leahey, T.H. (2000) *A History of Psychology: Main Currents in Psychological Thought*, 4th edn. Englewood Cliffs: Prentice-Hall. Best full-scale general history currently available. *To be taken as further reading for most subsequent chapters.*

Richards, G. (1989) *On Psychological Language and the Physiomorphic Basis of Human Nature*. London: Routledge. Only one chapter of this is explicitly on history of Psychology but it presents my general 'metapsychological' position (although leaves the 'reflexivity' issue itself relatively unexplored).

Smith, R. (1988) 'Does the History of Psychology Have a Subject?' *History of the Human Sciences* 1(2): 147–177. Highly influential paper challenging notions of historical continuity and disciplinary coherence as well as highlighting the functions served by traditional histories.

Smith, R. (1997) *Fontana History of the Human Sciences*. London: Fontana. A comprehensive and sensitive overview of the history of all the human sciences which has already established itself as a classic.

The only comprehensive bibliographical reference work is:

Watson, R.I. (1974, 1976) *Eminent Contributors to Psychology* (2 vols). New York: Springer. Vol. 1 contains bibliography of works by major psychologists who died before 1970, vol. 2 secondary sources.

For early Psychology journals see:

Osier, D.V. and Wozniak, R.H. (1984) *A Century of Serial Publications in Psychology: 1850–1950. An International Bibliography*. New York: Kraus International. In fact this contains founding dates etc. of journals going back to the late eighteenth century, 1107 in all, plus 739 of incidental relevance described more briefly.

Classic history of Psychology

The following are among the most important of the many titles published:

Baldwin, J.M. (1913) *History of Psychology*. London: Watts. By one of the founders of American Psychology. Fairly brief and mainly focused on philosophy.

Boring, E.G. ([1929]1950) *A History of Experimental Psychology*, 2nd edn. New York: Appleton-Century-Crofts. Single most influential account and an invaluable reference work. Primarily 'internalist' but made use of the concept of the *Zeitgeist* or 'spirit of the times' in addressing contextual factors.

Boring, E.G. (1942) *Sensation and Perception in the History of Experimental Psychology*. New York: Appleton-Century-Crofts. Spin-off from the previous work, similarly valuable for reference purposes.

Brett, G.S. (1912–1921) *History of Psychology* (3 vols), abridged R.S. Peters (1953). London: Allen & Unwin. Primarily a history of the philosophy of mind, only reaching modern Psychology in the last volume. Peters' edition has a supplementary chapter attempting to cover the period from 1900 to 1950.

Hearnshaw, L. (1964) *A Short History of British Psychology 1840–1940*. London: Methuen. The only pre-1980s monograph on British Psychology, on which it remains essential reading. Includes some institutional history.

Kantor, J.R. (1963, 1964) *The Scientific Evolution of Psychology* (2 vols). Chicago: Principia Press. 'Presentist' approach casting Kantor's own 'interbehavioural' version of behaviourism as the logical outcome of Psychology's development.

Klein, D.B. (1970) *A History of Scientific Psychology: Its Origins and Philosophical Background*. London: Routledge & Kegan Paul. Excellent on the philosophical roots of Psychology.

Müller-Freienfels, R. (1935) *The Evolution of Modern Psychology*. New Haven: Yale University Press. A European-authored work which adopted a distinctive issue-centred approach, rather more sophisticated than most American texts of the time.

Murphy, G. and Kovach, J.K. (1972) *Historical Introduction to Modern Psychology*, 6th edn. London: Routledge & Kegan Paul. The first edition, by Murphy only was published in 1928. The most widely read general history from the time of first publication until the 1970s, with a somewhat broader agenda than Boring.

Schultz, D. (1975) *A History of Modern Psychology*. New York: Academic Press. One of the last fully traditional histories.

Watson, R.I. (1963) *The Great Psychologists. Aristotle to Freud*. Philadelphia & New York: Lippincott. Watson was largely responsible for placing history of Psychology on a serious academic footing in the US, and although his orientation was fundamentally progressivist and celebratory it was not rigidly so. This textbook was highly successful with a 5th revised edition, co-authored with Rand B. Evans, appearing in 1991.

Newer approaches

This is a selection only. One particularly valuable series is *Studies in the History of Psychology*, published by Cambridge University Press.

Ash, M.G. and Woodward, R.W. (eds) (1987) *Psychology in Twentieth-Century Thought and Society*. Cambridge: Cambridge University Press. Important collection of papers filling out the cultural and contextual dimensions of the story.

Bunn, G.C., Lovie, A.D. and Richards, G.D. (eds) (2001) *Psychology in Britain: Historical Essays and Personal Reflections*. Leicester: British Psychological Society and London: The Science Museum. Published to mark the British Psychological Society's 2001 Centenary. Includes essays exploring numerous contextual and biographical aspects of British Psychology.

Buss, A.R. (ed.) (1979) *Psychology in Social Context*. New York: Irvington. Marked the first major departure from internalism.

Graumann, C.F. and Gergen, K.J. (eds) (1996) *Historical Dimensions of Psychological Discourse*. Cambridge: Cambridge University Press. Although variable in quality this is one of the few books explicitly addressing the nature of Psychological discourse itself from a historical perspective.

Jones, D. and Elcock, J. (2001) *History and Theories of Psychology: A Critical Perspective*. London: Edward Arnold. Both comparable and complementary in approach to the present work this has a significantly different weighting of topics, with more in-depth analysis of several major issues. A very useful introductory textbook.

Koch, S. and Leary, D.E. (eds) (1985, rep. 1998) *A Century of Psychology as a Science*. Washington DC: APA. Numerous papers, many of which adopt fresh approaches. Koch himself had been adopting a critical perspective over many years following his editorship of the monumental *Psychology: A Study of a Science* (6 vols, New York: McGraw-Hill, 1959–1963), an experience which disenchanted him with the view that Psychology was, or could be, a coherently unified discipline.

Kusch, M. (1999) *Psychological Knowledge: A Socal History and Philosophy*. London: Routledge. A deeply insightful work focusing on the Würzburg School's relationship with the Wundtians and the 'imageless thought' controversy.

Leary, D.E. (ed.) (1990) *Metaphors in the History of Psychology*. Cambridge: Cambridge University Press. Stimulating collection of papers on the metaphorical nature of Psychological discourse, though few contributors are really prepared to bite the bullet.

Murray, D.J. (1983) *A History of Western Psychology*. Englewood Cliffs: Prentice-Hall. Departed from earlier approaches by significantly broadening the agenda of topics covered.

Pandora, K. (1997) *Rebels Within the Ranks: Psychologists' Critique of Scientific Authority and Democratic Realities in New Deal America*. Cambridge: Cambridge University Press. Reminds us that more radical American psychologists in the United States during the 1930s (notably Gardner Murphy, Lois B. Murphy and Gordon Allport) were engaged in a battle somewhat similar to that now occurring between 'social constructionist' or 'critical' psychologists and laboratory-based experimentalists.

Richards, G. (1987) 'Of What is the History of Psychology a History?' *British Journal for the History of Science* 20: 201–211. Explores the implications of the ambiguities of the term 'psychology' as referring to both discipline and subject matter.

Richards, G. (1992) *Mental Machinery: The Origins and Consequences of Psychological Ideas. Part One 1600–1850*. London: Athlone Press. Originally planned as the first volume of a two-part work (now abandoned) this attempted to rethink the pre-1850 period in the light of recent developments in the history of science and the nature of psychological language.

Richards, G. (1997) *'Race', Racism and Psychology. Towards a Reflexive History*. London: Routledge. Endeavoured to provide a comprehensive survey of the ways Psychology has engaged 'race' and 'racism' issues, drawing attention to the varieties of forms this has taken and the often ironic character of events (see Chapter 21).

Robinson, D.N. (1995) *An Intellectual History of Psychology*, 3rd edn. London: Arnold. Conservative but sophisticated and scholarly.

Rose, N. (1985) *The Psychological Complex: Psychology, Politics and Society in England 1869–1939*. London: Routledge & Kegan Paul. A telling and highly influential sociological account, adopting a broadly Foucauldian approach.

Rose, N. (1990) *Governing the Soul: The Shaping of the Private Self*. London: Routledge. Extends his previous work, focusing on Psychology's role as the source of 'technologies of subjectivity'.

Smith, R. (1992) *Inhibition: History and Meaning in the Sciences of Mind and Brain*. Cambridge: Cambridge University Press. An in-depth exploration of the ideological and cultural ramifications of the concept of 'inhibition' and the inseparability of its technical and its cultural meanings.

Soyland, J. (1994) *Psychology as Metaphor*. London: Sage. A further exploration of the 'metaphorical' character of Psychological discourse.

Woodward, W.R. and Ash, M.G. (eds) (1982) *The Problematic Science: Psychology in Nineteenth Century Thought*. New York: Praeger. Useful collection of papers opening up the origins of modern Psychology to contextual and constructionist scrutiny.

Zenderland, L. (1998) *Measuring Minds. Herbert Henry Goddard and the Origins of American Intelligence Testing*. Cambridge: Cambridge University Press. A fine re-examination and re-evaluation of the career of H.H. Goddard and the processes by which intelligence testing became established in the United States.

Additional references

Churchland, Patricia S. (1986) *Neurophilosophy Toward a Unified Science of the Mind/Brain*. Cambridge, MA. & London: MIT Press.

Churchland, Paul M. (1988) *Matter and Consciousness*, rev. ed. Cambridge, MA: MIT Press.

Information

The major journals in this field are *The Journal of the History of the Behavioral Sciences*, *History of the Human Sciences*, *History of Psychology* and *History and Philosophy of Psychology*. Important research resources in Britain are the Wellcome Institute for the History of Medicine Library in Euston Road, London; the University of London Library at Senate House, Malet Street, London; the Centre for the History of Psychology, Staffordshire University, Stoke on Trent (which houses the British Psychological Society archives). In North America the Archives of American Psychology at the University of Akron, Ohio is the key institution, while several universities such as York (Canada), New Hampshire and Texas A & M have strong traditions of research in the field. The American Psychological Association's (APA) Section 26 promotes History of Psychology within the discipline itself, as does the British Psychological Society's History & Philosophy of Psychology section in the UK. In Holland, the University of Groningen has a major research centre, as does the University of Passau in Germany. The European Society for the History of the Human Sciences and its North American sister society Cheiron are the principal international organisations.

Websites

There are numerous websites, including a number providing direct links to others. Currently the most useful jumping off points for history of Psychology are the APA Section 26 site located at:

www.yorku.ca/dept/psych/orgs/apa26/apadiv26.htm Chris Green, who runs this site has put the texts of many classic books and journal papers online. To access the catalogue directly go to:

www.yorku.ca/dept/psych/classics/index.htm

and the European Society for the History of the Human Sciences site at:

http://psychology.dur.ac.uk/eshhs

Other interesting sites include:

http://elvers.stjoe.udayton.edu/history/welcome.htm

www.psychology.okstate.edu/museum/history/index.html (typically celebratory however)
www.slu.edu/colleges/AS/PSY/510GUIDE.html

Sites with good links include:
www.salve.edu/~walsch/psych.history.html
www.chss.montclair.edu/psychology/museum/museum.html (this is particularly good for pictures of early equipment and apparatus).
http://maple.lemoyne.edu/~hevern/index2.html

A 'History of Psychology' search will identify numerous online descriptions of US
university courses, with assignments, reading lists, etc. These are an interesting
browse to get a feel for how the topic is currently being taught and conceptualised.

A handy starting point for US Psychology generally is the APA site at: apa.org

From this it is easy to access the sites of the various APA divisions, which often
include brief histories of their fields.

The BPS History and Philosophy of Psychology Section site is;
www.chelt.ac.uk/ess/soss/hps

The Centre for the History of Psychology, Staffordshire University catalogues
are on:
www.staffs.ac.uk/schools/divisions/psychology/chop.html

Searches under individual psychologists' names are also often productive.

Chapter 2

Before Psychology: 1600–1850

- Non-existence of Psychology prior to 1850
- Traditional historical approaches to this period
- Reasons for the non-existence of Psychology prior to 1850
- Philosophical traditions
- The significance of physiological studies
- Educational writings
- Attempts at understanding madness
- Social philosophy and other genres

No discipline calling itself Psychology existed prior to the mid-nineteenth century. What we might clumsily call 'reflexive discourse' – discourse about human nature, 'Mind' and the Soul – has always existed but, barring isolated exceptions, before 1800 this was not 'scientific' in any modern sense, let alone experimental. This is, on the face of it, surprising. In *The Advancement of Learning* (1605) and *Novum Organum* (1620), Francis Bacon had advocated a 'general science concerning the Nature and State of Man' at the outset of the 'Scientific Revolution'. Yet few experiments of a recognisably 'Psychological' kind are on record before 1850, and even non-experimental empirical research was sparse. In Britain the very word 'Psychology' was rare prior to the early 1800s, when the poet-philosopher Samuel Taylor Coleridge imported it from Germany (where philosophers had long used *Psychologie*). The significance of this absence must be stressed since, as previously mentioned, Psychology was traditionally depicted as emerging seamlessly from earlier 'reflexive discourse', often starting with the ancient Greeks.

The line that the questions remain the same but the methods of answering them change is unsatisfactory, for had these earlier thinkers been asking the same questions Psychologists ask then devising the obvious empirical methods of investigation, at least some of them, would have been easy. Even in 1700 they could have run rats through mazes, circulated questionnaires, seen how many trials it took to learn word-lists, or invented (albeit crude) instruments to measure reaction times – all methods typical of modern Psychology. The reason they did not was that they were not asking these questions in the first place.

This is not to claim a complete lack of historical connection, only that their predecessors were not doing what Psychologists began doing in the late nineteenth century, still less what they do today. They were not failing to answer the same questions but asking different ones, about the nature of Virtue, the relations between the immortal soul (if it existed) and the body, whether all our ideas came from sensory experience or whether some were innate and self-evident, what kind of a substance the mind was, how to master one's 'passions', how to educate children, or, at a cruder level, how character was manifested in the face. In addressing these they often engaged in what looks like Psychological theorising, being led to discuss topics such as perception, the structure of the mind, even, occasionally, child and animal behaviour. Such discussions set the terms in which psychologists began tackling the same topics, which is where the historical link lies. But caution is needed on reading too much into this: (a) these matters mostly arose in the context of issues no longer figuring, at least in the same way, on Psychology's agenda, and (b) nobody saw such investigations as contributions to a single discipline, Psychology.

Many modern Psychological inquiries are occasionally anticipated in earlier works, but the connections (if any) between these and subsequent research are frequently obscure. Too often historians cast them as part of Psychology's history, even though they had little or no impact on the later work and were unknown to Psychology until the historian disinterred them. The interesting question such anticipations raise is really why they did *not* have an impact, but to answer this would take the traditional historian in an unwelcome direction, highlighting the differences rather than the continuities between modern Psychology and previous work. The only two topics on which a convincing case can be made for a continuous

Table 2.1   Pre-1850 genres of 'Proto-Psychology'

Æsthetics	Animal behaviour
Education and child rearing	Linguistics
Logic	Medicine (Psychiatry)
Mesmerism	Philosophy
Phrenology	Physiognomy
Physiology	Popular 'advice' books on marriage, etc.
Punishment of crime	Rhetoric
Social and Political Philosophy	Theology

A thorough account of pre-1850 'Psychological' thought would have to consider texts of all these kinds, as well as, for example, works speculating on the origins of human society and institutions, meditations on the meanings of proverbs and theories about the 'racial' diversity of 'mankind'.

lineage of proto-scientific inquiry and theorising since 1600 – indeed since antiquity – are memory and visual perception.

The easiest way of treating this period is in terms of prevailing disciplines and genres of 'reflexive discourse' (Table 2.1). Unfortunately a whole range of these must be left aside here, including fiction, drama, poetry and oral history. These often provide valuable evidence about the psychological ideas of the times and how far new philosophical or physiological ideas about human nature had penetrated popular culture, but were not intended to extend knowledge about human nature as such. Even this proviso leaves a nigh unmanageable body of material. The most important genre was philosophy and, as the eighteenth century progressed, physiology became increasingly influential. But while these traditionally dominate historical attention there are numerous relevant works on education, child-rearing, language, æsthetics, madness, physiognomy, manners, and logic, as well as volumes of, now mostly unreadable, theology. Excepting some of the educational texts these, unlike the literary and oral genres, are of course over-whelmingly white male in authorship. First though, why did no discipline of Psychology materialise before 1850?

One obvious culprit is religion. During the 1600s theologians used the word 'Pneumatology' for a supposed science or study of the Soul. Relations between science and religion are always rather fraught. One topic theologians were very touchy about was any 'Baconian' approach that threatened their monopoly regarding the nature of the Soul, a boundary which was heavily policed during the Scientific Revolution. This is, ironically, very evident in the work of the French philosopher René Descartes in the 1620s to 1640s, who regularly figures as a hero because of his doctrine of 'mechanism' and physiological speculations on 'reflexes' and how the body affects the mind. At the centre of his philosophy lies his famous distinction between mind and body. The body and material world consist of an extended substance governed by mechanistic laws amenable to scientific study. The mind, however, is an 'unextended substance' and can only be investigated by Reason; it is thus *excluded* from the province of natural philosophy. Of course many, such as

Thomas Hobbes, disagreed with him, but the materialist opposition continued to argue in philosophical terms, they did not engage in Psychological research.

Second, throughout the period (though decreasingly so) it was unclear that Man (the word always used) was actually part of 'Nature', and thus in the province of science. This uncertainty was again religious – humans, having immortal souls, are semi-divine, partly above 'animate Nature'. Natural philosophy, however, is the study of Nature. To treat 'Man' scientifically was thus to risk accusations of heresy and, aside from the eighteenth-century radical French philosophers, few were prepared to risk it. Even physiologists, though happy to tackle sensation, balked at extending their theories to the mind itself. This doctrine also implied that the human mind was universally the same, that all humans were basically identical psychologically, even if there were differences in temperament, or due to environmental circumstances (pre-c. 1790 'racial' differences were usually explained either environmentally or by descent from different sons of Noah). Any philosophically derived 'laws of the mind' (e.g. those of 'association of ideas') were thus universal in scope, and if the reasoning by which they were derived was sound, empirical research was superfluous.

The question of 'Man's place in Nature', to use T.H. Huxley's phrase, was answered in terms of the long-standing idea of the Scale of Nature (*Scala Naturæ*) or 'Great Chain of Being', an ascending scale of perfection from bugs at the bottom to God at the top. Man, being part divine, bridged the gap between animals and angels, matter and spirit. The angel-God gap was held to be immeasurable, otherwise, many believed, this scale was unbroken, though this presented difficulties. Towards the end of the eighteenth century this image underwent an important change. Whereas previously it had been static, representing the structure of an unchanging divinely ordered world, new ideas of progress, growing awareness of historical time and accumulating geological discoveries now gave it a dynamic dimension. Nature as a whole was progressing towards perfection, the Scale of Nature was, so to speak, being ascended over time. This laid the deeper foundations for subsequent evolutionary notions but did not immediately challenge 'Man's' semi-divine status. On the contrary it gave this more dramatic connotations – as in early nineteenth-century German Idealism where 'Man' becomes the very agent by which 'Absolute Spirit' is realising itself. (For some of the pious, however, the rising consciousness of change had the reverse effect – it signified a process of decay heralding the imminence of the Day of Judgement.)

Thirdly, there is a problem about language related to my remarks in Chapter 1, which may be simplified thus: new psychological ideas are generated, we saw, by reflexively applying metaphors from the public world. But the philosophy underpinning the Scientific Revolution involved a rejection of fanciful metaphors – scientists were to use only simple unambiguous language. Because the human mind was believed to be universally the same, existing psychological concepts were accepted uncritically as basically adequate. Philosophers like John Locke in the late seventeenth century restricted their psychological language to a few basic, seemingly unproblematic, terms such as 'idea' and 'sensation'. The upshot was that this combination of the doctrine of universality and anti-metaphorical linguistic attitudes (shared, for different reasons, by all major schools of linguistic thought) inhibited the exploration *within disciplinary contexts* of the Psychological potential of new scientific ideas. While new psychological ideas and words appeared, they usually did so, as always, as trendy metaphors – often from physiology or medicine (e.g. 'irritable'). They were not introduced by would-be scientists of the mind utilising fresh ideas from science and technology in formulating new Psychological theories (as psychologists typically do, as we shall see). This is ironic because some, including Locke, recognised the fundamentally metaphorical nature of psychological language.

Fourthly, which must suffice, many now argue that not until around 1800 did the notion of the individual mind as a unitary entity crystallise in western thought. This is linked, they claim, to the rise of capitalism and economic individualism, and breakdown of earlier collective social structures. The discipline of Psychology is not therefore seen as possible prior to the nineteenth century because its subject matter was not yet thinkable as a unified object of investigation. This is a complex and contentious issue which, although we cannot further explore it at this point, is a major theme among contemporary historians of the human sciences. (See Chapter 11 for further discussion of this.)

Traditions of 'reflexive discourse' before 1850

While it is beyond the scope of the present work to provide a detailed account of this period, nonetheless an overview of it is necessary for an understanding of Psychology's point of departure.

The most significant genre was philosophy, of which three traditions were dominant during this period, each contributing significantly to the corpus of psychological concepts with which the first psychologists had to work:

- Rationalism. This is the label generally given to a lineage of French and German philosophers, the most important being Descartes, N. de Malebranche (French), B.B. Spinoza (Dutch Jewish), G.W. Leibniz, C. Wolff, J.N. Tetens and I. Kant (German). Like all such labels it oversimplifies – any major philosopher's thought is in many respects unique. What unified them was a belief that basic metaphysical questions (e.g. the nature of existence, the origins and limits of knowledge, the nature of truth) can be answered by reason acting alone. If sufficiently logical and rigorous we can attain knowledge of such matters, the certainty of which actually surpasses anything based on our fallible senses.
- Associationism. This is generally considered to begin with John Locke (1689) and was developed in Britain by Bishop Berkeley, F. Hutcheson, the Scottish sceptic David Hume and David Hartley during the first half of the eighteenth century, to reach its final form in the work of James and John Stuart Mill in the nineteenth century. This also enormously influenced radical eighteenth-century French materialist philosophers such as E.B. de Condillac, O. de La Mettrie, Baron D'Holbach and C.-A. Helvetius. The central tenet of this school was that all psychological phenomena originated in atom-like or 'corpuscular' sensations which were built up into complex ideas by a few simple 'laws of association'.

- Scottish 'common sense' realism. This began as a reaction against reductionist associationism, its first major exponent being Thomas Reid (1764). During the period from 1764 to the 1840s this approach underlay much of the work of 'Scottish Enlightenment' thinkers, David Hume being the main exception. This school included Dugald Stewart, Adam Ferguson, Henry Home (Lord Kames) and Adam Smith plus a host of lesser lights, with James McCosh and Sir William Hamilton its final major representatives in Scotland in the 1840s and 1850s. These writers typically opted for a compromise between rationalism and empiricism. On the one hand they accepted the existence of innate faculties or 'powers', but espoused an empirical *non*-reductionist approach to the identification and study of these. In many respects the work of this school anticipated that of modern Psychology more closely than either of the other two. For reasons discussed in Chapter 4 it also came to dominate the indigenous American 'Mental and Moral Philosophy' tradition of the nineteenth century. Curiously, however, it receives less attention than associationism and rationalism in most histories. This neglect appears to be for three reasons. First, none of its exponents was a philosopher of quite such stature as Locke, Hume or Kant. Second, by the 1890s reductionism was seen as a central scientific virtue so those wishing to stress Psychology's scientific character preferred to cite the associationists as their favoured ancestors. Third, the US 'Mental and Moral Philosophy' tradition was cast as the establishment against which America's 'new psychologists' of the 1880s and 1890s were rebelling.[1]

These three traditions created a legacy of often conflicting images of human nature and psychological phenomena and how they should be studied. In particular, the relative importance of experience and innate factors, and of empirical research, logical analysis or introspection as methods, emerged as central issues. These were not purely abstract debates but related to the cultural settings in which the various schools flourished. In pre-revolutionary France, most philosophers were intent on undermining the still feudal *ancien régime* and espoused strong materialist and anti-religious positions. For them an associationist philosophy was the most congenial epistemological framework. By contrast, the Scots were eager to reconcile philosophy with Protestantism and were at the same time keen to find a rational basis for studying human society in the light of the dramatic changes accompanying the Industrial Revolution. For them a non-reductionist but practical orientation seemed most appropriate. The university-based German philosophers, in a feudal, but non-centralised, culture as yet almost unaffected by industrialisation, were in the most ivory-towered position and inclined to adopt a purely intellectual mode of tackling philosophical issues which offered no threat

---

[1] A note on terminology is in order here: 'empiricism' is the doctrine that knowledge is derived from experience; 'sensationalism' the doctrine that experience ultimately consists of atomistic sensations (in all sensory modes); 'associationism' the doctrine that these sensations are combined by a number of 'laws of association' to yield complex ideas and concepts. While these clearly tend to go together they are logically distinct, in particular empiricism does not necessarily imply the other two. See also Glossary.

to the ruling princes, electors and margraves of the various German states. Unlike the Scots and Germans, few English philosophers were university-based and, unlike the French, they were disinclined to extreme radicalism (although exceptions such as William Godwin and Mary Wollstonecraft eventually surfaced). Nor were their religious allegiances as heartfelt as those of the Scots. Hostile to what they viewed as airy-fairy speculation they saw associationism as the philosophy most in keeping with Newtonian natural philosophy. In fact there is scant English philosophy of much significance between Hartley (1749) and James Mill (1829). The associationism versus 'common sense' division is, I should add, perhaps clearer in retrospect than it was at the time. For example, Thomas Brown's very influential *Lectures on the Human Mind* (1822) straddled the divide quite impressively (although it has been co-opted into the associationist camp by most historians).

Conceptually each contributed to the emergence of Psychology. As far as rationalism is concerned we need note the following: (a) Kant gave mind a more active role than it possessed in most rival systems, in which it passively obeyed quasi-natural laws; (b) Kant, particularly, disputed the logical possibility of a science of the mind, which was unquantifiable and beyond direct investigation; (c) rationalist philosophical analyses, being non-reductionist, provided a conceptually subtler account than those of reductionist associationists and materialists. These were clearly a mixed blessing for the prospects of a scientific Psychology. Following Kant, German philosophy reacted in two ways: first, some, such as F.W.J. von Schelling, rejected his view that Mind (or Spirit) was unknowable 'in itself', and went to romantic idealistic extremes, rhapsodising about Man being the vanguard of that cosmic process by which the Absolute was realising itself. Although this 'transcendental idealism' (of which G.W.F. Hegel was to be the most significant advocate) had a number of positive features, stimulating renewed consideration of human nature in all its complexity, most British and many French thinkers viewed it, somewhat unfairly, as inflated windbaggery. Others, however, sought to circumvent Kant's rejection of the possibility of a scientific Psychology, J.F. Herbart, F.E. Beneke and H. Lotze being the most eminent. It was from this strand, in combination with advances in physiology, that a discipline calling itself Psychology would shortly establish itself in Germany.

Associationism's legacy lay primarily in its reductionist mode of analysis. Although the original laws of association ('contiguity', 'contrast' and 'similarity') fell into disuse, the notion that learning and memory could be explained in fundamentally associationist terms persisted. From Alexander Bain onwards many anglophone psychologists saw their task as involving the translation of associationist ideas into more scientifically sophisticated, often physiological, terms, culminating in behaviourist learning theory. For Herbert Spencer the challenge was to reconcile it with his grand evolutionary cosmology, abandoning its more extreme environmentalist implications.

The Scottish realist school's contribution was more diffuse. As well as their deeper role in the history of US Psychology, their catalogue of innate 'powers' of the mind long continued to provide a framework for organising the topics in general Psychological texts, while their practical orientation (including interest in child development and social psychological phenomena) adumbrated the possibility of an applied discipline of the kind Psychology eventually became.

The foregoing sketch, in which little attempt has been made to discuss the details of the numerous philosophical systems included under this triad of umbrella terms, must suffice for present purposes. The point I wish to stress here is that none of these philosophical traditions is attempting to study psychology in a thoroughgoing 'natural philosophical' or 'scientific' fashion. The Scottish school occasionally came close but even here there was little resembling 'research' as we now understand it.

For the beginnings of this we need to look at physiology which, by the late eighteenth century, was making serious headway in conceptualising biological processes. As it did so psychological issues of various kinds soon assumed prominence. Most significantly, as the eighteenth century drew to a close there was growing debate about brain-functioning. One important manifestation of this was Franz J. Gall's 'craniology', later known as phrenology. He claimed that functions were highly localised in different 'cerebral organs', the relative sizes of which indicated an individual's character and determined the shape of their cranium, from which their character could thus be read. It enjoyed a particularly sympathetic reception in Scotland where its list of functions closely matched the Reidians' 'powers'. Its foremost Scottish advocate was George Combe. Phrenology enjoyed great popularity as a 'scientific' approach to 'character' from c. 1810 until the early 1850s (a little longer in the US) and influenced several pioneer Psychologists (notably Alexander Bain, Herbert Spencer and the US educationist Horace Mann) during their early years, although they later abandoned it. In many respects it was a 'dry run' for Psychology. Traditionally dismissed as a naive pseudo-science by disciplinary historians it is now understood to have played a vital contextual role in popularising the notion of a secular 'science of the mind' as well as pioneering what is now known as the 'functionalist' approach. Opponents such as the French biologist M.J.P. Flourens disputed localisation on experimental grounds, and eventually succeeded in discrediting the theory. Later the localisation theory returned to favour, but in a very different form (see Chapter 9). Associated with, though distinct from, phrenology was 'physiognomy'. This ancient notion that character could be read from the face was reformulated in Romantic terms in the late eighteenth century by the Swiss pastor J.C. Lavater (Fig. 2.1). Although, as a doctrine, this was quite distinct from phrenology, later popular phrenological writings often tended to include some physiognomic content.

Among other key discoveries were the differentiation between the afferent and efferent (or motor) nerves – those carrying information from sense organs to the brain and those controlling the muscles – accomplished independently by Charles Bell and the French physiologist François Magendie by the 1820s. A little later came the fuller development of the concept of reflex action by Marshall Hall in the 1830s and 1840s which put the issue of 'unconscious' action clearly on the map as well as possibilities of theorising about the biological basis of learning.

Finally, the experimental study of the senses, beginning with the early nineteenth-century work of E.H. Weber in Germany and lesser-known French researchers, had two important consequences: first, methodologically, it paved the way for Psychological experimentation and, second, it succeeded in bringing the experimental approach across the border from physiological topics to psychological ones, e.g. reaction times and sensory thresholds (the area later called

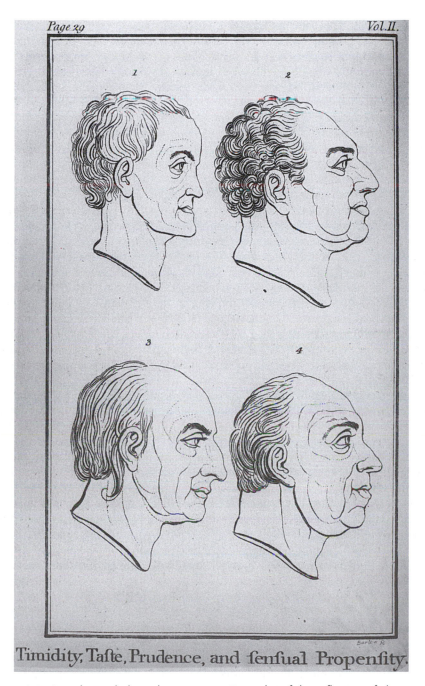

Figure 2.1 Nearly Psychology, but not quite. Examples of the reflection of character in the face according to the Swiss physiognomist J.C. Lavater's *Essays on Physiognomy* (1797). Photo: George Singer. Reproduced by permission of the Centre for History of Psychology, Staffordshire University.

psychophysics). This laid the basis for Gustav Fechner's and Wilhelm Wundt's work in the 1850s which is generally held to represent the birth of experimental Psychology. Mention must also be made of Johannes Müller, a German physiologist whose multi-volume handbook of human physiology (1834–1840) brought together and evaluated the early nineteenth-century developments, serving as the primary reference work on the topic.

From around 1800, such developments in physiology began to make increasing inroads into philosophy's academic monopoly on psychological issues. By and large, however, direct confrontation was held at bay, neither camp wanting to see the other as an enemy. While philosophy and physiology may be seen as Psychology's major roots, it is vital to understand that other disciplines and interests were also involved. I will indicate just some of them.

Child Psychology has its deeper origins in the various ideas regarding education which flourished during this period. Two key figures are Locke who published *Some Thoughts Concerning the Education of Children* in 1693 and the French philosopher Jean Jacques Rousseau, one of the first 'romantics', whose extraordinarily influential *Emile* (1762) expounded, in fictional form, his ideal of how boys should be educated. This is often taken as the founding text of 'modern' or 'progressive' educational theory. At the end of the eighteenth century in Britain numerous books appeared on education (including education of women, and often written by women), drawing on Locke's and Rousseau's ideas, and occasionally those of other philosophers (e.g. Reid). It is this genre which mediates between philosophy and practice, trying to apply philosophical ideas on learning to the real world of education. Educational theory and pioneering educational projects flourished in mainland Europe after Rousseau, major names including J.H. Pestalozzi, J.F. Herbart and F. Froebel (see Chapter 16). In France the famous incident of the feral child Victor of Aveyron, taken under his tutelage by J.M.G. Itard, further stimulated interest in child development and the question of how far 'human nature' was a product of civilisation and how far it was inborn. While research into the significance of early educational writings for the history of Psychology remains fairly meagre they indisputably stimulated public awareness of the potential practical relevance of philosophical ideas about the mind, thereby creating a climate in which demands for professional expertise on the child could develop. Thus, when Psychology did emerge, it was here that it found its first applied 'market'.

An area in which innovatory Psychological concepts were especially needed was the treatment of madness, always a singularly difficult, and often not very popular, task of medicine. From the mid-eighteenth century onwards the history of Psychiatry acknowledges a great many 'pioneers' such as P. Pinel who released the lunatics from their chains at the Bicêtre (a large Paris asylum) after the French Revolution, Samuel Tuke who founded the humanitarian 'Retreat' at York, and J.C. Reil, a German psychiatrist who proposed radical therapeutic methods. Most psychiatric writers prior to the 1850s developed theories and/or classifications of mental illness and its symptoms which incorporated models of the structure of the mind, often containing original elements. Such notions as the psychosomatic nature of symptoms, the existence of an unconscious, the causative role of trauma, the super-ego/ego/unconscious division and many others are first aired, albeit hazily or in different terminology at this time. We return to this in Chapter 14.

Finally we should note the numerous works on social philosophy and pioneer sociology. As social change accelerated during the eighteenth century and the effectiveness of religious authority declined, many, including Scottish Enlightenment thinkers such as Adam Smith, felt compelled to seek other bases for what they called 'civil society'. Implementing such a project usually involved formulating some new core notion of 'human nature', leading the Scots for example to adopt the principle of 'sympathy' as a social equivalent to 'gravity' in physics. It was a topic that combined concern with morality or 'virtue' with practical understanding of human social behaviour. A fine example of this is Smith's *Theory of Moral Sentiments* (1759), which contains many penetrating observations on social phenomena and what modern psychologists call 'attitudes'. His concerns clearly verged on those of Social Psychology. The 'utilitarian' image of human nature proposed by Jeremy Bentham, very different from Adam Smith's, was the one favoured by associationists. Most notorious was Bernard de Mandeville's *Fable of the Bees: or, Private Vices, Public Benefits* (1723), a cynical satire in which the disastrous social consequences of a general outbreak of virtue were explored, an early version of the recurrent argument that humans are basically selfish and competitive. Other prominent social theorists of the period included Rousseau (who introduced the notion of the 'social contract'), C.L. de S. Montesquieu, Adam Ferguson and William Godwin. The views of human nature offered by social philosophers cover the range from pessimism (Mandeville) to utopian optimism (e.g. W. Godwin), one popular image being the 'the noble savage' which was inspired by explorers' accounts of the apparently idyllic lives of 'savages' (notably, in Captain Cook's case, Tahitians). This image, which greatly impressed Rousseau, powerfully affected the Romantic movement which flourished from c. 1780 to the 1830s. Finally, this period sees the first 'speculative histories' of the human race, outlining its progress from savagery to civilisation, including the origins of language – precursors of the subsequent, often only slightly less speculative, evolutionary accounts that have been produced since the mid-nineteenth century. Social philosophising necessarily involved authors in adopting some core, non-religious, notion of human nature, displaying their own 'human natures' in so doing. Clearly, in a case like this, the histories of Psychology and psychology become inextricable.

Other genres and schools of thought might easily be added: 'Mesmerism', or 'animal magnetism' (popular from the 1770s to 1840s); the linguistics of James Harris, Horne Tooke, Lord Monboddo and the German J.G. Herder; the proto-criminology of the Italian C. Beccaria; and various seventeenth-century works on 'the passions' and gesture (notably John Bulwer's). The lesson of all this, though, is that after c. 1600 ideas about human psychology were changing in many different ways and on many fronts. Some underlying trends are discernible – a gradually mounting willingness to treat human nature as a phenomenon to be studied by 'natural philosophers' rather than philosophers and theologians alone, growing interest in processes of change and development, interest in the linkage between psychological and biological phenomena, and a gathering concern with those practical matters such as education, mental illness, crime, even (in the case of phrenology) incipient 'personnel selection', which later provided Psychology with markets for its expertise. Methodologically, however, it is only in the early nineteenth century that, especially in German physiology, the experimental methods of physical science start being applied to psychological issues, while statistical methods of data-analysis (other than simply descriptive) are largely absent until the 1880s.

Even by 1850 these varied interests and approaches had not cohered into a single discipline. They each tackled different kinds of question and operated with differing, if often related, conceptual frameworks. The word 'Psychology' was gaining wider circulation, but its meaning was more restricted than that which it has today, primarily denoting mental (or 'intellectual') philosophy. Something was needed to integrate all these realms of inquiry. That something was, as we will see in the next chapter, the rapid rise to ascendancy of evolutionary thought triggered by the work of Charles Darwin and Herbert Spencer in the 1850s. However, it was not the absence of such an integrating theory alone which delayed Psychology's appearance; it is now clear that prior to the early 1800s European cultures had in fact no 'place' for such a discipline. Insofar as the cultural roles modern Psychology plays were enacted at all (and many were not), they were dissipated across that variety of other disciplines we have indicated here.

Further reading

Space precludes detailed references to the vast body of work referred to in this chapter. These are readily accessible in the following texts and numerous histories of specific disciplines.

General

Hearnshaw, L.S. (1987) *The Shaping of Modern Psychology*. London: Routledge & Kegan Paul. Has some useful material relating to this earlier period.

Klein, D.B. (1970) *A History of Scientific Psychology: Its Origins and Philosophical Background*. London: Routledge & Kegan Paul. Especially good on philosophy.

Porter, R. (ed.) (1997) *Rewriting the Self. Histories from the Renaissance to the Present*. London: Routledge. Three-quarters of the papers are on the pre-modern period.

Richards, G. (1992) *Mental Machinery: The Origins and Consequences of Psychological Ideas, Part One: 1600–1850*. London: Athlone Press. An attempted rethink of how this period should be approached. Includes coverage of phrenology and mesmerism.

Smith, R. (1997) *Fontana History of the Human Sciences*. London: Fontana. Especially good on the period under discussion here.

Physiology

Boring, E.G. (1942) *Sensation and Perception in the History of Experimental Psychology*. New York: Appleton-Century Crofts. Basic reference work on the roots of these research fields.

Fearing, F. (1930) *Reflex Action. A Study in the History of Physiological Psychology.* London: Baillière, Tindall & Cox. A dated but very useful reference work.

Neuberger, M. (1981; 1st German ed. 1897) *The Historical Development of Experimental Brain and Spinal Cord Physiology before Flourens.* Translator and editor. Edwin Clark. Baltimore: Johns Hopkins University Press. Clark's comprehensive annotations on subsequent scholarship render this particularly useful.

Madness

See Chapter 14 references.

Education

While much has been written on the history of education, little seems to have been done regarding its role in Psychology's history. See Chapter 4 of Richards (1992) reference above and Chapter 16 references.

Social philosophy and sociology

Bryson, Gladys (1945, rep. 1968) *Man and Society: The Scottish Inquiry of the Eighteenth Century.* Princeton: Princeton University Press; rep. New York: Augustus Kelley. Despite its date this remains the most accessible point of departure for further reading on the Scottish school.

Language and linguistics

Aarsleff, H. (1983) *The Study of Language in England 1780–1860*, 2nd edn. Minneapolis: University of Minnesota Press/London: Athlone Press.

Land, S.K. (1986) *The Philosophy of Language in Britain: Major Theories from Hobbes to Thomas Reid.* New York: AMS.

Chapter 3

Founding Psychology: Evolution and experimentation

- Evolutionary thought
- Role of evolutionary thought in the emergence of Psychology
- Alexander Bain
- Gustav Fechner and the origins of experimental Psychology
- Wilhelm Wundt and his problematic status
- The statistical tradition of Francis Galton
- Contextual factors and their consequences for the nature of Psychology

In the 1860s two developments occurred which supplied (a) an integrating framework for emerging types of Psychological inquiry and (b) scientific procedures for pursuing them. These were, respectively, the success of evolutionary thought associated with Charles Darwin and Herbert Spencer, and the appearance in Germany of the experimental methodologies identified with Gustav Fechner and Wilhelm Wundt, followed by the British development of parametric statistics. These will be considered in turn.

Evolutionary thought

Darwin's *Origin of Species* (1859) proposed the doctrine of 'natural selection' to explain organic evolution scientifically. Current forms of organic life, including by implication (although he was as yet unready to spell it out) humans, had evolved from previous life-forms through æons of time by a mechanism which appeared, in itself, quite blind. And these earlier forms left various legacies in their living descendants. Although Darwin convinced the majority of scientists of the validity of the evolution-hypothesis, 'natural selection' was immediately attacked as insufficient (though not rejected as a factor), while some pre-existing evolutionary ideas were readily assimilated into it. It would be misleading to see 'evolutionary thought' and 'Darwinism' as synonymous. The 'natural selection' paradigm's eventual victory only came in the 1920s. In particular it was unclear (even to Darwin) that inheritance of acquired characteristics (so-called 'Lamarckian inheritance') could be rejected. Evolution's major populariser was Herbert Spencer, whose evolutionary *The Principles of Psychology* (1856) was followed from the 1860s by numerous weighty volumes expounding his 'synthetic philosophy' – a grandiose vision of evolution as an inexorable cosmic process in which matter became progressively more heterogeneous and complex. The history of nineteenth-century evolutionary thought – a vast, multi-faceted, topic – has received attention from a multitude of writers, particularly since 1960. For present purposes a fairly small number of central evolutionary ideas can be identified which supplied the unified theoretical framework Psychology needed:

* Humans were descended from primates and could thus be considered zoologically. They were not semi-divine and beyond the remit of science.
* 'Spontaneous variation': the raw material for natural selection was the occurrence in each generation of random variations. (The 'gene' concept later clarified this, but lack of genetic understanding handicapped evolutionary theory until the 1920s.)
* Recapitulation: this idea, originated by C.E. von Baer and popularised by German biologist Ernst Hæckel, held that each individual recapitulates in its development from conception to maturity the evolutionary stages through which its species has passed. Often summed up as 'ontogeny reflects phylogeny', this became known as the 'biogenetic law'.
* 'Degeneration': if natural selection is suspended 'unfit' organisms survive and reproduce, the quality of the population declines and 'degenerate' lines are established, subverting the usual evolutionary process which guarantees 'survival of the fittest' (Spencer's, not Darwin's, phrase).

- Although not strictly required by Darwinian theory, evolution was, perhaps inevitably, seen as essentially progressive. In the human case organic evolution had been succeeded by 'social evolution' – an 'ascent' from savagery via barbarism to modern industrial civilisation. This image was influentially promoted by the American L.H. Morgan (1877).

These notions galvanised interest in human nature on a wide range of fronts. To summarise briefly:

1   They encouraged the investigation of the evolution of 'mind' and how far human characteristics were present in rudimentary form in 'lower' animals or, conversely, how far humans retained 'lower' traits. This stimulated the comparative study of human and animal behaviour later called 'Comparative Psychology'. One aspect of this was a fascination with 'instincts'. The concept of 'instinct', long used to refer to divinely implanted innate patterns and categories of behaviour, was given a far harder scientific meaning and significance. Darwin's protégé George Romanes eagerly pursued this theme, followed towards the century's end by C. Lloyd Morgan (see Chapter 15).

2   They focused attention on the diversity of the human stock as the raw material from which future generations would be 'naturally selected'; this underlay Francis Galton's pioneer studies of individual differences and the development of statistical procedures for analysing them.

3   Recapitulation gave new significance to child-study as a method of looking back in time and tracking the psychological evolution of humankind. Important figures in this include James Sully, G. Stanley Hall and Wilhelm Preyer (see Chapter 16).

4   The structure of the nervous system could now be understood in terms of older and newer components, the brain itself evolving by successive additions and modifications to the brain-forms of lower organisms. Spencer's influence was considerable here, because his theory (we now know erroneously) proposed that 'associations', if sufficiently strong, could forge new, heritable, nervous connections. This integrated the environmentalist position of the leading associationist philosophers (principally James and John Stuart Mill) with the hereditarian implications of developments in physiology and neurology.

5   The notion of degeneration gave the investigation of human nature an added urgency, as well as an explanatory framework, in dealing with such social issues as crime, madness, 'idiocy' and alcoholism. Galton figures prominently here as the founder of 'eugenics', another influential savant being the Italian criminologist Cesare Lombroso.

6   The evolutionary image of human history as progressing through various stages (an idea rooted in eighteenth-century 'speculative histories') could also be applied to social behaviour, e.g. Gustav Le Bon saw crowds as collectively regressing to a more primitive mentality (see Chapter 12).

7   Finally most late nineteenth-century psychologists espoused the evolutionary perspective as their general theoretical framework. These included William James and James Mark Baldwin in the US, G.H. Lewes and James Sully in

Table 3.1 Psychological topics integrated by evolutionary thought

Animal behaviour Sheds light on 'mental evolution'.
Brain functioning Brain structure interpreted in terms of differing evolutionary levels.
Child development Child recapitulates psychological evolution.
Criminality Explained by 'degeneracy' and 'atavism'.
Crowd behaviour Regression to a more 'primitive' evolutionary stage.
'Idiocy' Explained by 'degeneracy' and 'atavism'.
Individual differences Represent the 'variation' on which natural selection operates.
Mental illness Explained by 'degeneracy' and 'atavism'.
'Race differences' Races are at different stages of evolution or separate evolutionary branches of humankind.
Sex differences Due to differing evolutionary functions – sometimes women were considered less evolved.

Britain, Theodore Ribot and Gabriel Tarde in France and non-Wundtians such as Karl Groos in Germany. There were some exceptions to this however, such as James Ward and G.F. Stout, who continued to adopt more philosophical orientations.

The diverse studies of children, animals, physiology, social behaviour and madness were thus unified as aspects of a single project: exploring the implications of the evolutionary perspective for human nature (see Table 3.1). We return to its impact on these fields in the relevant subsequent chapters. Inevitably this resulted in a tendency towards nativist 'instinct' explanations, but also advanced the 'functionalist' approach (however see Glossary for the complexities of this term). What this means in this context is basically that a psychological phenomenon can be explained by identifying its survival value for the organism. In the event, English-language Psychology texts up to 1900 are dominated by those written from an evolutionary perspective. Its role in Psychology is one aspect of evolutionary thought's broader cultural impact as reinforcing, for example, such beliefs as the 'naturalness' of competitive capitalism and the natural superiority of the white 'races'. Galton's 'eugenics' concerns were the principal manifestation of this in Psychology.

A further figure who cannot be omitted is the Scot Alexander Bain. Whilst never a fully committed evolutionist his two earliest books, *The Senses and the Intellect* (1856) and *The Emotions and the Will* (1859) comprehensively surveyed psychological issues from an empirical perspective, incorporating the latest physiological findings. Often labelled an 'associationist', Bain's thought also retained elements of the Scottish 'common sense' tradition. His approach was not experimental; rather he strove to systematise and classify psychological phenomena. Although he wrote numerous other works these were his most influential and revised versions continued in use as textbooks until the 1890s. In 1876 he founded the journal *Mind* in collaboration with G. Croom Robertson, a major forum for Psychological papers until the end of the century when specialist Psychology journals began appearing, *Mind* specialising in philosophy thereafter (see F. Neary, 2001, for the fullest account of the founding of *Mind* and its somewhat ambiguous character).

Experimental methodology

The role of evolutionary thought is absolutely crucial to the birth of modern Psychology (and modern 'psychology' too in fact), but was underplayed by earlier disciplinary historians in contrast to the rise, in Germany, of an experimental methodology. They chose to stress Psychology's scientific credentials by emphasising German experimentalism's vital role in gaining Psychology a foothold among the natural sciences. Its origins lie in a meeting between physiological studies of the senses, notably by E.H. Weber, and philosophical concerns with refuting Kant's arguments that scientific Psychology was impossible. The work marking the advent of experimental Psychology is generally taken as Gustav Fechner's 1859 *Elemente der Psychophysik*, 'Elements of Psychophysics'. Here, building on Weber's work, he investigated the relationship between changes in stimulus magnitude as objectively measured and as experienced. Weber had already discovered that the 'just noticeable difference' ('j.n.d.') – i.e. the amount of change necessary for a change to be perceived – was a function of the size of the stimulus, e.g. a half inch increment in length is easily spotted if the initial length is an inch, but not if it is fifty foot. What Fechner succeeded in doing was deriving a unit, based on the sensory threshold ('limen') for any sensation to be experienced at all, which could be used to quantify experienced, as against objectively measured, magnitude. With this he derived the 'Weber–Fechner Law', a generalised formula for relating perceived to objective changes in stimulus magnitude. Although this 'law' has, to a limited extent, withstood the test of time, it was the three experimental procedures he employed that had the most long-term impact and still continue to be used. These procedures, the 'method of constant stimuli', the 'method of limits' and the 'method of average error' are described (though the names used vary) in most experimental textbooks as well as in histories such as Boring (1950). Significantly, however, Fechner's aim was in fact still philosophical, as he thought he was helping solve the mind–body problem. His legacy, though, was to bequeath to posterity the subdiscipline 'Psychophysics'.

Soon after this Wilhelm Wundt, usually cast as Psychology's 'founding father', began his systematic laboratory studies of consciousness using experimental introspection. He believed this methodology was only applicable to psychophysical phenomena such as sensation, reaction times, and attention, holding that memory, thinking, language, personality, social behaviour and the like belonged to the humanities (in German, the *Geisteswissenschaften*) rather than sciences (*Naturwissenschaften*). The date of 1879 is normally given for the establishment by Wundt of the first Psychological laboratory at Leipzig. Wundt's experiments involved not 'subjects' but 'observers', trained to objectively introspect on what passed in their consciousness during the experiment (for a full account see Danziger, 1991). Wundt's older contemporary Herman Helmholtz, one of the century's most eminent scientists, in whose Heidelberg laboratory Wundt was an

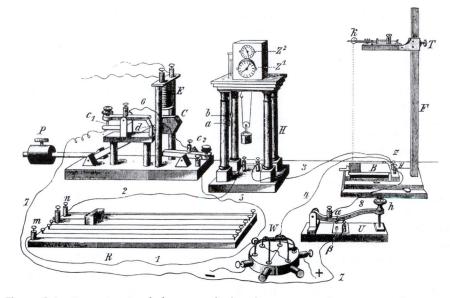

Figure 3.1 Promoting Psychology as a high-tech experimental science: an illustration from the fourth (1893) edition of Wilhelm Wundt's *Grundzüge der physiologischen Psychologie*. Reproduced by permission of Douwe Draaisma.

assistant for thirteen years, also published fundamental work on perception and hearing (see Chapter 8). Wundt was, additionally, very keen on introducing high technology equipment into the laboratory, which helped promote the image of Psychology as a hard scientific discipline (Draaisma and Rijcke, 2001) (Fig. 3.1).

Wundt's significance rests largely on his creation of the experimental laboratory and the fact that this attracted numerous American postgraduate students who, on returning home in the 1880s and 1890s, laid the foundations of American Psychology. Wundt is an interesting and controversial figure. His experimental Psychology, for which the English-speaking world remembers him, is only a fraction of his colossal output. He wrote extensively on philosophy and logic and capped a long career by producing a 10-volume *Völkerpsychologie* ('folk psychology'), of which only Volume 1 (on language) was translated into English. As it transpired, Wundt's disciples, notably the English-born E.B. Titchener who emigrated to the US, failed to establish his introspective methodology permanently beyond Germany, and his American ex-students soon abandoned the most Wundtian features of his Psychology. Even in Germany the following generation broke away from his doctrines. Most notably, the Würzburg school of O. Külpe, K. Marbe, N. Ach and K. Bühler, while introspectionist, rejected his view that all conscious contents were reducible to elementary processes of sensation and established the role of what they called 'conscious attitudes' in determining experience in experimental situations (to grossly simplify a highly complex theoretical issue). Other German-speaking thinkers, including E. Mach, C. Stumpf, W. Dilthey and F. Brentano, also disagreed with Wundt on numerous theoretical grounds, besides those adopting the evolutionary approach. Wundt's canonical eminence partly stems from the fact that E.G. Boring, Psychology's most influential historian, was Titchener's student. Since 1970 Boring's version of Wundt has been seriously contested, disagreement over what he actually believed and how important he really was still persisting. Certainly in Germany experimental Psychology spread to other universities no faster than elsewhere, and the first autonomous Psychology degree was not offered until the Nazi period. For English-speaking psychologists, it is I think fair to observe that Wundt has unduly dominated our picture of late nineteenth-century Psychological thought.

For the historian, Wundt's place in Psychology's history provides an interesting case study. Since the discipline itself, guided by its historians, has accepted him as its heroic founding father, this must be accepted as a *psychological* fact in its own right as far as generations of psychologists are concerned. Yet current historical research on how he acquired this role reveals a rather muddier picture. Unlike Newton, Lavoisier, Darwin or Einstein, Wundt, despite his legendarily prodigious productivity, left no enduring legacy at either the theoretical level or by way of empirical discoveries. Why, then, his long-standing eminence? Yes, he *did* succeed in establishing an academic presence for experimental research on psychological topics and produced lengthy textbooks and theoretical works on the subject. Beyond that, however, his status appears to derive more from the symbolic significance he acquired for others than the success of his Psychology. The discipline *wanted* a founding father with good experimental scientific credentials, and his American ex-students naturally revered him as their most influential teacher even while subsequently abandoning most of what he taught them. This tangled on-going debate at least demonstrates how difficult, perhaps impossible, it is to differentiate between the contributions of actor and audience to an historical achievement.

More influential methodologically in the long run was the British statistical tradition launched by Galton and Pearson, rooted in earlier work by the Belgian statistician A. Quetelet, and continued by C. Spearman, C. Burt, W.H. Winch, G. Udny Yule, and R.A. Fisher. This has dominated modern experimental Psychology and psychometrics, yielding all those *t*-tests, correlation coefficients, ANOVAs (analyses of variance) and such which have plagued the lives of so many students who joined Psychology 'in order to help people'. It arose in the context of evolutionary concerns, more specifically in the need to measure variation within populations regarding hereditary traits. From the start Galton's statistical methods had a dual purpose: as well as enabling researchers to quantify the degree and nature of data-variation, they also seemingly provided a tool for investigating the extent to which heredity was operating. Initially Galton focused on family pedigrees to establish how far eminence ran in families and was therefore, he believed, hereditary. He soon moved on to ponder the respective roles of 'nature and nurture' (effectively initiating this perennial debate), while his eugenic concerns demanded techniques for describing and comparing populations as a whole (see also Chapter 18).

The rapid expansion of statistics as an analytic, as well as descriptive, technique around 1900 provided psychologists with precisely the kind of quantitative tools they hankered after as necessary for their scientific credibility. A synergistic relationship developed: new statistical techniques opened up new research possibilities, while psychologists' heightened aspirations spurred the development of new statistical techniques adequate to the tasks they sought to undertake. The two primary directions this took were (a) measuring individuals on traits with regard to their standing in the population as a whole (psychometrics) and (b) comparing how groups (either the same group or different groups) performed under different experimental conditions. In the former, statistics became the primary research instrument in its own right, providing both techniques for designing psychometric tests and the tool by which the very things to be measured could, it was believed, be reliably identified or discovered. In the latter, while enabling the quantification of how 'significant' experimental results were, the statistical techniques available also guided the design of the experiments themselves (see Chapter 18).

By 1900 methodological issues had become the major priority for mainstream academic psychologists in the US and Britain, while theoretical issues had become less urgent. The majority still worked within a broad evolutionary framework, but experimentalists (if not psychometricians) were shifting their attention to the 'nurture' side of things. What seemed most important was accumulating quantifiable empirical data on matters hitherto rarely subjected to empirical scientific investigation: memory, learning, child development, fatigue, emotion and such. Data first, theory second, was the over-riding attitude. And while previously the mind or 'consciousness' was seen as the discipline's subject matter, the study of behaviour was making increasing inroads, supplementing if not replacing the mind itself.

Contextual aspects

So far this chapter has adopted a fairly 'internalist' approach, concentrating on theoretical and methodological factors *within* the tradition of Psychological enquiry which enabled it to intellectually (if not yet institutionally) integrate under a single disciplinary label. Even so, hints have been made of factors beyond these. It is time to take a closer look at them.

It is a simple fact that virtually all those involved in creating Psychology were white middle and upper class males, sharing the values and attitudes of their gender and social class. A few observations about this group may be made immediately. First, they saw themselves as being at the peak of humanity not only economically and culturally but, increasingly, in evolutionary terms. Second, they were acutely aware that they were responsible for managing societies of unprecedented size and complexity – again seen as the pinnacle of humanity's evolutionary development. Third, they really did see women and non-whites as intellectually deficient and possessed of various innate traits unfitting them for destinies other than domestic or menial (see Chapters 17 and 21). When scientifically minded men of this character turn to study their fellow humans their approach must inevitably be coloured by the attitudes, values and priorities associated with such a position, and it is surely not somehow deeply 'anti-scientific' to try and take this into account. It is a Psychological observation in its own right.

From this hierarchical world-view their attitude was essentially managerial. The appeal of Psychological expertise lay in its promise that those possessing it would be able to more effectively manage the populations under their control. This 'management of individuality', as Nikolas Rose calls it, should not be mistaken for ruthless oppression, rather it took the form of extreme paternalism, albeit with preparedness to take harsh decisions regarding the recalcitrantly unmanageable. Psychological expertise would enable them to educate the young efficiently, diagnose and deal with harmful deviancy and pathology, inform their policies towards, and treatment of, various social groups and subject populations, and enable them to direct those they governed into the most fitting walks of life, as well as improving industrial efficiency by a better understanding of phenomena such as fatigue and attention (see Chapter 13). It was this potential applicability of Psychological expertise that provided academic Psychology's underlying cultural momentum, moving it ever further from traditional philosophical concerns with the nature and structure of consciousness or the mind. Instead, from Galton onwards, it progressively gravitated towards developing practical expertise. Over and above any intrinsic scientific flaws, Wundtianism simply had little to offer such a project.

This agenda was reinforced by the cultural meanings which rapidly accrued to evolutionism. From their lofty height, men like Galton, Spencer and Lombroso surveyed the tumultuous scene beneath with some apprehension. The foundations were in real or potential danger of being undermined by the proliferating lower orders, inferior human stock, who seemingly outbred their superiors. This threatened not just a historically transient ruling class or economically privileged clique but civilisation itself, the entire human evolutionary achievement. Humanity's very future was at stake. Thus the eugenic and degenerationist thinking of Galton and many like him across Europe and North America profoundly affected their conception of the task of Psychology. We will see in later chapters how this infused Psychology's initial views of crime, madness, women, children and 'race'.

An intriguing feature of the situation as far as the relationship between Psychology and psychology is concerned is that evolutionism brought to prominence an image of human nature which was actually quite new: beneath our civilised veneers lurks a 'beast within'. The social position of the class to which Psychology's founders belonged was thus reflected in their image of the structure of the psyche. Enlightened reason had to control and manage the lurking instinctual and bestial forces of irrationality – and the now enlightened could locate them in the mind or in the seething masses they sought to manage with equal ease. As well as in numerous other cultural forms, we can find this 'beast within' image in turn-of-the-century Psychological writings ranging from the French Psychologists G. Tarde and G. Le Bon to Sigmund Freud himself, with his entirely negative view of the unconscious. In this climate opposition thought naturally turned increasingly to the celebration of the irrational and 'primitive' (e.g. in painting and music).

A further, less obvious consequence of these developments was that Psychological writers became blind to certain insights into the reflexivity of the enterprise which had, to a limited extent, been achieved by earlier philosophers. The foundational position of Psychology in relation to the natural sciences, for example – the fact that scientific thinking and behaviour must logically be part of the subject matter of any would-be science of thinking and behaviour – was lost from view as the imperative to prove its scientific credentials intensified. This was an insight central to, for example, David Hume's philosophy as well as to that of the contemporary American 'mental and moral philosopher' Noah Porter. One error of Psychology's founders was to confound the Olympian mode of consciousness produced by their social class position with 'scientific objectivity' itself. Only they, it seemed, could see the entire picture 'objectively' from their exalted position. All below were to some degree incapable of 'objectivity', and hence vulnerable to irrationality. Only the ruling paternal eye could really encompass the totality. This position was sustainable precisely because their evolutionary perspective enabled them to see their situation as a natural one, rooted ultimately in biology, rather than the product of purely social and historical forces. If they were on top, this of itself *proved* their essential superiority.

This is not to say that Psychology's rise was entirely due to 'top down' factors of this kind. If the ruling classes saw such a discipline as potentially assisting them in discharging their paternal managerial duties to the national family, faith in science was spreading at the grass roots too. It was to this that phrenology owed its earlier success, and the subsequent acquiescence of the populace to Psychological testing needs to be understood in the light of gradual mass-familiarisation with quasi-scientific phrenological and physiognomical personality analyses since the beginning of the nineteenth century. Aspirations towards better education, control of criminality, improved understanding of mental distress and the like were shared by everyone enthused by modern 'scientific' industrial culture or experiencing the problems it brought in its train (see also Chapter 11 on another aspect of the situation, the problem of the 'Self'). In this respect masters and subjects were in accord. But as to which side *they* were on – psychologists were as yet unconscious of any conflict of interests.

There was, though, an underlying difficulty. To be useful Psychology would have to be applicable. This implied that expert *environmental* intervention in psychological affairs would eventually be effective in determining the course of events. On the other hand, the prevailing evolutionary framework was fundamentally *hereditarian* or 'nativist', implying that environmental influences could have a limited psychological effect at best. This has been an axis of controversy ever since. Broadly speaking, professionals whose job is descriptive and diagnostic, such as psychometricians in the Galtonian tradition, have tended to be 'nativist'. If you are claiming to measure someone's intelligence, for example, you will be unfavourably disposed to the prospect of this changing significantly next week or next year because of environmental influences. By contrast, those whose jobs are interventionist have tended to be 'nurturists', since such jobs would be pointless if their environmental interventions were ineffective. The immediate lesson of this here is that it suggests that their theoretical orientations are not likely to be unaffected by the kinds of 'external' pressures on Psychologists (with which they will tend to identify anyway) to direct their efforts towards those goals prioritised by their own class and culture or, more loosely, the 'psychological constituency' they represent. In the nineteenth century these tended towards managerial description, classification and diagnosis within hereditarian evolutionist assumptions, in the twentieth century this was increasingly supplemented, though not displaced, by interventionist and self-liberatory goals, for which environmentalist orientations are more congenial.

Conclusion

Psychology's late nineteenth-century debut was a distinctively 'modern' development. It involved creating images of human nature consistent with and reflecting life in the new industrial-scientific cultures. Evolutionary thought provided a rich 'modern', 'scientific' way of viewing the world and humanity's place within it which yielded the first and perhaps most profound of such images. The experimental methodology introduced by Wundt similarly represented an appropriately radical departure from the past in how human nature should be studied, even if his own introspective methodology proved inadequate. In early twenty-first century retrospect these developments clearly carried a heavy price, especially in the case of evolutionary thought. However valid its core hypothesis, the cultural meanings it acquired rapidly constrained evolutionary thought, especially about humans, within the class, 'race' and gender-specific interests of those promulgating it. Women were less evolved than men, Africans less evolved than Europeans, criminals degenerate offspring of tainted stock, and within each of us lurked a bestial savage striving to shake off reason's shackles.

It was not to be in Europe, however, that Psychology first succeeded in establishing itself institutionally as an autonomous academic discipline but in the United States. Why and how it did so is the topic of the next chapter.

Further reading

Evolutionary thought

Boakes, R. (1984) *From Darwinism to Behaviourism: Psychology and Minds of Animals.* Cambridge: Cambridge University Press. A sound basic history of Comparative Psychology.

Bowler, P. (1983) *The Eclipse of Darwinism: Anti-Darwinian Evolution Theories in the Decades around 1900.* Baltimore & London: Johns Hopkins University Press. An extremely useful review of the complex state of evolutionary thought in the late Victorian and Edwardian periods. Important background reading for understanding the intellectual context in which Psychology emerged.

Cravens, H. (1978) *The Triumph of Evolution: American Scientists and the Heredity–Environment Controversy 1900–1941.* Pennsylvania University Press. Useful supplementary reading on twentieth-century American developments.

Pick, D. (1989) *Faces of Degeneration. A European Disorder c. 1848–c. 1918.* Cambridge: Cambridge University Press. The best general review of the 'degeneration' panic.

Richards, R.J. (1987) *Darwin and the Emergence of Evolutionary Theories of Mind and Behavior.* Chicago: Chicago University Press. The most exhaustive examination of the topic, this must now be considered a classic text.

Young, R.M. (1970, rep. 1990) *Mind, Brain and Adaptation in the Nineteenth-Century.* Oxford: Oxford University Press. The best account of the physiological Psychology side of the story.

Wundt and German Psychology

Boring, E.G. (1929, 2nd edn 1950) *A History of Experimental Psychology*. New York: Appleton-Century-Crofts. Has extensive coverage of all the German-speaking pioneers.

Bringmann, W.G. and Tweney, R.D. (eds) (1980) *Wundt Studies*. Toronto: Hogrefe. Contains several crucial papers on the Wundt controversy. R.D. Tweney and S.A. Yachanin's 'Titchener's Wundt' (pp. 380–395) is a judicious evaluation of the relationship between them.

Danziger, K. (1990) *Constructing the Subject: Historical Origins of Psychological Research*. Cambridge: Cambridge University Press. Excellent on Wundt's methodology and its rivals.

Draaisma, D. and de Rijcke, S. (2001) 'The Graphic Strategy. The Uses and Functions of Illustrations in Wundt's *Grundzuge*'. *History of the Human Sciences*, 14: 1–24. Explores Wundt's efforts to promote an image of Psychology as a high-tech experimental natural science.

Rieber, R. (ed.) (1980) *Wilhelm Wundt and the Making of a Scientific Psychology*. New York: Plenum Press. For the 'revisionist' debate on Wundt.

Primary texts

For full bibliographic data see 'Further reading' texts.

Major early Psychological works espousing evolutionism

Child development

Chamberlain, A.E. (1900) *The Child: A Study in the Evolution of Man*.

Darwin, C. (1877) 'A Biographical Sketch of an Infant'. *Mind*, 2.

Groos, K. (1901) *The Play of Man*.

Hall, G.S. (1904) *Adolescence* (2 vols).

Preyer, W. (1888) *The Mind of the Child* (vol. 1).

Sully, J. (1895) *Studies in Childhood*. Reprinted 2000, with Introduction by S. Sugarman and Biographical Introduction by E. Valentine. London: Free Association Books.

Animal behaviour

Darwin, C. (1872) *Expression of the Emotions in Man and Animals* (1872).

Groos, K. (1896, English edn 1898) *The Play of Animals*.

Lloyd Morgan, C. (1894) *Introduction to Comparative Psychology*.

Lubbock, J. (1882) *Ants, Bees and Wasps*.

Romanes, G.J. (1882) *Animal Intelligence*.

Individual differences

Galton, F. (1883) *Inquiries into Human Faculty.*
King, J.H. (1893) *Man as an Organic Community* (2 vols). London: Williams and Norgate; New York: G.P. Putnam's. This somewhat bizarre text has only recently been 'rediscovered'; it is, however, highly significant as an example of the lengths to which evolutionary recapitulationist logic could be taken.

See also:
Fancher, R. (1985) *The Intelligence Men: Makers of the IQ Controversy.* New York: Norton.

Physiological psychology

Carpenter, W.B. (1874) *The Principles of Mental Physiology.*
Ferrier, D. (1876) *The Functions of the Brain.*

General theory

Baldwin, J.M. (1902) *Development and Evolution.*
James, W. (1890) *Principles of Psychology* (2 vols).
Lewes, G.H. (1874–1879) *Problems of Life and Mind* (5 vols).
Spencer, H. (1855) *Principles of Psychology.*

Social psychology

Le Bon, G. (1896) *The Crowd.*
Ward, L. (1892) *The Psychic Factors of Civilization.*

Mental illness, 'deviance' and gender

Dugdale, R.L. (1877) *'The Jukes'. A Study in Crime, Pauperism, Disease and Heredity.*
Ellis, H. (1890) *The Criminal.*
Ellis, H. (1896) *Man and Woman.*
Galton, F. (1896) *Hereditary Genius.*
Lombroso, C. (1876) *L'Uomo Delinquente* (The Delinquent Man).
Lombroso, C. and Ferrero, W. (1895) *The Female Offender.*
Maudsley, H. (1892) *Responsibility in Mental Disease, 5th edn.*
Nordau, M. (1895) *Degeneration.*
Wilson, A. (1910) *Unfinished Man.*

Wundt's and Fechner's major works

Fechner, G. (1859) *Elemente der Psychophysik*.
Wundt, W. (1862) *Beitrage zur Theorie der Sinneswahrnehmung*.
Wundt, W. (1863) *Lectures on Human and Animal Psychology*. Trans. J.E. Creighton and E.B. Titchener 1896.
Wundt, W. (1874) *Grundzüge der physiologischen Psychologie*. Generally considered to be the first modern Psychology textbook, this went through numerous subsequent revised editions.
Wundt, W. (1896) *Grundriss der Psychologie*.
Wundt, W. (1900–1910) *Völkerpsychologie* (10 vols).

Other major German texts

Brentano, F. (1874) *Psychologie vom empirischen Standpunkt*.
Ebbinghaus, H. (1885) *Memory: A Contribution to Experimental Psychology* (English trans. 1913, rep. 1964).
Helmholtz, H. (1863) *Die Lehre von den Tonempfindungen*.
Külpe, O. (1893, English edn 1895) *Outlines of Psychology*.
Mach, E. (1885, English edn 1906) *The Analysis of Sensations*.
Müller, G.E. (1878) *Zur Grundlegung der Psychologie*.
Stumpf, C. (1883, 1890) *Tonpsychologie* (2 vols).

French Psychology

Binet, A. (1888) *Études de psychologie experimentale*.
Ribot, T. (1873) *English Psychology*.
Ribot, T. (1883) *Diseases of Memory*, 2nd edn.
Ribot, T. (1886) *German Psychology of Today*.
Taine, H. (1871) *On Intelligence*.
Tarde, G. (1890) *Les Lois de l'Imitation*.

Additional reference

Morgan, L.H. (1877) *Ancient Society or Researches in the Lines of Human Progress from Savagery through Barbarism to Civilization*. Chicago: Charles H. Kerr.

Chapter 4

William James and the origins of American Psychology

- William James's life and character
- James's *Principles of Psychology* (1890) and its contents
- James's significance
- Origins of the 'New Psychology'
- Major figures besides William James
- Why Psychology established itself so successfully in the United States

William James (1842–1910)

Just as A.N. Whitehead famously said that Philosophy consisted of footnotes to Plato, it might similarly be argued that, in some respects, modern American Psychology is a series of footnotes to William James's two-volume masterpiece *The Principles of Psychology* (1890). To understand James's historical role it is necessary to consider briefly his life and personality – his own 'psychology'. He was the eldest son of a rich New England family, his father being a keen follower of the eighteenth-century Swedish mystic Emanuel Swedenborg. After William came Henry, the novelist, whose wider fame excels William's own. Thirdly came Alice, now remembered as a diarist and something of a feminist heroine. Two younger brothers, Wilkie and Garth, had less eminent lives. One feature of their childhoods was that their father led them a wandering, albeit affluent, life criss-crossing Europe (and the Atlantic) numerous times. His educational ideas were somewhat eccentric. While keen on his children gaining a wide knowledge of life, science and culture he had a horror of them ever committing themselves to specific careers. As soon as one of them showed real interest in a topic he tended to discourage them from pursuing it too deeply and shunted them onto something else. Knowing about chemistry was fine, wanting to become a chemist was not.

It was an intellectually stimulating life-style, gaining the eldest children early mastery of French and German, but also confusing and disruptive. By his late teens William was suffering serious emotional problems and displaying numerous psychosomatic symptoms. In the terminology of the day he was clearly 'neurasthenic', or in current parlance neurotically anxious and depressed. He dropped out of Harvard where he had been studying medicine and comparative anatomy, tried painting, at which he had considerable skill, then abandoned that too. In 1865 he journeyed up the Amazon with the great zoologist Louis Agassiz, fell ill, concluded that zoology was not his forte either, decided to be a philosopher and returned worse than ever. He remained a virtual invalid almost until he was 30, when he really started pulling his life together. In 1869 he finally qualified as a doctor at Harvard Medical School (although never practised), becoming an instructor in anatomy and physiology at Harvard in 1873. Psychodynamic theorists might see his prolonged incapacitation as an ultimately creative 'moratorium' period, but only someone in his socially privileged position could get away with it.

During the early 1870s, James and his friend C.S. Peirce (future founder of 'pragmatism' and, arguably, semiotics), honed their philosophical skills in the 'Metaphysical Club' run by the brilliant, but eccentric, evolutionist Chauncey Wright in Cambridge, Massachusetts. In 1875, four years before Wundt's Leipzig laboratory was founded, James began giving instruction in physiological Psychology, using a small demonstration laboratory which Americans sometimes invoke as the first Psychological laboratory, although it was not experimental and little more than a large cupboard. He was soon promoted to Assistant Professor of Physiology. In 1878, the year of his marriage to Alice Gibbens, he began writing the *Principles*, and in 1880 switched to Assistant Professor of Philosophy, becoming full Professor in 1885 only to change titles once more, in 1889, to Professor of Psychology. Ironically, after 1890 his interests moved increasingly towards Philosophy, particularly the advocacy of pragmatism, and in 1897 the German anti-Wundtian Hugo

Munsterberg arrived at his behest to take over the experimental side. (University College London acquired most of Munsterberg's equipment for the first English Psychology laboratory.) In 1901–1902 he returned to Psychology in his famous Gifford Lectures at Edinburgh, published as *The Varieties of Religious Experience*, otherwise his last years were devoted to philosophy.

Throughout adulthood James continued the wandering habits of childhood, only once spending six years continuously in the United States. He was a personal friend or acquaintance with nearly all the leading academic and literary figures of his day (contacts often facilitated by his charming brother Henry who had settled in Europe).

One way of reading James's career is to see him as resolving the question of 'what shall I be?', rendered so acute by his father's educational strategy, by becoming a professional mind, an expert on what it was like to be conscious. And very good at it he was too (see Fig. 4.1). The mature William James was an attractive personality, open-minded, tolerant of paradox and inconsistency – which he sought to articulate rather than hide – and ever sympathetic to the psychological troubles of others. His open-mindedness is evident in his continued interest in psychic research long after it ceased to be fashionable.

Why was James initially so disturbed? I have indicated some personal reasons already, but these served to render him peculiarly conscious of the wider underlying anxieties of the post-Darwin era (see also Chapter 11 on this point). The 'determinism vs. free will' debate, intensified by the successes of contemporary deterministic science, particularly preoccupied him in his early twenties. A reading of the French philosopher Charles Renouvier showed him a way out – and he resolved, he says, as his first free act, to believe in free will. The philosophy of pragmatism which Peirce and he (along with John Dewey) later developed was very much aimed at rescuing the notion of free will in human affairs. This in itself casts James in an ambiguous light as far as scientific Psychology is concerned, for his commitment to the adequacy of science to account for human nature was always less than wholehearted.

A final background point needs to be made to set James in perspective. The New England culture in which he grew up (and which his father embodied) was deeply infused by the earlier nineteenth-century movement known as New England Transcendentalism, a later American version of Romanticism, of which the leading figures had been Ralph Waldo Emerson (who dandled the infant William on his lap), Henry Thoreau and Nathaniel Hawthorne. This legacy is, I believe, fairly clear in James's own writings. The *Principles* is acknowledged as a literary masterpiece, and often echoes the style of Emerson's essays.

Why James is so significant is partly because his position is so obviously ambivalent regarding Psychology, and because the ambiguities and paradoxes he raised have remained with the discipline ever since (G.W. Allport, 1943). Unlike most American 'founding fathers' he was uneasy about mounting the 'science' bandwagon. Yet he was as cosmopolitan a thinker as it was possible to be, in touch with all contemporary developments in philosophy, Psychology and physiology and sufficiently on the ball to review Freud and Breuer's seminal paper on hysteria in 1893, the year of publication. The *Principles of Psychology* itself is a highly ambiguous work. Wundt allegedly exclaimed on reading it, 'It's literature,

Figure 4.1 The professional introspector: a self-portrait by William James (c. 1866). Reproduced by permission of the Houghton Library, Harvard University (shelf-mark reference: fMS Am 1092.2) and Bay James, copyright trustee of the William James estate.

it's beautiful, but it's not Psychology!' (in German of course). Much of it had earlier appeared in journal paper form, hence many of the ideas it contained were already known to his contemporaries. In some ways it was the high point of the older introspective philosophical approach, but it comprehensively surveyed and integrated the new scientific Psychological information available from Germany, France, Britain, Italy, Russia and North America. In this latter role it served as a point of departure, both goad and challenge, for the succeeding generation even when they rejected its underlying orientation. Such unity as it possesses is not that of a scientific theory, but more a matter of stylistic consistency and 'voice', the personality or 'psychology' of James himself. Let us then consider some of its contents.

Although I cannot cover them in any depth, among the most enduringly influential chapters were the following:

The stream of thought

This expounds one of James's best known ideas, the stream of thought or, as it became more widely known, the stream of consciousness. His basic argument, one he sees as refuting rigid determinism, is that because every experience changes the organism, the organism never has the same experience twice – for on the second occasion on which the same stimulus is presented the organism itself is different. No psychological state recurs in precisely the same form. If we try to capture the course of consciousness five basic points emerge that, though possibly obvious, need to be spelled out:

(a)   every thought belongs to a personal consciousness;
(b)   within that consciousness thought is always changing;
(c)   it is 'sensibly continuous' – we do not experience any gaps in it;
(d)   it always appears to deal with objects independent of itself;
(e)   it selects from these all the while.

Pursuing these points (especially b and c), James observes that consciousness does not appear 'chopped up in bits': 'It is nothing jointed; it flows. A river or stream are the metaphors by which it is most naturally described . . . Let us call it the stream of thought, of consciousness, or of subjective life' (James 1890: 463). The character of this 'stream' and the difficulties we have in introspectively grasping it are then spelled out, deploying a variety of further metaphors, e.g. the bird's life 'of alternate flights and restings' used to capture the distinction between 'transitive and intransitive' passages of consciousness (it is transitive ones which are peculiarly recalcitrant to introspection), and the bamboo stalk with its joints, analogous to sudden events which change, but do not break, the continuity of consciousness. Among other things this argument raised serious problems for associationism, which becomes just one more metaphor for certain features of the stream, not the full story. This idea had considerable influence, e.g. James Joyce's *Finnegans Wake* has been seen as an attempt to trace this stream in all its detail, while it also, quite fortuitously, helped popularise the psychoanalytic notion of 'free association' – with which it sometimes got confused.

Emotion

This chapter contains the James–Lange Theory of Emotion (Karl Lange, a Danish psychologist, having proposed something similar), one of the few relatively hard hypotheses James proposed. It demonstrates his ability to argue convincingly for an initially implausible idea: that rather than emotions determining bodily reactions, the reverse is the case. Like the English psychologist William McDougall a little later, he saw instincts and emotions as inextricably linked: 'every object that excites an instinct excites an emotion as well', but emotions fall short of instincts in 'terminating in the subject's own body' instead of entering into 'practical relations with the exciting object'. In brief he argues that '... we feel sorry because we cry, angry because we strike, afraid because we tremble ...' (vol. II, p. 450). The following passage indicates how difficult it is to differentiate Psychology and 'psychology':

> In rage, it is notorious how we 'work ourselves up' to a climax by repeated outbreaks of expression. Refuse to vent a passion and it dies. Count ten before venting your anger, and its occasion becomes ridiculous. Whistling to keep up courage is no mere figure of speech. On the other hand, sit all day in a moping posture, sigh and reply to everything with a dismal voice, and your melancholy lingers. There is no more valuable precept in moral education than this, as all who have experience know: if we wish to conquer undesirable emotional tendencies in ourselves, we must assiduously, and in the first instance cold-bloodedly, go through the outward movements of those contrary dispositions which we prefer to cultivate. The reward of persistence will infallibly come ... Smooth the brow, brighten the eye, contract the dorsal rather than the ventral aspect of the frame, and speak in a major key, pass the genial compliment, and your heart must be frigid indeed if it do not gradually thaw!
>
> (vol. II, p. 463)

This conveys not just a Psychological theory of the emotions, but at least two other levels of meaning: (a) echoes of how he himself finally overcame his prolonged moping, sighing, and melancholy 'dispositions' by an act of will; and (b) a typical late nineteenth-century piece of moral discourse, representative of the 'psychology' of the times – an extended exhortation to 'count to ten before losing your temper, pull yourself together, straighten your back, stop frowning!'

Another quotable passage is this:

> Prof. Sikorsky of Kieff has contributed an important article on facial expression of the insane to the Neurologisches Centralblatt for 1887. Having practised facial mimicry himself a great deal, he says: When I contract my facial muscles in any mimetic combination, I feel no emotional excitement, so that the mimicry is in the fullest sense of the word artificial, although quite irreproachable from the expressive point of view. We find, however, from the context that Prof. S's practice before the mirror has developed in him such a virtuosity in the control of his facial muscles that he can entirely disregard their natural association and contract them in any order of grouping ...
>
> (vol. II, p. 465)

This surely tells us more about the state of Psychiatry in Kiev than it does about the expression of emotion!

The James–Lange theory has not fared well, and there was a long consensus that certain animal experiments by Walter Cannon had disproved it. Even so, it is difficult not to feel that James was onto something. The phenomenology of emotion is often consistent with his doctrine: following a bump in the car, we feel fine, then realise our legs are trembling and that we are actually in a state of shock, or we think we are displaying great *sang froid* in dealing with some upsetting incident until, on meeting a friend, we discover ourselves bawling our eyes out. Again, try grinning miserably or cheerfully scowling.

The self

James's discussion of the 'self' launched a topic that later figured centrally in Social Psychology (e.g. G.H. Mead's studies in the 1930s and much current 'postmodernist' work on the topic, discussed further in Chapter 11). James's fellow pioneer James Mark Baldwin (1897) also tackled it. He begins by distinguishing between the self 'as known', i.e. as an object of knowledge (the 'empirical ego' or 'me'), and the self as 'knower' (the 'I', the 'pure' or 'transcendental ego'). This last concept, traceable to Kant (and indeed to Buddhism), James later rejects as unnecessary. It transpires that there is an hierarchy of empirical selves, 'the material me', 'the social me' and 'the spiritual me'. On further examination there are innumerable social selves, virtually a different one for every acquaintance and type of situation. My 'self' extends to my belongings, my favourite football team perhaps, or my country. All that with which I feel a personal identification or sense of belonging is an aspect of 'me' – if it is damaged, lost, fails or whatever I feel it as my own loss or failing. There is also a nice little equation:

$$\text{Self-esteem} = \frac{\text{Success}}{\text{Pretensions}}$$

Habit, Methods and Snares, Memory

The other chapters I will mention more briefly. That on habit lays the groundwork for the early work on learning by Edward Thorndike (done in James's basement) which led him to formulate the Laws of Effect and Exercise. It contains some powerful sermonising on habit as the 'enormous fly-wheel of society' which keeps 'the miner in his darkness, and nails the countryman to his log-cabin and his lonely farm through all the months of snow; it protects us from invasion by the natives of the desert and the frozen zone' (vol. I, p. 121). Again, the Psychological and 'psychological' seem to fuse. He is far less at odds with associationism here than in the Stream of Thought chapter.

The 'Methods and Snares' chapter is particularly important, though more difficult than most of the others, in containing an influential account of the introspective method. Notably he draws attention to one very dangerous 'snare': 'the psychologist's fallacy' – a tendency to confuse the 'idea' which one is reporting with the object of the idea (also known as 'stimulus error'), this arising because we use the same words for both. The idea of a wall is not built up from ideas of bricks. In dealing with phenomena such as emotion, however, this distinction becomes more obscure. The psychologist must avoid confusing 'his own stand-point with that of the mental fact about which he is making his report'. For James, introspection is still *the* primary method of Psychology, but I feel this chapter unwittingly elucidates the sheer difficulty of valid introspection for those less remorselessly introspective than James himself. Some current writers (e.g. Jill Morawski) see this argument (which was widely accepted) as a means by which the first psychologists outflanked the 'reflexivity' problem: in effect it claimed that psychologists could, by their training, achieve a distinctive mode of objective professional consciousness from which to view consciousness itself. The chapter also contains an entertaining account of the new German experimental methods (James says they could never arise in a nation capable of being bored) which explicitly articulates his deep ambivalence towards experimentalism and the 'pendulum and chronograph philosophers'. He knows the discipline's future lies in this direction and, as mentioned, appoints Munsterberg for just this reason, but temperamentally he has no feel for it (even though he happily cites reports of experimental findings).

Finally, the Memory chapter introduces the distinction between short-term or 'echoic' memory and secondary or long-term memory (STM and LTM), including an interesting discussion on the duration of STM and how long the 'rearward portion of the present space of time' extends. James gave it an upper limit of twelve seconds but J.M. Baldwin (reviewing the book) disagreed, arguing for four seconds at most.

Taken overall the *Principles* played a major role in setting the agenda of issues for the next generation of 'functionalist' Psychologists, although it was far from the only textbook available. James sets his ideas in a broad evolutionary frame-work in which the basic function of mind is to gain knowledge. It covers nearly the whole field, although some areas such as animal and child Psychology are absent (but it does contain the famous comment that a new-born baby's life is 'one great blooming, buzzing confusion' (vol. I, p. 488), with which few would now agree).

To sum up: James's contribution to Psychology was a central, but complex, one. His own deeper aims were to rescue free will, to set limits on rigid deter-minism, and, like his 'Mental and Moral Philosophy' predecessors, to promote Psychology as a route for morally beneficial self-knowledge and understanding. Yet he is fascinated by the findings of contemporary empirical research, citing and quoting a vast array of contemporaries whose work fuels his own creative thought. Whatever he finds 'introspectively' he is keen to reconcile with the latest findings in physiology, German psychophysics, or French clinical studies of double con-sciousness. It is a cliché to say people are 'transitional' or that their thought com-bines new and old, but in James's case it is for once deeply true. The traditional aspects of his work (introspection, moralising, self-conscious use of literary style, personal distaste for experimentation) genuinely contrast with its original aspects (orientation towards scientific evidence, preparedness to rethink basic issues, acceptance of an evolutionary perspective, and curiosity about hitherto neglected or unfashionable phenomena and topics). He was indeed a brilliant introspector, and excellent at evoking such vague borderline phenomena as having something on the tip-of-the-tongue or how attitudes change with age. Equally, it remains a moot point how far James belongs to the nineteenth century or the twentieth. Although a fairly near contemporary of Freud – very much a twentieth-century figure – his overt long-term influence has been far less. And yet it is surprising how American Psychology periodically indulges in a spell of re-reading and reassessing James. For Americans he is a cultural hero as well as a psychologist, America's first major home-grown philosopher. 'Nothing human is alien to me' – James certainly strove to exemplify this ancient adage in his own life and thought, even if his cultural setting and privileged position meant that some human things remained invisible to him.

In historical retrospect James seems to loom in stature far above his contemporaries in American Psychology. At the time however, charismatic and central though he was, his standing as a scientific psychologist of the new school was a matter of debate. Let us now step back and look at how the 'New Psychology', as it called itself, became established so successfully and rapidly in the United States between 1880 and 1900.

The founding of the 'New Psychology' 1880–1900

Most pre-1980s accounts tend to accept uncritically the pioneers' claims to represent a revolutionary break with the past, with nothing done in the US prior to their own endeavours being of much value. Recent writers have begun to contest this picture. Ever since the early nineteenth century American universities and colleges had imposed on their students a compulsory course of 'Mental and Moral Philosophy'. The reason for this was that these institutions (invariably having denominational affiliations, most frequently Presbyterian) felt it necessary to counter the materialist and atheist arguments of many leading European thinkers by demonstrating the consistency of Christianity with philosophy and logic. They had good grounds for anxiety as at around 1800 there had been major campus riots by avowedly atheist students (including Bible-burning and arson). The philosophical tradition which most college presidents (who taught such courses) adhered to was the Scottish 'common-sense' school (see Chapter 2) that dominated the Mental and Moral Philosophy curriculum prior to the 1880s, although German idealism and some French philosophers (like the 'eclectic' Victor Cousin) also had a presence. The traditional image is of this school as hidebound, dogmatic, and anti-scientific, one writer variously describing it as 'a great cloud', 'a frigid wave', a 'kind of Protestant scholasticism' (R.C. Davis, 1936). The 'New Psychology' was cast as breaking the stranglehold of this sterile force.

Recently a number of us have been doing that daunting thing – reading the forbidding tomes produced by this despised school. The organisational and institutional factors involved in the shift from Mental and Moral Philosophy to Psychology have also come under scrutiny. We are now beginning to appreciate that, even in the 1860s, a number of American writers, including some Mental and Moral Philosophers, were starting to address contemporary European developments such as the evolution question. During the 1870s there are numerous indications of movement and leading establishment figures are writing books that, while admittedly pious, are far from anti-scientific and dogmatic. Even more interestingly, several pioneer New Psychologists were inspired by, or were protégés of, leading Mental and Moral Philosophers. Three notable cases are G. Stanley Hall, first inspired by John Bascom (now virtually forgotten), James Mark Baldwin, a protégé of the eminent Mental and Moral Philosopher, James McCosh, and George Trumball Ladd, recruited to Yale by the notoriously conservative Noah Porter. Institutionally, the post-Civil War period saw a rapid expansion of tertiary education, with numerous secular universities, such as Johns Hopkins, being founded, accompanied by growing pressure for post-graduate level teaching, hitherto absent, and a decline in the college president's authority. My own view is that, while Psychology established itself as a replacement for Mental and Moral Philosophy under these changing conditions, there were some important respects in which it continued to play a similar 'moral education' role. Furthermore, many textbooks published as 'Psychology' between 1880 and 1900 closely resemble their predecessors in agenda and structure, even if they are more secular in approach and more 'scientific' in tone. In other words, there were fairly high levels of continuity between old and new, and the New Psychology's revolutionary rhetoric was frequently more an expression of aspiration than achievement; not until the following century was any 'revolution' really accomplished. German and British influences were indeed crucial, but such influences were discernibly at work from the 1860s.

We may now turn to those, besides James, most involved in the rise of the New Psychology: G. Stanley Hall, James Mark Baldwin, John Dewey, George Trumball Ladd, E.B. Titchener, James McKeen Cattell and E.W. Scripture (see Table 4.1). While these are the best known there were numerous others who

Table 4.1 The founders of Psychology in North America, and their institutions.

James Mark Baldwin	Toronto University, Johns Hopkins University*
Mary W. Calkins	Wellesley College
James McKeen Cattell	Columbia University*
John Dewey	University of Chicago*
G. Stanley Hall	Johns Hopkins University, Clark University*
William James	Harvard University*
Joseph Jastrow	University of Wisconsin
George Trumball Ladd	Yale*
Morton Prince	Tufts University from 1902 after medical career
E.C. Sanford	Johns Hopkins University, Clark University
E.W. Scripture	Yale*
E.B. Titchener (English expatriate)	Cornell University*
Margaret F. Washburn	Wells College, Cornell University, University of Cincinnati

* These may be considered as the major figures.

cannot be discussed here, such as Morton Prince, E.C. Sanford, Joseph Jastrow and the only two women figuring significantly, Mary Whiton Calkins and Margaret Floy Washburn. (Some sociologists, notably Lester Ward, would warrant inclusion in a comprehensive account.) It must be stressed that, while succeeding in presenting a fairly united front to the outside world, this group disagreed among themselves regarding most matters of importance such as the role and nature of experimentation, 'pure' versus 'applied' conceptions of Psychology's goals, whether or not behaviour as well as consciousness was part of their agenda, and how Psychology and philosophy were – or should be – related (see J.M. O'Donnell, 1985).

Organisationally, the prime mover of the New Psychology was G.S. Hall (who had done a doctorate under Wundt), founder of the American Psychological Association (APA). He also created Psychology departments at Johns Hopkins and Clark universities and numerous journals, most importantly the *American Journal of Psychology* (1887) and *Pedagogical Seminary*, later *Journal of Genetic Psychology* (1891). His primary area of interest was developmental Psychology, espousing recapitulationism and initiating the first large-scale programme of empirical research; indeed he is widely credited with launching what is known as the 'Child Study Movement'. His *magnum opus* was the two-volume *Adolescence* (1904). In 1910 he invited S. Freud, C.G. Jung and other psychoanalysts to the Clark University 20th Anniversary celebrations, providing them with their first opportunity to expound the doctrine in the New World. Hall was undoubtedly an opportunist and a highly effective political animal in promoting Psychology's interests between 1880 and 1910, capable of trimming his sails to the prevailing wind when necessary (e.g. variously claiming Psychology was entirely secular or affirming its doctrinal respectability according to the audience being addressed). His emphasis on child development was well calculated to highlight the new discipline's practical value. His last major Psychological work was *Senescence* (1922).

James Mark Baldwin was, like Hall, an ardent evolutionist and founded the Toronto and Princeton laboratories. Unlike Hall he was a keen laboratory experimentalist, but it was his *Mental Development in the Child and the Race* (1894) and *Social and Ethical Interpretations of Mental Development* (1897) which were his most influential Psychological works. A prolific writer, he shifted increasingly towards philosophy although remaining Professor of Psychology at Johns Hopkins until 1908. In 1894 he co-founded the *Psychological Review* with J. McK. Cattell to compete with the *American Journal of Psychology*. Theoretically his most significant contributions were his innovations in evolutionary theory and the groundwork he laid for subsequent Developmental and Social Psychology studies of the 'self' (J. Broughton and D.J. Freeman-Moir (eds), 1982).

The keenest advocates of Wundtian Psychology were the English *emigré* E.B. Titchener (at Cornell) and Scripture (at Yale), both Leipzig veterans. Titchener carried the Wundtian introspectionist flag (calling his approach 'structuralism') until his death in 1927, but was virtually the only US-based psychologist to do so beyond about 1900. Nonetheless, his textbooks were central in promoting undergraduate laboratory-based courses. Titchener's Wundtianism is now generally considered to have parted from the original by recouching it in terms more akin to British associationism than that had been. Though theoretically marginalised he remained highly respected within the discipline and theoretical differences did not prevent friendly relations with, for example, the behaviourist J.B. Watson. Scripture's Psychological career was less successful. Following an almighty row with his superior, G.T. Ladd, at Yale regarding the department's experimental orientation he left, eventually becoming an expert on speech disorders, based for a time in London, and ending his career as Professor of Experimental Phonetics in Vienna. His *Thinking, Feeling, Doing* (1895) was the first thoroughly experimentally-oriented textbook while the similarly pitched *The New Psychology* (1897) is partly responsible for this term's use as a name for the founding movement as a whole.

J. McK. Cattell, another of Wundt's ex-students, was based at Columbia, where he founded a laboratory. After an initial phase of psychophysical research, his interests turned to individual differences, educational Psychology and testing (see Chapter 18). From 1900 his main forte became that of a journal founder and editor (most importantly of *Science, American Naturalist* and *American Men of Science*). As a pacifist opponent of the war he lost his Columbia post in 1917, but continued promoting the discipline's interests in the applied field and was president of the 1929 Ninth International Congress of Psychology. In 1981 his early diaries and letters (1880–1888) were published, providing interesting insights into his Wundt years.

John Dewey played an early role in the New Psychology by virtue of his 1886 *Psychology*, considered by Boring to be the first English text promoting the new approach aside from the Englishman James Sully's *Outlines of Psychology* (1884). It was, though, hardly radically different in agenda from the Mental and Moral philosopher John Bascom's *The Science of Mind* (1881). His eminence is due more to his later formulation of a version of pragmatism with which to advance the applicable 'functionalist' view of Psychology as against the German approach. His 1896 paper 'The Reflex Arc Concept in Psychology' was a profound, if often misunderstood, attack on the objective reality of the stimulus/response distinction. At Chicago he was instrumental in establishing the distinctive Chicago functionalist tradition. His associations with G.H. Mead and the sociologist W.I. Thomas at this time (1894–1904) were of particular importance. By 1900 his educational interests were coming to the fore and he eventually became an eminent educational philosopher as well as the embodiment of the liberal-progressive American intellectual tradition.

G.T. Ladd's significance for Psychology rests largely on his early textbooks and establishment of Psychology at Yale. His original interests in physiological Psychology and experimentation were soon ousted by philosophical and theological concerns. Theoretically he is generally included in the early functionalist evolutionary camp, but played little direct role in furthering the applied Psychology project that derived from this.

The preceding sketches do barely more than identify the leading *dramatis personæ* in the story. Nevertheless they may indicate how diverse in character the US founders in fact were. O'Donnell (1985) has provided the most extensive re-examination of this founding phase currently available and from his pages emerges a picture of constant feuding and dissent among these figures and their associates. He is also downbeat about the significance of the flurry of Psychology laboratories that appeared during the 1880s and 1890s, seeing them as having a pedagogic initiatory role rather than a productive research one.

How then *did* Psychology establish itself so rapidly and successfully in the United States? While to some extent the jury is still out on this question, a few closing observations on the issue may be offered.

1 Expansion and organisational changes in the university and college system provided an institutional opportunity for the new generation of aspiring psychologists unmatched anywhere in the Old World. They were able to co-opt the existing Mental and Moral Philosophy curriculum and convert it into a more secular discipline which could be harnessed to wider progressivist cultural aspirations for a scientifically managed technological society, as well as benefitting from a rapid increase in the number of secular universities where they could establish Psychology on the ground floor.

2 The 1880s–1900 phase is one during which the 'purist' European concept of Psychology as a 'science of the mind' is rapidly being squeezed (though not eliminated) by an evolution-influenced functionalist concept of the discipline as a potential producer of marketable expertise. This shift is apparent not only between psychologists but in the careers of individuals such as Dewey, Munsterberg and Cattell, with James's *Principles* (1890) serving as a kind of fulcrum.

3 The usual image of a group of like-minded experimentally-oriented revolutionaries collaborating to forge modern American Psychology is thus deceptive. The existence of the APA as an umbrella organisation facilitated the promotion of a public image of unity but behind the scenes, as previously mentioned, these figures were at loggerheads on all the fundamental issues. America, though, was big enough to contain this diversity and as the numbers of Psychology graduates grew, along with methodological variety, North American Psychologists themselves soon functionally adapted, turning their discipline's inherent pluralism into an asset.

Further reading

Allport, G.W. (1943) 'Productive Paradoxes of William James'. *Psychological Review* 50: 95–120. (Whole issue devoted to James.)

Boring, E.G. (1929, 2nd edn 1950) *A History of Experimental Psychology*. New York: Appleton-Century-Crofts.

Brozek, J. (ed.) (1984) *Explorations in the History of Psychology in the United States*. London: Associated University Presses.

O'Donnell, J.M. (1985) *The Origins of Behaviorism. American Psychology 1870–1920*. New York: New York University Press. This is essential reading.

Psychological Science, Vol. 1 (3) 1990. Issue devoted to James on the centenary of publication of *Principles*, numerous authors on different topics.

Rieber, R.W. and Salzinger, K. (eds) (1977) *The Roots of American Psychology: Historical Influences and Implications for the Future*. New York: New York Academy of Sciences. Volume 291, particularly Parts I and IV.

William James's principal works

Psychology

James, W. (1890) *The Principles of Psychology* (2 vols.). New York: Henry Holt.
James, W. (1892) *Psychology: Briefer Course*. London: Macmillan.
James, W. (1899) *Talks to Teachers on Psychology*. London: Longmans Green.
James, W. (1902, reprint 1960) *The Varieties of Religious Experience*. London: Fontana.
James, W. (1908) *Human Immortality*. London: Dent.

Philosophy, etc.

James, W. (1896) *The Will to Believe and other Essays*. New York: Longmans Green.
James, W. (1907) *Pragmatism*. New York: Longmans Green.
James, W. (1910) *A Pluralistic Universe*. New York: Longmans Green.
James, W. (1926) *The Letters of William James* (2 vols, ed. Henry James). London: Longmans Green.

Selected secondary references on William James

Allen, G.W. (1967) *William James: A Biography*. London: Hart-Davis.
Cotkin, G. (1990) *William James: Public Philosopher*. Baltimore: Johns Hopkins University Press.
Dooley, P.K. (1974) *Pragmatism as Humanism: The Philosophy of William James*. Chicago: Nelson-Hall.
Feinstein, H.M. (1984) *Becoming William James*. Ithaca: Cornell University Press. Excellent psychological study of James's formative years, reproducing many of his own drawings.
MacLeod, R.B. (ed.) (1969) *William James: Unfinished Business*. Washington DC: American Psychological Association. Papers on aspects of James's Psychological work.
Perry, R.B. (1935) *Thought and Character of William James* (2 vols.). Boston: Little, Brown. Classic review of James's life-work.
Poirier, R. (1988) *The Renewal of Literature: Emersonian Reflections*. London: Faber. Locates James in a distinctive Emersonian literary tradition.
Richards, G. (1991) 'James and Freud: Two Masters of Metaphor'. *British Journal of Psychology*, 82: 205–215. This issue contains other papers, first given at a 1990 BPS Symposium on the centenary of the *Principles*, by G. Bird and E.R. Valentine.
Simon, L. (ed.) (1996) *William James Remembered*. Lincoln, Nebraska & London: University of Nebraska Press. A collection of personal recollections of William James in various roles.

Simon, L. (1998) *Genuine Reality. A Life of William James.* New York: Harcourt Brace and Company. The most recent biography of James, benefitting from the additional scholarship since G.W. Allen (1967) and much additional research.

Other pioneer American psychologists and their precursors

Major secondary sources on this are:

Boring, E.G. (1948) 'Masters and Pupils among American Psychologists'. *American Journal of Psychology*, 61: 527–534 (reprinted in E.G. Boring (1963) *History, Psychology, & Science: Selected Papers*, R.I. Watson and D.T. Campbell (eds). New York: Wiley). Summarises the academic lineages of the first US Psychologists, though tends to ignore connections with Mental and Moral Philosophy.

Broughton, J. and Freeman-Moir, D.J. (eds) (1982) *The Cognitive-Developmental Psychology of James Mark Baldwin.* New Jersey: Ablex. A major reappraisal of Baldwin's work and historical significance.

Cattell, J. McK. and Sokal, M.M. (eds) (1981) *An Education in Psychology: James McKeen Cattell's Journal and Letters from Germany and England 1880–1888.* Cambridge, MA: MIT Press. Quite fun as well as intrinsically informative.

Davis, R.C. (1936) 'American Psychology 1800–1885'. *Psychological Review*, 43(6): 491–493. Out-of-date in its views, but useful for reference purposes.

Evans, R. (1984) 'The Origins of American Psychology'. In J. Brozek (ed.) *Explorations in the History of American Psychology.* Lewisburg: Bucknell University Press, 17–60. Provides an excellent insight into the early nineteenth-century context.

Fay, J.W. (1939) *American Psychology Before William James.* New Brunswick, NJ: Rutgers University Press. Still the only comprehensive account.

Mills, E.S. (1969) *G.T. Ladd: Pioneer American Psychologist.* Cleveland: Press of Case Western Reserve University. The only biography of this complex figure.

Richards, G. (1995) '"To Know Our Fellow Men to do them Good": American Psychology's Enduring Moral Project'. *History of the Human Sciences*, 8(3): 1–24.

Rieber, R.W. (1998) 'Americanization of Psychology before William James'. In R.W. Rieber, and K. Salzinger (eds) *Psychology: Theoretical-Historical Perspectives.* Washington DC: APA, 191–216. Focuses primarily on T.C. Upham, the most influential of the early nineteenth-century 'Mental and Moral' philosophers.

Roback, A.A. (1952, rev. 1964) *History of American Psychology.* New York: Collier. Unusually for histories of this period this does contain useful, if selective, coverage of the pre-1880 period.

Zenderland, L. (1999) *Measuring Minds: Henry Herbert Goddard and the Origins of American Intelligence Testing.* Cambridge: Cambridge University Press. Well evokes the atmosphere of 1890s American Psychology in the opening chapters.

Major works by founders of the 'New Psychology'

Full bibliographic data in 'Further reading' texts. This is very selective and only lists early works.

Baldwin, J.M. (1902) *Development and Evolution.*
Baldwin, J.M. (1894) *Mental Development in the Child and the Race.*
Baldwin, J.M. (1897) *Social and Ethical Interpretations of Mental Development.*
Dewey, J. (1886) *Psychology.*
Dewey, J. (1896) 'The Reflex Arc Concept in Psychology'. *Psychological Review.*
Dewey, J. (1899) *The School and Society. Being three lectures supplemented by a statement of the university elementary school.*
Dewey, J. (1906) *The School and the Child.*
Hall, G. Stanley (1904) *Adolescence* (2 vols.). Most of his early work was in journal paper form, notably in his own *Pedagogical Seminary.*
Jastrow, J. (1901) *Fact and Fable in Psychology.*
Ladd, G.T. (1887) *Elements of Physiological Psychology.*
Ladd, G.T. (1898) *Outlines of Descriptive Psychology.*
Prince, M. (1885) *The Nature of Mind and Human Automatism.*
Prince, M. (1905) *The Dissociation of a Personality. The Hunt for the Real Miss Beauchamp.*
Sanford, E.C. (1898) *Course in Experimental Psychology.* First appeared in *American Journal of Psychology,* 1891.
Scripture, E.W. (1895) *Thinking, Feeling, Doing.*
Scripture, E.W. (1897) *The New Psychology.*
Titchener, E.B. (1898) *A Primer of Psychology.*
Titchener, E.B. (1901–1905) *Experimental Psychology* (4 vols).
Washburn, M.F. (1908) *Animal Mind.*

Chapter 5

Behaviourism

- J.B. Watson's 'Behaviorism' of 1913
- Watson's impact on US Psychology
- Varieties of behaviourism after Watson
- The decline (and persistence) of behaviourism
- Behaviourism's public image
- The wider impact of behaviourism

US Psychology's founding phase culminated in 1913 in the movement called 'behaviourism', the impact of which extended well beyond those identifying themselves as behaviourists. While experimental Psychology was well established by 1910, the forms this took varied and research reports remained unstandardised. Basic psychophysics aside, it was difficult to compare findings of different researchers or replicate experiments. Much experimental work of the post-1900 period was explicitly 'functionalist', a label adopted by J. Dewey's Chicago colleague J.R. Angell. A fairly eclectic approach, this persisted as the dominant orientation of US experimental Psychology until World War Two, avoiding most traditional philosophical issues in favour of adaptational accounts of both mental phenomena and behaviour – often in applied Psychology contexts. 'Behaviourism' may be seen as an extreme form of this functionalism. Its enduring effect was as much methodological as theoretical, although it was largely as a theoretical-level movement that it was launched. In this chapter we will look primarily at three aspects of behaviourism: (a) how John B. Watson, its founder, envisaged 'behaviourism' in 1913; (b) the variety of forms it subsequently took; and (c) the difficulties that led to a weakening of its influence after 1945, including some comments on its public image and legacy.

In the early 1900s US culture was pervaded by an almost utopian enthusiasm about its destiny (quite literally – the concept of America having a 'Manifest Destiny' was widespread). It saw itself engaged in creating the first truly modern technological industrial civilisation and was thus highly future-oriented and intensely concerned with the practical utility of science and technology. Watson, a temperamentally rebellious young man from humble South Carolina roots, fully shared this aspiration. We cannot deal here with his earlier academic career, but suffice to say that, by 1913, he was very discontented with the state of the discipline on several counts.

1   He had little sympathy with its continuing philosophical (as he saw it) concerns with the nature of consciousness and the mind–body problem (he would have liked, he wrote, to bring up students 'in ignorance of the entire controversy'). These, he believed, kept Psychology bogged down in intractable metaphysical debates of little practical consequence.

2   Closely linked to this was his commitment to a positivist view of science as only capable of studying overt, visible, measurable phenomena. Since consciousness, or 'the mind', was not amenable to such scrutiny it could not be investigated scientifically – we can really only study behaviour.

3   He had been greatly impressed by contemporary biological work, notably that of Jacques Loeb, whose *Comparative Physiology of the Brain and Comparative Psychology* (1901) advanced a highly reductionist approach to Psychological questions as ultimately answerable in physiological terms. Watson felt that, by comparison, experimental Psychology (with a few exceptions in applied areas) was still floundering in an amateurish way and that its standards of both conceptual and methodological rigour were poor.

4   He believed Psychology was too human-centred. A central point of reference here was the rapidly developing discipline of genetics. Just as genetics was concerned with the general phenomenon of heredity, not with heredity in

one species, so Psychology, Watson argued, should be concerned with behaviour in general. And just as geneticists were confining their empirical research to a single convenient species – the fruit fly – so Psychologists could adopt the white rat. Geneticists were not interested in the fruit fly as such, simply using it as a representative 'reproducing organism' with which to investigate genetics in general. So the white rat could serve as a convenient 'behaving organism' to study behaviour in general. Even if its flaws have since become obvious, this argument was certainly not a stupid one.

5   Finally, he was increasingly unhappy with the hereditarian bias in Psychology (the legacy of its commitment to evolutionary thought). The reasons for this are somewhat complex but one major factor is that Watson was seeking scientific techniques for, to use his own phrase, ritually repeated by psychologists ever since, 'predicting and controlling behaviour'. This of course stemmed from his belief in science as a provider of practical knowledge. As already noted, if you wish to change and control behaviour you will naturally try to downplay the importance of immutable genetic factors. Here Watson was really only taking functionalism to its logical conclusion in seeking immediate adaptational explanations for psychological and behavioural phenomena. Moreover, it has also been suggested by J. Hirsch (1967) that he misunderstood a classic experiment by the geneticist W. Johanssen, mistakenly interpreting it as showing that environmental factors were the major determinants of behaviour. Whatever the truth, while Watson initially accepted a role for heredity, albeit limited, this became attenuated in time to a belief that 'unlearned' behaviour is restricted to a few physiologically governed reflexes.

These dissatisfactions come to a head in his manifesto paper 'Psychology as the Behaviorist Views It' (1913). I do recommend this to the reader; it is fairly short and almost polemical in style, so easily manageable. He attacks Psychology at all levels: its methods, its language, and the tasks it sets itself. By the end it is clear that, for Watson, Psychology is really an adjunct to biology, its findings serving to illuminate the organism's biological structure – or, as he puts it, they 'become functional correlates of structure and lend themselves to explanation in physico-chemical terms'. Methodologically there is great need for uniformity in procedure and reporting of results – and the results which interest the 'behaviourist' are such things as learning curves and rapidity of habit formation. Introspection is totally out.

The problem for Watson at this stage is how to tackle higher order phenomena such as thinking and language. Nonetheless he feels confident that in due course these will become amenable to behaviourist methods and suggests that in principle thinking could be understood as 'subvocal speech' – speech, of course, being an overt behaviour (although this somewhat oversimplifies his position). This proved one of the least tenable of his doctrines and is fraught with fairly obvious difficulties.

Watson's paper served to rally some younger psychologists, such as R.M. Yerkes, A.P. Weiss, W.S. Hunter and M. Parmelee, for whom it seemed to point the way to the discipline's future, although its initial impact has, as F. Samelson

(1981, 1985) has shown, been exaggerated and very few fully accepted Watson's extreme reductionism. (A contemporary, Max F. Meyer, had also independently arrived at much the same position, although he has tended to be overshadowed.) The experimental study of learning, pioneered by E.L. Thorndike in the 1890s, soon dominated their research. When the work of Russian physiologist I. Pavlov came to their attention his theoretical concepts were eagerly assimilated. The initial success of Watson's project rested in large part on the perception by fellow American psychologists that he had finally succeeded in hauling Psychology firmly into the natural sciences. His rejection of mentalistic concepts and insistence on restricting attention to overt behaviour seemed to mark the discipline's final abandonment of philosophical concerns as well as reflecting the dominant positivist view of the nature of science. We can only scientifically study observable phenomena: feelings, emotions, mental images, fantasies and the like, being subjective and only accessible to the single individual experiencing them, are thus beyond our concern. All that matters is overt behaviour. We can of course study what people say they experience (because speech is a form of behaviour), but this is a different level of inquiry from studying their experiences as such. It must be stressed, however, since the point is often misunderstood, that few American experimental psychologists rejected mental phenomena in such strong terms as Watson himself. They did though believe their scientific significance to be obscure and that overt behaviour could be explained most scientifically without invoking them.

Behaviourism rapidly evolved a technical language incorporating that of Pavlovian theory, comprising terms like stimulus, response, reinforcement (positive and negative), conditioning (classical and operant), and habit strength. As it happened, however, the theoretical unity Watson aspired to introduce was relatively short-lived, behaviourist theorising soon taking a variety of directions. While these divisions lacked the emotional intensity of those surrounding the Freudian tradition they nevertheless concerned fairly fundamental issues. It is to these we turn next.

Table 5.1 Major early behaviourists and their institutions

John B. Watson	Johns Hopkins University
J. Dollard	Yale University
W.K. Estes	Rockefeller University
E.R. Guthrie	University of Washington, University of Nebraska
E. Hilgard	Stanford University
Clark L. Hull	Yale University
W.S. Hunter	University of Texas, University of Kansas, Clark University, Brown University
M.F. Meyer	University of Missouri
N. Miller	Yale University
O.H. Mowrer	Yale University
B.F. Skinner	Harvard University
K.W. Spence	University of Virginia, University of Iowa
E.C. Tolman	Stanford University
A.P. Weiss	Ohio State University

Figure 5.1 'Little Albert', the famous subject of J.B. Watson and R. Rayner's experiment in which he was conditioned to fear a rabbit. This photo appeared (without him being named) in J.B. Watson's *Psychological Care of Infant and Child* (1928). Reproduced by permission of the Centre for History of Psychology, Staffordshire University.

The varieties of behaviourism

Behind the rapid divergence lay the fact that Watson himself left academic life following a divorce scandal in 1920, having had an affair with, and subsequently married, Rosalie Rayner (his co-worker in the famous Little Albert study in which an infant boy was conditioned to fear a fluffy rabbit) (Figure 5.1). This cost him his job at Johns Hopkins University (where he had succeeded James Mark Baldwin – also effectively dismissed over a sex scandal) and he joined the advertising agency J. Walter Thompson to become highly successful in applying behaviourist principles to advertising.

Academic behaviourism thus lacked a figure who could play a dominating role such as Sigmund Freud always played for Psychoanalysis. The divergences were of several kinds.

* Some remained unhappy about excluding internal events and simply looking at overt stimulus-response (S-R) relations. Without wishing to readopt mentalistic concepts they sought ways of reincorporating internal processes into the picture. A major figure in this respect was E.C. Tolman, who had been impressed by the Gestalt psychologists' holistic approach (see Chapter 6). His research led him, for example, to conclude that organisms acquired a 'cognitive map' of their surroundings merely by moving around it, a process he called 'latent learning'. He came to refer to such internal factors as

'intervening variables' and 'hypothetical constructs' (the distinction between which, though important, would require too lengthy an exegesis for inclusion here). Instead of S-R alone we now had 'S-O-R' models ('O' meaning 'organism'). Underlying this Tolman was primarily concerned with developing a behaviourism which could handle purposiveness, and evade the over-reductionist character of Watson's original version, by then under fierce Gestaltist attack. Clark L. Hull also strove to incorporate the internal in a highly elaborate, algebraicised theory, mentioned again shortly, introducing concepts like 'fractional anticipatory goal response', for example.

- Some of the divergency simply arose from extending behaviourism to other topics than learning. Thus Karl Lashley, a neuro-physiologist, adopted the behaviourist framework in his brain functioning research. He claimed that brain functioning was only localised in very broad terms, large tracts of the brain showing what he called 'equipotentiality' – they could be utilised to serve a great many functions and assume those of the part which had been removed (see Chapter 9). This, of course, fitted in nicely with Watson's environmentalism. From the mid-1930s Lashley began challenging the adequacy of behaviourism, but until then his behaviourist physiological Psychology was a powerful and authoritative factor in maintaining the movement's prestige. In a different direction lay G.H. Mead's 'social behaviourism', concerned with the social construction of the self. This was miles away from Watson's ideas on what Psychology should be and there is much controversy about what precisely Mead meant by calling his approach 'behaviourist'.

- Another dimension of divergence was in terms of theoretical complexity. The polar opposites here are B.F. Skinner and Hull. Skinner's approach became virtually atheoretical, purely concerned with empirically studying the shaping of behaviour by reinforcement contingencies, with no attention at all to supposed internal events and no elaborate theory construction. Hull's theory, by contrast, was a highly ambitious attempt at producing a 'hypothetico-deductive' theory with postulates, theorems and quantification. His algebraic system included such symbols as sO_R for 'momentary behavioral oscillation' and sU_R for 'unlearned receptor-effector connection', and could generate equations such as $J = s\underline{E}R_d = D \times V_2 \times K \times sH_R \times 10^{-.15d} \times V_1$ ('the influence on reaction potential reduction caused by the delay in reinforcement'). Be thankful you are not entering the discipline in the 1960s (or worse, the 1950s) when we were still expected to master the rudiments of this!

There is now wide agreement that the almost baroque theory Hull developed sat unconvincingly with the rat-learning experiments on which it was based. Soon after his death his system received one of the most pitilessly destructive analytical refutations ever to befall a Psychological theory, written by his erstwhile disciple Sigmund Koch (W.K. Estes *et al* 1954). Nevertheless some Hullian terminology entered the general vocabulary of the discipline. B.F. Skinner fared much better. His single-subject operant conditioning methods proved extremely versatile and he was able, to some extent, to produce the goods in terms of applicable techniques for predicting and controlling behaviour. Skinner was a much subtler and more complex thinker than he initially appeared to most of the present author's generation during the 1960s and 1970s. His views on language, for example, are, on re-examination, proving to be more consistent with the modern linguistic philosophy account than was once thought. The late U.T. Place in particular developed them with a degree of philosophically informed sophistication which Skinner himself never managed (e.g. Place, 1992). By the time he died Skinner seemed to be a lone survivor of a fast-fading approach, but already his reputation seems to be rising again. His integrity in restricting his discourse to the terminology of his own system led, I think, to some misunderstanding, particularly during the 1960–1980 phase when he was demonised as the archetypal amoral dehumanising manipulator, an image his earlier behaviourist Utopian novel *Walden Two* (1948) seemed to justify.

Despite this internal variety, only sketched here, there was for a long time a feeling that behaviourism represented the most advanced 'paradigm' for experimental Psychology. While it certainly pervaded the intellectual atmosphere of American Psychology it never in fact dominated Psychological practice to the extent which is often claimed. In R.S. Woodworth's standard college textbook *Experimental Psychology* (1938), for instance, only around 20% of the text is clearly strictly behaviourist in its concerns. The majority of America's working researchers between the two world wars were more eclectic functionalists, still inclined to judiciously include 'experience' alongside 'behaviour' as part of Psychology's subject matter. But, as said at the outset, its impact extended beyond theory to affect the whole manner in which research was conducted and reported. After Watson there was no return to the personalised, discursive and idiosyncratic journal papers of the pre-1910 period. By the 1950s the tide was turning against behaviourism. A number of issues were arising with which behaviourists could not adequately deal, or at any rate as adequately as their rivals. (Skinner is the main exception here, partly precisely because he was not interested in theory-building.) Before pursuing these it might be helpful to suggest that behaviourism should be considered not so much as a theory in itself but as a conceptual framework in which theorising could be undertaken; a 'unified discourse' and set of methodological practices within which propositions could be formulated and theoretical debates conducted and, hopefully, settled.

The decline of behaviourism

Although the presence in America of exiled European Psychologists constituted a background challenge to behaviourism, I will refer here only to two core difficulties.

The 'organisation of behaviour' problem

According to classical behaviourism, complex behaviour involves associatively conditioning each successive component item to its predecessor. By the 1950s it was apparent that this simply cannot explain many higher order human behaviours such as piano playing or, even more obviously, language learning. Building these up by laboriously creating associative chains would take more time than anyone has available. As we will see in Chapter 7 this was the weak point in behaviourism's armour, quickly latched onto by the new cognitive psychologists like George A. Miller. It was also addressed in D.O. Hebb's extremely popular *Organization of Behavior* (1949), a post-war attempt at synthesising the contending behaviourist and Gestalt schools of thought in the light of advances in neurology. The cognitivist attack was boosted by the fact that in designing computers to perform complex actions the first generation of programmers soon developed much better ideas about how such outcomes might be neurologically implemented. The superiority of the new cognitive Psychology in dealing with the organisation of complex behaviour dealt behaviourism a most damaging blow.

The return of instincts

The second difficulty arose from the new ethological research into animal behaviour by people such as Konrad Lorenz and Nico Tinbergen, which called into question behaviourism's doctrinaire environmentalism. While earlier instinct theorists had dealt with instincts such as aggression, hunger and sex, this new generation gave the instinct concept a much more specific meaning. This is discussed in Chapter 15; suffice to say here that in the light of the new ethology it was fairly obvious that behaviourism had been seriously misled by pinning its faith on the white rat.

Watson's initial rationale, that we could use the white rat as a convenient 'behaving organism' for studying behaviour as such, contained a hidden logical error. The very reason why the white rat was so convenient to use was because it happened to be a highly adaptive animal: pretty omnivorous, able to adjust rapidly to new environments, and very generalised (as zoologists call it) in its behaviour – in short *because* its behaviour was highly environmentally determined. To invoke findings on the white rat as evidence of the primary role of the environment in determining behaviour was thus to beg the question (a fallacy known technically as *petitio principi*) – a three-toed sloth, a Galapagos tortoise or a lobster would yield a very different picture, but that of course is the reason why you cannot use them in the first place! (While Skinner had always had a penchant for pigeons the same argument applies.) Behaviourists initially responded by expanding the number of species they used. But further scrutiny revealed that even in the white rat and pigeon there were in-built constraints on the S-R connections it could learn. All species, it transpired, were 'prepared' and 'counterprepared' to learn, or not learn, certain kinds of behaviour. Conditioning a pigeon's pecking response to enable it to obtain food by pecking a button is easy – but try conditioning its wing-preening to food and you are in trouble, they are 'counterprepared'. Rats, on the other hand, can learn that a food is noxious in a single trial even though the negatively reinforcing consequences of ingestion are considerably delayed, they are 'prepared'. Neither phenomenon is explicable without invoking innate factors.

Eventually, even among those operating within the behaviourist tradition, it became clear that extreme environmentalism was untenable and that heredity played a crucial role in determining, and setting constraints on, animal behaviour. The 'nature–nurture' debate had, though, acquired important political connotations by the 1960s. Unfortunately, behaviourists were, in this regard, caught wrong-footed as they were being popularly cast as dehumanising technocrats serving the 'system' in its oppressive schemes. Thus while environmentalism was at this time the, so to speak, 'politically correct' position, behaviourism – the most radically environmental school of all – failed to benefit. 'Politically correct' environmentalism was more sociological in character, focusing on the social environment and social psychological processes in order to combat such things as racism and sexism. Even while environmentalist, behaviourism was thus unable to benefit much from the prevailing pro-environmentalist cultural climate. But on the other hand, neither could it withstand the criticisms of the new 'nativist' ethologists (who, ironically, were able partially to evade the consequences of their *prima facie* 'incorrectness' – at least until the mid-1970s – for reasons outlined in Chapter 17). Skinner, it is true, acquired a certain cult following as a result of *Walden Two*, while J. Wolpe's behaviour therapy, and 'token economy' regimes in juvenile custodial institutions, continued to develop fairly pragmatically, but the core area of behaviourist learning theory had lost its 'paradigmatic' position by around 1965.

Even so, as K. Baistow (2001) has explored in some detail regarding the British scene (although what she says holds true for North America also) the death of the behaviourist tradition has been greatly overstated. 'Behavioural' approaches to the management – and self-management – of all kinds of behavioural problems (e.g. children's unruliness, smoking and helping people with learning difficulties) is flourishing as never before. This has been achieved by the abandonment of theoretical dogmatism in favour of the more pragmatic approach, and a corresponding change in how the technique is presented. The 'expert' predictor and controller once so feared has yielded to the expert sharing their knowledge of a practical skill with non-psychologists (such as teachers) or directly with clients (e.g. smokers).

But how valid was that perception of earlier behaviourism as an instrument of oppressive control? Closer examination of the lives and characters of the leading neo-behaviourists such as Hull, Skinner, Tolman, Ernest Hilgard and O.H. Mowrer, reveals a rather more complex picture. Certainly none were personally inspired by a vision of being able to exert governmental control over the masses, even Skinner seeing his work as facilitating better self-control. Tolman and Hilgard both ran foul of the political establishment during the McCarthyite era, Hull was at worst a scientistic utopian and Mowrer, after hundreds of hours of psychoanalysis, moved on to pioneer group theory. Certainly they were mostly politically liberal in North American terms. This is, in fact, a clear instance of how a modest degree of historical research can rapidly subvert glib rhetoric, however emotionally appealing it may be.

The impact of behaviourism

What was behaviourism's broader impact? Popular culture has two main images of the psychologist. Most widespread remains the psychoanalyst intent on discovering hidden meanings and messages in innocently intended behaviour. The other is the white-coated scientist running rats round mazes and discovering numerous cunning ways to control behaviour – which of course derives from behaviourism. Like all Psychological theories, behaviourism acquired a popular meaning beyond its practitioners' control. In behaviourism's case it promoted the image of 'human being as maze-bound rat': somewhere experts in behavioural control are subtly affecting our lives using scientific techniques we know not of. (Even worse, we may believe that somewhere there exists a body of expertise on 'mind control', 'brain-washing' and the like of which the unscrupulous can take advantage.) It was an apt, not entirely misleading, metaphor for late twentieth-century urban life. Also, we can now say things like 'I feel as if I've been conditioned' – meaning that somewhere along the line we have, unknowingly, been got at. For Watson, of course, the very notion of 'feeling you've been conditioned' would have been a contradiction in terms since the term 'conditioned' could, by definition, only refer to overt behaviour. (See Chapter 16 for behaviourism's specific impact on child Psychology.)

Philosophically behaviourism's rise coincided and was seen as harmonising with that of logical positivism and 'operationalism', a school of philosophy of science which insisted that only concepts definable in terms of verifiable public phenomena were really meaningful and which sought to define the logical structure of valid scientific theory construction and testing. For the bearings of this on behaviourism the best initial account is B.D. MacKenzie (1977). Among other things MacKenzie argues in depth that Watson's move was more extreme than was strictly required by positivist doctrines. Even so, in its halcyon days behaviourism was welcomed by figures as philosophically astute as Bertrand Russell. The historical relationship between logical positivism and behaviourism has been more exhaustively examined by L.D. Smith (1986), the most definitive analysis of the issue to date. Smith concludes that, while sharing certain concerns, they developed in parallel with relatively little direct influence from logical positivism on behaviourism (which in any case originated earlier).

Leaving the neo-behaviourists aside, was Watson himself a manipulator or a liberator? The answer to this is genuinely unclear. It is easy to find alarmingly manipulationist statements in his writings, but equally explicitly he saw himself as breaking the shackles which bound humanity in 'steel bands' of superstition, myth and folklore and was an advocate of sexual, but not 'libertine', freedom. Like Skinner he saw an understanding of behaviourist principles as a route by which people could free themselves from unwanted habits and desires. As an aspiring technology of behavioural control and prediction its advocates, casting themselves as pure scientists, might have claimed that like all scientific knowledge it could be used for both good and ill, and that this decision was society's responsibility. In the end, however, our mistake is perhaps to suppose that behaviourism was meant to be a philosophy of life (though for Watson and Skinner personally it clearly approached this). It was not. To begin with, at least, it was an attempt at creating a technology by which behaviour could be controlled and behavioural problems rectified and, as suggested previously, a conceptual and methodological framework within which scientific Psychological theorising and research could be conducted. The current widespread acceptance of 'behavioural' techniques has, ironically, been achieved by in effect stripping behaviourism of all its most grandiose aspirations and recasting its principles as practical skills rather than the one scientific route capable of unravelling human nature (K. Baistow, 2001).

Conclusion

Behaviourism served an important historical function for Psychology in moving it *methodologically* into the realm of the natural sciences – really in a sense by insisting that psychologists actually *behave* like scientists. The *theoretical* price paid was an abandonment of concern with many genuinely profound philosophical and theoretical questions about Psychology's status and nature that had previously preoccupied the discipline, and commitment to a reductionism which many felt deeply unsatisfying and which seemed to discard the baby with the bath water. For about four decades – from 1913 to the early 1950s – behaviourist approaches made the running in American experimental Psychology although, as indicated, it was never a homogenous doctrine, nor lacking rivals. As a theoretical orientation it eventually foundered on the twin rocks of the problem of how complex behaviour was organised and the inadequacy of its extreme environmentalism. Not all hands were lost in this foundering, however; on the contrary, numerous survivors manage to continue aspects of the behaviourist project in less dogmatic fashion. In any case, as with all Psychological doctrines, behaviourism's impact is a psychological fact in its own right and the concepts and images of human nature which it yielded have, for better or worse, irreversibly entered our culture.

Additional points

Watson's own 'psychology' was in many ways highly conflicted. Anyone wishing to explore this topic in depth should read one of his biographies. For example: he is theoretically anti-emotion but in practice highly emotional as a brief browse through his writings shows: he dismissed imagery as unimportant but suffered a life-long fear of the dark which he was unable to cure by behaviourist means, and so on.

The Russian 'Reflexology' school of Pavlov and I.M. Sechenov represented a somewhat analogous development in Russia (and after 1917, the Soviet Union) to the rise of behaviourism in the US. Pavlov, primarily a physiologist, was vital to behaviourism's success by virtue of his research on canine conditioning which supplied much of its conceptual framework. Pavlov frequently stars in histories of Psychology and accounts of his work are easily accessible. It is significant that both societies were, when these approaches originated, in the throes of idealistically trying to create a scientific, technological, modern mass culture, albeit from opposing ideological bases, and that in both Psychology took up the task of devising the appropriate techniques of behavioural control. However, it would be misleading to conflate the two traditions since Soviet Pavlovian Psychology acquired a character of its own, in some respects more sophisticated than the American Watsonian one. Interestingly, H.J. Eysenck and J.A. Gray, the leading mid-twentieth century British behaviourist sympathisers, soon ditched Hull for Pavlov during the 1950s.

Further reading

Buckley, K.W. (1989) *Mechanical Man: John Broadus Watson and the Origins of Behaviorism*. New York: Guilford Press. Probably the best biography.

Estes, W.K., Koch, S., McCorquadale, K., Meehl, P.E., Mueller Jr, C.G., Schoenfeld, W.N. and Verplanck W.S. (1954) *Modern Learning Theory. A Critical Analysis of Five Examples*. New York: Appleton-Century-Crofts. Contains Koch's devastating demolition of Hull's system.

MacKenzie, B.D. (1977) *Behaviourism and the Limits of Scientific Method*. London: Routledge & Kegan Paul. An invaluable conceptual critique and evaluation.

Schwartz, B. (1989) *Psychology of Learning and Behavior*, 3rd edn. New York & London: Norton. For the state of play in behaviourist Psychology towards the end of the last century this comprehensive textbook is the best starting point.

Smith, L.D. (1986) *Behaviorism and Logical Positivism: A Reassessment of the Alliance*. Stanford, CA: Stanford University Press. The definitive work on this topic.

Watson, J.B. (1913) 'Psychology as the Behaviorist Views it'. *Psychological Review* 20: 158–177. Reprinted in W. Dennis (ed.) (1948) *Readings in the History of Psychology*. New York: Appleton-Century-Crofts. Absolutely essential.

For full bibliographic details of works cited below see 'Further Reading' texts and general histories.

Major early behaviourist books

Beach, F.A., Hebb, D.O., Morgan, C.T. and Nissen, H.W. (eds) (1960) *The Neuropsychology of Lashley: Selected Papers of K.S. Lashley*. New York: McGraw-Hill. As Lashley's work was nearly all in journal paper form this is the most accessible source.

Guthrie, E.R. (1935, rev. edn 1952) *The Psychology of Learning*.

Guthrie, E.R. (1938) *The Psychology of Human Conflict*.

Hunter, W.S. (1919, rev. 3rd edn 1928) *Human Behavior*.

Mead, G.H. (1934) *Mind, Self and Society from the Standpoint of a Social Behaviorist*.

Meyer, M.F. (1921) *The Psychology of the Other One*.

Parmelee, M. (1913) *Science of Human Behavior*.

Tolman, E.C. (1932) *Purposive Behavior in Animals and Men*.

Watson, J.B. (1919) *Psychology from the Standpoint of a Behaviorist*.

Watson, J.B. (1924) *Behaviorism*.

Watson, J.B. (1928) *Psychological Care of Infant and Child*.

Weiss, A.P. (1925) *A Theoretical Basis of Human Behavior*.

Later 'neo-behaviourists'

Hilgard, E.R. (1940, with D.P. Marquis; rev. edn G.A. Kimble, 1961) *Conditioning & Learning*. The standard textbook.

Hilgard, E.R. (1948, 2nd edn 1956, 3rd edn 1966 with G.H. Bower), *Theories of Learning*. The standard mid-twentieth-century textbook.

Hull, C.L. *et al* (1940) *Mathematico-Deductive Theory of Rote Learning. A Study in Scientific Methodology*.

Hull, C.L. (1943) *Principles of Behavior*.

Hull, C.L. (1951) *Essentials of Behavior*.

Hull, C.L. (1952) *A Behavior System*.

Skinner, B.F. (1938) *The Behavior of Organisms*.

Skinner, B.F. (1948) *Walden Two*.

Skinner, B.F. (1957) *Verbal Behavior*.

Skinner, B.F. (1959, enl. 1961) *Cumulative Record*. A collection of major journal papers.

Skinner, B.F. (1971) *Beyond Freedom and Dignity*.

Skinner, B.F. (1953) *Science and Human Behavior*.

On Skinner, see also:

Bjork, D.W. (1993) *B.F. Skinner. A Life*. New York: Basic Books.

O'Donohue, W. and Ferguson, K.E. (2001) *The Psychology of B.F. Skinner*. Thousand Oaks, CA and London: Sage. Very pro-Skinner. Has a full bibliography of Skinner's publications and review of his legacy.

Skinner, B.F. (1976) *Particulars of My Life*. London: Jonathan Cape. The first volume of his autobiography, this provides a fascinating picture of the origins of Skinner's surprisingly complex character.

Weiner, D.N. (1996) *B.F. Skinner. Benign Anarchist*. Boston: Allyn & Bacon.

Spence, K.W. (1956) *Behavior Theory and Conditioning*.

Stevens, S.S. (ed.) (1951) *Handbook of Experimental Psychology*.

See also: Koch, S. (ed.) (1959) *Psychology, A Study of a Science*. New York: McGraw-Hill. Vol. 2 contains several (sometimes final) theoretical statements by major figures, including Tolman.

Russian behaviourism

General

Smith, R. (1992) *Inhibition*. London: Free Association Books. See especially Chapters 3 and 5.

Pavlov school

Asratyan, E.A. (1953, Russian 1949) *I.P. Pavlov: His Life and Work*. Moscow: Foreign Language Publishing House. Interesting not only for what it says about Pavlov but also for its relentless ideological tone.

Frolov, Y.P. (1937) *Fish Who Answer the Telephone and Other Studies in Experimental Biology*. London: Kegan Paul, Trench & Trübner. Popular account of contemporary Russian research on conditioning.

Frolov, Y.P. (1937) *Pavlov and his School. The Theory of Conditioned Reflexes.* London: Kegan Paul, Trench & Trübner. A useful review of the state of Soviet behaviourism by the 1930s.

Gray, J.A. (1964) *Pavlov's Typology. Recent Theoretical and Experimental Developments from the Laboratory of B.M. Teplov,* with an introduction by H.J. Eysenck. Oxford: Pergamon Press. Explores the application of Pavlovian theory to personality.

Ivanov-Smolensky, A.G. (1954) *Essays on the Patho-Physiology of the Higher Nervous Activity according to I.P. Pavlov and his School.* Moscow: Foreign Language Publishing House. Won the 1949 Stalin Prize – not, of course, necessarily a recommendation.

Pavlov, I.P. (1927, rep. 1960) *Conditioned Reflexes: An Investigation of the Physiological Activity of the Cerebral Cortex.* Oxford: Oxford University Press.

Pavlov, I.P. (1928) *Lectures on Conditioned Reflexes: Twenty-five Years of Objective Study of the Higher Nervous Activity (Behaviour) of Animals.* London: Martin Lawrence. These two works are the key English-language Pavlovian texts.

Platonov, K. (1959) *The Word as a Physiological and Therapeutic Factor. The Theory and Practice of Psychotherapy according to I.P. Pavlov.* Moscow: Foreign Language Publishing House. Post-World War Two extension of Pavlovian approaches into Clinical Psychology.

The first English account of the Psychological relevance of Pavlov's work appears to be:

Yerkes, R.M. and Morgulis, S. (1909) 'The Method of Pawlow [*sic*] in Animal Psychology'. *Psychological Bulletin* 6: 257–273

Sechenov

Sechenov, I.M. (ed. K. Koshtoyants) (1960) *Selected Physiological and Psychological Papers.* Moscow: Foreign Language Publishing House. Sechenov (*fl.* 1860s–1880s) is generally considered the 'father' of Russian Psychology and a major influence on Pavlov.

Bekhterev

Bekhterev, V.M. (1933, trans. of 1928 4th edn, 1st Russian edn., 1917) *General Principles of Human Reflexology, An Introduction to the Objective Study of Personality.* London: Jarrolds. Pavlov's main rival.

Further secondary sources

Baistow, K. (2001) 'Behavioural Approaches and the Cultivation of Competence'. In G. C. Bunn, A.D. Lovie and G.D. Richards (eds) *Psychology in Britain. Historical Essays and Personal Reflections.* Leicester: British Psychological

Society/London: The Science Museum, 309–329. Explores the persistence and revival of behavioural approaches in Britain since behaviourism's supposed demise.

Bakan, D. (1966) 'Behaviorism and American Urbanization'. *Journal of the History of the Behavioral Sciences* 2(1): 5–28. Proposes an interesting contextualised thesis regarding behaviourism's initial appeal, although Samelson's later papers (see below) refute much of Bakan's case.

Burnham, J.C. (1968) 'On the Origins of Behaviorism'. *Journal of the History of the Behavioral Sciences* IV(2): 143–151. A good introduction.

Cohen, D. (1979) *J.B. Watson. The Founder of Behaviourism*. London: Routledge & Kegan Paul. A useful biography, but largely superseded by K.W. Buckley's book (see above).

Creelan, P. (1975) 'Religion, Language and Sexuality in J.B. Watson'. *Journal of Humanistic Psychology*, 15(4): 55–78. An analysis of Watson's hostility to religion as rooted in a childhood background infused with maternal evangelical zeal.

Harris, B. (1979) 'Whatever Happened to Little Albert?' *American Psychologist* 34: 151–160. Classic re-examination and demythologising exposé of Watson's famous 'Little Albert' experiment.

Hirsch, J. (1967) 'Epilog: Behavior-genetic analysis'. In J. Hirsch (ed.) *Behavior-Genetic Analysis*. New York: McGraw-Hill, 416–435. Argues that Watson's radical environmentalism arose from a misunderstanding – 'a fantastic *non sequitur*' – of an experiment on genetics by W. Johanssen (see p. 419).

King, W.P. (ed.) (1930) *Behaviourism: A Symposium*. London: S.C.M. Press. A useful contemporary document on the behaviourism debate. Published in the US as *Behaviorism: A Battle Line*, a few contributions are omitted from the English edition.

Place, U.T. (1992) 'Eliminative Connectionism: Its Implications for a Return to an Empiricist/Behaviorist Linguistics'. *Behaviour and Philosophy* 20(1): 21–35. A sophisticated defence and restatement of the Skinnerian account of language.

Roback, A.A. (1937) *Behaviorism at Twenty-Five*. Cambridge, MA: Sci-Art. A scornful attack on Watson in particular.

Samelson, F. (1981) 'Struggle for Scientific Authority: The Reception of Watson's Behaviorism, 1913–1920'. *Journal of the History of the Behavioral Sciences* 17: 399–425. Debunks the notion that Watson immediately attracted many ardent disciples.

Samelson, F. (1985) 'Organizing for the Kingdom of Behavior: Academic Battles and Organizational Policies in the Twenties'. *Journal of the History of the Behavioral Sciences* 21: 33–47. Further pursues issues raised in the previous paper.

Watson, J.B. and McDougall, W. (1928) *The Battle of Behaviorism*. London: Kegan Paul Trench & Trübner. A classic encounter.

Wickham, H. (1928) *The Misbehaviorists: Pseudo-science and the Modern Temper*. New York: Lincoln MacVeagh, Dial Press/Toronto: Longmans, Green. A contemporary attack on the doctrine.

Chapter 6

Gestalt Psychology

- The context and manner of the emergence of Gestalt Psychology
- Central concepts of Gestalt Psychology
- Gestalt Psychology's approach to cognition
- The fate and impact of Gestalt Psychology in the United States
- The significance of the Gestalt Psychology story

The nature of Gestalt theory

Coincidentally with behaviourism's rebellion in the United States, another very different rebellion, Gestalt Psychology, occurred in Germany. We may at the outset identify one underlying difference: behaviourism sought to become more scientific by emulating the behaviour of natural scientists, Gestalt psychologists by adopting the most advanced theoretical ideas of contemporary physics. Unlike behaviourists, they neither ignored consciousness nor reduced psychological phenomena to atomistic elementary units such as S-R connections, moves they felt were profoundly mistaken. In this chapter I will outline some of the central concepts developed by the three major Gestalt psychologists, Max Wertheimer (the movement's founder), Wolfgang Kohler and Kurt Koffka, who were, as far as one can tell, in complete accord. I will then discuss its fate and some other figures associated with the school.

First, to set the scene: German psychologists and philosophers were far from united in accepting W. Wundt's essentially reductionist approach to the nature of mind, and his doctrines were strongly disputed (see Chapter 3). One topic in particular continued to fox both Wundtians and anti-Wundtians alike – the perception of form. The Austrian Graz school was especially concerned with this. The problem is captured in Von Ehrenfehls' observation that we can recognise a tune regardless of key, tempo or instruments – the form persists though all the elements have changed. This resisted solution from a 'bottom-up' direction and seemed to imply that the brain somehow contained innate forms to which it matched stimuli – hardly credible given the variety of forms we can identify.

At first sight this appears to be a recondite technical question: how can we account for form-perception within an analytical theoretical framework? This, however, is but the tip of the iceberg of the far profounder issue of 'meaning' itself, and the appropriateness of scientific reductionism for an understanding of the mind. It is clear from their writings (particularly Koffka, 1935) that Gestaltists viewed current events very differently from the future-oriented Americans. Although the movement started in 1911, they were soon working in the heartland of Europe in

Table 6.1 The Gestalt school and their institutions

Solomon Asch	Swarthmore College
K. Duncker	University of Berlin; Swarthmore College (1938–1940)
Kurt Koffka*	University of Giessen; Smith College (1927–1941)
Wolfgang Kohler*	Universities of Frankfurt, Berlin, Gottingen; Swarthmore College (1935–1955)
Kurt Lewin	University of Berlin; Cornell University (1932–1935), University of Iowa (1935–1944); MIT (1944–1947)
Wolfgang Metzger	University of Frankfurt, University of Munster
Max Wertheimer*	University of Berlin, New School of Social Research, NY

*The three central figures, Wertheimer being the acknowledged founder of the school.

the grim aftermath of World War One and saw their culture as under serious threat. Reductionist Psychology of the behaviourist as well as Wundtian type was, moreover, part of that threat since it eliminated all consideration of human values:

> Meaning and significance could have no possible place in such a molecular system; Caesar's crossing the Rubicon: certain stimulus–response situations; Luther at Worms: so many others; Shakespeare writing 'Hamlet'; Beethoven composing the Ninth Symphony; an Egyptian sculptor carving the bust of Nephretete, would all be reduced to the stimulus response schema.
>
> (Koffka, 1935: 26)

They thus cast themselves as defenders of meaning and culture against a rising tide of arid and philistine scientific reductionism – a situation exacerbated by the wider anarchy engulfing Europe at the political, military and economic levels. It is essential, I think, to remember this, and it is rarely made clear in history texts. (See M.G. Ash, 1996, for the definitive study of Gestalt Psychology's own cultural significance.)

If opposed to reductionism they were not opposed to science itself; on the contrary, they were closely associated with the leaders of modern physics: Wertheimer was a lifelong friend of Albert Einstein and Köhler had studied under Max Planck, inventor of quantum theory. Unlike Watson they suffered few personal doubts about either their own scientific credentials or those of their project, and were thus less concerned with methodology as such. They did not feel driven to prove Psychology could be a science, they felt securely part of 'science' already. Ironically this counted against them in the long run.

Now let us consider a few of their central concepts. In doing so, the way they reconceptualised form-perception will emerge.

1   *Field.* Their single most important move was to adopt the new approach, pioneered by Einstein, known as 'field theory' (although the 'field' notion dates back to J.C. Maxwell's work on electromagnetism in the 1840s and 1850s). This concept of 'the field' lies at the heart of all Gestalt theory. What, though, is a 'field'? Traditionally, to simplify drastically, scientific explanation had taken the form of identifying the linear cause–effect sequences that determined phenomena. Field theoretical physics, by contrast, reconceptualised the problem by viewing phenomena as arising from a network, or field (*Feld*), of forces – gravity and electromagnetism, for example. Linear sequences are replaced by 'fields' with an overall structure or form – thus iron filings scattered around a magnet align themselves with the form of the magnetic field. The Gestaltists therefore saw their task as identifying those fields of forces that determine behaviour and mental phenomena, and the laws governing these. Psychological phenomena could be said to occur at the intersection of several kinds of 'field' – biological, perceptual, environmental, and so on. Approaching things in this way enabled the retention of 'mental' phenomena as a central topic, for the structure of conscious phenomena is one outcome or product of these interacting force-fields, which they in turn reflect as iron filings around a magnet reflect the magnetic field.

It also meant that reductionism could be avoided, for it was essentially a holistic approach. This last is an important point and provided their solution to the form-perception question: *rather than seeing wholes being built up from parts, the structure of the whole will determine what the parts are, should you analyse it.* And certain phenomena only exist at this level: if two dots are placed alongside one another we immediately have the relational property of left-and-rightness; there is no way of determining whether a dot is the left or right dot by scrutinising it ever more closely in isolation. In short, the adoption of the field notion – which, as is clear from Koffka (ibid.), they did not see as a mere metaphor but as a route for incorporating Psychology into the unified discourse of the sciences – promised to enable them to tackle issues of value, meaning and consciousness in a truly scientific manner.

2   *Isomorphism.* This is a concept adopted from the branch of mathematics known as 'topology', which is concerned with the properties of different forms rather than with quantification. In topology two forms are, technically, 'isomorphic' if one can be mapped onto the other, or, expressing it more loosely, share a common structure. The forms *s*, *c*, and *l* are thus isomorphic with each other, as are *p*, *b*, 9, and *d*, since the first are all variations on a single line, the second variations on a line with an end-loop. This idea was deployed by Gestalt psychologists to link conscious experience with physiological level phenomena, and is closely associated with the field concept. Putting it briefly, their doctrine of isomorphism is that conscious, 'phenomenological', experience, is isomorphic with underlying physiological processes. The classic example was the phenomenon of apparent movement (the 'phi-phenomenon'), now familiar from moving neon signs. Nothing has moved in the outside world, but we experience movement. Wertheimer suggested this was because something was happening at the physiological level 'isomorphic' with the movement – perhaps the leakage of current between two poorly-insulated circuits. Köhler eventually developed an elaborate theory of the brain as operating in terms of constantly fluctuating electrical fields isomorphic in structure with conscious experience. Although a clever move, this doctrine proved one of their weakest points as, from the 1940s, findings from neurological brain research proved incompatible with it.

3   *Prägnanz.* In exploring their field approach the Gestaltists claimed to have discovered or identified a general principle, *Prägnanz*, which governed the structure of psychological phenomena, namely that they are always organised in the neatest, tightest, most meaningful way. We lack a precise English equivalent for this (although it is related to the word 'pregnant' as in 'the situation is pregnant with possibilities'). This general principle was elucidated further by a number of 'laws of *Prägnanz*' (although these could not exhaust the meaning of the general principle itself). Most fundamentally, *some* organisation always occurs, however random the stimuli – we hear pulsation in white noise, we see figures in haphazard markings on a wall, etc. These 'Laws' became the most widely known of Gestalt theory's ideas, especially, though not exclusively, as applied to perception. They include the following:

(a) Figure/ground distinction. We always experience one part of the over-all stimulus array as a figure against a background. If information is ambiguous we experience continuous oscillation as in the well-known Maltese cross, Necker cube or face/vase figures. The figure/ground distinction applies to all modalities. In hearing we identify the sound of someone speaking as a 'figure' against a 'ground' of other noise. Our selectivity in doing this often becomes apparent in tape-recordings of lectures or discussions: playing them back we hear all sorts of noises – coughs, doors closing, lifts, traffic – of which we were originally unaware.

(b) Contrast and closure. We tend to ignore or over-ride minor breaks in a figure (closure), but if they are sufficiently significant we exaggerate their scale (contrast). Contrast, more generally, includes the tendency to exaggerate perceptible differences between stimuli (e.g. in adjacent areas of light and darkness what looks grey alongside a very white area will look bright white when set against a black one). There are a multitude of illustrations of this to be found in books on perception. 'Closure' also manifests itself over time in our need to finish 'unfinished business'. This produces the 'Ziegarnik effect' – we recall interrupted, unfinished tasks better than completed ones (reported by Kurt Lewin's student B.V. Ziegarnik in 1927 in the main Gestalt journal *Psychologische Forschung*).

(c) Constancy. What they called 'well-articulated' forms tend to resist change, particularly if familiar; thus even when viewed in different lights and from different angles we still 'see' the same form persisting. We do not become baffled when we see a saucer edge-on. Without constancy our perception of the world would be highly chaotic, shifting from moment to moment as objects appeared from different angles. This is also closely related to the next 'law'.

(d) Transposition. We are, for example, able to recognise letters of the English alphabet regardless of stylistic variation (e.g. f, F, f, *F*, **F**), even if they retain hardly any 'elements' in common with the usual letter-forms (as when depicted as shadows on three-dimensional forms of the letters). We recognise a familiar face whether presented in a photo, a painting, in the flesh or as a cartoon, in profile or face-to-face. This is a very important aspect of the Gestalt argument: relationships are more important than parts. Regarding recognition of tunes this phenomenon, as already noted, played a major early role as it was especially difficult to account for in terms of the 'bottom up' approaches previously adopted.

There are numerous other 'laws' but these should suffice to convey the message. While perception became a central topic for Gestalt theorising (as learning had for behaviourists), it was not restricted to this. The idea that the field structure of the situation played a major role in learning was the theme of one of the most famous Gestalt experimental programmes – Köhler's experiments carried out during the First World War on Tenerife (where the British had interned him). He demonstrated first that chickens could learn that a reward was in the lighter or darker of two boxes (i.e. they had learned a relationship, not a single S-R association), but then undertook experiments on chimpanzee problem solving. The best-remembered of these are Sultan's realisations that he could obtain bananas by pulling them into his cage with a stick, or stacking up boxes when they were hanging beyond reach. The point of these experiments was to show how the solutions occurred when the subject as it were mentally reorganised the structure of the situation – which could be aided for example by laying the stick pointing towards the banana rather than at right angles to it. This sudden 'insight learning' (the 'aha!' experience, as it is sometimes called) proved a considerable challenge to behaviourist learning theory.

In their later work the Gestaltists, especially Wertheimer, concentrated increasingly on cognition and problem solving, exploring how a problem's presentational structure facilitated or hampered its solution. As an illustration of this, Wertheimer retold an anecdote about the mathematician Gauss. When Gauss was an infant in the kindergarten the teacher instructed the class to add up 1+2+3+4+5+6+7+8+9+10. Little Gauss immediately shot his hand up and gave the correct answer – 55 – explaining that as 1+10 is 11, 2+9 is 11 etc., there are five pairs of 11 and 5×11 is 55. Instead of attempting to solve the problem sequentially as posed he had first reorganised its structure. Among the influential cognitive research undertaken from a Gestalt perspective was that of K. Duncker on factors affecting problem solving. This involved presenting subjects with hypothetical problems (e.g. 'how can you apply high intensity X-rays to an internal tumour without damaging intervening tissue?') and asking them to 'think aloud' as they tried to solve them. Again these highlighted the need to reorganise the elements in the situation if a solution was to be achieved. It is fair to say that Gestalt Psychology in many ways laid the groundwork for modern Cognitive Psychology, although we will see in Chapter 7 that cognitivists radically altered the terms in which thinking was addressed (see D.J. Murray (1995) for a full account of the role of Gestalt Psychology in the origins of Cognitive Psychology).

The fate and legacy of Gestalt psychology

What then happened to Gestalt Psychology? Koffka went to the US in the 1920s but maintained strong links with his colleagues, so until the early 1930s the school was able to make considerable headway as a scientific alternative to behaviourism even, to some extent, in the US (as we saw in the case of E.C. Tolman). Nazism forced Wertheimer and Kurt Lewin into exile (both being Jewish), Köhler (almost uniquely among non-Jewish German psychologists) quitting in solidarity. (Within Germany the theory was taken over by Wolfgang Metzger who opportunistically reformulated its holistic approach to endorse Nazi doctrines, recanting post-war and continuing to pursue his academic career.) While eventually finding academic posts they were unable to adjust easily to the US context, although their ideas greatly influenced Social Psychology, particularly via the work of Kurt Lewin (see below). Solomon Asch, who performed the famous conformity experiments, also strongly endorsed the Gestalt approach (see Asch, 1952). In a way, though, they were partly victims of their success – their best insights were readily incorporated into mainstream thought while, as just indicated, their approach to cognition was overtaken by the post-war generation of US cognitive psychologists. At the theoretical level their central doctrine of psycho-physiological isomorphism was refuted by neurophysiologists, while their 'field theory' approach in general proved difficult to sustain, less clearly the single most advanced mode of scientific thinking than had earlier seemed to be the case. There was no Gestaltist Skinner to carry the flag further and by Köhler's death in 1967 the movement had long ceased to exist as an identifiable school. Its anti-reductionism and insistence on addressing values and meanings were nevertheless continued by the Humanist school, one of the leaders of which, Abraham Maslow, studied under Wertheimer in the early 1940s in New York at the New School of Social Research.

Closely associated with, though not exactly a member of, the Gestalt School, Kurt Lewin also had some success in the US in developing his own 'topological' approach, which incorporated the field concept. During the 1940s Lewin applied this to topics ranging from personality to learning and group dynamics. Again the central message is that behaviour can only be understood in terms of the total field or 'life space' of the behaving entity, be it an individual, group or organisation. Lewin developed various methods of representing and analysing this 'life-space' and its dynamics, as well as exploring the methodological implications of such an approach. (Tolman, incidentally, enjoyed a long intellectual sparring partnership with Lewin.) Gestaltism's long-term effect on US Social Psychology was to ensure that a phenomenological and holistic theoretical strand continued alongside the dominant empiricism of most post-war attitude theorists. This began to bear fruit somewhat later during the 1960s (see Chapter 12).

The school was often criticised for alleged experimental sloppiness and thus castigated as 'unscientific'; this is an error – it was rather that they had a different, more relaxed, concept of what being scientific meant. My personal view is that Gestalt Psychology was in many respects far more sophisticated and creative than behaviourism. Of course it backed the wrong horse at a deeper theoretical level, but it was a highly excusable – and in the event a quite productive – error. Its legacy to the studies of perception, cognition and Social Psychology should not be underestimated even though it often remains unacknowledged. And finally, of course, we must remember that their demise as a school was primarily due to historical circumstances beyond their control. This is even truer of their many German contemporaries (like Wilhelm Stern or Karl and Charlotte Bühler), unassociated with specific 'schools', who, as far as the English-speaking world is concerned, have been largely forgotten.

It is possible that some readers are baffled as to why I have not mentioned Fritz Perls' Gestalt therapy. The word 'Gestalt' is probably now better known in this connection than any other. In fact there is hardly any connection at all between Gestalt Psychology and Gestalt therapy. In some ways they are quite opposite in temper: Gestalt Psychology is among the most rigorously cerebral of Psychological doctrines, whereas Gestalt therapy was very much a reaction against intellectualism and stressed the emotional and irrational. Perls' use of the term refers to the therapeutic procedure itself in which the client is required to focus clearly on some aspect of their experience or situation as a 'figure' and address its psychological meaning. This also involves the Gestaltist notion of 'closure' or 'completing unfinished business' (e.g. the therapist might take the role of a deceased parent to enable the client to finally express all the things they wanted, but were unable, to say to that parent). While there are some affinities between them in their use of such notions as 'figure/ground' and 'closure' these are deployed quite differently in Gestalt Therapy. Fritz Perls himself was not closely associated with the German Gestalt school, and although his first book (written in South Africa) is dedicated to Wertheimer, his major theoretical point of reference was Freud.

What does the story of Gestalt Psychology tell us about Psychology itself? One important point which emerges is the difficulty of successfully transferring theoretical perspectives between cultural contexts. Unlike the physics of their famous colleagues, the Psychology of the Gestaltists did not fare well beyond the German-speaking culture in which it had arisen (and the collapse of which caused its enforced exile). This suggests that, sophisticated scientists though they were, their Psychology was rooted in the 'psychology' of their culture in a way in which contemporary German physics was not. How they viewed their task and subject matter simply differed in some central respects from the views prevailing in the US. This did not mean that their ideas were rejected, quite the contrary, but that they became refashioned and assimilated in a rather piecemeal manner into US Psychology. Something similar happened to psychoanalysis (see Chapter 14). A second point is that Gestalt research yielded several popular iconic representations (now quite divorced from its theory) of 'what Psychology is about': Köhler's apes, the 'figure/ground' distinction, the stimulus material used in their perception studies, and some of Duncker's experiments, for example, continue to appear in textbooks or adorn their covers. Even if anglophone Psychology in the end rejected the theory, its products thus remain part of the discipline's 'self-image'. Finally, Gestalt Psychology provides an unusually explicit example of the way in which Psychology derives its ideas from elsewhere (in this case from physics). While this often only involves exploring a new metaphor, in this case it was a quite conscious attempt at incorporating Psychology into the 'unified universe of discourse' of physical science – 'field' was *not* just a metaphor. In this respect its failure is perhaps especially instructive – for those who want instruction – regarding the difference in nature between Psychology and the physical sciences.

Further reading

Asch, S.E. (1952) *Social Psychology*. Englewood Cliffs: Prentice-Hall. See especially Chapter 2.

Ash, M.G. (1996) *Gestalt Psychology in German Culture 1890–1967: Holism and the Quest for Objectivity*. Cambridge: Cambridge University Press. The most definitive and comprehensive account to date and likely to remain so.

Henle, M. (1977) 'The Influence of Gestalt Psychology in America'. In R.W. Rieber and K. Salzinger (eds) (1977) *The Roots of American Psychology: Historical Influences and Implications for the Future*. New York: Annals of the New York Academy of Sciences, 291: 3–12. Useful complementary reading to Ash's book.

Henle, M. (1985) 'Rediscovering Gestalt Psychology'. In S. Koch, and D.E. Leary (eds) (1985, reprinted 1998) *A Century of Psychology as a Science*. Washington

DC: APA 100–120. Mary Henle has long striven to keep the Gestalt tradition alive in the US.

Koffka, K. (1935) *Principles of Gestalt Psychology*. New York: Harcourt Brace. See especially chapters 1–3 for a comprehensive statement of the Gestalt approach. These are perhaps the best starting point for anyone wishing to explore the topic further.

Köhler, K. (1917, English edn 1925, reprinted 1957) *The Mentality of Apes*. Harmondsworth: Penguin. One of Psychology's enduring classic texts, this includes, but covers much more than, Sultan's exploits in banana acquisition.

Murray, D.J. (1995) *Gestalt Psychology and the Cognitive Revolution*. New York: Harvester Wheatsheaf. The most thorough examination of the relationship between Gestalt Psychology and cognitivism.

Sokal, M. (1984) 'The Gestalt Psychologists in Behaviorist America'. *American Historical Review* 89: 1240–1263. Very useful, and quite amusing, follow-up to Henle (1977).

Major Gestalt texts

Duncker, K. (1926) 'A qualitative (experimental and theoretical) study of productive thinking (solving of comprehensible problems)'. *Journal of Genetic Psychology* 33: 642–670.

Duncker, K. (1945) (trans. Lynne S. Lees) 'On Problem-solving'. *Psychological Monographs* 270.

Henle, M. (ed.) (1971) *The Selected Papers of Wolfgang Köhler*. New York: Liveright.

Koffka, K. (1928) *The Growth of the Mind*. London: Kegan Paul Trench & Trübner.

Köhler, W. (1938) *The Place of Value in a World of Facts*. London: Kegan Paul, Trench & Trübner.

Köhler, W. (1940) *Gestalt Psychology*. New York & Toronto: Mentor Books.

Köhler, W. (1947) *Dynamics in Psychology*. New York: Liveright.

Lewin, K. (1935) *A Dynamic Theory of Personality*. New York: McGraw.

Lewin, K. (1936) *Principles of Topological Psychology*. New York: McGraw.

Lewin, K. (1951, rep. 1964) *Field Theory in Social Science*. New York: Harper.

Petermann, B. (1932) *The Gestalt Theory and the Problem of Configuration*. London: Kegan Paul, Trench & Trübner. Influential critique of Gestalt Psychology. Petermann turned Nazi, and became Professor of Psychology and Pedagogy at Göttingen in 1939.

Wertheimer, M. (1959, enlarged edn, 1st edn, 1945) *Productive Thinking*. New York: Harper. Key text on the 'cognitive' aspect.

On Lewin, see also:

Hall, C.S. and Lindzey, G. (1957) *Theories of Personality*, 1st edn. New York: Wiley. An extremely good introduction to Lewin's system despite, or more probably because of, its date. See Chapter 6.

Also cited:

Perls, F.S. (1947) *Ego, Hunger and Aggression. A Revision of Freud's Theory and Method*. London: Allen & Unwin.

Chapter 7

Cognitive Psychology

- Emergence of Cognitive Psychology
- Core conceptual innovations underpinning the cognitivist approach
- Founding Cognitive Psychology texts
- Growth and character of Cognitive Psychology

It is appropriate to move directly from Gestalt to Cognitive Psychology, for the past quarter century the most prominent school in experimental Psychology. Unlike behaviourism this arose more or less simultaneously in the US and Britain, although the role of British figures such as Kenneth Craik, Frank George, W. Grey Walter and the late Donald Broadbent as well as Alan Turing's work – notably his 'Turing Machine' and 'Turing Test'[1] concepts – has been largely overlooked in the US-authored histories which hitherto have been virtually the sole sources of historical information on its origins. R. Hayward (2001) has now helped redress this imbalance, eliciting the distinctive character of the British work. It would be quite wrong to imagine that Psychologists previously ignored cognition. As we saw, the Gestaltists paid it much attention, while in 1923 Charles Spearman had published *The Nature of 'Intelligence' and the Principles of Cognition* and in Switzerland Jean Piaget began studying the cognitive development of children in the 1920s. One could go back further to papers by Alfred Binet from the 1890s, R. Jardine's forgotten *The Elements of the Psychology of Cognition* (1874), and even Herbert Spencer (1855). Traditional philosophy, moreover, commonly treated logic and cognition as nearly synonymous (e.g. G. Boole, 1854). Why then did Cognitive Psychology appear so revolutionary in the 1950s – a view sustained by most of its historians? Certainly it was not the choice of cognition as a subject matter that was new.

The answer is twofold:

- Cognitivism was seen as breaking behaviourism's hold on experimental Psychology, supplanting it as the most productive theoretical orientation. This view has been keenly promoted by cognitivism's advocates. In retrospect the 'rebellion against entrenched behaviourism' story appears to have been somewhat exaggerated (see Chapter 5), though has some validity for the US situation at least.
- More genuinely revolutionary was the adoption of a new set of theoretical concepts, a new technical language. Cognitive Psychologists were thinking about thinking in a quite novel way. It is on this I wish to concentrate.

To begin somewhat obliquely, by the late 1930s technology was approaching current levels of complexity, especially in radio, television and aero-engineering. World War Two intensified this with inventions such as radar, the need to coordinate radar with air-defences, problems posed by night-flying, the need for code-breaking machines (as at Bletchley Park, UK where Turing worked) and finally the Manhattan Project. One feature of these innovations was the ever-escalating level of mathematical calculation involved, stimulating the development of ever-more versatile calculating machines. Another consequence was that design problems regarding control and integration of complex technical systems – and the interaction between human and machine – were brought to the fore. From this setting, in which technology, mathematics and theoretical concern with design principles

---

[1] You are faced with two keyboards (or equivalent) by which to communicate with an unseen source – one a human, the other a machine. If after your conversation you cannot tell which is which the machine has passed the 'Turing Test'. This is discussed in Chapter 19.

were interwoven, the concepts emerged that would underlie Cognitive Psychology. Generally these were not, note, initiated by psychologists but by electrical engineers like Claude Shannon, mathematicians like Norbert Weiner and J. von Neumann, and logicians such as Turing. Kenneth Craik, a brilliant young psychologist at Cambridge, is the principal exception to this generalisation, his short book *The Nature of Explanation* (1943) amounting almost to Cognitive Psychology's first manifesto. The invention that finally integrated these strands was, of course, the electronic computer, the first versions of which date from the mid-1940s, with the 1948 invention of the transistor rendering possible computers as we now know them. From this came three central ideas which were to alter the conceptualisation of cognition: information, feedback and programming.

1   *Information.* Although the term 'information' is recorded from 1387, prior to about 1940 the notion of measuring it would have seemed absurd (although a statistical usage by R.A. Fisher appeared in 1925). In 1948 Shannon of MIT endowed 'information' with a precise technical meaning enabling it to be quantified (a development brewing since the 1930s). In retrospect his move looks simple: information can be measured in terms of the uncertainty it eliminates. Adopting 'binary logic', this is formally convertible into the question of how many yes–no decisions are required to specify the information. As a simple illustration: to specify a given square on an 8×8 chess board we need to ask six yes/no questions of the form 'is it in the top half?'/'is it in the left half?' (each of which halves the remaining possibilities). In IT jargon this means that specifying a square requires six 'bits' (for 'binary digit') of information. Mathematically developing this insight soon took things into more complex realms, but the core conceptual point is actually quite straightforward. Converting this into hardware terms was easy: Yes/No (1/0 in binary), was equivalent to On/Off states of electrical switches.

By using Information Theory things like 'channel capacity', 'storage capacity', and 'noisy signals' could start to be discussed. One important innovation was the notion of 'redundancy', meaning 'surplus' information. If a 'signal' only contains the precise minimum of information necessary, any interference will render it meaningless; additional 'redundant' information ensures successful transmission despite a degree of degradation. Thus in written English many letters are strictly speaking redundant: in small ads these are often eliminated to save space as when 'desirable semi-detached house with 3 bedrooms, 2 reception rooms and a small garden' becomes 'des. semi 3 beds 2 recep. sm. gard'.

This notion of measuring information first entered Psychology in psychophysics and reaction time (RT) studies: it became possible, for example, to study RT as a function of the information in a stimulus array – how much longer does it take to react to one of eight possibilities than to one of four, one of two or in the absence of any choice? Other kinds of question rapidly followed: What is the information capacity of short term memory (STM)? How is information most effectively memorised or presented? What are the channel capacities for various sensory modalities? How fast is information of different kinds processed? Many such questions – never even askable before

– soon came onto the agenda and were often of direct practical importance (e.g. in relation to instrument design). The upshot was to recast the study of cognition as the study of human information processing.

2   *Feedback.* E.C. Tolman had, as we have seen, striven to incorporate 'purpose' into behaviourist theory. But this was difficult. Prior to the 1940s, the puzzle was that 'purposiveness' was apparently incompatible with scientific determinism; it suggested that something later in time could cause something earlier in time, which is counter to the unidirectionality of time and the very notion of cause–effect sequences – a cause cannot come after its effect. To say you are studying to get a degree three years hence seems to imply that an event three years ahead is causing your present behaviour. Purposive or 'teleological' explanations had thus been systematically eliminated from physical science over the previous two centuries. Tolman introduced various technical expressions to try and circumvent this but none caught on. At this point, in the early 1940s, technology provided what looked like a non-mysterious solution – the notion of negative feedback. The term 'feed-back' is first recorded in 1920 in the sense of feed-back through microphones, when a microphone picks up output from its amplifier and we get that familiar 'howl' effect. The first usage in the sense we are concerned with occurs, according to the *New Oxford English Dictionary*, in 1943. Credit for realising its potential really belongs jointly to Norbert Weiner and Craik, although Weiner gained most of the historical kudos by creating a new discipline, Cybernetics (from a Greek word meaning 'rudder', etymologically related to 'governor'), to promote its exploration.

Weiner had spotted the theoretical significance of some devices long familiar as gadgets for controlling the operation of machines such as steam engines. The earliest example, from ancient Greece, was a method for rigging a ship's rudder to maintain it on a constant course: should it veer to port the rudder counteracted this by moving it to starboard and vice-versa. Steam engines incorporated a 'planetary valve', invented in the eighteenth century, which maintained the engine at constant speed; if it accelerated the balls on the valve were thrown wider which closed down the throttle, if the engine slowed, the opposite happened, opening up the throttle. In each case what happens in formal terms is that the system's output is 'fed back' in such a way as to return it to a desired state. Now this greatly resembles purposiveness – the boat keeps heading for Athens, returning on course when diverted; the steam engine strives to maintain a particular speed despite momentary variations. But there is nothing mysterious about this, it is achieved by a simple 'feed-back loop'. Weiner differentiated between positive and negative feed-back. The howling amplifier is an example of positive feed-back, where the feed-back loop increases the divergence in output yet further. This is not necessarily bad: theories of human evolution, for instance, frequently postulate positive feed-back loops between such things as brain-size, access to nutritional foods and intelligence. More immediately significant, though, is the negative feed-back loop which counteracts divergence, maintaining the system in a desired state (e.g. the homeostatic biological mechanisms for keeping temperature constant, adjusting vision to changing

Figure 7.1 *Speculatrix*, one of W. Grey Walter's cybernetic 'tortoise' robots built c. 1950. Reproduced by permission of The Science Museum/Science and Society Picture Library.

light levels etc.). During the early 1950s several British scientists, most importantly W. Grey Walter, designed and built small cybernetic robots ('cybernauts') (Fig. 7.1) to demonstrate how apparently 'purposive' behaviour could be artificially achieved (see R. Hayward 2001).

The Psychological relevance of this was obvious: purposive behaviour was no longer mysterious, but could be studied using the notion of feedback. But what was it that was being 'fed back'? What else, but information. The psycho-physiological system could be conceptualised as one which processed information about both the external environment and its own current state and output via feed-back loops (some sensory, some neuromuscular etc.). So the image of human-as-information-processor incorporated the concept of feed-back as a central feature. But there is still one feature missing. Information must somehow be *represented*, be it about a required internal end-state or about the world outside and the organism's transactions with it.

3   *Program*. Again, there were technical antecedents: in late eighteenth-century France complex looms were devised (known as Jacquard looms after their inventor) incorporating numerous frames. They were controlled by a chain of perforated wooden blocks passing through the loom, the pattern of holes determining which frames would rise and fall. This was exactly

analogous to the punched tape or card later used for programming computers. These wooden blocks were perhaps the first 'software'.

Since the Middle Ages hosts of dancing or musical 'automata' had been constructed by inventors and engineers. These involved building into the machine some kind of unfolding sequence of instructions such as the pins on a music-box cylinder. Unlike the blocks on a Jacquard loom, however, they could not be rearranged. These may be thought of as the original 'hardware' programs.

With the advent of computers 'programming' acquired major significance. The first usage in this sense is from a 1945 report on the ENIAC computer (the first modern 'electronic' computer). For psychologists the concept proved immediately useful, for it seemed to be strictly analogous to the concept of a 'plan': we could now handle complex higher order behaviour in terms of programs or plans which the organism 'ran through' – and these could be nested within one another and on any time-scale.

As indicated, programming occurs at two levels. First, at the 'hardware' level of the system's design it governs the system's structure and the repertoire of operations it can perform. This includes how it will process information input from outside and may involve a wide range of feed-back mechanisms. Second, there is the 'software' level, the means by which information is inputted into the system, instructing it to run through its repertoire of operations in a certain way. If learning to read is a 'hard-programming' educational phase, books are a form of 'software'. Acquiring one's native language is very closely linked with brain-maturation and almost literally involves programming the 'hard-wiring' of the brain areas involved in language use.

This core group of concepts, along with numerous subsidiary and related ones, provided a new framework, drawn from outside Psychology, in terms of which topics such as thinking, memory, learning, neurological organisation and the like could be tackled. (The analogy between electrical circuits with their on/off switches and the nervous system's on/off synapses had already been advanced in the mid-1940s.) The task now was to embark on a research programme which would explore the implications of this – what we know as Cognitive Psychology. Ultimately, I suppose, we could see it as an exploration of the 'human as computer' metaphor, although it ranges somewhat more widely than that. Initially, for Craik (who knew 'calculating machines' rather than computers) it was the brain's ability to model external world phenomena which he saw as the crucial insight, leading him to equate 'models' with 'explanations' (and thereby cut through the abstract formalism of the logical positivists' concept of scientific explanation). It was this kind of thinking that then enabled the computer itself to be viewed as a 'model' of the brain. By the 1950s humans could thus be viewed as information processing systems operating according to complex sets of programs derived from a variety of sources, from genetic to social, and sustained in this by sophisticated self-monitoring 'feedback' capacities. While a very abstract way of couching things, this seemed to leave the door open for most of the phenomena which psychologists might wish to study. (It eventually returned to such philosophical

Table 7.1 Founders of Cognitive Psychology in the US and Britain and their institutions.

United States
(MIT – Massachusetts Institute of Technology)

Jerome K. Bruner	Harvard University
E. Galanter	Harvard University, Stanford University
Warren McCulloch	University of Illinois, MIT (from 1952)
George A. Miller	Harvard University
A. Newell	Rand Corporation, Carnegie-Mellon University
W. Pitts	University of Chicago, MIT (from 1947)
Karl Pribram	Center for Advanced Studies in the Behavioral Sciences, Stanford University
Claude Shannon	MIT
Herbert Simon	Rand Corporation, Carnegie-Mellon University
Norbet Weiner	MIT

United Kingdom

W. Ross Ashby	none, psychiatrist in private practice
Kenneth Craik	Cambridge University
Donald Broadbent	Cambridge University
Frank George	University of Bristol
W. Grey Walter	Burden Neurological Institute, Bristol

chestnuts as the nature of consciousness and the mind–body relationship.) Ultimately it remains debatable whether 'purposiveness' can really be completely translated into feedback and programming terms, but undoubtedly the perceived possibility of doing so broke a major conceptual log-jam.

The first indications of the impact of this new approach within what was then termed the 'Psychology of Thinking' appear in works such as J.K. Bruner *et al* (1956), a study of what (somewhat debatably) they called 'concept formation'. The majority of the book concerned a research programme using a special pack of 81 cards varying across three values on each of four features – colour (red, green, black), shapes (discs, squares, crosses), numbers of border-lines (1, 2, 3), number of shapes (1, 2, 3) – the subject being required to identify a target 'concept' (e.g. 'All cards with two shapes and one border'). While clearly cognitive in spirit this work did not, however, widely deploy the new technical concepts. These were more clearly in evidence in G.A. Miller (1956), his now classic paper on the information capacity of STM. Two years later A. Newell *et al* (1958) introduced their 'General Problem Solver' program which, it was claimed, had found a new, more elegant, proof for one of the theorems in A.N. Whitehead and B. Russell's *Principia Mathematica*. This launched the Artificial Intelligence project which has flourished unabated ever since. In the same year Donald Broadbent began using information-processing flow-charts (D. Broadbent, 1958). From this point the cognitive movement accelerated rapidly, its founding phase being sealed by a work we should discuss in a little more detail.

Plans and the Structure of Behavior *by G.A. Miller,* *E. Galanter and K. Pribram (1960)*

Although cognitivism had been developing for over a decade, this work provided the first systematic and comprehensive statement of its perspective, soon acquiring the status of a launch manifesto for cognitivism in American Psychology. The central argument is that human behaviour can best be understood in terms of the nesting and clustering of 'plans' – programs of action through which the organism runs in order to reach its goals. Whereas the central unit in behaviourism had been the S-R connection, these authors proposed what they called the TOTE (Test-Operate-Test-Exit) unit. The TOTE unit is a simple feedback loop. Suppose I am hammering a nail, first I 'test' the situation (is it straight?), then I 'operate' (hit the nail), then I test again (is it in far enough?), if it is, I then 'exit' – there may of course be several test-operate sequences before exiting. But this whole unit will probably be a subcomponent in a larger plan – I am nailing a strip of wood to the wall into which I intend screwing some hooks. This plan involved an earlier trip to a hardware store to buy the materials and will end when I 'exit' after testing that the hooks bear the weight of the family's coats. At which point I may realise that a glass door-panel will bang into the last hook! This will modify my hook-mounting plan such that in future it includes a TOTE unit representing 'check against swinging doors', to be implemented before nail-banging starts.

One reason why this alternative to S-R was so powerful was that it could handle complex behaviours; the pianist playing a rapid arpeggio does not learn this by associating each note to the previous one, rather they run through an 'arpeggio program' (and note the similarity between musical notation and the punched-tape kind of programming technique). Another aspect of this is one Miller explored in some detail – how we organise information by 'chunking' it. Music hall 'perfect memory' entertainers had long ago developed techniques of memorising large amounts of information in this way, and indeed these go back to classical times. It also has a fairly close relationship with Gestalt ideas on structuring of problems so they can be solved in the most efficient way.

The book had great success, pulling together recent developments in linguistics (notably Noam Chomsky's work), neurology, memory, problem solving research, even hypnosis, to show how they were amenable to the cognitive approach. As it happened the TOTE unit itself did not establish itself as a technical term, primarily because other expressions proved more useful as Cognitive Psychology expanded throughout the 1960s. Nevertheless, the book is widely acknowledged as signalling the point when the academic tide finally turned in cognitivism's favour. Reading it could in some cases trigger an almost Damascene conversion as Margaret Boden (2001) has testified.

Cognitivism's rise to dominance

One measure of the maturation of a new theory or school is the appearance of undergraduate college textbooks. In 1967 Ulric Neisser's *Cognitive Psychology* appeared, fulfilling this role for cognitivism, although he backtracked somewhat from the pure information-processing model, stressing the selective and synthesising aspect of human processing which artificial systems lacked. In the mid-1970s Neisser became far more sceptical, but for the time being his textbook was read as confirming cognitivism's broad potential and for the next twenty years it effectively made the running in mainstream experimental Psychology, closely allied with Artificial Intelligence (AI) studies and, increasingly, with neurophysiology. The work of later figures such as J. Fodor, D. Kahnemann, Z. Pylyshyn, M. Minsky, and in Britain, A. Baddeley, P.C. Wason, P.N. Johnson-Laird, D. Marr and M. Boden cannot, unfortunately, be surveyed here. They have variously extended cognitivism to the study of such things as memory (Baddeley), syllogistic reasoning (Wason and Johnson-Laird), creativity (Boden), the 'modularity' model of mind (Fodor) and perception (Marr). The cognitivist approach to language, as represented by, for example, F. Smith and G.A. Miller (1966) provided the theoretical basis for the Artificial Intelligence project, but long suffered from a failure to engage with the insights of contemporary (largely British) linguistic philosophy (see Chapter 19). Within cognitivist theorising there is now a theoretical debate concerning the relative merits of 'computational' and 'connectionist' approaches, and the excitement about 'parallel distributed processing' (PDP) models has not yet abated. For these issues readers should consult one of the numerous recent textbooks.

For us what should be noted is how a movement that began as offering a new conceptual framework for studying higher mental processes gradually developed into something with a far more comprehensive semi-philosophical character (although this was there in embryonic form in Craik's work). By the 1980s writers such as Paul and Patricia Churchland were claiming to have virtually solved such perennial issues as the 'mind–body problem' and, in effect, casting 'cognitive neuroscience' as the panacea for all human ills. Are we beginning to discern a pattern here? As with psychoanalysis (see Chapter 14), behaviourism and Gestalt Psychology, for example, Psychological schools of thought seem prone to expanding from the relatively restricted scientific issues which serve as their starting points into putative philosophies of life.

Cognitive Psychology's arrival was engineered quite self-consciously by a relatively small group of American and British psychologists, while non-psychologists like Shannon and von Neumann played a continuing role. Even so, others were moving in the same direction, some of whom became identified as fellow-travelling cognitive psychologists once the movement was established. Chomsky was always invoked as an ally because of his theory of the deeply programmed nature of grammar and opposition to behaviourist accounts of language (notably Skinner's). George Kelly's 'Personal Construct Theory' has a strong cognitivist character, while C.E. Osgood et al's The Measurement of Meaning (1957) was moving in a cognitive direction also, despite the retention of much Hullian terminology. L. Festinger's 'Cognitive Dissonance Theory' (see Chapter 12) and A. Ellis's 'Rational-Emotive Therapy' were catching the same wind. Bruner soon 'rediscovered' Jean Piaget and incorporated Piagetian Psychology into American cognitivism.

By the 1980s cognitivism was so intertwined with AI research and neurophysiology that to many devotees links with the rest of Psychology seemed tenuous. As they saw it, especially in the US, the rest of Psychology had gone 'soft' and was under the joint thumbs of Humanistic Psychology and social constructionist, feminist influenced, Social Psychology. Due in part to the fact that a succession of APA Presidents were drawn from the latter camps a split developed, and in some universities Psychology was divided between 'Cognitive Science' and Social Science or Social Studies departments. In Britain this has not widely happened, but tensions are there.

From my own viewpoint Cognitive Psychology represents a very major example of how novel technologies and scientific discoveries can change how we think about ourselves. Perhaps it should go without saying that cognitivism's success has both reflected and reinforced a 'contextual' climate dominated by the rise of information technology. Some recent writers have also seen its US origins in an altogether darker light as rooted in a distinctly militaristic view of human nature in which humans are reduced to the status of expendable pieces of equipment (P. Galison, 1994). Since the late 1980s criticisms of the school have begun to mount, not only from its traditional critics such as Humanistic psychologists and behaviourists, but from a variety of social constructionists, phenomenologists and philosophers (see A. Costall and A. Still (1987) for a sample). Even if its career has plateaued ('peaked' would be falsely to prophecy an imminent decline), cognitivism is no more likely to disappear than any other school of Psychological thought – it is far too congenial a doctrine for too large a contemporary psychological constituency to permit this to happen.

Further reading

Boden, M.A. (1977, 2nd edn, 1987) *Artificial Intelligence and Natural Man*. London: MIT Press; New York: Basic Books. Sophisticated overview of the issues by a staunch cognitivist.

Boden, M.A. (1989) *The Creative Mind: Myths and Mechanisms*. London: Weidenfeld & Nicolson. Proposes a cognitivist theory of 'creativity'.

Costall, A. and Still, A. (eds) (1987) *Cognitive Psychology in Question*. Brighton: Harvester. An influential collection of critical papers, invaluable for anyone seeking an introduction to theoretical controversies regarding the nature, status and claims of Cognitive Psychology.

Eysenck, M.W. and Keanes, M.T. (2000) *Cognitive Psychology: A Student's Handbook*, 4th edn. Hove: Psychology Press. Textbook representing the current state of Cognitive Psychology.

Galison, P. (1994) 'The Ontology of the Enemy: Norbert Wiener and the Cybernetic Vision'. *Critical Inquiry*, 21: 228–266.

Galotti, K.M. (1999) *Cognitive Psychology In and Out of the Laboratory*. Belmont, CA: Brooks/Cole-Wadsworth. Useful as a more popularly pitched alternative to Eysenck and Keanes (above).

Gardner, H. (1987) *The Mind's New Science: A History of the Cognitive Revolution*. New York: Basic Books. The best general, if somewhat celebratory, history of the school although ignoring the British story.

Garfield, J.L. (ed.) (1990) *Foundations of Cognitive Science. The Essential Readings*. New York: Paragon House. A convenient starting point for the study of the major theoretical issues.

Hayward, R. (2001) '"Our Friends Electric": Mechanical Models of Mind in Post-war Britain'. In G. Bunn, A.D. Lovie and G.D. Richards (eds) *Psychology in Britain. Historical Essays and Personal Reflections*. Leicester: British Psychological Society/London: The Science Museum, 290–308. Counteracts the American-centred accounts hitherto available.

Hirst, W. (ed.) (1988) *The Making of Cognitive Science: Essays in Honor of G.A. Miller*. Cambridge: Cambridge University Press. Worth dipping into, though variable.

Johnson-Laird, P.N. (1988) *The Computer and the Mind*. London: Fontana. A useful book by one of Britain's veteran cognitivists.

Murray, D.J. (1995) *Gestalt Psychology and the Cognitive Revolution*. New York: Harvester Wheatsheaf. The most thorough examination of the relationship between Gestalt Psychology and cognitivism.

Posner, M.I. and Shulman, G.L. (1979) 'Cognitive Science'. In E. Hearst (ed.) *The First Century of Experimental Psychology*, New York: Erlbaum. For me this gets off on the wrong foot by saying history is boring and dull, but it provides some good factual information and an interesting insiders' view of the story.

Some early cognitivist texts

Ashby, W. Ross (1952) *Design for a Brain*. New York: Wiley. Early exposition of how computing and information theory could be used to simulate mental processes.

Attneave, F. (1959) *Applications of Information Theory to Psychology: A Summary of Basic Concepts, Methods, and Results*. New York: Holt, Rinehart & Winston. Short summary of IT and its applications to psychophysics which introduced many psychologists to IT concepts.

Broadbent, D.E. (1958) *Perception and Communication*. London: Pergamon. Major early British text.

Bruner, J.S., Goodnow, J. and Austin, G. (1956 rep. 1962) *A Study of Thinking*. New York: Science Editions. Pioneering study of 'concept formation' from a cognitivist orientation.

Craik, K. (1943) *The Nature of Explanation*. Cambridge: Cambridge University Press. Short but enormously significant text which largely determined the orientation of the first British cognitive psychologists and their colleagues in other disciplines. Craik was killed in a cycling accident in 1945 at the age of 31.

Chomsky, N. (1957) *Syntactic Structures*. The Hague & Paris: Mouton. Classic exposition of his linguistic theories (in their first version).

McCulloch, W. and Pitts, W. (1943) 'A Logical Calculus of the Ideas Immanent in Nervous Activity'. *Bulletin of Mathematical Biophysics* 5: 115–133. Exploration of the nervous system-calculating device analogy, routinely cited as a founding text.

Miller, G.A. (1956) 'The Magical Number Seven, Plus or Minus Two: Some Limits on our Capacity for Processing Information'. *Psychological Review* 63: 81–97. Often considered to be the single most important paper in demonstrating the value of the information-processing approach in addressing a clearly defined topic (the capacity of human short-term memory).

Neisser, U. (1967) *Cognitive Psychology*. New York: Appleton-Century-Crofts. The first cognitivist textbook. Neisser subsequently shifted away from the cognitivist camp.

Newell, A., Shaw, J.C. and Simon, H.A. (1958) 'Elements of a Theory of Human Problem Solving'. *Psychological Review* 65(3): 151–166. Introduced the 'General Problem Solver' program.

Osgood, C.E., Suci, G.C. and Tannenbaum, P.H. (1957) *The Measurement of Meaning*. Urbana: University of Illinois Press. Curiously blends a broadly cognitivist orientation with much Hullian vocabulary.

Shannon, C.E. and Weaver, W. (1949) *The Mathematical Theory of Communication*. Urbana: University of Illinois Press. Full theoretical statement of the information technology perspective.

Smith, F. and Miller, G.A. (eds) (1966) *The Genesis of Language. A Psycholinguistic Approach*. Cambridge, MA: MIT Press. Major early cognitivist text on psycholinguistics.

Wason, P.C. and Johnson-Laird, P.N. (1972) *The Psychology of Reasoning: Structure in Content*. Cambridge, MA: Harvard University Press. Explores human syllogistic reasoning etc.

Von Neumann, J. (1958) *The Computer and the Brain*. New Haven: Yale University Press. He also introduced 'Games Theory', undiscussed in the main text, which had its own distinct influence on Cognitive Psychology and cognitively pitched Social Psychology.

Among the most extreme advocates of cognitive science have been the Churchlands. See the following 'position statements':

Churchland, P.M. (1988, rev.edn) *Matter and Consciousness*. Cambridge, MA: MIT Press.

Churchland, P.S. (1986) *Neurophilosophy. Toward a Unified Science of the Mind/Brain*. Cambridge, MA and London: MIT Press.

For the state of play at the height of Cognitive Psychology's fortunes, just prior to subsequent schismatic tendencies, see:

Anderson, J.R. (1980) *Cognitive Psychology and its Implications*. San Francisco: Freeman.

Precursors besides Piaget and Gestalt Psychology

Selected key texts in chronological order:

Boole, G. (1854) *An Investigation into the Laws of Thought*. London: Macmillan. Embodies the view that the laws of logic are the laws of thought and introduces the idea of binary logic.

Spencer, H. (1855, 2nd edn 1870) *The Principles of Psychology*. London: Williams & Norgate. Has, in retrospect, a distinct, if largely unacknowledged, cognitive air.

Jardine, R. (1874) *Elements of the Psychology of Cognition*. London: Macmillan. Completely forgotten but historically interesting as half-way between traditional philosophical concerns and Psychological ones.

McCosh, J. (1886, rev. 1892) *The Cognitive Powers*. New York: Scribner's. American Mental and Moral Philosophy in transition to Psychology.

Binet, A. (1886) *La Psychologie du Raisonnement*. Paris: Alcan.

Binet, A. (1903, rep. 1922) *L'Étude Expérimentale de l'Intelligence*. Paris: Schleicher Frères, A Costes. Binet also published papers on calculators and chess players (1894) and, as well as the first intelligence test (with T. Simon), a study of the development of children's intelligence (1905). As a pioneer proto-cognitivist Binet, unlike the Gestaltists, is often overlooked, perhaps because few other French psychologists pursued the topic subsequently.

Spearman, C. (1923) *The Nature of 'Intelligence' and the Principles of Cognition*. London: Macmillan.

Spearman, C. (1930) *The Creative Mind*. Cambridge: Cambridge University Press. Spearman's distinctive theoretical approach was highly original and widely read but failed to make a long-term impact on the topic, being a difficult blend of the experimentally empirical and the scholastically formal.

Bartlett, F. (1932) *Remembering*. Cambridge: Cambridge University Press. Anticipated cognitivist studies of memory. Hailed in the 1970s as a neglected pioneering text, though its social constructionist dimension was discreetly ignored.

Vinacke, W.E. (1952) *The Psychology of Thinking*. New York: McGraw-Hill. Possibly the last overall review prior to the rise of Cognitive Psychology, summarising the state of play on the eve of the 'cognitive revolution'.

See also:

Mandler, J.M. and Mandler, G. (1964) *Thinking from Association to Gestalt*. New York: Wiley. A set of representative historical readings.

Events

1948: Hixon Symposium at California Institute of Technology on 'Cerebral Mechanisms in Behavior' (see L.A. Jeffress (ed.) (1951) *Cerebral Mechanisms of Behavior. The Hixon Symposium*, New York: Wiley). Crucial founding event. Subsequent symposia at Harvard, MIT, and elsewhere promoted and consolidated cognitivism's status.

1958: In the UK, the National Physical Laboratory Symposium on 'Mechanisation of Thought Processes'. Published by HMSO (2 vols) (1959). Not mentioned by Gardner. The list of participants is very illuminating.

1960: Bruner and Miller found Harvard Center for Cognitive Studies.

Part two

SOME TOPICS

The next six chapters discuss how Psychology has addressed a variety of specific topics: perception, the brain, memory, personality, social psychology and various topics presented to Applied Psychology by society at large. These show Psychology dealing with issues ranging from the physiological via simpler and more complex psychological processes to the individual as a whole, and social interaction, while Applied Psychology shows how Psychology tackles issues of practical importance and urgency in the 'real world'. This selection is nonetheless somewhat arbitrary, for example 'emotion' could have served as well as 'memory' in many respects. By tracking these over time we can see in each case why and how the way in which Psychology has done this has changed. It transpires that this is not due to some simple process of 'scientific progress' alone but also constantly reflects changing historical circumstances and priorities. Sometimes, indeed, we might wonder whether any 'scientific progress' of the usual kind has actually occurred at all.

Chapter 8

Looking at perception

Visual perception has received the attention of scientists and 'natural philosophers' (as well as doctors) for longer than any other psychological topic except memory. The 'Moon illusion' (the larger appearance of the Moon, and in fact the Sun, when near the horizon) was known in ancient times, discussed in the *Philosophical Transactions of the Royal Society* in the late seventeenth century, and has frustratingly resisted satisfactory explanation to the present day (H.E. Ross and C. Plug, in press). With the advent of lenses and optical instruments incorporating them, much attention was paid to optics, the lens-character of the cornea being recognised from early on. Optics and the anatomy of the eye were thus one of the earliest fields of natural philosophical study and experimentation, these frequently verging on being Psychological. How far perception was learned or innate was discussed by John Locke and his Ulster associate W. Molyneux; whether a congenitally blind person suddenly given sight would be able to identify shapes becoming known as 'Molyneux's Question'. A little later the philosopher G. Berkeley (1709) addressed the function of binocularity.

During the eighteenth century philosophers argued about whether visual perception was direct or representational, i.e. whether we see what is really before us (the 'direct perception' position) or only a representation of it in the brain (the 'indirect perception' position). The latter position can lead to an infinite regress – we have to postulate some internal equivalent of the eye to 'see' the representation and another to see that 'eye''s representation of the representation and so on *ad infinitum*. The 'direct' perception position (strongly advocated by Thomas Reid) is also fraught with difficulties since it was appreciated from early on that nothing in the eye itself directly constitutes a 'picture' of the outside world, while perception is obviously prone to errors. As we shall see, a more sophisticated version of this controversy continues to be a major axis of debate.

Not surprisingly, then, it is in the study of perception that we find the first stirrings of experimental Psychology in the early 1800s, primarily in Germany. This was partly because experimental physiology had naturally turned its attention to such phenomena, moving beyond traditional anatomy, and partly because the validity of sensory perception was becoming an issue of concern to scientists in general. It is in this form that science's data present themselves, so for the scientist to report data accurately and 'objectively' it is necessary to know what perceptual errors and distortions might enter into the situation. It is no coincidence that colour blindness was discovered by the chemist J. Dalton, who suffered from it. Historians of experimental Psychology have often not appreciated how intimately the early growth of German experimental Psychology was bound up with the rise of the modern scientific laboratory itself and the problems of instrumentation and reliability of data-reports to which this was giving rise. (The oft-told tale of how reaction-time studies originated in Astronomy also needs to be understood in this context.) A false impression is given that the 'scientific laboratory' was a fully developed pre-existing institution which Psychology simply copied.

With its venerable links to optics the study of perception has never been monopolised by Psychology, and during the latter nineteenth century Psychological researchers such as Herman Helmholtz, Ewald Hering and W.H.R. Rivers continued to work in association with physiologists, ophthalmologists and physicists. Subsequently the approaches and interests of these disciplines parted; by the

1920s perception research had become highly fragmented, but between the late 1850s and about 1900 it constituted a fairly unified project. This was due to two main factors: first, it was geographically located almost exclusively in German-speaking countries (exceptions being F.C. Donders in Holland and W.H.R. Rivers in England), and second, it was dominated by a far-reaching and complex theoretical battle between the doyen of German scientists, Herman Helmholtz, and his rival Ewald Hering which served as the focus for everyone in the field whatever their disciplinary allegiances. The Helmholtz and Hering camps were well-defined. Those identifying with neither sought a mediating role, but their publications were invariably read as tending to support one side or the other. German experimental Psychology did not therefore begin as an entirely autonomous venture, but as a particular approach to psychophysical phenomena also being studied by physiologists and physicists, the methodologies of all three disciplines developing jointly.

But what was the dispute about? At heart it was about the 'nativism versus empiricism' issue, and to some extent it created this perennial controversy in its modern form (though Francis Galton too was instrumental in this). Helmholtz espoused a highly empiricist position in which perception was largely the product of learning and experience; Hering, on the other hand, was cast as a 'nativist' (although disputed the validity of the dichotomy). The dispute centred on two main topics: space perception (which we must leave aside here) and, increasingly, colour vision. In essence Helmholtz (drawing on an earlier theory of the English 'natural philosopher' Thomas Young, further developed in the 1840s by physicist J. Clerk Maxwell), argued for three primary colour sensations, red, green and blue (or violet), while Hering argued for three basic processes, one determining blue-yellow perception, one red-green, and the third black-white (brightness). Each of these he conceived as reciprocally inhibiting, thus we cannot experience mixtures of red and green or blue and yellow, although we can experience bluish greens and reddish yellows. The nativism versus empiricism issue entered in the following way. Hering was insistent that the task of perceptual theories was to explain phenomenological or subjective experience, which he believed could only be done by relating this experience to physiological processes – the 'psycho-physical interface'. From this perspective our colour perceptions were essentially built-in. The Helmholtz view was that the task was to account for the fidelity of perceptual experience to the objectively existing physical world. This left the door open for a greater role to be played by higher level processing and learned adaptation, as well as a leaning towards a more reductionist, physics-based, theoretical orientation. Thus the absence, in the 'Young–Helmholtz Theory', of yellow as a primary sensation did not matter as this could be explained as due to higher-level processing. As far as the physics of the eye was concerned the tri-colour theory sufficed. This oversimplifies a highly complex issue, of course, but highlights how an apparently clear-cut scientific question – how do we perceive colours? – can be formulated, and theoretically framed, in radically incompatible terms.

As far as the innate versus learned controversy is concerned, R.S. Turner (1994) argues that even now the controversy has not been entirely resolved, although current understanding of colour-perception incorporates both Helmholtzian 'tri-chromaticity' (at the retinal level) and Hering's 'opponent-process' account (at the lateral geniculate nucleus level). In many respects it was irresolvable because the underlying theoretical positions and the language used to refer to phenomena were incommensurable. As historians of science have it, the dispute resisted 'closure'. (Turner, incidentally, suggests that the very nature of their research resulted in the Helmholtz and Hering camps actually seeing the world differently in some crucial respects.) By the 1930s it looked as if Helmholtz's approach had won the day; however, post-World War Two developments have swung the pendulum back to positions bearing a closer resemblance to Hering's account. But even if it ultimately evolved from it, the present situation cannot be easily mapped onto this earlier controversy.

A further, contextual, side-point is worth noting. One reason why colour-vision became so important in the 1880s was a result of a Swedish train crash which, it was believed, happened because a colour-blind railway employee misread a signal. Suddenly the question of railway safety (an intense Europe-wide anxiety during this period) pushed the issue of colour vision to the top of the perception-research agenda, although G. Wilson was expressing similar concerns as early as 1855.

Until about 1905 research (of various kinds) on the senses dominated laboratory-based experimental Psychology. Subsequently, if no longer so over-whelming, it has remained at the heart of Psychology's experimental inquiries and was, as we saw, especially important for the Gestalt school. It constantly impinges on other topics: the involvements of motivation, learning and personality with perceptual performance have been studied from a multitude of directions including the psychodynamic and social. Perceptual processing has been studied in the context of cognitive and information-processing theories, and as bearing on quite fundamental theoretical issues (as in the 'direct' versus 'indirect' debate). It encompasses psychophysiology at one extreme and extra-sensory perception (ESP) at the other.

From the present angle of interest an obvious question arises: can we find evidence of social and contextual factors operating even in relation to research on such an apparently basic and universal function as perception? The answer is 'yes', but a reflexive point is necessary in order to clarify why. The traditional 'Martian' might ask, 'How does the human species' perceptual system work?' In answering this the alien would, presumably, first study our biological sensory apparatus. But when it comes to the subsidiary question, 'how do humans deal with perceptual problems and difficulties?', at least part of the answer is that they have now evolved a collective strategy which they call 'doing Psychological research on perception'. (Another strategy has been technological expansion of perceptual capacities using instruments such as telescopes, microscopes, radar and thermal imagers – the invention and distribution of which are again collective in nature.) In other words, research on perception is itself part of our species' current perceptual system, coming into play primarily when perception is proving problematic. This ranges from the colour blindness case mentioned above to the problems facing World War Two fighter pilots (studied by Kenneth Craik for example) and the physiology of perceptual processing in a medical (or quasi-medical) context (as studied by, for example, Colin Blakemore). One might also recall that M. Wertheimer's

Figure 8.1 Games psychologists of perception play: a stunningly effective version of the spiral illusion by Nicholas Wade (1982) (these are in fact concentric circles). Reproduced by permission of Nicholas Wade.

research on apparent movement, which initiated the immensely influential Gestalt approach to perception, coincided with the advent of moving film. This is not, I stress, a denial that 'basic' or 'pure' research on perception is in some sense possible, or has and is being undertaken. It is only to draw attention to the enveloping, almost tautological, sense in which research on perception is framed within current concerns regarding perceptual phenomena and performance. These *include* current scientific concerns emanating from sources such as broader cognitive theorising, AI and physiology. More obscurely, perhaps, they also include current philosophical assumptions about the very nature of the relationship between the world as perceived and the world as it really is (an issue underlying the Helmholtz–Hering controversy). From this perspective 'the Psychology of perception' itself serves a psychological function as a collective aspect of the very process it studies.

There is a risk, though, of casting the Psychology of perception in too sombre a light. Of all Psychology's topics it is probably the most ludic in nature (see Fig. 8.1). Like everyone else psychologists revel in playing games with visual images, exploiting the effects of toying with our perceptual mechanisms and playing tricks on our eyes – a realm which Richard Gregory and Nicholas Wade, to name but two, have made their own.

We cannot offer here anything approaching a comprehensive review of current research on perception, only sketch the major theoretical issues being tackled. Two approaches now dominate the field. Firstly, the 'ecological' approach initiated by the late J.J. Gibson, which found its fullest expression in Gibson

(1979). This is generally held to represent a 'direct' perception position. The visual system has evolved over millions of years to enable us to extract 'invariants' from the information-rich dynamic flow of light in which our eyes are constantly bathed. These pertain to those features of our environment most relevant to survival in our ecological niche. Gibson adopts the term 'affordances' to refer to these, claiming that we directly see objects in terms of what they enable us to do: grasp them, stand on them, eat them, etc. Ultimately this invariant information is about the properties of light-reflective surfaces. This aspect of perception was, Gibsonians argue, ignored in earlier research because it concentrated on unrealistically simple laboratory tasks lacking 'ecological validity'. While this achievement obviously involves complex physiological processes, Gibsonians claim there is little need to postulate internal representational systems of a cognitive kind – the perceptual system directly ascertains or experiences the real properties of external objects insofar as they are relevant to the ecological needs of the organism in question.

This ran directly counter to the more orthodox tradition of empirical research as typified by Richard Gregory, for example. Those in this camp argue that the vast range of visual illusions and effects signifies that perceptual experience is the output of a highly sophisticated and complicated set of constructive processes whereby the organism creates an image representing the external world from a fairly chaotic barrage of incoming light sensations located at the retina. Progress made in unravelling the neurophysiology of perception since the Nobel Prize-winning research of D.H. Hubel and T.N. Wiesel (1962) is interpreted as supporting this. However, the most influential opposition to Gibson has, since the late 1970s, come from those in the cognitivist AI school, in particular those developing an approach initiated by David Marr, who died (aged 35) in 1980 and whose posthumously published *Vision* (1982) is widely considered the most important single text on perception since Hubel and Wiesel's work. Those seeking a full account of his theory should consult one of the numerous current perception textbooks such as Gordon (1989), Bruce and Green (1990) and Sekuler and Blake (1994). Marr's model comprises four stages: firstly the 'image' on the retina consisting purely of a range of light intensities; secondly 'the primal sketch' in which the distribution of changes in light-intensity is analysed to yield information about likely surfaces; thirdly the now famous (or, since many find its meaning so elusive, notorious) '$2\frac{1}{2}$-D sketch' in which surfaces are represented from the immediate standpoint of the observer; and fourthly the full 3D representation of the world as containing persisting stable objects. Stated thus baldly it may be difficult to understand all the fuss, but it entailed an insightful analysis of the kinds of question involved in researching perception, and when elaborated it facilitated the incorporation and integration of a large range of research findings.

To simplify somewhat, we are faced with two broad camps: the Gibsonians and the cognitivists exploring Marr's ideas and models such as Parallel Distributed Processing (e.g. J.L. Rumelhart, 1986 and D.E. McClelland). Gibsonians may be seen as continuing a tradition of interactionist thought (going back to J. Dewey) in which the stress is on the inter-relatedness of organism and environment, or even on challenging the objectivity of this very distinction. In Britain a number of psychologists such as A. Costall, J. Good and A. Still have used Gibson's work as a basis for developing what they call a 'mutualist' theoretical position of a general kind (the anthropologist T. Ingold also has affinities with this camp). This is, in some respects, an attempt at moving beyond simple social constructionism which implies a one-way process. Mutualism views the organism and its environments as mutually interacting and changing each other in an on-going fashion. In perception theory, however, it is widely felt that Gibson was unable to deal satisfactorily with those higher levels of meaningful perception involving knowledge and experience of the world. Nonetheless, even his opponents acknowledge the value of Gibson's demands for ecological validity and his insistence that perception is but one aspect of the total ensemble of our active engagements with the world. The cognitivist approaches for their part are a facet of the wider cognitivist neuro-psychology movement, closely linked to AI. While Marr was certainly not guilty of this, the risk here is an unjustifiably reductionist account which, ironically given the generally positivist aspirations of those involved, ends up espousing a secular parody of Berkeley's idealism – everything is in the brain.

Where does this leave the two perennial issues of innate versus learned and direct versus indirect views of perception? There are few now who would see the first as a fundamental question. Most accept that perceptual phenomena range from the 'hard-wired' to those which are almost completely products of learning, training and culture. Some of the hard-wired aspects of perception also appear to require certain environmental conditions to be met if they are to mature, especially during the early months of life. Reading is a perceptual activity *par excellence*, but you have to know the language of the text to be able to do it. On the other hand there are numerous visual illusions (like the 'Moon illusion') which resist all efforts at 'unlearning'. The real task facing psychologists is to gain some purchase on the spectrum from simple physical object or property perception (this is round, or blue) to those capacities for perceptual discrimination requiring expertise and knowledge, but no less immediate for those capable of them (e.g. bird spotters, art connoisseurs, ice-skating contest judges and field geologists). This can be a collective as well as individual achievement – we wonder how on earth anyone was fooled by Victorian fake photographs of mediums exuding 'ecto-plasm' or those of the Cottingley fairies, which now quite simply *look* like fakes. Presumably the stars were seen as seven miles up by our Mediæval forebears, while to us they look awesomely distant. Gordon (1989) raises the question 'How is it that so many things from a particular era seem to have something in common: the period style? The cars, buildings, dresses and factories of the 1920s all seem to cohere in a subtle but unmistakable manner' (p. 249). One might add that since this extends to 1920s music as well, it is even more puzzling. It has been suggested that we should differentiate between our perceptions of the natural world in which we evolved (to which the Gibsonian account might well apply) and the human-made world, but it is hard to believe things are quite as dichotomous as that. The real lesson is perhaps that perception (in any modality) cannot be studied in isolation from other psychological processes except with regard to a relatively constrained (though vital) set of questions about its neurological implementation. The innate versus learned issue ceases to be a matter of fundamental principle and dissolves into a mass of micro-level questions regarding specific phenomena.

The enduring 'direct versus indirect' issue appears to be of a somewhat different conceptual order. Some of its continuing heat perhaps arises from the lingering persistence of obsolete philosophical connotations which, on closer inspection, do not clearly relate to the points now actually at issue. We tend initially to understand the controversy in terms of analogies drawn from everyday experience. We think of 'indirect' perception by analogy with, say, watching a shopping mall through a CCTV monitor or navigating by radar, 'direct' perception being unmediated looking at the shopping mall or objects on the route ahead with our eyes. The 'indirect' position is thus thought of as claiming that the 'picture' we see of the world is like that generated by some kind of inbuilt TV system. This clearly will not do. Gibsonians have, rightly I think, seen this thinking as a legacy of philosophical dualism in which the mind 'sees' a picture in the head 'representing' the external world. However few modern psychologists in either camp actually espouse mind–body dualism of this kind. So how do 'indirect' theorists conceptualise the 'direct' perception which they are denying? What, in their terms, would count as 'direct perception'? And conversely how do 'direct' theorists conceptualise the 'indirect perception' which *they* are denying? What would *they* consider as counting as 'indirect perception'? I would suggest that this is a pragmatic issue of definition. In one sense *all* perception must be indirect since it occurs in the brain, involves complex neurological processes etc. – but what could 'direct perception' mean in this context? Alternatively these mediating processes might constitute the method *by which* direct perception is achieved. On this basis even CCTV monitors and radar screens could, in McLuhanish fashion, be construed as extensions of our nervous systems and *all* perception be said to be direct. One is bound to wonder whether this amounts to anything more than a dispute about how theoretically to deploy the metaphors 'direct' and 'indirect' – which is not an empirical question at all but a matter of convention.

It then transpires that what Gibsonians and the Marr or Gregory schools are arguing about has little to do with the older philosophical debate. It is a more technical debate about how the 'extraction of invariants' in the optical array presented to the retina is accomplished and how it should be described, not about how far perception 'really' resembles the objectively existing external world or whether what we see is 'really there'. The latter is generally understood to be a false question, since we cannot know what the objectively existing external world is 'really' like *except* via our perceptual processes. (We can, of course, play tricks with visual cues, but these are only remarkable because they *do* contrast with normal, presumably error-free perception, this presumption itself being a *necessary* one. One should also be alert to the danger of equating *incomplete* perception, e.g. colour blindness, with *erroneous* perception, e.g. in the Ames Room set-up.) In some respects the schools are at cross-purposes. Gibsonians are relatively uninterested in the neurological details of invariant extraction, and more concerned with the holistic level of organism–environment transactions. It thus makes sense to argue that since any species' very survival depends on these transactions, its perception of that environment will evolve in the direction of ever greater accuracy. However 'invariants' are actually extracted, they pertain directly to real features of the perceptual world. The Marr camp is, by contrast, more concerned with understanding the 'how' of the situation as a problem challenging information-processing theory. From this perspective the output of the system must, almost by definition, be some kind of 'symbolic representation'. But again we risk being misled by a metaphor; 'representation'. Literally this means to present again, to re-present – which assumes an initial 'presentation'. A scene 'presents itself' to me and I 're-present' it by drawing a picture or map (the status of photos is oddly ambiguous here). Taken too literally, therefore, this position seems to be suggesting that there are *no* presentations – only *re*-presentations.

This situation has certain features reminiscent of the ancestral Helmholtz–Hering controversy in that the controversy hinges not on 'facts' but on deeper, almost philosophical, differences. The two parties are asking different kinds of question in the contexts of differing assumptions about what they are trying to explain or understand. The Gibsonians apparently see perception as a central issue in the elaboration of a broader vision of human nature as a whole, as dynamically and actively engaged in, and part of, the world. There are no hard and fast divisions between organism and environment, the innate and the learned, stimulus and response. For cognitivists, by contrast, perception is the most challenging, complex and subtle of information-processing accomplishments. It is managed by a neurological system which possesses properties demonstrably similar to those implementable in electric circuits. The challenge is to understand the architecture of this system – an achievement promising direct pay-offs in the fields of, say, engineering and medicine. The most salient property of the output of this system, however, is the phenomenological or conscious experience itself. At this point the study of perception connects up with ongoing debates in philosophy and AI circles about the nature of consciousness.

Both approaches may, finally, be seen as responses to contemporary challenges to the human perceptual system. In Gibson's case one need was to relate Psychological work on perception to the real perceptual worlds in which people lived, worlds being rapidly changed by technology (his research began in the context of military research on the spatial perception of pilots). As these technologies required actively engaging the world in novel ways, the dynamic nature of perception came to the forefront. Driving a car at 60 mph raises the role of the flux in the optical array to consciousness in a way which lumbering along in a cart at 7 mph does not. But he was also able to incorporate an evolutionary and 'ecological' dimension into his thinking coincidentally with the rise of ethology and post-behaviourist interest in evolutionary theory. In the case of cognitivist approaches the challenges range from the medical to extending the capabilities of AI systems. But I will end with a rather different observation: perception has been our species' primary epistemological tool – we gain knowledge by looking and by changing, enhancing and playing with ways of looking. Science has, since the Renaissance, proceeded in tandem with artistic developments of visual media – from the discovery of perspective to time-lapse photography. In studying perception itself we are again engaged in a tightly reflexive enterprise. The perception of objects and the perception of meanings have proved impossible to separate, as have the meanings of objects and how we perceive them. What then is going on when we treat perception itself as an object, and whence arise the meanings of what we see when we do so?

Note

Though this discussion is restricted to visual perception, which has dominated the field, most of the conceptual points raised apply to other modes. It might be remarked that since E.G. Boring (1942) there has been very little historical work on auditory perception (let alone smell, touch and taste). I have also only considered the core area of theories of the visual system, though as indicated most psychological topics have a perception dimension to them, from attitude studies to developmental Psychology, from personality (e.g. the Lüscher colour test) to psycholinguistics and non-verbal communication. What I have tried to do here is indicate how even a psychological topic as apparently scientifically 'hard' as perception is not immune to constructionist and reflexive binds. I must again stress – particularly since I suspect colleagues in the perception field will be inclined to read this chapter as an attack – that, crimes against the primate cortex aside, I have no desire to subvert research in this fascinating area. On the contrary, I am if anything trying to suggest how some conceptual difficulties, particularly the direct–indirect perception controversy, may be overcome.

Further reading

Boring, E.G. (1942) *Sensation and Perception in the History of Experimental Psychology*. New York: Appleton-Century-Crofts. The most exhaustive historical account available.

Bruce, V. and Green, P.R. (1990) *Visual Perception: Physiology, Psychology and Ecology*, 2nd edn. Hove & London: Lawrence Erlbaum. An excellent textbook.

Gordon, I.E. (1989) *Theories of Visual Perception*. Chichester: Wiley. A highly accessible critical overview of the major theoretical positions. A good starting point for anyone new to the topic.

Hamlyn, D.W. (1957) *The Psychology of Perception. A Philosophical Examination of Gestalt Theory and Derivative Theories of Perception*. London: Routledge & Kegan Paul. An interesting, if rather neglected, conceptual analysis of what we mean by 'perception' itself, and how this has been neglected by psychologists.

Koffka, K. (1935) *Principles of Gestalt Psychology*. New York: Harcourt and Brace.

Ross, H.E. and Plug, C. (in press) *The Moon Illusion Through the Ages*. Oxford: Oxford University Press. This promises to be an extremely interesting monograph.

Sekuler, R. and Blake, R. (1994) *Perception*, 3rd edn. New York: McGraw-Hill. A good recent general textbook.

Turner, R.S. (1994) *In the Eye's Mind: Vision and the Helmholtz–Hering Controversy*. Princeton: Princeton University Press. A brilliantly researched monograph, insightful at many levels.

Wade, N.J. (ed.) (1983) *Brewster and Wheatstone on Vision*. London: Academic Press.

Wade, N.J. (ed.) (2000) *The Emergence of Neuroscience in the Nineteenth Century* (8 vols). London: Routledge/Thoemmes Press. Reprints, with commentary, of numerous classic texts.

Additional references

Berkeley, G. (1709, reprinted 1957) 'An Essay Towards a New Theory of Vision'. In M.W. Calkins (ed.) *Berkeley: Essay, Principles, Dialogues, with Selections from Other Writings*. New York: Charles Scribner's, 1–198. A philosophical classic, essential for the historian of the topic.

Blake, R.E. and Ramsey, G.V. (eds) (1951) *Perception. An Approach to Personality*. New York: Ronald Press. This remains an interesting compendium including papers by a number of eminent figures.

Costall, A. and Still, A. (eds) (1987) *Cognitive Psychology in Question*. Brighton: Harvester. Contains a variety of critiques of cognitivism.

Craik, K. (ed. Stephen L. Sherwood) (1966) *The Nature of Psychology. A Selection of Papers, Essays and Other Writings*. Cambridge: Cambridge University Press. See the Bibliography by Mrs S.J. Macpherson for titles like 'A note on windscreen design and visibility from fighter aircraft' (1941).

Gibson, J.J. (1950) *The Perception of the Visual World*. Boston, MA: Houghton-Mifflin. Gibson's first full-length book containing the initial exposition of his approach.

Gibson, J.J. (1979) *The Ecological Approach to Visual Perception*. Boston, MA: Houghton-Mifflin. His final theoretical statement.

Gregory, R. (1970) *The Intelligent Eye*. New York: McGraw-Hill. One of Gregory's earlier works, but of enduring interest.

Gregory, R. (2001) 'Adventures of a Maverick'. In G.C. Bunn, A.D. Lovie and G.D. Richards (eds) *Psychology in Britain: Historical Essays and Personal Reflections*. Leicester: British Psychological Society and London: The Science Museum, 381–392.

Hubel, D.H. and Wiesel, T.N. (1962) 'Receptive Fields, Binocular Interaction and Functional Architecture in the Cat's Visual Cortex'. *Journal of Physiology* 166: 106–154. Represented a major break-through in the understanding of the neurological architecture facilitating perception.

Marr, D. (1982) *Vision*. San Francisco: W.H. Freeman. Rapidly became the point of reference for subsequent cognitivist theorising on perception.

Rumelhart, D.E. and McClelland, J.L. (eds) (1986) *Parallel Distributed Processing*. Cambridge, MA: MIT Press. This collection of papers effectively launched the 'PDP' approach.

Wade, N. (1982) *The Art and Science of Visual Illusions*. London: Routledge & Kegan Paul.

Weber, E.H. (Intro. J.D. Mollon, trans. H.E. Ross and D.J. Murray) (1978) *The Sense of Touch. De Tactu, Der Tastsinn*. London: Academic Press for the Experimental Psychology Society. Definitive English translations of Weber's two classic texts.

Wilson, G. (1855) *Researches in Colour-blindness: With a Supplement of the Danger Attending the Present System of Railway and Marine Coloured Signals*. Edinburgh: Sutherland and Knox.

Chapter 9

Psychology and the brain

- Early interest in the brain
- Phrenology and its significance
- Oscillations between localisation and non-localisation views of brain-functioning
- Images of how the brain works
- The impossibility of physiologically reducing of psychology to brain-functioning
- The role of brain research in Psychology, and vice versa
- A final problem

Psychology has always been shadowed by the question of brain functioning. From the late 1600s the brain was understood as the major physical location of psychological phenomena, although the site of the emotions in particular remained debatable. With Franz Joseph Gall's craniology (later called phrenology) in the 1790s the brain, along with the senses, became the principal meeting-point between physiology and Psychology. Studying the brain presented unique difficulties. The physical functions of most organs are reflected in their morphology – e.g. how the heart pumps and the lungs transfer oxygen from the air to the blood. By contrast, brain morphology is unrevealing, presenting a gelatinous mass within which only the grossest structural elements such as the hemispheres, the major 'lobes' and the cerebellum, are easily discernible. Only around 1800 did Gall and other physiologists begin finding order in the chaotic folds of the cortex. Thus while the brain was understood to be the nexus of the nervous system, and accepted as the seat of consciousness, how it operated remained totally obscure. Phrenology's account may now seem no more than a crude and arbitrary allocation of faculties to different parts of the cortex, lacking any genuine theory about its workings, but it highlighted, as R.M. Young has explained in depth, a central theoretical problem: that of *empirically* identifying the various psychological functions themselves.

The problem arose because the existence of the traditional faculties, reason, will, emotion, sensation (memory and imagination were sometimes added) typically tended to be taken as self-evident, they had not been 'discovered' by empirical enquiry. Associationist thinkers from Locke onwards denied the reality of faculties altogether, seeing everything as rooted in sensation. The choice was thus between the traditional catalogue and associationist reductionism. The Scottish 'common sense' school, rejecting both accounts, produced a more extended catalogue of the psychological 'powers' deployed in our transactions with the world (see Chapter 2). Gall more explicitly stressed the need to identify these empirically, seeing them as modes of adaptation serving the organism's needs. This 'functionalist' analysis was radically different from those previously dominant, but Gall's faculties (or 'organs') actually turned out to closely resemble T. Reid and D. Stewart's 'powers' and, not surprisingly, phrenology caught on very quickly in Scotland, George Combe being its leading exponent. Young argues that the central theoretical issue of empirically identifying the units of functional analysis relevant for studying brain anatomy was never adequately resolved. With phrenology's fall from grace brain physiologists first fell back on the traditional list, and then recouched the reductionist associationist model in new terms by replacing 'association of sensations and ideas' with 'stimulus–response' connections. This move retained a 'functionalist' character by focusing on the organism–environment relationship, but left no place in brain physiology for the kinds of psychological faculty-category which Gall and his successors elaborated. The brain was simply conceived as a neurological storage and clearing house where sensory inputs and motor-responses were matched up, the telephone exchange switchboard becoming a frequently invoked analogy around 1900.

Physiologically, the main difficulty with phrenology was that experimental demonstration of localisation of brain functioning was extremely difficult, and ablation experiments by the French anatomist M.J.P. Flourens in the 1840s were widely believed to disprove localisation altogether – only general behavioural deficits ensued from removing parts of an animal's brain, not specific losses. By the 1860s, however a counter-shift was initiated following the discovery of the speech area ('Broca's area'), and in 1870, G. Fritsch and E. Hitzig reported highly localised motor regions of the cortex, discovered using new electro-stimulation techniques. These findings left the theoretical issue of functional units unresolved since the phenomena these areas governed were defined purely in terms of physical movement such as 'opening of mouth and retraction of tongue' or 'turning of eyes downward and to opposite side'. The speech area was interpreted in terms of muscular control of speech organs. By the end of the nineteenth century a new generation of neurologists including David Ferrier and H.C. Bastian were espousing what they termed a 'new phrenology'; we could indeed identify the cortical regions controlling certain behavioural movements, but these were conceptualised as categories of behavioural response which could be connected to stimuli, no longer as *psychological* functions.

In the 1920s and 1930s Karl Lashley swung the pendulum back against localisation. His research on rats apparently demonstrated the 'equipotentiality' of different areas of the brain, in other words destruction of cortical areas was followed, with a few exceptions as in Flourens' findings, by a general performance deficit, not a specific one. Furthermore it appeared that functions served by destroyed areas could in time be taken over by the remaining brain.

In the 1940s and 1950s Wilder Penfield and various associates again reversed the picture, their work on the stimulation of human brains exposed during surgery disclosing very fine-grained localisation: specific memories would be evoked, or highly distinct smells. Taken in conjunction with the growing data from brain-damage cases, this was initially greeted as a route for finally unravelling the functional structure of the brain, but the interpretation of such findings proved problematic. Basically there is a general problem of inferring the function of a component of a complex system from the consequences of removing or manipulating it. Break a button on your sound-system and you will be unable to control the volume but volume is not 'localised' in that button; a car engine with a flat battery will not fire, but firing is not 'localised' in the battery, and lack of fuel or spark-plugs has the same result. In the absence of some understanding of how the system works as a whole we are merely floundering in the dark. In the past, purely empirical data have but rarely, as in the case of hemispheric differences, been able to give us relatively unambiguous information regarding structural organisation. Only in the 1990s have such methods as computer-assisted tomography appeared which seem to offer a way of surmounting this hurdle by being able non-intrusively to monitor brain activity as a whole.

Next question then: how does the brain work? The history of the study of the brain from this perspective has really been the record of the application of technological and scientific metaphors, particularly those related in some way to the recording, processing and transmission of information (as we saw in the case of Cognitive Psychology) (see Fig. 9.1).

Somehow, it is argued, the formal organisation of the brain resembles that of the technological phenomenon in question. Thus we move from the early 'telephone exchange' models through Gestalt's 'field theories' to cognitivist computing

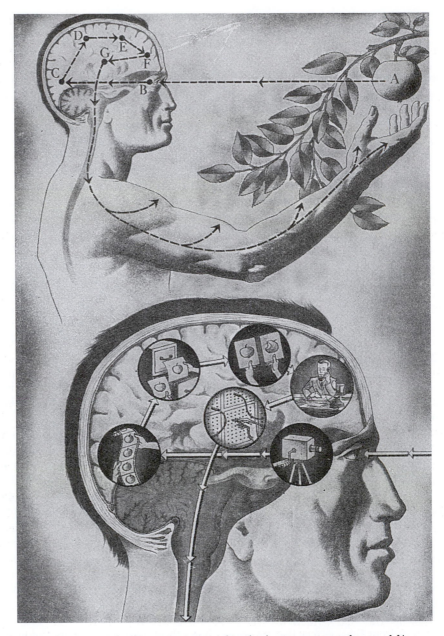

Figure 9.1 Using technology to conceptualise the brain: a quaint fusion of film, telephone switchboard and contemporary office organisation from A.H. Bowley *et al* (c. 1946). Reproduced by permission of the Centre for the History of Psychology, Staffordshire University.

models of progressively greater complexity and Chaos Theory, not forgetting Karl Pribram's hologram theory of memory (see Chapter 10 p. 130). Physiology meanwhile provides increasingly detailed information on the brain's cell-structure, neurochemistry and, since the development of electro-encephelograph (EEG) techniques in the 1940s, its electrical activity. The current task for researchers in this area using the advanced techniques alluded to earlier is primarily to try and integrate the physiological data with models of the formal organisation of the brain's information processing (parallel processing, connectionism and the like). We seem to be approaching a point where expert familiarity with information systems might finally facilitate recognition of the kind of 'machinery' present in the brain – just as familiarity with pumps and lenses enabled seventeenth-century physiologists to recognise similar machinery in the heart and eyes.

Since the mid-1980s writers such as Roland Penrose have raised the possibility that brain functioning cannot be understood without taking account of the principles of quantum physics. If this proves justified it would mark a return to Gestalt Psychology's tactic of incorporating the latest ideas from physics. Reviewing these latest developments is beyond our present scope, but one should note that they entail an interesting shift in our image of the universe which has not been widely recognised. We are now used to the idea that beneath the everyday world of objects lies an arcane realm of atomic and subatomic particles and waves only comprehensible by mathematicians and physicists. We have dealt with this, as the term 'beneath' indicates, by adopting a 'layer-cake' model in which we can ignore the nature of micro-level processes in understanding more macro-level ones. But if Penrose (1994) and G.M. Edelman (1992) are right this is too crude, at least as far as organic phenomena are concerned, in that such micro-level processes continue to play a pervasive role even in determining the most large-scale phenomena (and you cannot get much bigger than consciousness itself – in which, as St Augustine said long ago, are 'the sky, the earth, the sea, ready at my summons'!). If the 'layer cake' image is being eroded then so, in a sense, is the reductionist aspiration itself, to which this image is absolutely central involving as it does the notion of a hierarchy of 'higher' and 'lower' explanatory 'levels'.

And yet the original conceptual problem of defining what the brain actually *does* psychologically speaking, what its *psychological* functions are, remains as elusive as ever. Implicit in much of the work on brain functioning is the assumption that since *all* psychological phenomena are ultimately located in the brain a complete understanding of the brain would be equivalent to a complete understanding of psychology. This leads Paul Churchland, for example, to argue that we will eventually replace what he sees as our crude unscientific folk-psychological vocabulary with an objectively correct vocabulary referring to the physiological events in our brain (which we will somehow learn to perceive introspectively with complete accuracy). Psychology would thus be completely reduced to brain physiology. Probably few would accept quite such an extreme position, but the temptation to take it is endemic to the field. Obviously the brain *is* ubiquitously involved in all psychological phenomena, but does this mean that all psychological functions and phenomena are, in the final analysis, exclusively physiological? Is it not possible that this conclusion is an error similar to that identified previously – of localising phenomena in single components of a larger system? People do not exist in isolation, and many – possibly most – psychological phenomena pertain to our interactions with others and our environment. A purely *individual* psychological system is actually inconceivable, which suggests that many psychological phenomena are not localised completely in individual brains but emerge within a larger system of interacting brains.

This raises the issue of 'meaning', which warrants a somewhat more extended discussion related to the earlier remarks on language (Chapter 1). Crucially, and highly damaging for reductionism, the two levels of psychological and physiological meaning cannot be fused. While it is common to use physiological expressions to communicate psychological meanings this only renders them ambiguous. 'This is giving me a headache' for example may refer to one's physical condition, but may also, psychologically, mean 'this problem is proving very difficult to solve'. As understanding of brain physiology spreads, expressions drawn from this body of knowledge will no doubt be adopted for psychological purposes – people already say things like 'she's a very right hemisphere person', meaning she is artistic, intuitive rather than rational and so forth. And I sometimes say 'there's a neurone not firing' to refer to a tip-of-the-tongue experience. (Again, computer buffs might say 'I can't access it' rather than 'I can't remember it'.) To put it technically, the truth conditions of the proposition 'she's a very right hemisphere person' differ according to whether it is understood as a physiological proposition (evaluated by testing her hemispheric dominance physiologically) or a psychological one (observing if she really is artistic, intuitive etc. in her overt behaviour and social relations). Whether a physiological expression is adopted in this way depends not on its scientific accuracy but on whether it adds a new expressive nuance or has become trendy due to popular attention etc. It is not at all clear why one should abandon 'you're making me very angry' and *universally* substitute 'the stimulus configuration you're presenting is stimulating my limbic system' – although there may be particular interpersonal situations in which a speaker might feel this best captures or expresses the nuances of what they feel. But this would probably be because something about their attitude to the listener could be communicated, *not* because it was 'scientifically correct'.

In short, there would appear to be large areas of psychological concern where knowledge of brain functioning as such is simply irrelevant even though brain-events are indisputably occurring. To claim the converse would be to claim, in effect, that all psychological problems, all hopes, fears, plans, virtues and vices, could, in principle, be cured, enhanced, altered and controlled by some form of surgical or pharmacological intervention. The problem with this claim is not so much that it is false (to some extent it is probably, in the era of Prozac, true) but that it is tantamount to denying the meaningfulness of the psychological level in the first place. Hopes, fears, plans, vices and virtues become mere side-effects of physiological processes which (given the requisite technology) we can hedonistically alter. Rather than change our circumstances or our behaviour, by tinkering with neurones and biochemistry we simply change how we experience the world (surely an oddly solipsistic strategy quite at odds with the resolute materialist 'realism' typical of those to whom we owe the technology itself). But even so, the object of the exercise is to bring about a *psychological* not a physiological result. This blurs an absolutely vital distinction between those instances in which the brain *is* genuinely implicated (primarily when something is going *wrong* physically) from those when it is not. Memory loss problems may symptomatise incipient Alzheimer's disease, but they may also arise from a life-style which places too many demands on the memory system.

Although comprised of them, psychology is not just brain-processes and the old problem of the status of psychological concepts and categories persists. We know a vast amount about the neurophysiology of visual perception, but we can say very little about the neurophysiology of 'beliefs'; indeed some writers like Steven Stich consider 'belief' to be a folk-psychological concept of no scientific value. The fact is, as just argued, that psychological concepts are often simply not *about* physiology or brain processes in the first place, but about, for example, construing and managing interpersonal relations. 'I sorely miss you, my dear, and anxiously await your return' is not a primitive 'folk-psychological' substitute for a 'more accurate' account of brain-events. The psychologist's tack in considering such a self-report should surely not be to seek brain processes associated with 'sorely missing' and 'anxiously awaiting' and the state of feeling someone is 'dear', but to inquire more deeply into the nature of the relationship being signified by this utterance – which obviously could be produced in a variety of situations (and in many tones of voice too). But even more technical Psychological concepts such as intelligence, prejudice, 'learned helplessness', territoriality, and 'motivated forgetting' are not just provisional terms awaiting a 'scientific' physiological synonym. Thus the problem remains of how to relate brain processes *per se* – consisting of neurone firings and neuro-chemical reactions – to the psychological phenomena which they 'subserve' (as William James put it). It would be foolish to dispute that very rapid advances are under way in detailed understanding of the brain-mechanisms that 'subserve' psychological phenomena of many different kinds. Computer-assisted tomography scanning (CAT scan), for example, is helping unravel the physiological basis of e.g. language pathology and, *inter alia*, how language functions are neurologically structured in the brain. Such knowledge may indeed answer some of our questions, but will hardly answer all of them, simply because they do not arise from physiological puzzles in the first place.

The role of brain research within Psychology is thus rather complex. The role of Psychology in brain research is perhaps more straightforward. Certainly much Psychological theorising is constrained within the terms of current understanding of the brain. It is a necessary condition for plausibility that theories, models and hypotheses be *consistent* with such understanding. It is even more a point in their favour if they heuristically suggest novel ideas for brain-functioning research itself (as much cognitivist work has done). No one would dispute that we now know an enormous amount about brain-functioning, nor that such knowledge is of relevance to Psychology. On the other hand there are, as we have seen, some aspects of the situation which remain problematical. A further conceptual difficulty should also be noted.

Knowledge about the brain influences the psychological categories we use to construe our psychological experience of ourselves and others. Most common in recent years has been the aforementioned notion of hemispheric division of function. Whereas in the nineteenth century the split was between the civilised and bestial halves of our nature, represented by our cortex and more central regions of the brain respectively, we now also see a split between left and right hemisphere modes of operating. This is a highly reflexive situation since, quite literally, what is going on is the brain construing its own modes of operation in terms of what it believes it has discovered about these modes of operation. If the 'constructs', to use G. Kelly's term, which we use to construe ourselves are themselves somehow physically embodied in the brain, when they are also derived from our studies *of* the brain it is hard to avoid the conclusion that brains are somehow altering their own operation to fit with how they believe they operate!

Another conceptual problem is locating the source of events. What, physiologically speaking, is volition or 'the Will'? Earlier brain researchers progressively pushed this issue ever upwards, so to speak, as their understanding of neurological functioning pushed higher and higher up the spine, medulla oblongata and cerebellum, finally leaving it aside altogether or getting bogged down in the minutiæ of the differences between involuntary and voluntary movement. It is a variation, of course, on the mind–body problem – somewhere in the brain, it seems, is the active conscious person, the agency for whose benefit the whole thing exists. Interestingly, even some prominent twentieth-century neurologists, such as Sir John Eccles, ended up opting for dualism. At present this 'agency' question is a matter of intense debate among those interested in AI and the nature of consciousness (see Chapter 19 for further discussion of this).

The relations holding between Psychology and brain-function research have never, I think, been entirely happy. Brain research has often been felt to hold the promise of eventually providing definitive answers to questions worrying psychologists, while psychological phenomena have often helped to guide the brain-research agenda. Nor have either of these lacked success. In the end, though, I cannot help feeling that Psychologists use contemporary accounts of the brain as metaphors or models for the psychological, or for human nature, which leads to the reflexive circularity noted earlier. Knowing what the brain looks like from the outside might well affect how we experience it from the inside, and vice versa, but neither standpoint can be fully substituted for the other.

Finally, we might ponder a curious fact which is rarely confronted. If the brain is the site of all psychological phenomena, then it must be able to analogue or represent *everything* of which we become aware. Insofar as our knowledge of the world (including brains) actually does resemble the world as it, unknowably, 'really is', it must be because the brain has the capacity to somehow be 'like' that world. Whatever aspects of the world the brain cannot 'be like' it can never know about. At this point we return to I. Kant and basic metaphysical conundrums. The immediate point, however, is only that this fact – virtually a tautology – must raise doubts about the ability of any models and theories drawn from a *subset* of our other fields of knowledge (physics, chemistry, computing, etc.) to provide a *complete* account of the brain, a point raised at least as far back as 1870 by Noah Porter (see Chapter 19). One could tangle things yet further, but it is perhaps more prudent for present purposes to call a halt here.

Further reading

Edelman, G.M. (1992) *Bright Air, Brilliant Fire: or the Matter of the Mind*. London: Allen Lane.

Penrose, R. (1994) *Shadows of the Mind: Search for the Missing Science of Consciousness*. Oxford: Oxford University Press.

Wade, N.J. (ed.) (2000) *The Emergence of Neuroscience in the Nineteenth Century* (8 vols). London: Routledge/Thoemmes Press. Reprints, with commentary, of numerous classic texts.

Young, R.M. (1970, rep. 1990) *Mind, Brain and Adaptation in the Nineteenth Century*. Oxford: Oxford University Press. Best account of the influence of phrenology via Herbart, Spencer and the work of Broca, Fritsch and Hitzig and Ferrier.

Chronological listing of some key texts

Willis, T. (1664 (Latin), 1681 (English), rep. 1965) *The Anatomy of the Brain*. Montreal: McGill University Press (ed. W. Feindel). The beginning of serious anatomical research on brain functioning.

Gall, F.J. (1809) *Recherches sur le Système Nerveux en Général, et du Cerveau en Particulier*. Paris: Schoell. Full statement of Gall's phrenological theory.

Flourens, M.J.P. (1824) *Experimental Researches on the Properties and Functions of the Nervous System in the Vertebrate Animal*. Paris: Crevot. First major 'anti-localisation' text.

Combe, G. (1836) *Elements of Phrenology*, 4th edn. Edinburgh & London: Maclachlan & Stewart, Longman & Co. Standard account of the developed phrenological model as popular in Britain.

Broca, P.P. (1861, trans. G. von Bonin, 1960) 'Remarks on the Seat of the Faculty of Articulate Language Followed by an Observation of Aphemia'. In *Some Papers on the Cerebral Cortex*, 49–72. Springfield, MA: Thomas. Discovery of 'Broca's area'.

Fristch, G. and Hitzig, E. (1870, trans. G. von Bonin, 1960) 'On the Electrical Excitability of the Cerebrum'. In *Some Papers on the Cerebral Cortex*, 73–96. Springfield MA: Thomas.

Carpenter, W.B. (1874) *Principles of Mental Physiology*. London, Kegan Paul, Trench. Abandons phrenological faculties in favour of traditional categories.

Ferrier, D. (1875) 'The Functions of the Brain'. In *Manchester Science Lectures 7th & 8th Series*. Manchester: Heywood. The 'new phrenology' accepting localisation of function but abandoning holistic faculties. His books *The Functions of the Brain* (1876, 2nd edn 1886) and *The Croonian Lectures on Cerebral Localisation* (1890) provide the fullest accounts.

Calderwood, H. (1879) *The Relations of Brain and Mind*. London: Macmillan. Comprehensive review of the state of knowledge post-Ferrier, falls back on mind–body dualism with regard to highest faculties and ends on a religious note.

Bastian, H.C. (1882) *The Brain as an Organ of Mind.* London: Kegan Paul, Trench & Trübner. A widely-read exposition of the 'new phrenology'.

James, W. (1890) *The Principles of Psychology.* New Holt. See especially Vol. 1, Chapters 2 and 3.

Sherrington, C. (1906) *The Integrative Action of the Nervous System.* Cambridge: Cambridge University Press. Although not specifically on the brain this epochal work radically changed the way in which the operation of the entire nervous sytem was conceptualised. Sherrington was closely associated with several British psychologists, and a concern with the mind–body relationship pervaded his work, most notably in his famous Gifford Lectures (1940) published as *Man on his Nature.* (See R. Smith, 2001, for a recent brief account of his work and its significance.)

Lashley, K. (1929) 'Brain Mechanisms and Intelligence'. In W. Dennis (ed.) (1948) *Readings in History of Psychology.* New York: Appleton-Century-Crofts. See also Lashley reference in Chapter 5.

Campion, G.G. and Elliot Smith, G. (1934) *The Neural Basis of Thought.* London: Kegan Paul. Attempt to formulate an account of the relationship between neural activity and thought. Anticipates Hebb's more influential 1949 work.

Hebb, D.O. (1949) *Organization of Behavior.* London: Methuen. Incorporates new neuro-physiological knowledge in integrating Behaviourist and Gestalt orientations. Brain develops by build-up of 'reverberating cell-assemblies'.

Penfield, W. and Rasmussen, T. (1950) *The Cerebral Cortex of Man.* New York: Macmillan.

Ashby, W. Ross (1952) *Design for a Brain.* New York: Wiley. Applies cybernetic concepts to the problem of simulating brain activity; reports his invention of the 'Homeostat' device.

Walter, G. (1953, 2nd edn 1961) *The Living Brain.* London: Gerald Duckworth. More popular, but influential review, with cybernetic/information theory emphasis.

Penfield, W. and Roberts, L. (1959) *Speech and Brain Mechanisms.* Princeton: Princeton University Press. Highly important reviews of direct brain-stimulation findings showing very high degrees of localisation.

Magoun, H.W. (1963) *The Waking Brain*, 2nd edn. Springfield: Charles C. Thomas. A succinct and popular synthesis of the state of knowledge at this date.

Dimond, S.J. and Blizard, D.A. (eds) (1977) *Evolution and Lateralization of the Brain.* New York: New York Academy of Sciences. Numerous papers representing the state-of-play in hemispheric differences research.

Bradshaw, J.L. and Nettleton, N. (1983) *Human Cerebral Asymmetry.* New York: Prentice-Hall. Later textbook reviewing the same area.

Jerison, H.J. and Jerison, I. (eds) (1988) *Intelligence and Evolutionary Biology.* Berlin: Springer-Verlag. See particularly T.W. Deacon's papers reviewing brain-evolution data; other papers set human brain functioning in evolutionary context.

Gazzaniga, M.S. (ed.) (2000) *The New Cognitive Neurosciences*, 2nd edn. Cambridge, MA & London: MIT Press. A massive compendium covering every aspect of the topic, edited by one of the field's most eminent figures. Likely to achieve enduring status as providing a definitive picture of the state of play at the beginning of the new millennium.

Secondary sources and additional references

Bowley, A.H. *et al* (c. 1946) *Psychology: The Study of Man's Mind*. London: Odhams Press.

Brazier, M.A.B. (1961) *A History of the Electrical Activity of the Brain: The First Half-Century*. London: Pitman.

Danziger, K. (1982) 'Mid-nineteenth-century British Psycho-physiology: A Neglected Chapter in the History of Psychology'. In W.R. Woodward and M.G. Ash (eds) *The Problematic Science: Psychology in Nineteenth Century Thought*. New York: Praeger, 119–146.

Fearing, F. (1930) *Reflex Action: A Study in the History of Physiological Psychology*. Baltimore: Williams & Wilkins. Still a useful historical research resource.

Magoun, H.W. (1958) 'Early Development of Ideas Relating the Mind with the Brain'. In G.E.W. Wolstoneholme and C.M. O'Connor (eds) *A CIBA Foundation Symposium on the Neurological Basis of Behaviour in Commemoration of Sir Charles Sherrington O.M., G.B.E., F.R.S. 1857–1952*. London: J. & A. Churchill, 4–27. Medieval and Renaissance views, with some nice illustrations.

Neuberger, M. (1897) *The Historical Development of Experimental Brain and Spinal Cord Physiology before Flourens*. E. Clarke (ed.) 1981. Baltimore & London: Johns Hopkins University Press. The most exhaustive and detailed study of the early period, Clarke's annotations and comments fully incorporate findings of later historical research.

Penfield, W. and Jasper, H.H. (1954) *Epilepsy and the Functional Anatomy of the Human Brain*. Boston: Little, Brown and Co.

Richards, G. (1992) *Mental Machinery: The Origins and Consequences of Psychological Ideas, Part One: 1600–1850*. London: Athlone Press. See chapters 4 and 6.

Smith, R. (2001) 'Physiology and Psychology, or Brain and Mind, in the Age of C.S. Sherrington'. In G.C. Bunn, A.D. Lovie and G.D. Richards (eds) *Psychology in Britain: Historical Essays and Personal Reflections*. Leicester: British Psychological Society and London: The Science Museum, 223–242.

Chapter 10

Memory: some points to remember

- The difficulty of studying memory comprehensively
- Types of memory
- Metaphors of memory
- Ebbinghaus and the origins of experimental research on memory
- Historical and cultural variability in the demands on memory
- Diversity of approaches to memory
- Memory research in Britain
- Improving memory
- Collective memory
- Legal aspects: witness reliability and child witnesses
- History as memory and a reflexive twist

Preliminaries

Considerable difficulties face the thorough investigation of so pervasive a pheno-menon as memory, which in its broadest sense comes close to being synonymous with consciousness. Without it the world would be a chaotic mass of meaningless sensations; we would know nothing about our surroundings or ourselves and, bar a few hard-wired reflexes, be unable actually to *do* virtually anything. Most con-temporary researchers in the field, such as Alan Baddeley (1997), acknowledge this. Underpinning everything from perception to personality, motivation to intel-ligence, memory is not just one, discrete, category of human behaviour. Indeed, outside Psychological laboratory experiments, it rarely manifests itself in isolation – we are invariably remembering for a reason, memory playing a part in our total psychological engagement with our situation, be it sitting an exam, watching a film, or going shopping. When, we may wonder, is memory *not* involved? As St Augustine acknowledged (see Chapter 9, p. 119), its sheer range is utterly awesome. Today's psychologists thus identify such sub-varieties as long and short term memory (LTM, STM), working memory, episodic memory, linguistic memory, implicit memory, autobiographical memory, visual memory, social or collective memory and recognition (see Table 10.1). Routinely differentiating memory and learning as separate fields of research or as distinct phases of the information acquisition and storage process can be rationalised on theoretical grounds, but perhaps more accurately reflects the historically contingent creation of two dis-tinct research traditions and an attempt to render the whole issue a little more tractable. Where the memory-learning distinction is most convincing is regarding

Table 10.1 The many types of memory psychologists have identified

(Those in bold have received the most attention from experimental psychologists.)
Auditory memory
Autobiographical memory
Collective memory
Echoic memory
Episodic memory
Implicit memory
Long term memory
Recognition*
Rote memory
Short term memory
Unconscious memory
Verbal (or linguistic) memory*
Visual memory
Working memory

*These in turn may be analysed into subsidiary forms, e.g. face-recognition and vocabulary versus syntactic verbal memory.
Other types have also occasionally been identified or discussed.

such things as, for example, routine behaviour and implicit everyday knowledge which require no conscious act of recall, their ultimate dependence on memory only becoming apparent in cases of pathological loss.

The wide range of forms memory takes are themselves mutually interrelated in a complex fashion. (And do we not occasionally even exercise a kind of 'meta-memory' – remembering when we remembered something?) But where and how is memory located and 'stored'? Most mainstream Psychological dealings with the topic have taken it as axiomatic that the first half of the answer is 'somewhere in the brain'. Only since around 1980 have some anglophone psychologists begun challenging the adequacy of this answer (in mainland Europe criticisms by writers such as M. Halbwachs were voiced somewhat earlier). They argue that the role of social and interpersonal factors in creating, storing, maintaining and retrieving memory has been severely underestimated, while we have always (and never more so than now) deployed all kinds of 'external memory systems' for the purpose – the printed word, diaries, photographs, tape-recorders, video-film, and public monuments. Of course brain processes are involved in their usage, but many kinds of memory do seem to require some measure of periodic social or technological rehearsal. This also bears on the phenomenon of 'context-dependent' recall – certain memories only being elicited in a particular place or situation. This was exploited in classical and Renaissance times by those wishing to enhance their memory (see Frances Yates' *The Art of Memory*, 1966). Ever since Frederic Bartlett's classic book *Remembering* (1932), virtually all psychologists have acknowledged that subjective memory involves, to some degree at least, a reconstructive process rather than simply consultation of a permanent, immutable record. There are, additionally, obvious individual differences in how memory appears to operate. Not only are there variations in quality, but in the role of visual imagery (for an extreme case see A.R. Luria's *Mind of the Mnemonist*, 1969) and things we find it easy or hard to memorise. We can also apparently 'improve' our memories using various techniques. Do we then actively devise our own techniques for memorising some time in early childhood? Do we have to learn and remember how to remember?

In the light of the foregoing it might, perhaps justifiably, be suggested that the category 'memory' is simply too sweeping, a folk-psychological term of scant scientific utility referring not to some unitary natural phenomenon but to a miscellaneous range of phenomena in which behaviour is in a way being partly determined by past events. To adopt such a position – not without its advocates in the neurosciences – would, ironically, tacitly concede the social constructionist case, confirming that 'memory' is not a 'natural' category, but a human invention which could be abandoned when it had lost its pragmatic utility. It is not my present job to solve this, but it is interesting to note that, as K. Danziger (2001) has stressed, 'memory', as a Psychological category, has remained virtually unchanged for longer than any other, dating back at least to Plato. (Whereas 'emotion', for example, was unknown to English-speakers before about 1700; people had 'passions' and 'affections', both of which meant something significantly, if subtly, different.) Moreover, the central metaphors for memory have also persisted since antiquity, namely the 'container' and 'inscription' images. Additional images have of course been suggested at various times, perhaps most remarkably Robert Hooke's complex materialist model presented to the Royal Society in 1682 (Hooke, 1705) which incorporated such analogies as vases, chains, sympathetically resonating bells, eclipses and phosphorescence (see G. Richards, 1992, pp. 67–69 for a summary). But this isolated speculative theoretical exercise was never further pursued. Although constant, the inscription image has undergone numerous mutations, tracking the historical emergence of new 'inscription' technologies such as printing, film and, in Karl Pribram's case, holograms (Pribram, 1980). Despite such transformations most theories of memory continue to rest on the notion of a 'container' in which memories are somehow stored in the form of 'inscriptions', this being analogous to some familiar public storage and inscription technology. (See D. Draaisma, 2000 for a full treatment of the 'metaphors of memory' issue.)

Bearing the foregoing in mind it is a little surprising that the early German Psychologists, notably J.F. Herbart and W. Wundt, did *not* consider memory to be an appropriate topic for experimental research, feeling that the concept implied the existence of a distinct 'faculty' of precisely the kind they were rejecting. Although T. Ribot had written on pathologies of memory, notably amnesia, in 1881, experimental Psychological research effectively originates only in 1885 with the publication of H. Ebbinghaus's monumental investigation, using himself as a subject, *Über das Gedächtniss*, 'On Memory' (English translation 1913, reprinted 1964). This involved him learning by heart innumerable nonsense syllables – a technique of his own invention – with detailed quantification of the number of trials required to reach success and subsequent forgetting. Theoretically this was based on an associationist model of memory. Despite Bartlett's rejection, variations on Ebbinghaus's method dominated experimental memory research virtually until the 1960s and are still used, his argument that using meaningful material unduly complicated the matter being widely and uncritically accepted (Figure 10.1). Through all its vicissitudes nonsense syllables have retained a major place in memory research, although we hardly ever memorise them in real life.

Even so, Psychology's memory research has not been confined to identifying the 'laws' of such rote memory learning and forgetting. The many ways psychologists have researched, and theorised about, memory should to some degree at least be understood as responses to wider concerns and agendas. Just as we usually 'remember' for a reason, we often 'research memory' because some aspect of it seems to require investigation, a new technology is perhaps making demands of a novel or more intense kind on a particular kind of memory, or (for whatever reasons) some memory phenomenon has become controversial (as in the 1990s with so-called 'False Memory Syndrome'). The demands on memory are not personal matters alone but are also determined by broader social and cultural conditions – imagine, for instance, the different roles rote-learning might play in non-literate and literate societies. These conditions affect both the sorts of thing we need to remember and the kinds of memory involved in doing so. An obvious example: pocket calculators and those built into every computer and shop-till have rendered increasingly redundant rote-learned 'mental arithmetic' skills, mastery of which was once considered essential. The demise of 'home-entertainment' in the face of mass entertainment media has similarly reduced the social importance of learning poetry and dramatic monologues by heart. Psychologists have rarely considered this dimension to the topic, which implies that the very functioning

Figure 10.1 Experimenting on memory in Germany early in the twentieth century. Many similar methods of presenting word-stimuli were devised at this time. From R. Schulze (1912) *Experimental Psychology and Pedagogy*, trans. R. Pintner, London: George Allen. Photo: George Singer. Reproduced by permission of the Centre for History of Psychology, Staffordshire University.

and meaning of memory has a degree of socio-historical variability. But this variability is itself detectable in how psychologists themselves have addressed the topic.

In the late nineteenth and early twentieth centuries evolutionary ideas led a number of thinkers (such as Henri Bergson, C. Blondel, Samuel Butler, Ewald Hering, T. Ribot and Richard Semon) to propose the existence of 'organic memory'. This move extended the meaning of an already very stretched term more widely than ever to cover almost *any* adaptive behavioural change, either in an organism's own life-time or in those of its ancestors, paving the way for such ideas as C.G. Jung's concept of the 'collective unconscious'. (We return to this later.) Despite the diversity of angles from which psychologists have approached memory it is nonetheless true that its laboratory investigation was long constrained by what many, such as Ulric Neisser (1982), regarded as an impoverished concept of the topic, concentrating almost exclusively on aspects of linguistic rote memory (continuing the Ebbinghaus tradition). This was perhaps analogous to classic behaviourism's focus on animal learning within the S-R paradigm. In each case the rationale was that more complex forms of the phenomenon would be explicable in terms of simpler core processes. The psychologist was studying the basic mechanisms underlying all 'higher' manifestations. Yet this laboratory-based experimental tradition did not have a complete monopoly. Within Social Psychology, for example, memory entered the picture in the context of studies of stereotyping, as in a much-cited study in which white subjects shown a picture of a white man holding a knife standing alongside an unarmed black man, recalled it as showing the black man holding the knife (G.W. Allport and L. Postman, 1947). An extensive fringe of such alternative approaches always surrounded the experimental 'Psychology of Memory' genre, reflecting memory's ubiquitous relevance. The last two decades have seen a sea change in the situation. Autobiographical and everyday memory and eye-witness reliability are now high on the research agenda, alongside more critical work on social and collective remembering. Other themes include the still unabated 'False Memory Syndrome' controversy previously mentioned, while studies of pathologies of linguistic memory have become central to brain-functioning and psycholinguistic research (largely as a consequence of new brain-imaging technologies). It is also fair to say that the rationale for laboratory experimentation has also shifted, the laboratory now being seen more as a site where new memory phenomena identified elsewhere can be rigorously isolated and studied.

Memory research in Britain

Memory research in Britain over the last century provides a very accessible illustration of how changes in the Psychological agenda relate to those in the wider world (Alan Collins, 2001). Collins identifies four phases in British research during the first half of the twentieth century. Initially interest focused on memory in educational contexts in order to optimise the way educational material was presented to schoolchildren during a period of radical educational reform; during and after World War One the psychotherapeutic treatment of 'shell-shock' victims switched attention to psychoanalytic ideas about unconscious memories, repression, and distortions of memory. Bartlett's 1932 *Remembering* then inaugurated a brief period of interest in 'ordinary' remembering and forgetting partly related, Collins argues, to a wider cultural preoccupation with 'remembrance' after World War One. Finally, in the 1940s, following wartime concern about human performance, especially in relation to new technologies and the emergence of Cognitive Psychology which this engendered (see Chapter 7), memory became a topic ideally suited to, and central to, cognitivist concerns with human performance and applied Psychological applications of this. Experimental laboratory research on STM in particular now assumed an extremely high profile, particularly after D. Broadbent's reformulation of this in information processing terms, leading to A. Baddeley's 'working memory' model developed during the 1970s.

If only in outline, this indicates how the vagaries in fortune of different ways of studying memory can be mapped onto the shifting demands which social conditions have made on Psychology (in Britain in this case) and the ways in which memory becomes problematical.

Problems with memory

Since memory is often viewed as a relatively 'pure' and asocial topic of inquiry, it is useful to pursue this last point a little further. Although we cannot explore them in any depth the following cases are worth noting (although numerous others could have been considered equally well).

Improving memory

As mentioned, techniques for improving memory date back to antiquity, being closely bound up with the art of rhetoric (in order to enable speakers to keep track of the topics they were addressing). Later they were integral to Renaissance Neo-Platonic thought, in which the magical aspiration was to reflect the cosmos in the mind as a move towards directly controlling it (Yates, 1964, 1966). One highly successful eighteenth-century practical manual was Richard Grey's *Memoria Technica: or A New Method of Artificial Memory* (1732), still in print a century later. In the early twentieth century the 'Pelman System of Mind and Memory Training' (backed by The Pelman Institute) enjoyed an enormous vogue into the 1930s. Advertisements for similar techniques still appear in the press. Unsurprisingly in the light of our opening observations, a 'bad memory' can be experienced as a major life-handicap, causing both anxiety and embarrassment. There is therefore a perennial market for methods of 'curing' it.

Somewhat curiously it took Psychology a long time to respond to this demand, although cognitive Psychology was, from early on, refining our understanding of traditional mnemonic and visualisation techniques long used by stage-performers. From a different angle we might also, in the light of Collins' account, concede that psychoanalysis was in some sense engaged in improving memory for therapeutic purposes. While all theories of memory involve a theory of 'forgetting' as well, such as 'decay', 'repression' (psychoanalysis) or 'interference' (cognitive theories), regarding improvement as such Psychological attention has tended to focus on the more extreme pathologies of amnesia and agnosia; conditions in which most (never, even in amnesia, all) or part of the memory system has failed. Other than in some forms of amnesia (e.g. transient global amnesia following shock) these are generally associated with brain damage. Physiologically-oriented psychologists from Ribot onwards naturally became closely involved in studying such conditions. As well as seeking methods of alleviating the problem and developing diagnostic tests to identify precisely how the memory system is affected, pathologies were seen as illuminating the neurological basis of memory and structure of language.

Again it was only in the late 1970s that improving memory became a topic for systematic investigation. The fact that memory obviously *can* be improved also promised a new direction from which to evaluate the various theories of memory proposed in the preceding phase. A major contribution to this was D.J. Herrmann *et al* (1992), which also contains a handy historical chapter by Herrmann and A. Sealeman. This reinforced a more widespread shift from passive to active concepts of memory (implicit in the social remembering approach). For Herrmann and Sealeman the recent work demonstrated that 'control over memory performance can be executed in a much more diverse fashion and over a much wider time interval than previously believed' (p. 15). Improvement may also be achieved from the opposite direction – the memorisability of 'external memory systems' themselves. Thus, as noted above, novel demands on memory made by technological innovations (like postal codes or information technology) have also resulted in psychologists becoming engaged at the design stage.

The collective past

I am going out on something of a limb here, for current Psychology of memory, broad though its concerns are, rarely considers this aspect of the topic directly. However, in my judgement, it does warrant an airing, particularly in a text of the present kind. We mentioned earlier the evolutionary notion of 'organic memory'. This relates to that broader concern with the collective past which is one of the few universal features of human societies. Its primary expression is an awareness of ancestors and ancestry, taking such forms as ancestor worship, complex kinship systems requiring genealogical tracking, cults of the dead, ancestral 'possession' and creation myths explaining a people's origins. This has never waned: war memorials, celebrations of historic events, our system of proper names and, of course, the discipline of history itself, all ultimately centre on our collective need to establish and sustain connections with our ancestral past (be it biological, social, intellectual or professional). As a hobby, genealogy flourishes as never before. Much of this is the academic province of anthropology, but the theme does have a somewhat covert Psychological presence.

Firstly, the evolutionary 'organic memory' idea facilitated a supposedly 'scientific' line of attack on the 'collective memory' issue. The Lamarckian strand in evolutionary theorising, which retained its mainstream respectability into the 1930s, raised the possibility of direct psychological access to our deep collective past, for ancestral experiences might somehow be genetically transmissable. Thus Sigmund Freud theorised that a primal act of collective patricide had permanently affected the character of father–son relationships, while Jung postulated the existence of a 'collective unconscious', the repository of ancestral wisdom, which manifested itself in 'archetypal' figures and symbols. But more sinisterly this 'collective unconscious' idea encouraged the notion of 'racial memory'. Reinforcing such speculations 'hypnotic regression' apparently yielded evidence for reincarnation. Explanations in terms of 'cryptamnesia' – the unconscious retention of material learned or witnessed in early life – were never sufficiently powerful to convince those committed to such doctrines. By the 1940s advances in genetics had rendered Lamarckism scientifically untenable. Whatever 'collective memory' and the 'collective unconscious' were they had to be social rather than genetic in nature. But their irreconcilability with genetics still failed to refute the reality of such phenomena – too many believed they had directly experienced them. Professional psychologists might protest, but belief in the 'collective unconscious' and the recovery of memories of past incarnations eventually became central to 'New Age' thinking.

For present purposes, what this demonstrates is Psychology's unwitting creation of a route by which quite traditional, and to most scientists 'primitive', modes of relating to the collective past could resurface in modernist cultures with a scientific gloss. In doing so Psychology was, perhaps, performing a necessary collective psychological role. During an epoch of dramatic and unprecedentedly rapid change, in which the present so overwhelmed the past, might not a counterbalancing recovery of a way of meeting our need for ancestral reconnection have been a psychologically healthy response? In providing this, early twentieth-century thinkers like Freud, Jung and Semon were reflecting and responding to a widespread anxiety. The tragedy was that this could be co-opted for quite sinister ends. In particular it could be read as implying that psychological 'race' differences were profound and ineradicable, as Gustav Le Bon had claimed (see Chapter 21). This undoubtedly played its part in Jung's own ambiguous initial responses to Nazism and anti-Semitism, as most contributors to A. Maidenbaum and S.A. Martin (eds) (1991) acknowledge.

The rise of social constructionism has, in a different way, again placed the topic of 'collective memory' on Psychology's agenda, exploring how story-telling and other social behaviours create and sustain memory as a way of maintaining social cohesion and group identity (U. Neisser, 1982; D. Middleton and D. Edwards, 1990; R.S. Wyer (ed.), 1995). The 'collective past' concerns families as much as society at large. The problems often faced by those lacking any knowledge of, or severed from, their family history, demonstrate how major a psychological role this kind of memory plays, providing much of the raw material for our very identities. Listening to the reminiscences and anecdotes of older family members, reciting our own to younger ones, jointly browsing through photograph albums, decorating our living spaces with family memorabilia, tracing our genealogies . . . all these add up to a highly developed, and often psychologically essential, memory-based system which imbues our lives with meaning and structure. Even when its oppressiveness incites a rejection, the rebellion is framed in terms which reflect it. It can require some contemplative meditation to evoke for oneself quite how profound and extensive this is, so embedded are we in the matrix of familial memory that we are hardly aware of its real importance. This is perhaps why its Psychological study took so long to materialise. But its emergence as a topic might also be traced to the strains being placed upon it by contemporary life: the increased physical dispersal of family members, the extent to which continuous social and technological change rapidly distances our present world from that of our childhood and, paradoxically, the massive expansion in the 'external memory systems' in which our past is 'inscribed' – boxes of old photograph albums, videos of family gatherings and the like. What effects, one wonders, do these have on our personal, subjective, 'autobiographical memory'? This is surely one field in which memory research is likely to continue expanding.

The legal angle: witness reliability and child witnesses

A further set of problems arises in the legal context. These have both stimulated, and partly resulted from, Psychological understanding of memory. One implication of the idea of collective remembering is that memory is in many respects 'dialogic', constituted by our conversations with each other. Police interrogation and the court room are certainly 'dialogic' settings. However genuinely questioners strive to efface their own presence in order to elicit an 'unbiased' recall of events from a witness's own episodic or autobiographical memory the setting, the 'game', inevitably affects the version of events produced and how memory operates. As long ago as 1909 and 1910 Hugo Munsterberg and Wilhelm Stern were raising the problem of 'suggestion' in the courtroom and the reliability of witness testimony, but not until the 1970s did the topic really capture the attention of those working in Forensic Psychology (see Chapter 13, and A.D. Yarmey, 1979). Somewhat disturbingly it had become apparent that the correlation between our level of certainty regarding the accuracy of our memories and their actual veracity was sometimes very low. The cautious, hesitant witness was as likely to be correct as the boldly assertive one. The effects of stereotyping (mentioned earlier) could also have distorting effects, especially in biasing descriptions of offender appearance in a stereotypically villainous direction. Reliability of identity parades (or line-ups) was also called into question. Child witnesses presented even more difficulties. Conventional wisdom was that their memories were intrinsically less reliable than those of adults, subject to intrusions of fantasy elements, and more prone to suggestion, plus they told authority figures what they believed would please them. Here Psychological research proved more reassuring. While child memory for detail was poorer, the accuracy of what was remembered was not. 'Adult-pleasing' and 'suggestion' could also be outflanked to some degree by using video-testimony and unthreatening familiar surroundings for questioning. But while Psychology perhaps helped improve the child witness's credibility it raised serious questions about the reliability of witness testimony in general. Without contemporaneous developments in forensic technology (e.g. most recently, DNA testing), 'offender profiling', and innovations such as CCTV cameras it is possible that Psychological findings would have subverted, rather than improved, the perceived trustworthiness of traditional court procedures and police detection methods.

Witness testimony research now flourishes in Forensic Psychology (a title which has replaced the hitherto embarrassingly ambiguous Criminal Psychology). Once again it has revealed how slippery a beast memory is, and its inseparability from the contexts in which memories originated and are being recalled. The current state of the topic may be gauged from C. Thompson *et al* (1998).

Conclusion

Psychology of Memory is, despite the existence of a distinct field of that name, a somewhat amorphous topic for reasons discussed in our preliminary remarks. The consequences for a social constructionist analysis are also slightly ambiguous. One common complaint about much earlier experimental work was that it was *not* relevant; it concentrated on too narrow a range of memory capacities, and the theories it produced about the structure of memory storage and retrieval were too technically restricted to account for more than an unrepresentative subset of memory phenomena. This could suggest that the various primacy, recency and interference effects it identified might indeed be asocial, 'natural', properties of the human rote-learning mechanism. Even so, perhaps it is *only* at this level that human memory *can* be treated as a 'natural' phenomenon – which is precisely why it *is* amenable to natural scientific methods of experimental investigation in the socially insulated laboratory. (Neuropsychological studies of effects of brain damage on memory could well be a similar case.) Once we move beyond this to memory's operation in real life the social dimension immediately forces itself upon our attention; memories become the product of 'dialogic' social processes, the demands placed upon it and the kinds of memory they prioritise become socially and historically contingent (even if within some broad parameters of variation) while social attitudes and beliefs can also come into play. If the great range of individual differences in memory use and organisation is partly related to differences in how we learned to remember in early childhood, interpersonal, social factors would then again enter the equation. Applying the older laboratory-based models to real issues, as began to happen early on in applied fields of cognitive Psychology, also invariably led to their radical modification and elaboration. But wherever one prefers to draw the line between 'social' and 'natural', one moral in all this is that psychologists concerned with memory should not forget its awesome dimensions, even if making headway on understanding its specific features requires donning intellectual blinkers to avoid bedazzlement. To varying degrees, most recent general textbooks on the topic explicitly acknowledge this, but for most of its history, when concerned with memory, psychologists kept their blinkers firmly in place, perhaps oblivious to the fact they were wearing them.

A final twist

In the light of what has been said, the Psychological study of memory, like perception (see Chapter 8), emerges as being a collective aspect of the phenomenon itself. Earlier I alluded to the discipline of history being an aspect of collective remembering. Moreover, as mentioned in the Introduction, one function of History of Psychology is to keep the discipline connected to its own 'LTM'. I will end by expanding on these thoughts, though sidestepping the contentious field of 'philosophy of history'. What I wish to consider is the entertainingly tangled query: what are we doing when we study the history of the P/psychology of memory? This involves 'remembering' both how memory operated in the past and how past Psychology has said that it operates. But, whatever the case with other varieties of memory, such historical remembering indubitably does involve a narrative reconstruction. In effect, we are attempting, on however a modest scale, to contribute to the Psychological understanding of memory by asking our fellow psychologists 'what kind of a phenomenon must memory be that it lends itself to a narration of this kind?' To be consistent with the present narrative's own story, however, I have to confront a further question: 'What is problematical about memory that renders this an appropriate way to address it?' Before answering it I must note that any answer must derive from the very narrative which it is intended to elucidate, since unlike the report of a laboratory experiment, 'data' and 'conclusions' are inseparable. In a text of the present kind at least, the historian cannot give even the appearance of separating the historical 'data' from a narrational exposition to which interpretation is intrinsic.

The problems of memory and its Psychological study to which the present account is relevant are then: (a) the sheer breadth of the kinds of phenomena to which the term refers and Psychology's tendency to lose sight of this; (b) the historical and cultural variability of memory phenomena; (c) the inseparability of memory from nearly all other psychological functions; and (d) the extent to which the Psychological agenda reflects contemporary real-world problems for memory functioning. Most contemporary workers in the field would agree that all, or most, of these are legitimate issues. The question is really how far they are prepared seriously to follow them through rather than merely concede them in principle while devoting their real energies to specific empirical research projects. But behind them, and behind the more specific kinds of problem discussed earlier, there perhaps lurks a genuine 'crisis of memory' which I am registering at some level. I balk at defining it, but several recent developments are worth noting: (a) a group of episodes including Holocaust denial, use of history to legitimise political policies (e.g. in the Israel–Palestine conflict, the Balkans and Ulster), and a resurgence in Britain of interest in Remembrance Day celebrations; (b) the 'false memory syndrome' controversy and concern over witness reliability in legal contexts; (c) a curious politically-loaded controversy among those who remember them about what 'really happened in the 1960s' (and, in Britain, the 1980s too), in which a struggle to define the immediate collective past is being played out; (d) the rumpus surrounding the turn of the millennium in the Christian calendar; (e) the fascination in Britain with national identity and the meaning of national history and the increasing number of books on histories of minority groups and their roles in wider events. What these share is that they all concern memory's role in defining the collective present. This involves history-as-memory, autobiographical memory, plus the general reliability of both subjective and external memory systems. When memory becomes problematic on this scale it signifies that 'reality' itself is being called into doubt. Its restabilisation is then sought in reaching a consensus on the collective past and its destabilisation exacerbated by inability to do so. We might therefore expect Psychological meta-commentaries on the nature of memory (such as this) to appear in response. Such meta-commentaries must, however, admit their own reflexively self-instantiating historical-memory status if they are to serve their purpose. Or have I forgotten something?

Further reading

I have included a relatively high proportion of uncited texts here since the topic's diversity would have resulted in the main text becoming swamped with references had every point been diligently referenced.

Baddeley, A. (1997) *Human Memory. Theory and Practice,* 2nd edn. London: Psychology Press. Baddeley, though a cognitivist himself, comprehensively and sympathetically overviews almost all aspects of the topic in this widely successful textbook.

Collins, A. (2001) 'The Psychology of Memory'. In G.C. Bunn, A.D. Lovie and G.D. Richards (eds) *Psychology in Britain: Historical Essays and Personal Reflections.* Leicester: British Psychological Society and London: The Science Museum, 150–168.

Collins, A.F., Gathercole, S.E., Conway, M.A. and Morris, P.E. (eds) (1993) *Theories of Memory.* Hove: Lawrence Erlbaum Associates. Useful overview of major positions.

Draaisma, D. (2000) *Metaphors of Memory.* Cambridge: Cambridge University Press. A comprehensive and groundbreaking historical study, with numerous illustrations. Essential reading for historians.

Herremann, D.J. and Chaffin, R. (1988) *Memory in Historical Perspective.* New York: Springer-Verlag.

Neisser, U. (ed.) (1982) *Memory Observed.* San Francisco: Freeman. A vehement critique of the irrelevancy of mainstream experimental approaches.

Neisser, U. and Hyman Jr., I.E. (eds) (2000) *Memory Observed: Remembering in Natural Contexts,* 2nd edn. New York: Worth Publishers. A far more bullish updated collection – Neisser himself almost gloats on the degree to which he feels he has swung the argument.

Yates, F.A. (1964) *Giordano Bruno and the Hermetic Tradition.* London: Routledge & Kegan Paul.

Yates, F.A. (1966) *The Art of Memory.* London: Routledge & Kegan Paul. These two books by Frances Yates have become the classic expositions of Renaissance Neo-Platonism and the role of memory in Neo-Platonist thought.

Classic and founding texts

Pre-Psychological

Grey, R. (1732) *Memoria Technica: or A New Method of Artificial Memory,* 2nd edn. London: Charles King.

Hooke, R. (1705) 'An Hypothetical Explication of Memory; How the Organs made use of by the Mind in its Operation may be Mechanically Understood'. In R. Waller (ed.) *The Posthumous works of Robert Hooke, M.D., F.R.S.* London: Smith & Walford (Printers to the Royal Society).

Organic memory

Bergson, H. (1896, 46th edn, 1946) *Matiére et Mémoire.* Paris: Presses Universitaires de France.

Butler, S. (1877, new edn, 1916) *Life and Habit.* London: A.C. Fifield.

Butler, S. (1880, 3rd edn, 1920) *Unconscious Memory.* London: Cape.

Hering, E. (1913) *Memory. Lectures on the Specific Energies of the Nervous System*, 4th edn. Chicago & London: Open Court Publishing Company.

Semon, R. (1904, 1st English edn, 1921) *The Mneme*. London: Allen & Unwin.

Experimental studies of memory

Bartlett, F.C. (1932) *Remembering: A Study in Experimental and Social Psychology*. Cambridge: Cambridge University Press. Now a classic text, usually taken as proto-cognitivist in character, but also somewhat social constructionist in approach.

Ebbinghaus, H. (1913, rep. 1964) *Memory. A Contribution to Experimental Psychology*. New York: Dover. First published 1885 as *Über das Gedächtniss*. Really launched experimental research on memory.

Edgell, B. (1924) *Theories of Memory*. Oxford: Clarendon Press. Useful review of the state of the topic in the early 1920s.

James, W. (1890) *Principles of Psychology*. New York: Henry Holt, chapter XIV. Introduced the distinction between long and short term memory. See Chapter 4.

Pathologies of memory

Berrios, G.E. and Hodges, J.R. (eds) (2000) *Memory Disorders in Psychiatric Practice*. Cambridge: Cambridge University Press. As well as up-to-date coverage of the topic this includes a chapter by Berrios on 'Historical Aspects of Memory and its Disorders' (3–38).

Bjorklund, D.F. (ed.) (2000) *False Memory Creation in Children and Adults. Theory, Research and Implications*. Mahwah, NJ: Lawrence Erlbaum Associates. Amounts to a fairly authoritative rejection of the 'recovered memory' phenomenon.

Luria, A.R. (1969) *The Mind of the Mnemonist*. London: Cape.

Ribot, T. (1881, 14th edn, 1901) *Les Maladies de la Mémoire*. Paris: Alcan.

Russell, W.R. and Espir, M.L.E. (1961) *Traumatic Aphasia. A Study in War Wounds of the Brain*. Oxford: Oxford University Press.

Sacks, O. (1985) *The Man who Mistook his Wife for a Hat*. London: Duckworth.

Cognitivist approaches

See also recent general texts in Chapter 7, Further reading.

Baddeley, A.D. (1986) *Working Memory*. Oxford: Oxford University Press. Major review of the 'working memory' research which Baddeley had initiated in the late 1960s. He has continued to develop his position since.

Collins, A.M. and Quillian, M.R. (1969) 'Retrieval Time from Semantic Memory'. *Journal of Verbal Learning and Verbal Behavior* 6: 240–247. A classic paper that greatly influenced research on linguistic memory.

Miller, G.A. (1956) 'The Magical Number Seven, Plus or Minus Two: Some Limits on our Capacity for Information Processing'. *Psychological Review* 81: 470–473. A landmark paper in establishing the cognitivist tradition within memory research.

Engelkamp, J. and Zimmer, H.J. (1994) *The Human Memory: A Multi-Modal Approach*. Seattle: Hogrefe & Huber. A recent cognitivist overview.

Social and collective memory

Freud, S. (1918, rep. 1950, 1st German edn, 1913) *Totem and Taboo*. London: Routledge & Kegan Paul. Includes the primal fraternal parricide hypothesis.

Halbwachs, M. (c. 1950) *The Collective Memory*. New York: Harper & Row.

Jung, C.G. (1959) The Archetypes and the Collective Unconscious. (*The Collected Works of C.G. Jung*, Vol. 9, Part 1.) London: Routledge & Kegan Paul. Includes papers from 1936 onwards.

Maidenbaum, A. and Martin, S.A. (eds) (1991) *Lingering Shadows: Jungians, Freudians, and Anti-Semitism*. Boston & London: Shambhala. A collection of Jungian essays focusing on Jung's 1930s dealings with Nazism. Cited in connection with the morally ambiguous nature of his concept of the 'collective unconscious'.

Middleton, D. and Edwards, D. (eds) (1990) *Collective Remembering*. London: Sage. Important collection of critical essays on various aspects of the topic.

Wyer, R.S. (ed.) (1995) *Knowledge and Memory: The Real Story*. Advances in Social Cognition Vol. VIII, Hillsdale, NJ & Hove, UK: Lawrence Erlbaum. Explores the role of 'story-telling' in memory, with heated debate between several of the authors.

Improving memory

Pelman Institute (c. 1930) *The Pelman System of Mind & Memory Training*. London: The Pelman Institute. This was issued as a series of booklets.

Herrmann, D.J., Weingartner, H., Sealeman, A. and McEvoy, C. (1992) *Memory Improvement: Implications for Memory Research*. New York: Springer-Verlag. Best starting point for further study of the topic.

Witness reliability and everyday memory

Groeger, J.A. (1997) *Memory and Remembering: Everyday Memory in Context*. London: Longman. Cognitivist, but undogmatic, in orientation.

Munsterberg, H. (1909) *Psychology and Crime*. London: Fisher Unwin. Published in the US as *On the Witness Stand*. Contains possibly the first discussion of the problem.

Stein, N.L., Ornstein, P.A., Tversky, B. and Brainerd, C. (eds) (1997) *Memory for Everyday Events*. Mahwah, NJ: Lawrence Erlbaum Associates.

Stern, W. (1910) 'Abstracts of Lectures on the Psychology of Testimony on the Study of Individuality'. *American Journal of Psychology* 21: 270–282. Usually cited with Munsterberg's book as introducing the topic into Psychology.

Thompson, C.P. *et al* (1998) *Eyewitness Memory: Theoretical and Applied Perspectives*. Mahwah, NJ and London: Lawrence Erlbaum Associates. A recent review of the debates.

Yarmey, A.D. (1979) *The Psychology of Eyewitness Testimony*. New York: Free Press, London: Collier-Macmillan.

Additional cited references

Allport, G.W. and Postman, L. (1947) *The Psychology of Rumor*. New York: Harper & Row.

Danziger, K. (2001) 'How Old is Psychology, Particularly Concepts of Memory?' Unpublished keynote address to the Annual Conference of the British Psychological Society, Glasgow, 29 March 2001.

Pribram, K. (1980) 'The Role of Analogy in Transcending Limits in the Brain Sciences'. *Daedalus* 109 (2): 19–38. Speculated about the 'hologram'-like nature of memory.

Reference

Young, M.N. (1961) *Bibliography of Memory*. Philadelphia & New York: Chilton. Comprehensive up to 1960.

Chapter 11

Personality: Psychology and who you are

- The appeal of the topic
- Why 'personality' rather than other terms?
- Types of personality theory
- Projective tests
- Other approaches to assessing personality
- The problem of the 'self'
- Reading books on personality
- Why the Psychology of personality was needed
- Personality theory today

Of all Psychology's topics the one perennially fascinating the general public is 'Personality', for here Psychology most closely resembles such fortune-telling and personal advice-giving predecessors as astrology, physiognomy and phrenology. What people most desire from an expert on human nature is information about themselves, and even if their destinies cannot be divined this expert should at least be able to diagnose personal strengths, weaknesses, flaws and virtues, and advise on how to live with them. Put more succinctly, they yearn to place themselves in the spectrum of humanity at large. Popular ambivalence about Psychology notwithstanding, when it comes to 'personality tests' there is a large and avid market. This apparent continuity with pre-Psychological traditions is no illusion, as we will see. But first we must consider the word 'personality' itself.

Why 'personality'?

In his enduring classic *Personality: A Psychological Interpretation* (1937) Harvard psychologist Gordon W. Allport identified 50 meanings for 'personality', stemming from the Greek 'persona' ('περσονα', the mask worn in Greek drama – hence Jung's adoption of it to refer to the 'face' people present to the world). 'Personality' has referred both to appearance and to inner, essential nature, and Allport identified numerous categories of usage such as 'derogatory', 'sociological', 'juristic', 'ethical', 'philosophical', 'biosocial' and 'theological'. In the early twentieth century Psychological acceptability of alternative terms began to wane. 'Temperament' was too identified with the ancient 'humoral' doctrine in which personality was determined by the relative proportions of the four bodily 'humours': blood, black bile, yellow bile and phlegm (which generated 'sanguine', 'melancholic', 'choleric' and 'phlegmatic' respectively). 'Character', for its part, had acquired too strong an ethical connotation for Psychological use as a general term to refer to individual uniqueness. In the 1930s (partly under Allport's influence) 'personality' became normal disciplinary usage. Prior to this the alternatives were still common, e.g. A.F. Shand's *The Foundations of Character* (1914) and A.A. Roback's history of the topic, *The Psychology of Character with a Survey of Temperament* (1927), although his separately published bibliography was entitled *Bibliography of Character and Personality* (1927). (See K. Danziger, 1997 for details of the transition.) A further expression, adopted by psychometricians, was 'individual differences', which has continued in use, even making inroads into the use of 'personality'. What we must grasp, though, is that Allport and others in effect *invented* or *constituted* 'personality' as we now understand it. This 'personality' was significantly different from 'character' and 'temperament' in being more general and both ethically and theoretically neutral. The word had a long history, but was now given a fresh 'scientific' meaning.

Types of personality theory

Before considering the 'place' of personality Psychology in modern western culture a brief sketch is needed of the major approaches psychologists have taken towards it. These have often been mapped in various ways and what ensues is

Table 11.1 Some major personality type classifications

Traditional 'humoral':   sanguine, phlegmatic, choleric, melancholic
Bain: mental, volitional, vital (ultimately derived from Plato)
Spranger: theoretical, economic, aesthetic, social, political, religious
Sheldon: ectomorphic, endomorphic, mesomorphic
Jung: 16 types based on eight possible patternings of the four 'functions'
        (thinking, feeling [rational], sensation, intuition [irrational]) and the
        extravert/introvert distinction
Freudian: oral and anal permutated with the modifers aggressive, retentive,
        passive, obsessional, plus 'phallic narcissist'. No rigorously exhaustive list,
        however.

only an outline. S. Maddi (1976) usefully distinguished theories focusing on the 'core' from those focusing on the 'periphery', at the same time classifying 'core models' into 'conflict' (of both 'intrapsychic' and 'psycho-social' varieties), 'balance' and 'fulfilment' types. Underpinning these variations, he suggested, were different underlying philosophical views of human nature. There has also been a longstanding tension between 'trait' and 'type' theories. The former, in spirit dating back to Francis Galton, was developed from the 1940s by figures such as R.B. Cattell, J.P. Guilford and H.J. Eysenck and views 'individual differences' as occurring along separate dimensions, each manifested by distinct 'surface traits'. These latter then serve as the starting point for generating personality questionnaires to ascertain an individual's position on each 'dimension'. Type theories, by contrast, classify individuals into holistic 'type' categories variously defined in terms of, e.g. 'value-directions' (E. Spranger), physiology (W.H. Sheldon), or mode of orienting to the world plus dominant psychological 'function' (C.G. Jung) (Table 11.1). Less globally, psychologists may identify specific 'types' (e.g. the authoritarian personality) or dichotomous dimensions yielding two types, e.g. field dependent vs field independent (H.A. Witkin and D.R. Goodenough, 1977) and internal vs external locus of control (J.B. Rotter, 1966). The boundary between trait and type can though become somewhat blurred. (For the type vs trait controversy of the 1970s and early 1980s see H.N. and W. Mischel (eds), 1973; D. Magnusson and N. Endler (eds), 1977; L. Cochran, 1984.)

   While psychologists may take 'personality' as their research speciality, virtually all general Psychological theories can, and have, been applied to the topic. For example, psychoanalysis produced type-categories based on infantile developmental phases (e.g. 'anal retentive' and 'oral aggressive'), learning theory became central to H.J. Eysenck's theory (enabling him to relate 'conditionability' to his 'extraversion' dimension), and cognitive Psychologists have identified various 'cognitive styles'. Currently we are witnessing a revival of genetic explanations of personality. At the opposite pole have been Marxist explanations of personality as a product of social relations, the fullest being Lucien Sève's *Man in Marxist Theory* (1978). Any general account of 'human nature' must somehow explain why people differ as well as explain what they have in common. Ironically this may end up actually subverting the notion that a general account is possible.

Projective tests

But how do psychologists determine someone's 'personality'? In Chapter 18 we will discuss how trait theorists developed personality questionnaires, the trait approach being theoretically rooted in factor analytic methodology for which questionnaires were, in the first instance, research tools. Some technical qualifications aside, this assumes, virtually as a central dogma, that developing a statistically reliable questionnaire amounts, operationally, to perfecting the measurement of something which objectively exists. From the 1930s into the 1960s broadly psychoanalytic or 'psychodynamic' psychologists adopted a different strategy, using 'projective tests' which assumed that people's fantasies and perceptions reflected their, often unconscious, personality dynamics and motivation. Projective tests may not always be visual in form – open-ended questionnaires can be used – but these predominate. For example, Henry Murray and his associates devised the Thematic Apperception Test (TAT) (Murray, 1938, 1943, see also Chapter 18). This consisted of an assorted battery of pictures, each of which the individual taking the test had to describe or tell a story about, this then being coded for the presence of expressions of the various 'needs' which Murray's theory postulated. Numerous variations on this method ensued, some devised for children (G.S. Blum, 1950; L. and S.S. Bellak, 1949) or adolescents (P.M. Symonds, 1949). In Shneidman's Make A Picture Story (MAPS) test figures representing numerous social roles, mythical figures, people of various ages, genders and dress (or lack of it), plus a few animals, are placed on background scenes (a street, bedroom, graveyard, bridge, etc.), again with an accompanying narrative (E.S. Shneidman, 1948). Somewhat analogous was British psychoanalyst M. Lowenfeld's World Test from 1929 and further developed during the 1930s, in which a 'world' could be created (usually by a child in this case) in a large sand-tray from 150 model buildings, vehicles, fences, people, trees and animals. In her later 'Mosaic Test' patterns are made using 465 variously coloured tiles of basic geometric shapes. Most famous is the Rorschach 'ink-blot' test, invented by Hermann Rorschach in 1921 and rapidly adopted in the US, S.J. Beck being its primary advocate (Beck, 1937). This purportedly discloses the personality's inner structure rather than specific contents. Contrary to popular belief, what is 'seen' in the ink-blot is considered less significant than how it is used (e.g. focus on fine detail vs treating it holistically, usage of the periphery or the centre of the image, or of the white spaces as well as the blot itself). Although Rorschach did have some links with psychoanalysis, the test was devised independently.

The main problem with projective tests is that they elicit a surfeit of information which resists reliable quantification, while responses mingle material of various kinds – mixing the straightforwardly 'expressive' and neutrally conventional with the genuinely 'projective'. They remain useful in therapeutic contexts where they can be incorporated into the therapeutic process in a qualitative and pragmatic fashion – shifting their status from 'tests' to therapeutic techniques – but in mainstream personality research they were largely in decline by 1970, although J.E. Exner successfully salvaged the Rorschach test (Exner, 1974–1982).

Two other strategies

While behavioural tests have had a limited use (e.g. the 'rod and frame test' for 'field dependency') variations on the questionnaire, never the 'trait' school's monopoly, have continued to dominate. A full survey of personality testing techniques would nonetheless turn up numerous idiosyncratic strategies, being one field in which psychologists have allowed their creativity free rein. An interesting *leitmotif* is the never-abandoned effort at scientifically systematising graphology. A French writer, J. Crépieux-Jamin, is generally credited as the pioneer, his work being followed up by Alfred Binet of intelligence test fame. The Germans Ludwig Klages and Robert Saudek were prominent during the 1920s and 1930s, while G.W. Allport, with British psychologist Philip Vernon, published studies on it in 1933. Earlier, American psychologist Jill Downey had devised a test of what she called 'will temperament' using handwriting (1919, 1923). Being an 'expressive movement' *par excellence* it seems reasonable to assume that handwriting reveals something about the writer's personality – indeed it often obviously *does* – but rendering our intuitions about this scientifically reliable proves forever elusive and it remains a marginalised approach. Another, more successful, technique which has achieved a permanent place is George Kelly's Repertory Grid Test (G. Kelly, 1955a, b; D. Bannister and F. Fransella, 1971), devised in connection with his 'Personal Construct Theory'. This involves selecting an 'odd one out' from trios of alternatives (typically names of relatives and associates) in order to elicit the major 'constructs' by which someone 'construes' – interprets and understands – the world. Unlike most other approaches this imposes no categories on the individual, aiming instead to elicit a picture of *their* unique system of 'constructs', their own unique psychology. While construct-systems vary in several typical ways related to their levels of elaboration, consistency and rigidity, these are not used to classify 'types'. Moreover, like projective tests, the 'Rep. Grid' may in itself serve a therapeutic function, as well as providing a technique for monitoring change. This last is an important point, for the goal of most personality assessment is to identify that which is more or less fixed and enduring. While the possibility of personality change is rarely excluded (and many theories aim quite explicitly to facilitate it), the term 'personality' essentially refers to something constant, distinct from transient moods, emotions and levels of arousal. Possessing some affinities with this is William Stephenson's 'Q-sort' method, which he began working on in the 1930s and fully formulated in Stephenson (1953). Only more recently has this become widely used, particularly among social psychologists.

The problematic self

Since the 1980s a serious theoretical issue has profoundly affected Psychological discourse on personality – the nature of the 'self'. This is not a new topic. William James discussed it (see Chapter 4) and within Social Psychology it remained a central theme of G.H. Mead's work of the 1920s and 1930s. Although for James 'the same brain may subserve many conscious selves, either alternate or co-existing' (1890, vol. I: 401), most psychologists had viewed the 'self' – meaning some enduring core personal identity – as a common natural component of, or principle within, the human 'psyche' or mind. Its status was admittedly somewhat hazy, hovering insecurely between the conscious ego and something more profound (as in Jung's theory). That it is not entirely equivalent to the conscious ego is reflected in the idea of people seeking their 'true' or 'inner' selves, giving 'the self' a certain ethical connotation as an authentic identity, contact with which might, for some reason, be lost. This self's essential feature was its unitary, enduring nature, only fracturing in pathological cases of 'multiple personality'. This assumption came under increasing strain after 1970 with widespread suggestions that the 'unitary self' notion evolved in Europe from the Renaissance onwards among middle and ruling class males (R. Porter, 1997). The idea of an autonomous private 'self' in control of its own destiny gradually ascends to dominance by the end of the Enlightenment and is reinforced by Romanticism. This contrasted with a previous mode of subjectivity in which personal identity was defined by membership of collectivities and control of one's fate lay with God or fate. Individuals' efforts to shape their fortunes were typically doomed to failure – the theme of dramatic tragedy from the Greeks to Shakespeare, in whom the tension reaches its highest pitch of moral ambiguity. This is also reflected in the negative attitude of predestinarian Calvinists and puritans to the 'self' – hence 'selfish'. During the eighteenth century attitudes towards the notion became more sanguine. Viewing human identity as centred on this rational, unified, ahistorical, autonomous, natural 'core' supported contemporary ideas of the rational economic man, 'free will' and the ability to forge one's own fate. This idea, critics argued, radically misled modern Psychology into 'individualism', ignoring both how social factors determined our 'modes of subjectivity', and the psychologies of women and non-European peoples (A. Mama's 1995 black feminist critique *Beyond the Masks* fuses these). While not entirely convincing as a historical analysis – phrenology fragmented the mind into 'faculties' and the idea of an evolutionary hierarchy of identities became common in the late nineteenth century – this did compel critical psychologists to scrutinise the concept of the self more sceptically. By the 1990s post-modern writers generally, including critical psychologists, were routinely asserting that the 'self' was a myth, at best a grammatical fiction. We all in fact possess numerous selves, continually revising and recreating our 'self' in the light of experience and circumstances. This actually echoes the sociological 'role theory' approach popular in the 1950s and 1960s, which deconstructed personality not into traits but into the various social roles that we are forever enacting. In Rom Harré's 'narrativist' theory our sense of 'self' is produced, and constantly modified, by the stories we continually tell ourselves and others about ourselves (R. Harré and G. Gillett, 1994; Harré, 2001).

This development had serious consequences for the idea of 'personality' as something more or less stable and continuous, centring on the 'self'. Ironically, the usually anti-constructionist trait theorists might view this with equanimity, having already undertaken their own mode of 'deconstruction', yet even they consider their 'traits' enduring. But does not this critical 'deconstruction' fall between two stools? If it means simply that our presentation and experience of ourselves vary across time and circumstance, the insight is commonplace and antique ('Each man in his life plays many parts', as Shakespeare famously wrote).

If a more radical and profound denial of some enduring identity is intended, then it is plain wrong – at least as regards our conscious phenomenological self-experience. For most of us the alleged post-modernist destruction of the unitary self is surely exaggerated. We may be eternally narratively reconstructing and revising this, and, always perforce living in the present, unable to compare our current 'self' with previous versions but we experience ourselves as remembering them. More importantly, this is a remembering of changes 'I' have experienced, not of the 'I' itself.

In short, it is unclear quite what the post-modernists are claiming to have achieved here. While it may remain true that the term 'self' lacks an objective referent beyond narrative construction or subjective memory, the theoretical position adopted in the present book is that this is true, to some degree at least, of virtually all psychological phenomena. Part of the problem, I feel, arises from the ambiguities of the term 'individualism' and how this relates to the far from clearcut concept of the 'self'. 'Individualism' has at least two, rather distinct, meanings. It may mean a belief in the 'sacredness' of individual rights to liberty and equality and the ethical virtues of self-fulfilment and self-sufficiency. This is how it was conceived in the Enlightenment by the authors of the American Constitution for example. But more latterly it has come to refer additionally to individual self-centredness and selfishness, denial of society's rights to exert more than an absolute minimum of control over one's own rights to do entirely as one pleases and an image of individual identity as at some level existing entirely apart from, and transcending, any social context. These are obviously different, although one can see how the former could degenerate into the latter – the real target for critical attack.

Reading personality psychology

What then has a century of Psychological debate about 'personality' yielded? Certainly a huge crop of novel images of human nature and concepts for discussing it, but one so variegated that clear lines of progress, or concrete 'natural knowledge' gains, are virtually indiscernible. Browsing the 'personality' literature is always stimulating, for we constantly encounter ideas and claims seemingly shedding a new (if often ephemeral) light on our own 'personality' when reflexively applied – as actually understanding the text invariably entails. One moment we are having to reappraise our family relationships, the next our mode of thinking, or we find we are introverted, field dependent, or obsessional. For the moment at least we feel compelled to take what we are reading seriously and believe it, if only to understand the psychological phenomena to which it refers. On rare occasions we may feel the scales falling from our inward eyes, on others conclude that we have been colluding with a piece of nonsense. But this raises a point hardly ever spelled out, although especially relevant to beginners in Psychology. This is that understanding a Psychological proposition in this reflexive fashion can lead us to conclude that it must be true, whereas really we have only successfully joined in the particular conceptual-linguistic game the theorist is playing which, while the game continues, in a sense *makes* it true. We are like an actor entering into a character

149

who then thinks that, having succeeded, they have, psychologically, *become* that character. But because you have grasped the meaning of, say, authoritarianism, extraversion or anal fixatedness, it does not mean that the concept has any 'objective' referent beyond the particular theoretical game being played. And even if it does, it may have a different meaning or significance in the contexts of other 'games'.

Why the psychology of personality was needed

In the context of the present work the central question must be why this twentieth-century proliferation of images of human 'personality' occurred, when until the late 1700s most people remained content with a relatively fixed range of personal identities defined by age, gender, appearance, social class, the traditional 'four temperaments' typology and occupation. The post-Renaissance emergence of the 'Self' did not initially affect this. Subtler explorations of the topic were the province of dramatists, poets, theologians and novelists, not matters for 'science'. From the 1780s first physiognomists (notably J.C. Lavater) and then phrenologists sought to bring science to bear on the question, but only at the end of the Victorian era did Psychology (in association with psychiatry) embark on wholesale systematic revisions of this heterogeneous traditional lore.

To answer this question we must return to our opening remarks on why we want 'knowledge' about personality in the first place. The reason, as we said, is our desire to know how, as individuals, we fit into the range of humanity at large, and what that range is. This, we hope, will yield insights into our own nature and (what is sometimes more to the point) that of others. One of the earliest 'Psychology' texts was the Spaniard Juan Huarte's *Examen de Ingenios*, translated as *The Examination Of Men's Wits* (1594) (and again in 1698 as *The Tryal of Wits*) in which the possibility of assessing men's (if not women's) aptitudes (now an aspect of 'personality') is first aired. Nonetheless, until the twentieth century Juan Huarte's project remained stalled, although his book was widely read into the early 1700s. What happened to change this situation? Again the answer is fairly obvious: the rise of industrialised urban civilisation during the nineteenth century and the ever-gathering momentum of socio-economic change which followed and continues still.

This shift bears directly on the problem of how we are to acquire and formulate self-knowledge. It becomes ever harder – especially, initially, for males – to locate one's identity within the traditional repertoire of possibilities. We enter the Dickensian urban chaos of a world of enigmatic strangers, each struggling to maintain some sense of dignity and meaning within an arbitrary, unjust, and often cruel social universe. Dickens' characters are rarely 'rounded', more embodiments of peculiar survival strategies (excepting the heroes – and even that falls apart in *Our Mutual Friend*). The questions 'what am I?' and 'what am I to be?', hitherto the indulgence of the philosopher or romantic intellectual, acquire genuine widespread urgency. For the intellectual they can intensify to fever-pitch as in S. Kierkegaard, F. Dostoevsky, F. Nietzsche and indeed William James, their anxiety reinforced by revolutionary new scientific discoveries and the impossibility of certainty either religious or philosophical. Within this disorienting milieu the need for new ways of mapping human diversity slowly manifests itself. This need, it should be stressed, is as much top-down as bottom-up. As Nikolas Rose has consistently argued and demonstrated, charting and quantifying psychological differences was a major task facing those charged with managing this new form of society: bureaucrats, lawyers and the police, teachers and psychiatrists, prison governors, asylum keepers and doctors.

In a nutshell, 'personality' became problematic because identifying and/or creating viable personal identities or 'selves' really had become problematic. It is not that people previously thought 'personality' was one thing and then psychologists arrived and told them otherwise – it is rather that people, now unsure of how to define their identities, wanted an authoritative 'scientific' voice to tell them ('science' having become the only voice of authority carrying credibility). It is this vacuum which twentieth-century personality theories sought to fill, theories formulated by people themselves sensitised in various ways to the need they sought to meet. *But the Psychological formulation of the very concept of 'personality' (subtly distinct from both 'character' and 'temperament') was itself the crucial move.* Again this relates to Rose's thesis that in supplying this need Psychology was engaged in creating modernist modes of subjectivity.

Note, however, that being produced in this way modern personality theories differ from such ancient systems as astrology, physiognomy and the humours in one especially significant respect – they are themselves infused with the personalities (or 'psychologies') of their creators. However wise, learned or 'scientific' personality theorists, like everyone else, cannot fully transcend the constraints of their time, gender and place. Theorists will prioritise those aspects of the problem of which they are most aware, approaching them against the background of a complex, idiosyncratic, biographical and social context. Reading them in any depth we eventually discover these limitations, and the less like theirs our own personalities are, the sooner we do so as post-1960s generations of female, gay and ethnic minority readers rapidly realised. The personality theorist is always an individual whose head cannot ultimately outflank our own, in total contrast to the impersonal anonymity of doctrines like astrology which evolved over many centuries, erasing the individuality of their innumerable creators. This anonymity partly perhaps accounts for the durability of astrology in particular – people do not feel they are being co-opted by another person's agenda.

To return to the main issue, we might then see modern personality theories arising after c.1918 as a psychological response to the increased difficulty people were having in actually finding their 'identities' and 'true selves'. (Jung's 1920 *Psychological Types* probably marks the beginning of this.) This is consistent with Jill Morawski's accounts of Psychology's cultural appeal in the United States at the turn of the twentieth century (e.g. J.G. Morawski and G.A. Hornstein, 1991; J.G. Morawski, 1992), as well as Rose's previously cited position. Almost a century later the situation has subtly changed. Whereas previous generations experienced rapid change as a disturbing deviation from some more normal condition of stasis, later twentieth-century cohorts accepted it as the 'normal' condition. It is in this context that the post-modernist critique of the 'self' emerges. A possibility previously too anxiety-making to contemplate now became an idea which it was almost entertaining to consider – perhaps we do not possess 'real selves', 'authentic' or 'enduring' identities, at all. We change throughout our lives in a fashion matching the changes in the world around us. In this intellectual atmosphere earlier modes of theorising about personality, generally reliant at some point on this notion even (if somewhat obscurely) in psychometric theories, seemed to become irrelevant. But have we all then lost the need for enduring 'identities'? On the contrary, another trend of the last quarter-century has been to seek this in identifying with a particular social minority, oppressed group or 'cause', be it sexual (gay, transexual, lesbian), ethnic (Asian English, Afro-Caribbean, Irish), related to health (physical or psychological) or a 'cause' such as environmentalism, although older explicitly ideological and political causes have waned. Life's 'meaning' is no longer in one's 'real self' but in struggling for this group's collective interests within the unending flux. It has become a cliché that in the US everyone now feels the need to belong to a minority of some sort. Self-definition by membership of a collectivity is not in itself new, but previously centred more comfortably on such things as occupation, social class, religious belief and national (as opposed to ethnic minority) identity. I would, however, suggest that its rejection of personal individuality has always rendered this strategy somewhat psychologically impoverished. (Of course I am not implying that engaging in collective causes and struggles necessarily involves centring one's entire identity on them in this way.) Its emergence is another aspect of the same weakened belief in the authentic 'inner self' which others happily live with. The baffled majority still struggle in the middle.

Psychology of personality today

Whatever else we may say about it, this state of affairs certainly leaves the 'Psychology of Personality' project in something of a fix, although the dialectical twists and turns are far from over. The rejection of the idea of fixed personalities is itself, I have just argued, a product of currently prevailing psychological conditions. But if critical and constructionist perspectives (to which we owe this very insight) are in the ascendent on the issue, the fact remains that the raw material, so to speak, from which we are to 'construct' our now mutable personalities includes the vast conceptual legacy of pre-1980 personality theories. In typical 'post modernist' fashion we are presumably free to take what we wish for our own purposes, even, paradoxically, to narratively recreate 'authentic' inner selves. And since so much contemporary epistemology views all knowledge as narrative in character, such 'selves' may be as 'real' as it can ever get. As suggested earlier, the error lay not in positing their existence, but in assuming that they 'objectively' pre-existed their narrational creation. Older style personality theories thus offer themselves for continued pragmatic ransacking, reappraisal and redevelopment, albeit in a different spirit to that in which they were first proposed.

One further lesson emerges from all this: the historical variability of 'personality'. Some 'traits' – being lazy, hard-working, amusing, boring, intelligent, miserable – no doubt possess near universality. But others, like 'pious', 'authoritarian', 'ambitious', 'noble', and 'creative', let alone 'field dependent', 'feminine' and 'neurotic', patently relate to specific social and historical conditions. In the case of 'authoritarianism' this was fully acknowledged by its proponents (M. Jay, 1973). Some – like 'feminine' – vary in meaning, others – like 'pious' – are only possible in specific contexts as in a society of atheists it would be meaningless. (See Chapter 18 for further examples of the historical contingency of 'traits' as measured by questionnaires.) The presence of both 'traits' and 'types' varies over time, but their meanings and how they correlate with one another also do so. One generation's heroic warrior might be another's war criminal, yesterday's man of iron will and determination is today's closed-minded authoritarian bigot, the scoundrel's admirably martyred loyal wife of 1870 seems a pitiable victim of patriarchal oppression a hundred years later. Personality-signifiers also change – what on earth did the once common English expression 'a milk in first type' mean?

Simple verdicts on Psychology's embroilments with 'personality' in terms of 'success' or 'failure', scientific 'truth' or 'falsity' are in the end vain. They must be accepted for the variegated corpus of accounts they are – direct expressions, usually produced in good faith, of twentieth-century western humanity's efforts to find a meaningful view of itself under sometimes quite extraordinary stress and upheaval, especially prior to 1960. Possessing this reflexive character, we cannot expect anything other than a correspondingly dramatic mixture of folly and wisdom, comedy and tragedy, the useful and the futile, and indeed good and evil.

To close on a lighter note. One of the most interesting books on personality I have met is D.B. Bromley's *Personality Description in Everyday Language* (1977). This reported research in which 100 people provided four short personality descriptions – of a man they liked, a man they disliked, a woman they liked and a woman they disliked. One among many of the things to emerge was how we can conjure up images of 'personality' on remarkably minimal information including 'he wears the most appalling sweaters knitted for him by his wife'. If the reader has not realised it already, I have a soft spot for 'personality theory', for all its invidious aberrations.

Further reading

Allport, G.W. (1937) *Personality: A Psychological Interpretation*. New York: Henry Holt. A key text, the opening historical discussion being especially valuable.

Danziger, K. (1997) *Naming the Mind: How Psychology Found its Language*. London: Sage. The section on how the term 'personality' ousted 'temperament' and 'character' is essential reading.

Maddi, S. (1968, 3rd edn, 1976) *Personality Theories: A Comparative Analysis*. Homewood, IL: Dorsey. The most sophisticated mainstream overview of the field.

Roback, A.A. (1927, rev. edn, 1928) *The Psychology of Character with a Survey of Temperament*. London: Kegan Paul, Trench & Trübner. An idiosyncratic but unsurpassed historical survey discussing much otherwise obscure and forgotten material.

Rose, N. (1996) *Inventing Ourselves. Psychology, Power, and Personhood*. Cambridge: Cambridge University Press. Essays addressing various aspects of the nature of the 'self' from a post-modernist perspective.

Additional references

Largely restricted to those cited in the text.

Allport, G.W. and Vernon, P.E. (1933, rep. 1967) *Studies in Expressive Movement*. New York and London: Hafner. Interesting attempt at getting to grips with the handwriting and personality issue in a scientific fashion.

Bannister, D. and Fransella, F. (1971, 2nd edn, 1980) *Inquiring Man. The Psychology of Personal Constructs*. London: Penguin. Highly influential British exposition of Kelly's theory.

Beck, S.J. (1937) *Introduction to the Rorschach Method. A Manual of Personality Study*. American Orthopsychiatric Association. The first comprehensive English language exposition of the Rorschach 'ink-blot' method.

Bell, J.E. (1948) *Projective Techniques: A Dynamic Approach to the Study of Personality*. New York: Longmans, Green. A good contemporary review, though misses later developments.

Bellak, L. and Bellak, S.S. (1949) *Children's Apperception Test*. Larchmont, New York: C.P.S. Inc.

Blum, G.S. (1950) *The Blacky Pictures. A Technique for the Exploration of Personality Dynamics*. New York: Psychological Corporation. A widely used projective test for use with children.

Bromley, D.B. (1977) *Personality Description in Everyday Language*. London: Wiley. Explores how ordinary people actually *do* describe and explain personality.

Cattell, R.B. (1946) *Description and Measurement of Personality*. London: Harrap. Major founding text of the psychometric 'trait' school.

Cattell, R.B. (1965) *The Scientific Study of Personality*. Harmondsworth: Penguin. Most accessible popular account of Cattell's theory, although this subsequently underwent further development.

Cochran, L. (1984) 'On the Categorization of Traits'. *Journal for the Theory of Social Behavior* 14: 183–209. A good critical review of the difficulties in defining traits in terms of overt behaviour.

Craik, K.H., Hogan, R. and Wolfe, R.N. (eds) (1993) *Fifty Years of Personality Psychology*. New York & London: Plenum Press. Celebratory, but contains several useful papers on Allport and Stagner.

Downey, J.E. (1919) *Graphology and the Psychology of Handwriting*. Baltimore: Warwick & York. A pioneering American attempt to render the topic 'scientific'.

Downey, J.E. (1923) *The Will-temperament and its Testing*. Yonkers: World Book Co. Exposition of Downey's 'will temperament' concept and the handwriting-based test she used to measure it.

Exner, J.E. (1974–1982, revised edn 1993) *The Rorschach: A Comprehensive System* (3 vols). New York: Wiley. The most thorough recent exposition of the Rorschach test and its theoretical basis by its leading advocate.

Eysenck, H.J. (1947) *Dimensions of Personality*. London: Routledge & Kegan Paul.

Eysenck, H.J. (1952) *The Scientific Study of Personality*. London: Routledge & Kegan Paul. The first expositions of Eysenck's highly successful personality theory, further developed in numerous later texts.

Hall, C.S. and Lindzey, G. (1957, 2nd edn, 1963) *Theories of Personality*. London & New York: Wiley. This remains a very useful, straightforward, but not uncritical, account of the classic personality theories.

Harré, R. (2001) 'The Advent of the Methodological Critique'. In G.C. Bunn, A.D. Lovie and G.D. Richards (2000) *Psychology in Britain: Historical Essays and Personal Reflections*. Leicester: British Psychological Society and London: The Science Museum, 393–401. Harré's own account of the background to his 'narrativist' approach.

Harré, R. and Gillett, G. (1994) *The Discursive Mind*. Thousand Oaks, CA: Sage. The major 'narrativist' text.

Huarte, J. (1594) *Examen de Ingenios (The Examination of Men's Wits)*. London: Adam Islip for Richards Watkins; (1698) *Examen de Ingenios, or The Tryal of Wits*, London: Richard Sale. Acknowledged as the first, but very premature, work to raise the possibility of assessing personality traits.

James, W. (1890) *Principles of Psychology*, New York: Henry Holt. See Chapter X on 'The Self'.

Jay, M. (1973) *The Dialectical Imagination. A History of the Frankfurt School and the Institute of Social Research*. London: Heinemann. Includes detailed discussion of the origins and nature of the 'authoritarian personality' concept.

Jung, C.G. (1923, 1st Swiss edn 1920) *Psychological Types, or the Psychology of Individuation*. London: Routledge & Kegan Paul. Highly influential typological analysis of personality. The widely used 'Myers-Briggs Type Indicator' test is based on this.

Kelly, G.A. (1955a) *The Psychology of Personal Constructs*, 2 volumes. New York: Norton. The original exposition of Kelly's theory.

Kelly, G.A. (1955b) *A Theory of Personality. The Psychology of Personal Constructs*. New York: Norton. A more popular synopsis of the previous work.

Klages, L. (1917, 13th edn 1929) *Handschrift und Charakter*. Leipzig: J.A. Barth. The major work by Germany's leading exponent of 'scientific' graphology.

Lowenfeld, M. (1935) *Play in Children*. London: Gollancz.

Lowenfeld, M. (1939) 'The World Pictures of Children'. *British Journal of Medical Psychology* 18: 65–101. These two texts include discussion of Lowenfeld's 'World Test'.

Magnusson, D. and Endler, N. (eds) (1977) *Personality at the Crossroads*. New York: Lawrence Erlbaum. Contains papers addressing the 'type' vs 'trait' issue and the 'cognitive social learning' attempt at moving beyond this.

Mama, A. (1995) *Beyond the Masks: Race, Gender and Subjectivity*. London: Routledge. Includes a black feminist critique of the notion of the 'self', as well as discussion of other issues.

Mead, G.H. (1934) *Mind, Self and Society from the Standpoint of a Social Behaviorist*. Best known work by the leading inter-war US theorist of the nature of the 'self'.

Mischel, H.N. and Mischel, W. (eds) (1973) *Readings in Personality*. Holt, Rinehart & Winston. Particularly useful for the 'trait' vs 'type' controversy.

Morawski, J.G. (1992) 'Self-Regard and Other-Regard: Reflexive Practices in American Psychology, 1890–1940'. *Science in Context* 5(2): 281–308.

Morawski, J.G. and Hornstein, G.A. (1991) 'Quandary of the Quacks. The Struggle for Expert Knowledge in American Psychology, 1890–1940'. In J. Brown and D.K. Van Keuren (eds) *The Estate of Social Knowledge*. Baltimore: Johns Hopkins University Press, Chapter 6. These two papers offer sophisticated examinations of the psychological conditions under which personality theory, and Psychology generally, emerged in the US.

Murray, H.A. (ed.) (1938) *Explorations in Personality. A Clinical and Experimental Study of Fifty College Men of College Age by the Workers at the Harvard Psychological Clinic*. New York: Oxford University Press. Report of an ambitious project to study personality from all angles, including the use of Murray's own Thematic Apperception Test and highly complex personality theory.

Murray, H.A. (1943) *Manual for the Thematic Apperception Test*. Cambridge: Harvard University Press.

Pervin, L.A. (ed.) (1990) *Handbook of Personality: Theory and Research*. New York and London: The Guilford Press. Apart from anything else this indicates how fragmented the field has become, covering everything from behaviour-genetics to politics.

Porter, R. (ed.) (1997) *Rewriting the Self. Histories from the Renaissance to the Present*. London: Routledge. A useful recent collection of historical essays on the 'self' issue.

Roback, A.A. (1927) *Bibliography of Character and Personality*. Cambridge MA: Sci-Art. Compiled to accompany his *The Psychology of Character*, but much scarcer. An invaluable reference work for historians.

Rorschach, H. (1942, 1st German edn, 1921) *Psychodiagnostics, a Diagnostic Test based on Perception*. Berne: Huber/New York: Grune & Stratton. Rorschach's own exposition of the Rorschach 'ink-blot' test and its rationale.

Rose, N. (1990) *Governing the Soul: The Shaping of the Private Self*. London: Routledge. Rose's historical account of the post-1939 period.

Rotter, J.B. (1966) 'Generalized Expectancies for Internal versus External Control of Reinforcement', *Psychological Monographs* 80(1) (Whole Number 609). Major statement of the subsequently very successful – but not unproblematic – 'locus of control' theory (which Rotter had been developing since the late 1950s).

Saudek, R. (1925) *The Psychology of Handwriting*. London: Allen & Unwin.

Saudek, R. (1928) *Experiments with Handwriting*. New York: Morrow.

Saudek, R. (1933) *Anonymous Letters: A Study in Crime and Handwriting*. London: Methuen. Saudek's work perhaps came nearest to placing graphology on a firm basis.

Sève, L. (1978) *Man in Marxist Theory and the Psychology of Personality*. Brighton: Harvester. Party-line Marxist analysis of the nature of personality, but highly detailed and often penetrating.

Shand, A.F. (1914) *The Foundations of Character, being a Study of the Tendencies of the Emotions and Sentiment*. London: Macmillan. Now largely forgotten, this was highly regarded in Britain up to 1939.

Sheldon, W.H. (1954) *Atlas of Man. A Guide for Somatotyping the Adult Male at all Ages*. New York: Harper & Brothers. One of the most extraordinary Psychology books ever to appear, this contains a systematic photographic survey of the various 'somatotypes', accompanied by brief statements about their personalities. Each is light-heartedly compared to an animal – 'palaeolithic tiger', 'dugongs and manatees' among them. Scandal prevented publication of a companion *Atlas of Woman*.

Sheldon, W.H. (1942, rep. 1970) *The Varieties of Temperament. A Psychology of Constitutional Differences*. New York & London: Hafner. The major exposition of Sheldon's 'somatotype' theory.

Shneidman, E.S. (1948) *The Make a Picture Story Test*. New York: The Psychological Corporation.

Shneidman, E.S. (1952) *Manual for the Make a Picture Story Method*. New York: Society for Projective Techniques and Rorschach Institute Inc. Shneidman's 'MAPS' test is one of the most intriguing 'projective' tests produced during the mid-twentieth century.

Spranger, E. (1928) *Types of Men. The Psychology and Ethics of Personality*. Halle: Niemayer/Steichart. Only English-language account of Spranger's typological theory.

Stagner, R. (1937) *Psychology of Personality*. New York & London: McGraw-Hill. Key founding textbook for the field alongside Allport's.

Stephenson, W.K. (1953) *The Study of Behavior: Q-Technique and its Methodology*. Chicago: Chicago University Press. The major exposition of the now increasingly popular Q-sort technique.

Symonds, P.M. (1939) 'Criteria for the Selection of Pictures for the Investigation of Adolescent Phantasies'. *Journal of Abnormal and Social Psychology*, 34: 271–274.

Symonds, P.M. (1949, rep. 1965) *Adolescent Fantasy. An Investigation of the Picture-Story Method of Personality Study*. New York & London: Columbia University Press. These give Symonds' account of his own projective tests, especially geared to the study of adolescents.

Witkin, H.A. and Goodenough, D.R. (1977) 'Field Dependence and Interpersonal Behavior'. *Psychological Bulletin* 84: 661–689. Introduced the 'field-dependency' concept.

Chapter 12

Social Psychology

- The complex character of Social Psychology
- Gustav le Bon and his agenda
- Early US Social Psychology: an example
- US Social Psychology in the 1930s: trends and changes
- Reasons for the appeal of Social Psychology in the US
- British Social Psychology in the 1960s
- Themes in post-1945 US Social Psychology
- The crisis in Social Psychology after 1970
- Current polarisation with Social Psychology between social constructionist and cognitivist approaches

Of all Psychology's subdisciplines, Social Psychology is that in which involvement with socio-cultural context is most intense. The priorities, problems and concerns of the societies in which social psychologists live largely determine the matters with which they deal. Their personal social positions, including gender, social class and ethnic group, will, moreover, play a part in determining *how* they deal with them, while, as members of society, they have ideological and political beliefs which may figure prominently in deciding the goals of their Psychological work. One result is that the ways in which social psychologists orient towards and conceptualise the subject are peculiarly diverse, sometimes even conflicting (see Table 12.1). A particularly important underlying axis of tension is whether the individual or the 'social' is prioritised. This has serious ramifications. Theoretically, the latter leads to more social constructionist (if not by name) positions, the former conforming more closely to the orthodox 'natural science' approach of experimental Psychology. Methodologically, the latter broadly favours field research and naturalistic observation, the former laboratory-sited research. Ideologically, the latter will also lean towards positions critical of the status quo and be prepared to invoke socio-economic factors in explaining social problems as opposed to individualist explanations in terms of personal psychology. Obviously too, the Sociology–Social Psychology boundary can become quite blurred from the second perspective.

Let us then consider the nature of Social Psychology at three times and places in this light: France around 1900, the United States between the two World Wars and both Britain and the United States since about 1950.

Table 12.1 Major angles from which Social Psychologists have addressed and conceptualised social psychological phenomena

- The individual's understanding of the social (attitudes, social cognition)
- Effects of the social on the individual (e.g. of joining a group)
- Role of the social in individual development (e.g. in creating the 'self')
- Dynamics of two-person (dyadic) interpersonal relations (e.g. social attraction)
- Small group dynamics as affected by group structure (e.g. hierarchical vs democratic)
- Psychological determinants of social phenomena (e.g. achievement motivation)
- Social functions performed in groups (role theory)
- General and large-scale social psychological processes (e.g. conformity, crowd behaviour, power-relations)
- Inter-group relations (e.g. group conflict)
- The social production of psychological phenomena (e.g. as argued by social constructionists)
- Social communication processes (e.g. sociolinguistic and discursive approaches)
- Psychological effects of social structural factors (e.g. class, ethnicity, gender-roles)
- Psychological effects of major events (e.g. war, natural disasters)

France around 1900

Although Social Psychology's origins date from the late 1700s and earlier nine-teenth-century German *Völkerpsychologie* it is widely held that in its modern form it begins with Gustav Le Bon's *The Crowd* (1896). Le Bon, a popular science writer, became an eminent pundit on political and social issues, on close terms with leading psychologists, politicians, philosophers and military figures whose friendships he cultivated at sumptuous gourmet dinners. A passionate patriot, loathing socialism and communism and desperate to renew French culture, this ideological agenda pervaded his Psychology. His concern with the crowd stemmed from several factors. First, ever since the French Revolution (1789) crowds had played a prominent part in French political life, with uprisings in 1830 and 1848, and the Paris Commune (1871) being the most notable events. Riots were endemic and the latter nineteenth century was constantly punctuated by violent strikes and left-wing demonstrations. In short, the crowd was playing a peculiarly prominent role in French history, creating a permanent sense of insecurity in its rulers, exacerbated by defeat in the Franco-Prussian War (1870), which had severely wounded patriotic morale.

Second, French Psychological thought as represented in works like G. Tarde (1890) and widespread clinical concern with hypnotism and kindred phenomena, combined with the evolutionary perspective, promised Le Bon seemingly profound insights into crowd behaviour. C.F. Graumann (1988) notes the additional impact of the 'contagion' metaphor drawn from the medical discoveries of L. Pasteur and R. Koch, which provided Le Bon with his notion of 'mental contagion'. Third, and centrally, he believed that understanding the 'laws' of crowd behaviour would enable national leaders to cultivate patriotic pride and self-confidence. *The Crowd* is thus offered as a resource for enabling France's rulers to maintain and exercise social power in fighting to preserve French civilisation from perfidious Socialism. (For Le Bon democracy is only the least worst option, while there is also a racial dimension to his thought, see Chapter 21.)

Le Bon's crowd is a seething, irrational mass governed by 'mental contagion' via the powers of 'suggestion'. Regressing to an earlier evolutionary stage, it can be manipulated by orators skilled in instilling the right suggestions, in a similar fashion to the hypnotist's control of hypnotic subjects. Individual identity dis-appears, buried within the superordinate, but more primitive, 'crowd mind'. Crowd behaviour is pathological and comprehensible in terms of the new scientific understanding of suggestion and hypnotism. He seeks to teach society's 'natural rulers' how to use and harness these laws to co-opt and direct the instinctive energies ever threatening to break loose. Civilised white (especially French!) male reason teeters on top of a fermenting unrest. Ruthless mass-manipulation and discipline are required to create the new 'race ideal' without which French civilisa-tion must perish.

His target audience was receptive, and his views played a major role in determining French military tactics in the First World War (during which he wrote morale-boosting propaganda); war was a battle of wills, armaments less important than will-power, morale, and the blindly loyal obedience of the troops. Mainstream French psychologists like A. Binet, G. Tarde, T. Ribot and G. Dumas endorsed his analysis. He was a friend of both Raymond Poincaré (later President) and the philosopher Henri Bergson. Freud cited him respectfully in *Group Psychology and the Analysis of the Ego* (1922). In retrospect, *The Crowd* emerges as one of the most sinister modern texts, second only to Hitler's *Mein Kampf,* for we now know that Hitler, Stalin and Mussolini avidly assimilated its message. Mussolini's heavily annotated copy still exists. Nevertheless, it is primarily a Psychology text offering a theory of crowd behaviour in what were understood as scientifically respectable terms. Thus Le Bon's ideological position can be seen by contemporaries as the scientifically objective and 'true' standpoint.

For several decades European psychologists such as, in Britain, William McDougall (1920) and Morris Ginsburg (1921) tended to follow in Le Bon's wake, seeing their task as understanding the 'group mind' and tracing the psychological roots of the rise and decline of nations and 'peoples'. The idea that the leader–follower relationship resembled that between hypnotist and subject was further developed by Freud (1922), while a tendency to equate social structure with individual psychological structure – the 'masses' representing the unconscious – was endemic among psychodynamic thinkers. C.G. Jung's 'collective unconscious' also had affinities with this concept (see Chapter 10). Meanwhile, across the Atlantic things were moving in a different direction.

The United States in the 1920s and 1930s

Prior to World War Two at least 35 books appeared in the United States with the phrase 'Social Psychology' in their titles, the earliest by C.A. Ellwood (1901). Previously the sociologist Lester Ward had published *Psychic Factors in Civilization* (1892), while what has been canonically accepted as the first US Social Psychology experiment was published by N. Triplett in 1898. The most eminent 1920s pioneers were Floyd Allport and Emory Bogardus. Particularly interesting for us, though, is James M. Williams' *Principles of Social Psychology* (1922). For Williams, Social Psychology is 'the science of the motives of people living in social relations' (p. 2). Motives are based on instincts which are moulded by learning and habit into 'dispositions'. Once established, these tend to be conservative although modern developments like immigration and greater information are weakening this. The mechanism underlying social relations is how conflicts of interest are negotiated. This, in brief, is his core Psychological model: a picture of behaviour as instinctively rooted but extremely flexible, with social relations being determined by the management of differences in interests. Nothing here about suggestibility or atavistic regression to earlier states, and very little interest in the crowd at all. Two-thirds of the chapters are organised under six broader headings of the form 'The Conflict of Interests in . . . Economic Relations/Political Relations/Professional Relations/Family Relations/Cultural Relations/Educational Relations'. He ends with 'The Social Reactions of Suppressed Impulses' – all social organisation requiring some 'suppression of impulses'. Even this is not tackled psychodynamically, being devoted to the effects of slavery, class control and military suppression.

Unlike Le Bon's world, Williams' is that of the professional businessman, teacher and American family life. No deep-seated military caste is present as in

France, and there is no mystical fantasising about national souls and 'race ideals'. Le Bon is not even referenced. Williams' interests are more immediately practical: 'labor relations', education, medical ethics and such, covering virtually every facet of social life including art and religion. Like much work during this period it hovers between sociology and Psychology, but his central explanatory level, is, as we saw, the psychological one. The major difference between this and the Social Psychology that began to appear later in the decade is that Williams does not see it as an experimental discipline. Rather, it requires immersion in specialist information from disciplines like economics, sociology and history. His bibliography is actually quite extraordinary – a book on artificial flower makers and others on coal-mine workers and tramps jostle with Thorndike and Titchener, Theodore Roosevelt's autobiography, a biography of Brahms and reports from the United States Supreme Court.

America's geographical isolation perhaps made the 'national character' issue, so dominant in Europe, relatively unimportant but in any case it was a society self-consciously building a new culture, not having to maintain long-standing sets of values, customs and social class interests. (Although in reality the defence of established WASP economic interests against African American and South European immigrant aspirations was quite passionate.)

By 1930 US Social Psychology's methodology is rapidly changing. Thorndike and Likert have introduced their methods of questionnaire design and attitude scaling, while much pioneer empirical research dates from this period, such as R.T. LaPiere's famous 1934 experiment on prejudice involving ringing up a restaurant to book a table for a party including Chinese guests. (Restaurants typically claimed to be full up over the phone, but happily seated the party when they arrived without prior notice.) The often-cited H. Hartshorne and M.A. May experiments on honesty in children were reported during 1929–1930 and M. Sherif (1936) published experimental studies of group effects on the autokinetic movement phenomenon (the apparent movement of a single spot of light in an otherwise totally dark visual field). Monographs also appear on such topics as the psychological effects of unemployment, mass media, public opinion formation, race prejudice, delinquency, industrial conflict and language. G.H. Mead's extensive study of the social processes by which the 'self' is formed dates from this period, but remained somewhat marginalised until the 1960s and yielded no immediate body of empirical experimental research. The influence of anthropological work on child-rearing and gender-roles by Margaret Mead and others must also be noted as a factor affecting accounts of the family and child development (as well as the 'race' issue) at this time.

Overall, what we are seeing during the inter-war period in the US is the creation of an experimental Social Psychology to provide both commentary on, and insight into, numerous social phenomena and problems from 'race' to radio, industrial relations to crime. This experimental Social Psychology abandons the European tradition, becoming resolutely individualist in level of analysis, the older approach's swansong being C. Murchison (1935). It is over-ridingly pragmatic and practical in orientation, though somewhat influenced by the general behaviourist climate. If there was an ideological agenda it tended, in the 1930s, to be a 'New Deal' Rooseveltian liberal one. K. Dunlap (1934), for example, is hostile to 'racial psychology', wary of the 'civilised' versus 'primitive' polarity, is very sympathetic to women, and views eugenics with scepticism. In fact American Social Psychology effectively splits (in the way identified at the beginning of the chapter) into individual psychology-oriented and more sociology-oriented camps (a division in the offing since the previous century). Leading figures in this latter camp, which tended to be more ideologically radical, included Gardner Murphy and G.W. Allport (see K. Pandora, 1997).

It is pertinent at this point to consider a central feature of US culture: the ubiquitous demands, arising from its distinct political and economic character, for feedback regarding the effects of behaviour. Politics requires constant information about reactions to political decisions and the state of public opinion. Effects of campaigning and lobbying demand rapid assessment. If true to some extent of all western democracies this operates in the US at a unique pitch – far more civil posts are elected than in Britain, and in some states changes in the law can be achieved by putting 'propositions' on the ballot. Similarly, from an earlier date than elsewhere, the US market economy hinged around market research and assessing the effectiveness of advertising and brand-image promotion. To a degree unknown in Britain, North Americans are voting from their first school-days onwards – from whether to permit gum-chewing in the playground to the class-mate most likely to succeed. In this climate attitude assessment assumes great importance and it was thus around this, above all, that US experimental Social Psychology crystallised in the 1930s. The specifically American context provided both the setting and rationale for the exploration of attitudes (indeed it yielded the very notion of 'attitudes' in its current Psychological sense as K. Danziger, 1997, explains) and all that comprises – measurement, how to change them, their motivational roots and structure. This is, in principle, ideologically neutral – anyone can use knowledge of attitude change techniques. Few shared French worries about the security of existing political institutions, national morale, and unruly mobs regressing to primitive bestiality and threatening civilisation. Rioting may happen of course, indeed it does, but is no longer construed in a degenerationist framework (I have identified only one pre-1940 US book on the crowd, Everett D. Martin (1920) which barely mentions Le Bon). For a Le Bon measuring people's attitudes would have seemed unimportant – by using 'crowd psychology' effectively rulers can instil whatever attitudes they want. Even if covertly, there is then an implicit ideological assumption in US Social Psychology's concern with attitudes: a belief in collective democratic procedures of decision-making as against, say, belief in a class of natural leaders obedience to whom is the natural order of things.

Britain and the United States in the 1960s

British Social Psychology only emerged as a distinct sub-discipline after the Second World War. While this largely reflected the importation of American methods and concerns, there were some distinctive features of British Social Psychology at this time. Firstly, British workers on the Social Psychology–Sociology borderline, such as Basil Bernstein in his studies of language (Bernstein, 1971, see Chapter 19), took social class far more seriously than their American counterparts and treated social class as a cultural as well as economic variable. While this may actually also be true of the US, cultural differences between British social classes were far more evident, being both longer established and sustained by lower levels of social mobility. While British social psychologists tended, ideologically, to be on the left in an oppositional role, in the US they tended, even if liberal, to support a prevailing egalitarian ideology in which the admission of fundamental social class differences was heretical. Secondly, the British initially did not always take that easily to the questionnaire-based research methodologies developed across the Atlantic. Some, like Michael Argyle, much preferred a more discreet observational style (although US psychologists also deployed observational techniques). This lent itself to the study of topics like interpersonal distance and non-verbal communication (see Argyle, 2001 for an interesting account of this phase). Thirdly, the long-standing nativist strand in British Psychological thought made some in the field more receptive to ideas from ethology than their transatlantic colleagues. As discussed in Chapter 15, this work had considerable impact during the 1960s. British social psychologists also came to address issues of group identity and inter-group conflict in a way that diverged significantly from transatlantic work on the same topics, this trend being particularly associated with Henri Tajfel's efforts to promote a European Social Psychology distinct from the American one. In France, Serge Moscovici (known for his theory of 'social representations') was also striking out in a direction separate from that of the individualist US experimental social psychologists. By and large, however, these factors did not entirely differentiate the British and US traditions, the former really representing a regional variant on the latter.

Post-war US Social Psychology revolved around a number of key themes: the complex of issues related to authoritarianism, conformity and prejudice; small group dynamics and the nature of 'leadership'; the broader area of attitudes; communication and media, and, on the Sociology borderline, the area known as 'role theory'. Only a few can be sketched here.

As discussed in Chapter 22, following the Holocaust psychologists were naturally preoccupied with trying to understand how Nazism arose and operated. Thereafter, a substantial sector of American Social Psychology became even more closely engaged with contemporary events, a move greatly stimulated by the presence of members of the exiled German 'Frankfurt School' and their associates (including Max Horkheimer, Theodore Adorno, Henri Marcuse and Erich Fromm). While Adorno *et al*'s *Authoritarian Personality* (1950) dealt primarily with anti-Semitism and identifying a distinct authoritarian personality type, priorities rapidly shifted as the Civil Rights movement grew and the African American's plight took centre stage. In this context Social Psychology effectively became part of the intellectual wing of the Civil Rights movement. Since the 1930s social psychologists had come to view 'prejudice' as a form of psychopathology and proposed linkages between prejudice and other negative personality attributes. In doing so they were, ironically, really adopting a tactic akin to Le Bon's even if from a diametrically opposite direction. Opponents of Civil Rights were not simply espousing a different opinion, they were people whom we could 'objectively' and 'scientifically' demonstrate had something wrong with them. (Le Bon's crowds and 'red' internationalist revolutionaries were similarly displaying a pathology, regressing to primitive evolutionary levels or unable to connect with the national or race soul.) This is not a criticism; the lesson is that issues such as 'prejudice' simply *cannot* be addressed from a neutral position – your very language will be loaded with evaluative meanings, while almost certainly your underlying motivation will be to some degree ideological. The temptation to objectify or naturalise ideological positions or values is endemic to 'social science'.

Among the attitude theorists one of the most stimulating was Leon Festinger whose 'cognitive dissonance theory' in effect married Cognitive Psychology to Freudian notions of 'rationalisation'. This had the appeal of coming to occasionally counter-intuitive conclusions, for example people read advertisements more *after* purchasing the product than before. He identified numerous 'dissonance reducing strategies' used to resolve cognitive dissonance, a situation arising when one cognitive element (e.g. I am a good mountaineer) implies the opposite of another (e.g. I just fell from a 3-foot ladder). This yielded an exhaustive elaboration of the rationalisations we use in such situations. As a scientific theory in the orthodox sense it was flawed, perhaps, in that it could account for any outcome (although Festinger and his associates undertook much empirical research). One of the best-known studies was of a sect which believed the end of the world was due on a certain date (L. Festinger *et al*, 1956). Taking advantage of this the sect's career was traced up to, including, and following the fateful day. The dissonance involved – 'I believed the end of the world was coming yesterday' and 'It didn't' – could hardly be greater. It was found that sect members unable to be with the others on the day in question quickly defected, whereas the rest became more evangelical and outgoing (having previously been an inward looking group) in the aftermath of the failed prophecy. Their faith had been tested and not found wanting, thereby averting God's apocalyptic wrath.

The study of language expanded rapidly in the post-war years, stimulated by the rise of Cognitive Psychology (see also Chapter 19). Roger Brown, Jerome Bruner and Charles Osgood published numerous works on its social psychological aspects: Brown (1958), Bruner *et al* (1966) and Osgood *et al* (1957) being among the most important. Studies of primate language acquisition were one strand in this. This American work was rather different from Bernstein's research on social class differences in language, concentrating on its developmental aspects and the nature of 'meaning'.

Another research area which briefly flourished between 1953 and 1961 was 'achievement motivation', or 'n.Ach.' ('need for Achievement'), a concept initially introduced by the personality theorist Henry Murray. David McClelland and his associates attempted to develop this into a major social psychological variable, believing that achievement motivation levels in different cultures and societies could be measured and compared. Again, the economic circumstances and Cold War climate of the 1950s obviously provided a favourable background. This was even truer of the large body of group dynamics and leadership research, primarily funded by either the United States Office of Naval Research or the United States Air Force, as well as the Rockefeller Foundation and Carnegie Corporation. Much of this was brought together in D. Cartwright and A. Zander (1953), which remains invaluable in providing a picture of the state of play in this field in the mid-1950s. (As discussed in the next chapter, the group behaviour strand had its origins in the aftermath of the Hawthorne Experiments, a major pre-war episode in Industrial Psychology.)

As the Vietnam War took its toll during the 1960s US Social Psychology became deeply embroiled – many in the discipline opposed the war, while others joined the military's 'psy ops' (psychological warfare) programme. Anti-war activists eagerly applied Psychological concepts and theories to government policies: authoritarianism, scapegoating, inappropriate cognitive dissonance reduction strategies, displaced aggression, etc. could all be unmasked. Together with continued involvement in the intensifying Civil Rights struggle, by the end of the 1960s this was pushing sections of American Social Psychology into a more oppositional role vis-à-vis official policies on both foreign and domestic issues. Precisely because Social Psychologists had raised so many irrational social processes to conscious awareness, collusion with their continued operation in public life became more difficult.

In the early 1970s, however, Social Psychology entered a period of crisis. Two decades of increasingly sophisticated and reflective thinking about social behaviour finally yielded a growing suspicion that an objective, scientific, 'neutral' view of social psychological phenomena was unattainable. At this point, with growing pressure from feminists, nonwhites and gays, Kenneth Gergen (1973) began to argue for a more up-front acknowledgement of the historical nature of the subject. By the mid-1970s much of the classic attitude literature was looking quite inadequate. Some, like Gergen, pushed for a thoroughly 'social constructionist' re-orientation of the subdiscipline, while others, adopting more complex approaches such as attribution theory, strove to recoup the situation by allying themselves with Cognitive Psychology.

Its immediate socio-political setting was not the only reason why post-war US Social Psychology expanded and developed as rapidly – and in the directions – it did. It had also, as has been indicated, attracted eminent exiled European psychologists, often unable to find positions in the discipline's more central areas. In some respects, therefore, it was a subdiscipline of a perhaps unusually high intellectual calibre. Submitting the issues vexing their host society to an outsider's gaze, these immigrants adopted an increasingly critical stance. For the Gestalt psychologists (notably Kurt Lewin, mentioned in Chapter 6) the emergence within the 'field' of social forces of social psychological phenomena irreducible to individual-level analysis was an obvious theoretical assumption, while the Frankfurt School exiles were deeply influenced by Marxist socio-economic theory. In Britain in the meantime, with a closer exposure to contemporary developments in European thought, the move towards a constructionist position was possibly more easily achieved, aided by the sociologically conscious character of British Social Psychological thought. On the other hand, European (including British) Social Psychology never achieved the cultural prominence it enjoyed in the US between 1950 and 1970.

Because Social Psychology is especially closely embedded in the concerns and priorities of its host societies, this does not mean that insights are not transferable – although sometimes they may not be. It does mean that being aware of this embeddedness, Social Psychologists now find themselves in a rather uncomfortable position, half inside, half 'objective observers' of, the contemporary social world which they study. Few now would be as happy as Le Bon to ally themselves uninhibitedly with established agencies of social power. On the other hand, few desire permanent outsidership, even those now explicitly identifying themselves as 'critical social psychologists'. In practice, one suspects, many contemporary social psychologists prefer focusing on specific micro-level problems (e.g. public perception of disabilities) where they can effectively work for change, to open ideological confrontation and grand theorising. Others, meanwhile, are further developing the constructionist approach by looking at some of the traditional topics of experimental Psychology, like memory (see Chapter 10), and how far they have a transpersonal social dimension which must be addressed (D. Middleton and D. Edwards, 1990; I. Parker and J. Shotter, 1990). Theoretically the field has now become fairly clearly polarised between the constructionists and the cognitivist heirs to the experimental tradition. Ironically the 'social constructionism' versus 'positivism' controversy is now at its most intense (well, would be if either side were still talking to the other!) in the very sub-discipline which is concerned with the social aspect of psychology. Perhaps this is because it is here that traditionalists have the most to lose. Certainly in many other branches of Psychology the constructionists are getting a far more sympathetic hearing.

Further reading

Allport, G.W. (1954) 'The Historical Background of Modern Social Psychology'. In G. Lindzey (ed.) *Handbook of Social Psychology Volume 1: Theory and Method.* Reading, MA & London: Addison Wesley. Useful but has since been criticised by writers such as C.F. Graumann (see below).

Farr, R. (1996) *The Roots of Modern Social Psychology.* Oxford: Basil Blackwell. Particularly good on G.H. Mead and the significance of C. Murchison's *Handbook* (see below).

Graumann, C.F. (1988, rep. 1989) 'Introduction to a History of Social Psychology'. In M. Hewstone, W. Stroebe, J.-P. Codol and G.M. Stephenson (eds) *Introduction to Social Psychology: A European Perspective.* Oxford: Basil Blackwell, Chapter 1.

Karpf, F.B. (1932, rep. 1972) *American Social Psychology: Its Origins, Development, and European Background.* New York: Russell & Russell. A comprehensive study of the earlier phase.

Lubek, I., Minton, H.L. and Apfelbaum, E. (eds) (1992) 'Social Psychology and its History'. Special issue of *Canadian Journal of Psychology* 33 (3): 521–661. Papers on various aspects of the topic.

Pandora, K. (1997) *Rebels within the Ranks: Psychologists' Critique of Scientific Authority and Democratic Realities in New Deal America.* Cambridge: Cambridge University Press. On the controversy between radical social psychologists and mainstream experimentalists during the 1930s.

Cited and additional references

Adorno, T.W., Frenkl-Brunswik, E., Levinson, D.J. and Sanford, R.N. (1950) *The Authoritarian Personality* (2 vols). New York: Science Editions. A classic text in which Frankfurt School neo-Marxist, psychoanalytic and American psychometric approaches were thoroughly interwoven (although the first, understandably, very discreetly!).

Argyle, M. (1967) *The Psychology of Interpersonal Behaviour*. Harmondsworth: Pelican.

Argyle, M. (2001) 'The Development of Social Psychology in Oxford'. In G.C. Bunn, A.D. Lovie and G.D. Richards (eds) *Psychology in Britain: Historical Essays and Personal Reflections*. Leicester & London: British Psychological Society and The Science Museum, 333–343. Nicely evokes the problems of post-1945 British Social Psychology.

Atkinson, J.W. (ed.) (1958) *Motives in Fantasy, Action, and Society*. Princeton: Van Nostrand.

Bernstein, B. (1971) *Class, Codes and Control*. London: Paladin.

Brown, R. (1958) *Words and Things*. New York: Free Press.

Brown, R. (1965) *Social Psychology*. New York: Free Press. One of the best 1960s textbooks, providing an excellent picture of contemporary concerns.

Bruner, J., Olver, R.H. Greenfield, P.M. *et al* (1966) *Studies in Cognitive Growth*. New York: Wiley.

Cartwright, D. and Zander, A. (eds) (1953) *Group Dynamics. Research and Theory*. Evanston IL: Row, Peterson; London (1954): Tavistock.

Dunlap, K. (1934) *Civilized Life: The Principles and Applications of Social Psychology*. Baltimore: Williams & Wilkins.

Ellwood, C.A. (1901) *Some Prolegomena to Social Psychology*. Chicago: Chicago University Press.

Festinger, L. (1957) *A Theory of Cognitive Dissonance*. New York: Row, Peterson.

Festinger, L., Riecken, Jr, H.W. and Schachter, S. (1956) *When Prophecy Fails*. University of Minnesota Press.

Freud, S. (1922; 1st German edn, 1921) *Group Psychology and the Analysis of the Ego*. London: Hogarth Press.

Gergen, K.J. (1973) 'Social Psychology as History'. *Journal of Personality and Social Psychology* 26: 309–320.

Ginsburg, M. (1921) *The Psychology of Society*. London: Methuen.

Graumann, C.F. and Moscovici, S. (eds) (1986) *Changing Conceptions of Crowd Mind and Behavior*. New York: Springer-Verlag.

Hartshorne, H., May, M.A. *et al* (1929–1930) *Studies in the Nature of Character*. New York: Macmillan.

LaPiere, R.T. and Farnsworth, P.R. (1949) *Social Psychology*, 3rd edn. New York: McGraw-Hill. Has an enormous bibliography.

LaPiere, R.T. (1934) 'Attitudes and Actions'. *Social Forces* 13: 230–237.

Le Bon, G. (1896) *The Crowd*. London: Fisher Unwin.

Martin, E.D. (1920) *The Behavior of Crowds: A Psychological Study*. New York: Harper.

McClelland, D.C. (1961) *The Achieving Society*. Princeton: Van Nostrand.

McClelland, D.C., Atkinson, J.W., Clark, R.A. and Lowell, E.L. (1953) *The Achievement Motive*. New York: Appleton-Century-Crofts.

McClelland, D.C. (ed.) (1955) *Studies in Motivation*. New York: Appleton-Century-Crofts.

McDougall, W. (1920) *The Group Mind.* New York & London: Putnam's.

Mead, G.H. (1934) *Mind, Self, and Society: From the Standpoint of a Social Behaviorist.* Chicago: Chicago University Press.

Mead, M. (1928) *Coming of Age in Samoa.* New York: Morrow.

Mead, M. (1930) *Growing up in New Guinea.* New York: Morrow.

Middleton, D. and Edwards, D. (1990) *Collective Remembering.* London: Sage.

Murchison, C. (ed.) (1935) *Handbook of Social Psychology.* Worcester MA: Clark University Press. A landmark text in the development of the field in the US.

Murray, H.A. (1938) *Explorations in Personality.* New York: Oxford University Press.

Nye, R.A. (1975) *The Origins of Crowd Psychology: Gustav Le Bon and the Crisis of Mass Democracy in the Third Republic.* London & Beverly Hills: Sage. The best account of Le Bon's work, character and career.

Osgood, C.E., Suci, G.C. and Tannenbaum, P.H. (1957) *The Measurement of Meaning.* Urbana, IL: University of Illinois Press.

Parker, I. and Shotter, J. (eds) (1990) *Deconstructing Social Psychology.* London: Routledge.

Pear, T.H. (1931) *Voice and Personality.* London: Chapman & Hall. Important pioneer British study on how personality was conveyed by the voice in radio broadcasts, inspired by the first American studies of mass communication. Pear, Professor of Psychology at Manchester University, was virtually the sole British pre-war social psychologist in the current sense.

Sherif, M. (1936) *The Psychology of Social Norms.* New York: Harper.

Tajfel, H. (1981) *Human Groups and Social Categories. Studies in Social Psychology.* Cambridge: Cambridge University Press.

Tarde, G. (1890, English trans. 1903) *The Laws of Imitation.* New York: Holt.

Triplett, N. (1897) 'The Dynamogenic Factors in Pacemaking and Competition'. *American Journal of Psychology* 9: 507–533. Often identified as the first Social Psychology experiment.

Ward, L. (1892) *Psychic Factors in Civilization.* Boston: Ginn & Co.

Williams, J.M. (1922) *Principles of Social Psychology.* New York: Knopf.

Chapter 13

Applied Psychology

- The nature of Applied Psychology
- Criminal Psychology: origins
- Criminal Psychology: major approaches
- Criminal Psychology: perennial themes
- Criminal Psychology: the critical perspective
- Industrial Psychology: origins and early expansion
- Industrial Psychology: The Hawthorne experiments
- Industrial Psychology: vicissitudes in Britain after 1945
- The tension underlying Applied Psychology

Quite misleadingly, 'Applied Psychology' implies a 'pure Psychology' the findings of which are then subsequently 'applied'. Psychology really arose as a discipline when society's needs to solve practical behavioural problems encountered the more abstract scientific and philosophical inquiries about the nature of the human mind (see N. Rose, 1985; Chapters 2 and 3 of this volume). The 'minds' presenting themselves to Psychology, at first those of children, criminals, the insane, the 'primitive' and the 'idiot', gradually extended to those of soldiers, factory workers, parents, the impoverished, the athlete and the 'consumer' (to list just some major categories). As this ever-extending remit established a major role for Psychology in twentieth-century life, the 'applied' always confronted the 'pure' with concrete issues and content, yielding new methods, concepts and hypotheses which 'pure' psychologists adopted (even 'motivation' – see K. Danziger, 1997, pp. 110–116); in D. Broadbent's words 'many problems which arose in the real world have been taken up by workers in the ivory tower, sometimes to the point where their origins have been forgotten' (Broadbent, 1971, p. 17). The boundary is in any case blurred: 'developmental Psychology' for instance, usually considered a sub-discipline of a 'pure' kind, is inextricably interwoven historically with the 'applied' fields of Educational Psychology and what used to be called 'subnormality'. Even 'perception' – a canonically 'pure' field – has been researched as much in 'applied' settings (like aviation) as within the 'pure' laboratory (see Chapter 8). 'Applied Psychology' is a field so diverse as to verge on granulation (see Table 13.1).

Table 13.1 Main fields of Applied Psychology

In rough chronological order of appearance

- *Educational* Strong 18th-century roots. Strong overlap with Developmental Psychology.
- *Criminal or Forensic* 18th-century roots, but primarily late 19th century.
- *Clinical* Lightner Witmer coined the term 'Clinical Psychology' in 1877 but its character has somewhat changed since, especially after the 1940s.
- *Industrial* First decade of 20th century.
- *Consumer and Psychology of advertising* First decade of 20th century.
- *Occupational or Vocational* Second decade of 20th century (but has some earlier roots).
- *Military* Second decade of 20th-century origins but emerges in the 1920s and 1930s as a distinct field.
- *Economic Psychology* Not a strong area, but began receiving attention in the 1950s.
- *Ergonomics* Earlier 20th-century roots but emerged as a sub-discipline in the 1950s (the word was coined in Britain in 1949).
- *Sport* Occasionally appears from 1920s on but became a major field during the 1970s.
- *Health* Although some psychosomatic aspects of health have long received attention this established itself as a major field during the 1970s and attracted increased attention during the 1980s.

The term 'Applied Psychology' is now used primarily for those in bold, the others being considered as distinct sub-disciplines.

In this chapter we will consider the history and character of only two fields: Criminal Psychology and Industrial Psychology (even so excluding the Vocational or Occupational branch of this), ignoring Military (but see Chapter 22), Sport and Health Psychologies, ergonomics and much else. Educational and Clinical Psychology have in any case become separate sub-disciplines. Criminal (now usually 'Forensic') and Industrial Psychology are interesting not only because they have penetrated modern culture so deeply, but because their chequered histories bring underlying issues so clearly to light.

Criminal Psychology

Degenerationist origins

Criminal Psychology began in the context of late nineteenth-century degenerationism (Pick, 1982); the most famous (or notorious) pioneer was the Italian Cesare Lombroso, whose first major work *L'Uomo Delinquente* (The Delinquent Man) appeared in 1876. For Lombroso the criminal physically displayed distinctive atavistic 'stigmata' signifying innate degeneracy such as a greater tendency to asymmetric features, lack of earlobes and, among women, greater hairiness and warts. Francis Galton (1883) also tried identifying criminal types physiognomically using composite photographs. Meanwhile, in America, a succession of degenerationist writers claimed to trace the inheritance of criminal and other degenerate behaviour across the generations of single families, starting with J.M. Friend's *The Chester Family* (1869) and, to more effect, R.L. Dugdale's *'The Jukes': A Study in Crime, Pauperism, Disease and Heredity* (1877). The last, and most influential, was H.H. Goddard's report on the 'Kallikak Family' (a pseudonym combining the Greek terms for good and bad) (Goddard, 1912) which purportedly tracked two lines of descent from a common male ancestor, one from an early liaison with a 'degenerate' woman, the other from his later respectable marriage (see L. Zenderland, 1998). Even during this phase degenerationism did not entirely monopolise the scene; H. Munsterberg's 1909 *Psychology on the Witness Stand*, for example, was already concerned with such things as the effects of 'suggestion' in the courtroom and eye-witness testimony, topics rarely pursued much further for many decades.

Major approaches

Other lines of attack largely supplanted degenerationism during the early 1920s. A distinct psychoanalytic tradition, dating in Britain from at least 1923 (J.C. Goodwin, 1923), remained influential for several decades (e.g. K. Friedlander, 1947), continued thereafter as one theoretical strand among many. The 1920s saw another theme gaining prominence: juvenile delinquency (B.B. Lindsey and W. Evans, 1925 being an early American example; see A. Platt 1977 for the origins of the concept). This provided Cyril Burt with the topic of his most successful book, *The Young Delinquent* (1925, reprintings of the last edition continuing until 1969).

Somewhat eclectic, this authoritatively combined psychometrics with a moderate hereditarianism and included hosts of statistical tables. In America, W.H. Sheldon and the Gluecks applied Sheldon's 'somatotype' based personality theory (see Chapter 11) to the topic (W.H. Sheldon, E.M. Hartl and E. McDermott, 1949; S. Glueck and E. Glueck, 1956) while others explored more sociological orientations (e.g. J.H. Bagot, 1941; J.B. Mays, 1954). In the US physician Frederic Wertham campaigned against the cultural causes of delinquency in several books, most famously *Seduction of the Innocent* (1955) about horror comics. Works relating delinquency to mental health also become commonplace (L. Grimberg, 1928; L. Bovet, 1951; J.D.W. Pearce, 1952).

The ultimately Lombrosan quest for distinct criminal types or personalities revived in the 1960s after a fairly brief phase during which social psychological and sociological accounts had dominated (e.g. D. Matza, 1964). A major figure in this was H.J. Eysenck (especially H.J. Eysenck, 1964, 2nd edn 1977; H.J. Eysenck and G.H. Gudjonsson, 1989). Eysenck postulates two major dimensions of personality variation, extraversion and neuroticism, each largely genetically determined and reflecting conditionability/base level of arousal and emotionality respectively. Since extraverts resist conditioning and require high levels of stimulation to arouse them, and because neurotics are emotional and unstable, extraverted neurotics naturally emerged as the most likely to become criminals under appropriate environmental and social circumstances. High psychoticism (his third, less rigorously theorised, dimension) was also implicated in certain types of 'psychopathic' crime. Others reached analogous conclusions using different personality scales, identifying a 'low self control' personality type with high impulsivity and low verbal skills.

General Psychological interest in crime, however, soon dramatically expanded beyond this, a new field named 'Forensic Psychology' achieving recognition in the 1990s. Topics tackled have now broadened to include a wider range of offences (e.g. driving offences, hostage-taking and child sexual abuse), the legal process itself (e.g. witness reliability, psychological aspects of policing and treatment of offenders) and factors related to the likelihood of falling a victim to crime. The methods used have become correspondingly diverse.

One theme weaving throughout all this is a tension between focusing on social factors or on the criminal's psychological character. Ascribing criminality to the personality of the criminal is, we should note, an implicitly pessimistic position, implying (especially when genetic factors are stressed) that rehabilitation measures are unlikely to succeed since criminal behaviour is an expression of an enduring 'criminal personality'. S. Maruna (2000) explores a major difficulty with this. Personality traits are, by definition, permanent, but the majority of crime is committed by young males in their late teens and early twenties, only a small minority offending thereafter. How then can trait explanations account for such typical 'desistence'? Maruna's move is to adopt a more 'three dimensional' narrativist approach to personality, taking changing circumstances, life-course and shifting narratives of self-identity into account, and enabling us to understand 'specific individuals in full social and developmental context'. This nonetheless maintains the assumption that the psychologist should focus on the individual criminal, and that the primary source of criminality is the individual psyche.

A related theme is the pathologisation of criminality, a recurrent topic since the later Victorian period when concerns about insanity pleas and crimes committed under hypnosis were widespread (e.g. H. Maudsley, 1892) and terms like 'kleptomania' and 'pyromania' were coined (the creation of such terms has attracted some attention from Foucaultian historians of late-Victorian psychiatric practice). This is an intriguingly ambiguous issue. That a given 'criminal' is highly disturbed or somehow mentally afflicted, needing treatment not punishment, is frequently indisputable. Yet, conversely, pathologising criminality can seem like the thin end of a very sinister wedge – dehumanising the criminal (and then other deviants as well perhaps) by denying their full rationality. Its medicalisation also implies that 'crime' is a 'natural' category, that what constitutes criminality is (like disease) self-evident. In reality it is defined quite explicitly by human laws, inconstant across time and place. Drinking alcohol was criminal in 1920s America, whereas teenage curfew-violation was unknown in twentieth-century Britain simply because no curfew laws existed (thus causing great difficulties for comparing 'delinquency' rates!). Male homosexuality was criminal in Britain until the 1960s. Even with offences like murder or robbery, which are nearly universally recognised, there are major variations in how seriously they are viewed (e.g. killing an unfaithful spouse may be condoned). And what of 'blasphemy'? For atheists such a crime cannot even exist. White-collar financial crimes such as embezzlement and fraud are, of course, rarely considered symptoms of mental illness.

The critical perspective

Bearing all this in mind, what is glaringly apparent to the historian is that contemporary Psychological texts (e.g. P.B. Ainsworth, 2000; C.R. Bartol, 1999; R. Blackburn, 1994) still generally fail to address the issues raised by revisionist cultural historians (especially M. Foucault, 1977) and radical sociologists (e.g. S. Cohen, 1985) regarding the broader cultural character of punishment and control, even if frequently raising matters, like 'medicalisation of criminality' and 'variability of what counts as crime', which point in this direction. It was Foucault who first highlighted the significance of the profound shift, around 1800, from punishment as an intimidating display of physical humiliation advertising the ruler's power, to punishment as a 'rational' technique of psychological control and 'disciplining' retargetting 'discipline' from the body to the mind, albeit by physical means. This move is exemplified by the immensely influential English utilitarian philosopher Jeremy Bentham's advocacy of the 'Panopticon' – an ideal prison design (subsequently realised in a few places) in which all inmates were constantly surveyed from a central tower. The shadow of the Panopticon hovers over all subsequent approaches to criminality in western societies. Thus viewed, Psychology has always been participating in the further evolution of techniques of psychological control and power, however ostensibly 'humane' particular methods and goals might appear to be. Criminal Psychology is thereby bound up with the wider, highly fraught, issue of how 'deviance' is created, defined and treated in modern societies. This is not to imply that critical contributors to the debate are 'pro-crime' but it does raise the question, rarely present in Psychological discourse, of whether any approach to it can be truly non-ideological. An underlying thrust of much of the more critical analysis is really that focusing on the offender's criminality obscures or masks the greater criminalities and inhumanities of the existing social order, which in some way *requires* the existence of such criminals in order to make its power visible and give it a purpose and justification.

Even now, such disturbing ruminations rarely perturb psychologists, who typically remain content to accept as 'natural' the social orders within which they dwell, although often striving for 'humanitarian' amelioration and reform. Much of what psychologists have said about the 'criminal personality' has, moreover, reinforced the view that criminality simply originates within pathological personalities. Even if involving social factors, the problem has no *fundamental* implications for the wider social system, notwithstanding platitudinous laments about the deleterious effects of poverty. Criminals are 'badness' visible, providing a point of moral consensus for an otherwise ideologically variegated population. As S. Cohen (1985) explores in detail, there is a crucial linguistic dimension to the whole business. Psychology, along with other disciplines and professions, has supplied numerous euphemisms, jargon and 'technobabble' which distances controllers from the nature of their own actions and those with whom they deal. Physical punishment can become 'aversive conditioning', incarceration becomes 'placement', emotional distress reduced to 'acting out'. Such concerns still rarely surface in mainstream Criminal Psychology. Even in a sophisticated text such as D. Canter and L. Alison (ed.) (2000), *The Social Psychology of Crime: Groups, Teams and Networks*, in which cultural anthropological and narrativist perspectives are represented, 'criminality' as such is treated as an unproblematic category. Psychology's 'place' as a discipline servicing society's needs on its own terms, rather than a position from which the psychological nature of 'criminality' can be addressed as it were *ab initio*, has hardly ever been challenged. This contrasts markedly with the extensive literature from cultural history and sociology of crime which has accumulated since the 1960s.

Unfortunately such viewpoints can easily be caricatured as 'soft' or morally 'relativistic', despite being usually driven by a fairly 'hard' liberationist ethic of their own. Nobody denies that a small minority of crimes are abhorrent by anyone's standards (e.g. sexual murders of children), or that there are necessarily limits on the social tolerability of behaviour. What is at stake is something rather deeper than this, a fear of the dystopian all-powerful dehumanising 'system', the ghost of the 'Panopticon'. We are haunted by such classic twentieth-century nightmares as Franz Kafka's *The Trial*, George Orwell's *1984*, and Anthony Burgess's *A Clockwork Orange* and have witnessed, in reality, the vulnerability of ideological and sexual 'deviance', intellectual nonconformity and political dissent, to criminalisation and pathologisation. Ongoing technological developments hardly mitigate such anxieties about social regimes of total surveillance. The extension of these regimes, in a slow, piecemeal fashion, can all too easily be rationalised by invoking the twin eternal 'fights' against illness and crime (which, as we have seen, are not entirely distinct). It is in failing to take this anxiety seriously, I think, that modern Criminal Psychology has erred most seriously.

The criticism bears less clearly on some of the issues more recently added to the agenda, and the tenor of current textbooks (e.g. P.B. Ainsworth, 2000) is certainly far more cautionary and up-front about the difficulties of providing adequate Psychological theories of criminality than that of more optimistic and gung-ho mid-twentieth-century texts. Somewhat surprisingly for a field which is among the oldest strands within Psychology, the mood among current researchers is almost one of pioneering excitement. Hopefully, in this more flexible and open-minded climate, critical voices may be heard with greater respect.

Industrial Psychology

Origins

Industrial Psychology's roots go back at least as far as the Italian A. Mosso's late nineteenth-century studies of fatigue, a topic further pursued by W.H.R. Rivers and William McDougall in the decade after 1900 (Rivers, 1908). Simultaneously a rather different development took place in the US: F.W. Taylor's 'efficiency engineering' approach to workplace organisation and performance, soon known as 'Taylorism' (Taylor, 1911; F. and L. Gilbreth, 1916). This aimed to maximise production by identifying the most efficient physical movements and layout for performing manual operations ('time and motion study'). Advertising, incidentally, was first addressed in a serious Psychological fashion by W.D. Scott in 1908. Hugo Munsterberg's *Psychology and Industrial Efficiency* (1913), is generally taken to inaugurate US Industrial Psychology in the more conventional sense. Germany had an Institute for Applied Psychology as early as 1906 and an Institute for Vocational Psychology in 1916, these merging in 1919 into the Psychotechnical Laboratories at Charlottenberg, near Berlin. Many other major German cities soon had similar 'Psychotechnical' research units. Fatigue continued as a major British concern, especially during World War One, the work of the Health of Munitions Workers Committee leading to the creation of the Industrial Fatigue Research Board (IFRB) under Charles Sherrington. In 1918 an Australian, Bernard Muscio (a former student of Myers), published a lecture series that effectively launched Industrial Psychology in Britain – *Lectures on Industrial Psychology*. Eminent British psychologist Charles Myers was deeply impressed, but so too was H.J. Welch, a director of the manufacturing company Harrisons and Crosfield. Events moved rapidly towards the founding of the National Institute for Industrial Psychology (NIIP) in 1920 under Myers' leadership, with Welch as initial financial backer – others, including the Carnegie Trust, soon following. Its 25-strong Scientific Committee was a virtual roll-call of major British psychologists from F.C. Bartlett to C.W. Valentine (and included Muscio). The IFRB, however, was in decline, being absorbed by the Medical Research Council (MRC) with severely reduced funding and retitled the Industrial Health Research Board (IHRB). Many members switched to the NIIP. In the US the Psychological Corporation was established in 1922 with similar aims and the veteran James McKeen Cattell as President plus an equally impressive list of members – G.S. Hall, J.B. Watson, W. McDougall, L.M. Terman and E.L. Thorndike among them.

The post-World War One years had in fact witnessed an enthusiastic international explosion of interest in the relevance of Psychology to industry and commerce. By the mid-1920s organisations of various types existed from the new Soviet Union to Australia, from Spain to Japan. International Conferences were held (in Barcelona, Milan and Berlin for example), while university courses and university-based research programmes were widely initiated. This reflected a general post-war climate in which repairing the destruction and building a saner, 'scientific', future were overriding concerns for workers, employers, scientists and politicians alike. The 'Taylorism' school was now cast as dehumanising, turning workers into machines, subordinating everything to maximisation of production regardless of the human cost (C.S. Myers, 1923; F. Watts, 1921). The NIIP, by contrast, aimed to promote 'the mental and bodily health and efficiency of every grade of worker'. The NIIP and Charlottenberg group could now enlist support from both sides of industry, trade unions and employers. Research was seen as comprising two strands: one ('technical') seeking to enhance worker efficiency, reduce fatigue and improve training and personnel selection, the other involving social and ethical studies of worker–management relations, group organisation, communication and participation. Industrial Psychology's task was not, for the Europeans, to help employers exploit their workers better, but to design work environments and practices in which all parties' interests were harmoniously met.

What though were industrial psychologists actually up to during the 1920s? The first volumes of the NIIP's journal *Industrial Psychology* (which appeared from 1922 onwards) give an impression of almost manic activity. There are commercially commissioned investigations (often surprisingly interesting) on such topics as packing chocolates, making tin boxes, and breakages in the catering industry, as well as the timing of work-breaks and payment arrangements (see Fig. 13.1). Greatly improved output and reduction of fatigue often reportedly ensued from relatively simple changes in work-bench design and layout, or placement of the materials. Especially where workers were on piece-rates this met everyone's satisfaction. Broader environmental factors (illumination, humidity and temperature) were also tackled while laboratory-based research into fatigue and other physiological aspects of work performance continued, often within university settings. Personnel selection and vocational guidance attracted people such as Cyril Burt and Winifred Raphael, who devised aptitude tests to assess specific skills (such as wiring, dress-making and packing) and questionnaires to identify suitable careers for impending school-leavers. C. Spearman designed vocational tests for the military and Civil Service. Finally, training courses and lectures were variously offered to would-be industrial psychologists, workers, managers and employers. (Advertising and design received some attention but were minor themes for the NIIP itself, market research being later explicitly excluded.) Despite variations in approach and weighting of different topics, such diversity typified Industrial Psychology wherever it was being practised at this time.

These 1920s developments represented Psychology's break-out from the clinic and school, as a coterie of highly-driven Psychologists established a permanent beach-head for their hitherto somewhat obscure discipline at the heart of industrial and commercial life, harbingers of a new scientific and technological culture which would remould society and leave past horrors behind. C.S. Myers in particular was ideally placed as an ex-colonel with wide experience in applied military research (on submarine location as well as shell-shock) and a career dating

Figure 13.1 Early British Industrial Psychology: selection testing at Rowntrees Cocoa Works, early 1920s. Reproduced by permission of the Borthwick Institute of Historical Research, University of York.

back to the 1898 Torres Strait expedition, combined with personal wealth and knowledge of the business world. To view him as an ivory-towered academic would have been ludicrous. Something similar, if less impressively, held for many contemporary psychologists across Europe and North America. They already understood that they were not only applying knowledge gained by 'pure' scientific research but that work in applied settings reciprocally enhanced Psychological understanding. Laboratory fatigue differed from factory fatigue, laboratory learning from workplace learning, and the human mind in the laboratory from that on the assembly-line. Moreover, they had to forge a new professional identity for themselves acceptable to all parties, striking a balance between claims of expertise and denials of scientific omniscience. Selling their services as the start of an exciting new project, in which much remained unknown, they were able to manage this, casting other parties as collaborators and ensuring tolerance of their failures as the inevitable price of pioneership.

The Hawthorne experiments

America's more ruthlessly capitalist economic atmosphere, already reflected in Taylorism, also affected the character of the best-known episode in Industrial Psychology's history: the Hawthorne experiments (1927–1932), undertaken by members of Harvard University Graduate School of Business Administration and identified primarily with Elton Mayo. Widely-viewed as a historical fulcrum for Industrial Psychology, and controversial ever since F.J. Roethlisberger and W. Dickson's *Management and the Worker* (1939) reported the findings, this requires some attention. The research took place at the Western Electric Company's Hawthorne (Chicago) Plant, following an earlier study of illumination effects. It fell into three phases. The 'Relay Assembly Test Room' study of 'rest pause effects' tracked the output of a selected group (separated from other workers) across 11 different 'rest pause' regimes. The result, hailed as a scientific discovery and christened the 'Hawthorne Effect', was that output apparently increased regardless of conditions (although not smoothly or for all participants). Being a selected group receiving special attention sufficed to improve workers' morale and performance. The complexity of the variables underlying the 'dramatic and continuous changes in the total psychological climate of the test room' (H.A. Landsberger, 1958, p. 11) was hard to unravel, but attitudes 'obviously' played a key role. These were then explored in an interviewing programme of a deliberately non-directive kind (reminiscent of Rogerian counselling). This in turn revealed the importance of group, as well as individual, processes, leading to the final phase, an observational study of the 'Bank Wiring' room. This 'discovered' that the group established and informally enforced a group norm for output, thus countering managerially introduced incentives and stabilising the production rate. In 1932 the deteriorating economic situation of the Depression brought the project to a halt.

The significance of this episode is multifaceted. It is credited with initiating the 'human relations' approach to industrial problems and organisation (leading, for example, to the creation of the 'personnel manager' role), inspiring Elton Mayo's influential 1933–1947 trilogy (see Further reading: Industrial Psychology) in which 'human relations' becomes a virtual ideology – a way of re-establishing spontaneous social harmony and cooperation within industrial civilisation, and being one important factor behind the rise of Social Psychological studies of group dynamics during the 1940s and 1950s. It is, in short, seen as refocusing Industrial Psychology on issues like leadership, group influences and worker morale. But from the early 1940s sociologists also attacked the entire approach as ideological and blinkered (see also D. Bramel and R. Friend, 1981). It accepted management goals unquestioningly, manipulated the workers and ignored unions (in fact Hawthorne was not unionised at the time), while Mayo's vision of conflict-free harmony was covertly anti-individualistic and quasi-totalitarian. (This objection partly reflected a contemporary panic about 'conformity', a major theme in post-war Social Psychology.) Landsberger (1958), though sympathetic to these criticisms, tried to ring-fence *Management and the Worker* off from Mayo's work and his 'human relations' school. It was a book of data, not of 'doctrine', its tone was provisional, descriptive and apologetic, and clearly left the reader 'with the impression' that Hawthorne was 'a thoroughly unpleasant place at which to work . . . and that the authors knew it'

(p. 53). R. Gillespie (1988, 1992) has now authoritatively undermined Landsberger's case, however, by doing that often subversive thing – examining the archives. These reveal *Management and the Worker* as a retrospective compromise between several different kinds of pressure. Its version of events is often inconsistent with the archival data of correspondence and communication between the various managers, Harvard academics and company researchers involved. Far from a logically structured sequence of scientific discoveries – the 'Hawthorne effect', the role of worker attitudes, group norm-setting – the project was slowly shaped over time by competing ideological commitments, short-term practical considerations, and compromises between various viewpoints and interests. The data themselves were invariably ambiguous, their final interpretation but one among several possibilities. Even the 'discoveries' were mostly already implicit knowledge in the management world. Gillespie's work is an excellent example, with wider implications, of in-depth historical research disclosing how something publicly displayed as objective scientific discovery was gradually forged over time from the social, psychological and political transactions between, in this case, managers, workers, academic researchers and company employed researchers.

World War Two and after

Despite the Depression US Industrial Psychology consolidated itself during the 1930s (see M.S. Viteles, 1932). More remarkably, from 1933 onwards the German Nazi regime co-opted 'Psychotechnik' into the service of the German military, this *Wehrmachtpsychologie* focusing on selection and training of military personnel (U. Geuter, 1992). Ironically, for the nation credited with 'founding' Psychology, only now were Psychology degrees separate from Philosophy established in German universities. The number of psychologists expanded by leaps and bounds. But most significantly, *Wehrmachtpsychologie* was basically identical to the Industrial Psychology being done everywhere else – devising selection tests, effective training procedures and so on. Use of 'racial' criteria (so central to Nazi race doctrines) was rapidly dropped as useless. *Wehrmachtpsychologie* lasted until around 1944 when the military were glad to conscript anybody they could get and 'selection' became irrelevant.

Elsewhere World War Two greatly boosted the demand for industrial psychologists, particularly with regard to personnel selection, training, and equipment design – the 'man–machine interface'. Both in Britain and America the cutting edge lay in problems posed for perception, vigilance and motor skills by high-technology equipment and aviation (see Chapter 22), the matrix from which Cognitive Psychology itself emerged. The Cambridge Applied Psychology Unit (APU) and comparable American centres continued this work throughout the post-1945 Cold War period. Beyond the prestigious APU, however, a gulf now seems to have opened in Britain between applied and academic psychologists, the former being seen as of lower status, concerned with one-off problems of little theoretical importance (P. Warr, 1971). At the popular level J.A.C. Brown's constantly reprinted Pelican *The Social Psychology of Industry* (1954) was nonetheless an important factor in ensuring the field's continued visibility, while the NIIP also struggled on.

Only in the late 1960s did Industrial (now increasingly referred to as 'Occupational') and associated areas of Applied Psychology begin to recoup the situation, not least because the cognitivist 'humans as information processors' model was proving so highly applicable, while work on topics such as memorisability of telephone numbers and postcodes, underground signalling systems and machine-translation of languages enabled cognitivists to refine previously simple abstract models of processes such as selective attention (D. Broadbent, 1971).

Even so, British Industrial Psychology's fortunes were hampered by a somewhat chaotic funding situation and decline in institutional support. The IHRB, still under the aegis of the MRC, was disbanded in 1959, two major university research units closed in 1969 and 1970 (at University College London and the University of Liverpool) and the long-faltering NIIP formally died in 1975. Financially everything seemed to hinge on the MRC, for which Applied Psychology was but a peripheral concern. Despite this the University of Sheffield did establish an MRC Social and Applied Psychology Unit in 1968 (succeeded by the Institute of Work Psychology in 1996) (P. Warr, 1999). Only slowly were other funding councils able to supplement the MRC's input. The APU, long sustained by military-related funding, also continued largely unhampered, moving into new governmentally-funded topics like driving behaviour during the 1970s. (In 1998 this mutated into the MRC Cognition and Brain Sciences Unit.) Industrial Psychology in post-1950s Britain otherwise became a commercial, rather than academic, activity (e.g. management consultancy, market research).

The stories elsewhere obviously differed, but this excursion into organisational and funding detail draws attention to the problematic nature of Industrial Psychology's position in late twentieth-century British society. At the intersection of public and private sectors it was pressured from several directions: practitioners sought status and connections with academic Psychology (which in turn required its inputs), governmental funding agencies demanded research on topics often owing their salience to political or economic factors rather than their Psychological interest, while the private sector required confidential research on issues of commercial, but again not necessarily Psychological, significance. Even its ardent exponents concede that this compromised its scientific status (D. Duncan, 1999).

Galvanised into existence between c. 1910–1918, Industrial Psychology initially soared optimistically on a brief wave of widespread post-World War One enthusiasm for scientific, technological solutions to the massive post-war problems. After the 1930s came a further surge, in which 'human relations' rather than 'time and motion' became the order of the day (see M.S. Viteles, 1954), while the 'backroom boys' of World War Two immersed themselves in selection, training and psychological aspects of operating secret technologies vital to the war effort. In Britain this war-time work arguably salvaged and revitalised what had virtually become a stalled project due to general economic conditions (S. Shimmin and D. Wallis, 1994). The post-1960 period presents a less clearcut picture. The discipline had, it is true, achieved a permanent place in industrial and commercial practice, but the pioneering evangelical fervour had dissipated. It continued to be the target of occasional ideological suspicion and attack (e.g. W. Hollway, 1991), but was low on the radical target-list after 1970. In the 1920s it could be an aspect of any psychologist's work, but was now a separate profession with only one foot in academia. Presently the situation remains in flux as university Psychology departments seek kudos by establishing research units of various kinds. Among the most likely to succeed appear to be those attracting funding within the local community, which may conceivably lead to Industrial and related areas of Applied Psychology once more gaining a strong academic presence.

Conclusion

Most of the substantial points have been made already. Drawing things together, Applied Psychology is clearly a nodal point at which Psychological ideas and approaches enter the wider cultural arena, and at which the latter affects Psychology's own agendas and priorities. It is via its applied fields that Psychology has managed so successfully to penetrate modern economic and social life. But as we have seen, both Criminal and Industrial Psychology have involved Psychology in playing roles which can, and have, laid it open to criticism as representing a 'tool of the system'. Where valid, this fault is not simply ethical but undermines Psychology's ability adequately to explore and theorise issues, for doing so would involve contesting the terms in which 'the system' prefers to have them understood. The 'system' truly welcomes knowledge, but not the knowledge that it is truly wrong. This tension between using applied Psychology uncritically in the service of the status quo and using it more critically as a route for reform, or even more radical critiques, has never fully abated. As we have seen, Applied Psychological work has indeed variously served, reflected and criticised the systems in which it has been undertaken, and continues to do so.

Further reading: Criminal Psychology

Bartol, C.R. (1999) *Criminal Behavior: A Psychosocial Approach*, 5th edn. Upper Saddle River, NJ: Prentice Hall. A good overview of the current state of the field.

Blackburn, R. (1994) *The Psychology of Criminal Conduct: Theory, Research and Practice*. New York: John Wiley and Sons. A widely used and highly praised textbook.

Cohen, S. (1985) *Visions of Social Control: Crime, Punishment and Classification*. Cambridge: Polity Press in association with Oxford: Basil Blackwell. An excellent introduction to the deeper critical issues.

Foucault, M. (1977) *Discipline and Punish: The Birth of the Prison*. London: Allen Lane. Essential reading for those entering the historical debates on the cultural meanings of punishment etc.

Degenerationist and other early texts

Dugdale, R.L. (1877, 5th edn 1891) *'The Jukes': A Study in Crime, Pauperism, Disease and Heredity*. New York and London: Putnam's. The first really influential case-history of a 'degenerate' lineage.

Ellis, H. (1890) *The Criminal*. London: Walter Scott. A somewhat more sober overview of the topic.

Friend, J.M. (1869) *The Chester Family, or the Curse of the Drunkard's Appetite*. Boston: W. White. Apparently the earliest of the degenerationist family case-histories.

Galton, F. (1883, rep. 1919) *Inquiries into Human Faculty and its Development*. London: J.M. Dent. Includes his composite photographs of 'criminal types'.

Garofalo, R. (1885) *Criminology*. Naples: publisher unknown. By a member of the Lombroso school.

Goddard, H.H. (1912) *The Kallikak Family: A Study in the Heredity of Feeble-Mindedness*. New York: Macmillan. The last major case-study of a 'degenerate' lineage. Highly important, see L. Zenderland (1998) for the most authoritative analysis.

Goddard, H.H. (1915) *The Criminal Imbecile: An Analysis of Three Remarkable Murder Cases*. New York: Macmillan. Actually a fairly humane plea for courts to take 'feeble-mindedness' in account.

Lombroso, C. (1876) *L'Uomo Delinquente*. Milan: Torin. The classic and most influential degenerationist treatise on crime. Lombroso was the greatest exponent of degenerationist criminology.

Lombroso, C. and Ferrero, W. (1895) *The Female Offender*. London: T. Fisher Unwin.

Maudsley, H. (1892) *Responsibility in Mental Disease*, 5th edn. London: Kegan Paul, Trench & Trübner. For contemporary anxieties about the extent of criminal responsibility etc.

Munsterberg, H. (1909) *Psychology and Crime*. London: Fisher Unwin. Published in the US as *Psychology on the Witness Stand*. This has a surprisingly modern agenda, with chapters on witness testimony, untrue confessions, 'suggestion' in court and crime prevention.

Pick, D. (1982) *Faces of Degeneration: A European Disaster c. 1848–c. 1918*. Cambridge: Cambridge University Press. The best general history of the degenerationism episode.

Zenderland, L. (1998) *Measuring Minds. Herbert Henry Goddard and the Origins of American Intelligence Testing*. Cambridge: Cambridge University Press. Includes excellent discussion on the nature of late-nineteenth and early-twentieth century US degenerationism and Goddard's 'Kallikak' family.

Juvenile delinquency

Bagot, J.H. (1941) *Juvenile Delinquency. A Comparative Study of the Position in Liverpool and in Wales*. London: Jonathan Cape.

Bovet, L. (1951) *Psychiatric Aspects of Juvenile Delinquency*. Geneva: World Health Organisation.

Burt, C. (1925) *The Young Delinquent*. London: University of London Press.

Friedlander, K. (1947) *The Psycho-analytical Approach to Juvenile Delinquency. Theory: Case-Studies: Treatment*. London: Routledge & Kegan Paul.

Glueck, S. and Glueck, E. (1956) *Physique and Delinquency*. New York: Harper & Row.

Grimberg, L. (1928) *Emotion and Delinquency. A Clinical Study of 500 Criminals in the Making*. London: Kegan Paul, Trench and Trübner.

Lindsey, B.B. and Evans, W. (1925) *The Revolt of Modern Youth*. Garden City, New York: Garden City Publishers.

Matza, D. (1964) *Delinquency and Drift*. New York: John Wiley & Sons.

Mays, J.B. (1954) *Growing up in the City. A Study of Juvenile Delinquency in an Urban Neighbourhood*. Liverpool: Liverpool University Press.

Pearce, J.D.W. (1952) *Juvenile Delinquency. A Short Text-book of the Medical Aspects of Juvenile Delinquency*. London: Cassell.

Platt, A. (1977) *The Child Savers: The Invention of Delinquency*, 2nd edn. Chicago: Chicago University Press. Best historical account currently available.

Sheldon, W.H., Hartl, E.M. and McDermott, E. (1949) *Varieties of Delinquent Youth: An Introduction to Constitutional Psychiatry*. New York: Harper.

Wertham, F. (1955) *Seduction of the Innocent*. London: Museum Press. In its time a controversial and highly publicised exposé of the effect of 'horror comics' on American youth.

Recent and general

Ainsworth, P.B. (2000) *Psychology and Crime. Myths and Reality*. London: Longman. An accessible and brief British overview.

Canter, D. and Alison, L. (eds) (2000) *The Social Psychology of Crime: Groups, Teams and Networks*. Dartmouth: Ashgate. Incorporates cultural anthropological and narrativist papers etc. in addition to more conventional approaches.

Eysenck, H.J. (1964, 2nd edn 1977) *Crime and Personality*. London: Routledge & Kegan Paul.

Eysenck, H.J. and Gudjonsson, G.H. (1989) *The Causes and Cures of Criminality*. New York: Plenum. The classic expositions of Eysenck's theory of criminal personality.

Maruna, S. (2000) 'Criminology, Desistance and the Psychology of the Stranger'. In D. Canter and L. Alison (eds) *The Social Psychology of Crime. Groups, Teams and Networks*. Dartmouth: Ashgate, 287–320. Effectively critiques the psychometric 'criminal personality' approach.

Further reading: Industrial Psychology

Shimmin, S. and Wallis, D. (1994) *Fifty Years of Occupational Psychology in Britain*. Leicester: British Psychological Society. A well researched and sometimes personal account by two veterans of the field. Includes general coverage of pre-1950 Industrial Psychology. I am unaware of an equivalent general text for the US.

British school

Broadbent, D. (1971) 'Relation between Theory and Application in Psychology'. In P. Warr (ed.) *Psychology at Work*. Harmondsworth: Pelican, 15–30.

Duncan, D. (1999) 'The Philosophy of the National Institute of Industrial Psychology and Post-Modernist Psychology'. *History and Philosophy of Psychology* 1: 79–85. Based on personal experience, a robust defence of the NIIP against the attack by Hollway (1991) (see next).

Hollway, W. (1991) *Work Psychology and Organisational Behaviour*. London: Sage. Foucaultian attack on Industrial Psychology as an atheoretical, behaviourist, and anti-women failure.

Muscio, B. (1918, revised edn 1920) *Lectures on Industrial Psychology*. London: Routledge/New York: Dutton. Really initiated the field formally in Britain.

Myers, C.S. (1923) 'The Efficiency Engineer and the Industrial Psychologist'. *Industrial Psychology* I (5) 168–172. Myers' attack on Taylorism.

Rivers, W.H.R. (1908) *The Influence of Alcohol and other Drugs on Fatigue. The Croonian Lectures delivered at the Royal College of Physicians in 1906*. London: Edward Arnold.

Smith, M. (1943) *An Introduction to Industrial Psychology*. London: Cassell.

Vernon, H.M. (1921) *Industrial Fatigue and Efficiency*. London: Routledge.

Warr, P. (ed.) (1971) *Psychology at Work*. Harmondsworth: Pelican.

Warr, P. (1999) *Work, Well-being and Effectiveness. A History of the MRC/ESRC Social and Applied Psychology Unit*. Sheffield: Sheffield University Press.

Watts, F. (1921) *An Introduction to the Psychological Problems of Industry*. London: Allen & Unwin.

Welch, H. and Miles, G.H. (1935) *Industrial Psychology in Practice*. London: Pitman.

American school

Bramel, D. and Friend, R. (1981) 'Hawthorne, the Myth of the Docile Worker and Class Bias in American Psychology'. *American Psychologist* 36: 867–878.

Gilbreth, F.B. and Gilbreth, L.M. (1916, 2nd edn 1919) *Fatigue Study. The Elimination of Humanity's Greatest Unnecessary Waste. A First Step in Motion Study*. London: Routledge.

Gillespie, R. (1988) 'The Hawthorne Experiments and the Politics of Experimentation'. In J.G. Morawski (ed.) *The Rise of Experimentation in American Psychology*. New Haven: Yale University Press, 114–137.

Gillespie, R. (1992) *Manufacturing Knowledge: A History of the Hawthorne Experiments*. Cambridge: Cambridge University Press. Thoroughgoing critical reappraisal of the Hawthorne experiments based on archival research, expanding on the points introduced in the 1988 paper.

Landsberger, H.A. (1958) *Hawthorne Revisited. Management and the Worker, Its Criticism and Developments in the Human Relations Industry*. Ithaca: Cornell University.

Mayo, E. (1933) *The Human Problems of an Industrial Civilisation*. New York: Macmillan.

Mayo, E. (1946, rep. 1949) *The Social Problems of an Industrial Civilisation*. London: Routledge & Kegan Paul.

Mayo, E. (1947) *The Political Problems of an Industrial Civilisation*. Boston: Harvard Graduate School of Business Administration.

Munsterberg, H. (1913) *Psychology and Industrial Efficiency*. Boston: Houghton-Mifflin. Generally seen as the founding text for Industrial Psychology in the US.

Roethlisberger, F.J. and Dickson, W. (1939) *Management and the Worker*. Harvard: Harvard University Press. Fullest report of the Hawthorne experiments.

Scott, W.D. (1908, 3rd edn 1912) *The Psychology of Advertising. A Simple Exposition of the Principles of Psychology in their Relation to Successful Advertising*. Boston: Small, Maynard & Co. First major Psychological work on advertising.

Taylor, F.W. (1911) *Principles of Scientific Management*. New York: Harper & Bros. Key text promoting 'Taylorism' in a quite evangelical fashion.

Viteles, M.S. (1932) *Industrial Psychology*. New York: Norton. Provides a good overview of the field as it had developed in America by the 1930s.

Viteles, M.S. (1954) *Motivation and Morale in Industry*. London: Staples Press. Well captures the impact of 'human relations' on the field.

Additional references

Danziger, K. (1997) *Naming the Mind. How Psychology found its Language*. London: Sage.

Geuter, U. (1992) *The Professionalization of Psychology in Nazi Germany*. Cambridge: Cambridge University Press.

Mosso, A. (1906) *Fatigue*. London: Swan Sonnenschein and New York: Putnam's.

Rose, N. (1985) *The Psychological Complex: Psychology, Politics and Society in England 1869–1939*. London: Routledge & Kegan Paul.

Part three

PSYCHOLOGY'S SUBJECTS

The next four chapters look at Psychology from the direction of some of those it has studied – its 'subjects': the mentally distressed, animals, children and women. (Its dealings with 'race' will be dealt with in Part Five.) More recently the term 'participant' has been increasingly used as replacement for 'subject', at least when dealing with humans, signifying a more egalitarian and cooperative relationship. Until the 1990s, however, 'subject' was almost always used and the power-relationship this implied remained unchallenged. The aim in this Part is to redirect attention away from, e.g. 'Developmental Psychology' itself towards the ways in which Psychology has related to and treated (in that case) children as such. This hopefully enables us to move towards a clearer picture of how Psychology, as a cultural institution, has reflected and influenced the way these subject groups are viewed and treated in modernist societies. Psychology's own theories thereby become, as it were, 'bracketed' in a way which enables us to see them as psychological phenomena in their own right. That is the intention anyway! The subject groups chosen more or less selected themselves: children have been prominent since Psychology's earliest days, as have the mentally distressed, while animals, as we will see, have a peculiarly profound psychological significance which Psychology has registered in various ways. Psychology's dealings with women (both as 'subjects' and psychologists) have, for their part, raised some of the most contentious and productive issues the discipline has faced over the last four decades.

Chapter 14

Psychology and the
meanings of madness

- Psychology's involvement with madness
- Historical perspectives and issues: attitudes towards and treatment of the insane
- Psychiatry and personality theory
- Anti-psychiatry in the 1960s and 1970s and its significance
- Psychoanalysis and related schools
- The endurance and impact of psychoanalysis
- What the case of psychoanalysis tells about the nature of Psychology

The images of psychologist, psychotherapist and psychiatrist have always been fused. Though annoying to psychologists this is not entirely unfounded since Psychology has long been intimately involved with psychopathology. Many of its concepts, theories and tests (especially those relating to personality) originated in this area, while Psychological theories have frequently been applied in therapeutic contexts. In this chapter I will first consider some of the questions raised by historical studies and the nature of Psychology's involvements with psychopathology and then turn specifically to Psychoanalysis.

Broadly speaking, Psychology's involvements may be identified as follows:

• Ideas about the nature of psychological processes often have their roots in clinical practice.
• Management of psychopathology presents psychologists with an important 'market' for their expertise (e.g. developing diagnostic techniques).
• The clinic often provides a testing ground for the application of psychological theories and models (e.g. behaviour therapy derived from learning theory).
• Psychopathology often supplies psychologists with ideas regarding normal psychological processes (e.g. aphasia in relation to language).
• Classifications of psychopathology may serve as a basis for theories of 'normal' personality differences (e.g. H.J. Eysenck's extraversion/neuroticism/psychoticism dimensions).

There are nonetheless some deeper aspects of the history of madness with which we must start. (Michel Foucault (1967) marked the beginning of post-progressivist studies in this field.) The heart of the matter is the fact that a society's concept of madness is necessarily also a statement of its concept of normality (though each eludes neat formulation). The boundary defines both sides and, to be meaningful, sanity needs a counter-concept of madness. This renders the history of madness both interesting and challenging.

First, it places a question mark above the notion of 'illness' as an objective reality when dealing with much of the behaviour which is or has been considered 'mad'. Nobody would quibble about whether smallpox is an illness, but even a cursory glance reveals great variation across time and place regarding which behaviours are considered mad. Conduct labelled as symptomatic of 'hysteria' or 'mania' in one epoch could result in canonisation or burning in another. Sometimes behaviour once thought 'mad' has since turned out to be an organic, not a psychological or 'spiritual', illness (e.g. epilepsy). At a more mundane level the acceptability of, say, talking to oneself, cross-dressing, or praying aloud in public, is subject to wide variation as is the 'normality' of much sexual behaviour. There are thus wide variations across time and culture in where the boundaries of 'normality' are placed.

Second, the cultural meaning of madness is itself quite flexible. One of the things Foucault first noted was the contrast between the late Renaissance (the 1500s–c. 1640) and the eighteenth century. During the Renaissance madness was something to which people related as an ever-present possibility; we find it particularly in painting (e.g. Hieronymus Bosch and the elder Breughel) and literature (most obviously in Shakespeare's plays where madness is fully integrated as part of the human condition, especially in *King Lear, Macbeth, Hamlet* and *Othello*, and at a lighter level in *A Midsummer Night's Dream*). One condition exerting great fascination at this time was 'melancholy', the topic of one of the greatest early 'Psychological' texts, Robert Burton's *Anatomy of Melancholy* (1621).

In the 1700s the picture changes dramatically, the mad becoming qualitatively different from the sane, objects of amusement, less than human for having lost the Enlightenment's most valued human attribute – 'reason'. Rather than a universal feature of the human condition, madness signifies exile from it. 'Melancholy', once resonant with profundity as the frequent stigma of artists and philosophers, is medicalised into 'melancholia'. It becomes a more-or-less physical condition, nick-named 'the Black Dog', arising from the state of one's nerves, bad diet, or the east wind. Meanings of 'psychopathology' can therefore change for a number of reasons, including broad cultural factors. More specifically they relate in a complex way to explanations of madness, which have included astrology (bad aspects to Saturn or the Moon – hence lunacy), demonic or divine possession, trauma, witchcraft (especially for male impotence), bad living habits, displacement of the womb (for female hysteria), divine punishment for sins and hereditary degeneration. In the present century new psychological, physical and genetic factors have been invoked from 'double-binding' to vitamin D deficiency (in relation to 'possession' phenomena). Implicitly (and sometimes explicitly) each carries its distinct meaning determining how the behaviour in question is perceived, evaluated, treated and located. Such causes vary along several dimensions: psychological vs. physical, optimistic vs. pessimistic, internal vs. external, ethically loaded vs. ethically neutral, empathic vs. objectifying. Although ætiologies of physical illness have been similarly subject to change, they have generally been seen as physical and ethically neutral (or divinely punitive in a fairly simple way). By contrast, their studies of the meaning of madness have increasingly led historians into such issues as the power relationship between doctor and patient, gender relations and interactions between treatment policy and wider cultural concerns.

Third then, Foucault and his numerous successors were led to dismiss the traditional progressivist story of a rise from ignorance to medical enlightenment. This drove the first wedge into the 'progressivist' approach generally, unsurprisingly because it was perhaps the easiest area in which to demonstrate progressivism's inadequacies. E. Shorter (1997) has attempted to recoup the progressivist story, but much of the fascinating material he covers only, in my view, reinforces the 'constructivist' case (e.g. how successive versions of the Diagnostic Standards Manual – the 'DSM' – were formulated).

We can now look in more detail at just some aspects of the topic: (a) changing attitudes to treatment; (b) input from psychopathology into the study of personality; and (c) the 'anti-psychiatry' movement of the 1960s and early 1970s.

Changing attitudes towards treatment

First, see Table 14.1 for some quantitative data.

Although this is undoubtedly a crude sample and one must be wary of reading too much into it, these figures at least demonstrate that reported 'recovery or

Table 14.1 Results of psychiatric hospital treatment

Hospital	Date	N	% R/I*	
Bethlem	1784–1794	1664	35	UK
Salpetrière	1803–1807	1002	47	France
The Retreat	1796–1811	149	48	UK
Salpetrière	1804–1814	2005	61	France
Dr Burrows	1820	242	92	USA
Hartford CT	1827	23	91	USA
Bethlem	1830s	562	70	UK**
Bloomingdale	1821–1844	1841	59	USA
Worcester, MA	1839–1843	922	49	USA
US asylums	1844	2092	41	USA
US asylums	1859	4473	57	USA
Worcester, MA	1880–1884	1319	20	USA
NY State	1912	7238	22	USA

Source: G. Tourney (1967)
* Recovered or improved
** Additional data from A. Morison (1838) Physiognomy of Mental Disease.

improved' (R&I) rates declined during the latter nineteenth century and that, for whatever reasons, New York State asylums in 1912 were doing worse than the main French asylum a century previously. Hardly a tale of medical advance!

To what can we ascribe this shifting pattern? First, the high early-nineteenth century figures reflect a retreat from the typical eighteenth-century attitude to madness towards a more positive view, associated with the rise of Romanticism. The gap between sane and insane narrows, reflecting Romanticism's emphasis on the emotional and irrational and the times' more egalitarian temper. Madness was reincorporated into the 'human condition'. A more psychologically oriented 'moral therapy' arose, challenging the Enlightenment's physical methods which had yielded little by way of therapeutic success (indicated in the first line of figures). The famed Dr Willis, who treated George III, was a leading exemplar of this new approach, while the best-known British asylum adopting it was Samuel Tuke's 'The Retreat' at York. In France reform was initiated by P. Pinel and his successor J.E.D. Esquirol at the Bicêtre and Salpetrière asylums in Paris. This more human-itarian approach and greater optimism about the possibilities of cure, together with therapeutic innovations, boosted R&I rates for several decades. The very high US figures need to be viewed sceptically since Burrows' patients, for example, were highly selected. Two developments then reduce the R&I rates: (a) the building of much larger asylums in which the moral therapists' idealistic blueprints are watered down as the medical profession reasserts professional authority; and (b) after c. 1840, an increasing belief that insanity is hereditary and, later, a sign of degeneracy. The latter both reduces prognostic optimism (hereditary conditions being incurable), and encourages a policy of confinement to protect the quality of the human stock by curbing 'degenerate' procreation.

A further factor is that the kinds of thing earning the label 'mad' early in the century included numerous behaviours offensive to bourgeois society, such as chronic gambling, alcoholism and sexual promiscuity, which later cease to figure. Since 'curing' these was a matter of inculcating some kind of moral reform, 're-educating' or 'brainwashing' (depending on how you look at it) the deviant into accepting respectable social values, the possibility of R&I was clearly fairly high. There are some quite complex aspects to the 'moral therapy' movement as an expression of a contemporary urge to inculcate new middle-class values of 'self control'. Foucault in particular recast Pinel's traditional heroic role more darkly, depicting him as the agent of a new bourgeois culture, using psychiatry as a channel for exercising social power.

During the latter nineteenth century, large institutions, therapeutic pessimism, and eugenic fears of degeneration thus mutually reinforced each other to impoverish the lot of the 'insane'. This in turn heightened the stigma of insanity, hence middle-class neuroses (as we would now call them), especially among women, were dealt with in the asylum less frequently. It was in relation to these that twentieth-century psychotherapies exerted much of their early appeal. In the twentieth century madness becomes an arena in which psychologists, heretical psychiatrists and orthodox medicine have constantly struggled for dominance, a struggle still unresolved – a point I return to when considering the anti-psychiatry movement.

To return to our figures then – the short answer to why they change as they do is that neither the meanings of madness nor cure (R&I) remain constant, and neither do the roles and functions of incarceration in an 'asylum'.

Input from Psychiatry into Personality Theory

The task of classifying mental 'illnesses' has been a fertile source of ideas regarding personality. In the early nineteenth century numerous models of personality and its dynamics (mostly now forgotten) were produced, especially by German psychiatrists (see H.F. Ellenberger, 1970; K. Doerner, 1981). (One should note here that the psychiatrist's or 'alienist's' relative independence, and until the present century, isolation, facilitated a high degree of intellectual autonomy, which continues in some areas of psychotherapy. Being funded by one's clients means being economically beholden to no single source, a situation obviously congenial to theoretical originality.) Different personality types come to be identified as especially prone to different kinds of insanity. While earlier psychiatrists often drew on folk-psychological typologies as a starting point, in the present century the traffic has been in the reverse direction. Psychiatrists and clinicians such as Sigmund Freud, E. Kraepelin, E. Kretschmer, and Carl Jung, and psychologists working in clinical settings such as H.J. Eysenck, have provided the major input into personality theory. Varieties of psychopathology are taken to represent the extremes of normal personality types or dimensions, as in Eysenck's model where schizophrenia and hysteria constitute extreme introvert and extravert modes of high neuroticism. Earlier Kretschmer devised a three-fold typology (linked to body-build): 'cyclothymes' (tendency towards manic-depression), 'schizothymes' (prone to schizophrenia) and 'collodethymes' (calm, unexcitable, but displaying explosive bursts of irascibility), identifying three sub-types for each of the first two.

Many of the 'personality tests' with which we are familiar originated as clinical diagnostic instruments: The Minnesota Multiphasic Personality Inventory, Eysenck's EPI, the 'Blacky Test' for aggression, and the Rorschach inkblot test to cite but four. Even IQ tests are not unlinked with this since Binet first devised them for identifying genuinely 'subnormal' children (though not now classed as insanity 'imbecility' was so classified until c. 1900 and its history follows a similar course). The 'projective' Thematic Apperception Tests (TATs) introduced by Henry Murray in the 1930s were based on the psychoanalytic notion that people unconsciously project their inner dynamics onto ambiguous stimulus material, an assumption underlying projective tests in general. (See Chapter 11 for further discussion of these.) George Kelly's Personal Construct Theory also arose from his clinical experience and was most vigorously developed in the United Kingdom by Donald Bannister and Fay Fransella in the clinical setting. Indeed, it is hard to identify any area of personality theory or research which did not either originate in the clinic or owe its subsequent success to its clinical usage – Cattell's 16 Personality Factor theory perhaps comes closest. Input from this source is thus not confined to psychoanalysis and related schools, but extends to mainstream medical psychiatrists such as Kretschmer and to much psychometrics as well.

The anti-psychiatry movement

In more recent times the problematic nature of madness is best illustrated by the 'anti-psychiatry' movement of the 1960s and early 1970s, associated with figures such as R.D. Laing, David Cooper, Thomas Szasz and Joe Berke. The roots of this reaction against mainstream medical psychiatry in Britain lay in the increasingly physiological orientation being adopted; many new psychoactive drugs had entered the psychiatrist's pharmacopoeia along with more-or-less intrusive physical techniques such as electroconvulsive therapy (ECT) and lobotomisation. One component of the intense cultural reaction against post-World War Two conformism, beginning in the mid-1950s, was hostility towards what many saw as the dehumanising nature of this physicalistic psychiatry, perceived as an agency for punishing deviance. Behaviours judged as socially unacceptable were, it was claimed, being medically objectified as mental illnesses. The American situation seems to have differed somewhat – in Britain this period coincided with a fairly sharp decline in the status of psychoanalysis, while in the US it was at the peak of its popularity. Physicalistic approaches were also making headway in the US, but with more competition from psychotherapy than in Britain.

In short, psychiatry still served the 'bourgeois' social control functions which Foucault had brought to the notice of discontented intellectuals as being its task around 1800. In the background was the primarily French philosophical movement of existentialism which greatly influenced Laing and had already forged links with psychiatry in mainland Europe (e.g. Ludwig Binswanger and Viktor Frankl). The result was a radical attack on mainstream practice, Laing's *The Divided Self* (1959) being the key text, in which it was claimed that all mental illness (especially 'schizophrenia', Laing's principal interest) was psychological in origin. Furthermore, such conditions possessed their own curative dynamic with which physical treatments interfered. A different approach was needed: provision of supportive environments within which the sufferer's 'self-cure' could be managed. Few such alternative institutions were created, but there were several short-lived attempts. For Laing 'schizophrenia' was the normal developmental outcome of being at the focus of confusing messages about one's identity, especially from parents. Special importance was given to 'double-binding', similar to what is popularly called a 'Catch 22' situation. An example would be a parent verbally insisting on the importance of the child being independent but not actually permitting it to be so. If the child is dependent it is criticised as clinging and lacking initiative, if it is independent it is accused of causing worry and anxiety. It cannot win. (See also Chapter 16.) The 'schizogenic mother' thus became a topic of considerable interest, and family dynamics in general were explored by Laing and his colleagues. For Cooper the family was the enemy of all self-fulfilment and he happily prophesied its end. 'Mental illnesses' reflected the problematic nature of the sufferer's 'being', thereby becoming almost philosophical rather than medical in character. Such arguments were bolstered by the American Thomas Szasz's provocatively titled *The Myth of Mental Illness* (1962). Szasz's thesis was that so-called 'mental illnesses' were really 'problems in living', not illnesses at all. The very act of labelling them 'illnesses' casts sufferers into a passive patient role, directly contrary to what is required if they are to regain control over their lives.

These developments occurred at a time when recreational drug use in the 'alternative culture' was widely happening in Britain for the first time, but this alternative culture was also an ideological and political movement. Drug experiences, notably LSD 'trips', were readily seen as yielding insights into 'schizophrenia' (thus Laing's approach was construed as enabling the patient to complete their 'trip'). But for those involved in the alternative culture the boundary between 'normal' and 'abnormal' was in any case becoming problematic. The 'sane' world's patent insanities at the time of the Cuban missile crisis and Vietnam War led many to happily reverse the whole evaluation – the 'mad' were sane martyrs, victims of trying to live honestly in an insane and evil world. For a while the 'schizophrenic' virtually became a hero figure. It is important to recognise that the era of 'flower power', hippies and 'permissiveness' was no mere eruption of youthful *joie de vivre*, but a quite desperate expression of the first post-war generation's deep fears, confusion and frustration. It was the period after all when 'paranoia' entered the popular vocabulary. Allen Ginsburg, leading poet of the immediately preceding 'Beat' movement began his most famous poem *Howl* with the line 'I saw the best minds of my generation destroyed by madness'. In the 1960s the best defence seemed to be to destroy madness itself by totally subverting the sanity–insanity boundary.

This could not last. For one thing it was unrealistic – most psychiatric patients are not engaged in heroic existential quests. For another, to categorically deny a physiological dimension to 'schizophrenia' or any other condition was to be a hostage to fortune, and by the mid-1970s neurochemical factors were beginning to be implicated. The meanings of these were (and remain) debatable, but confronted with ever-more sophisticated pharmaceutical methods little headway was to be made in pushing for expensive 'self-cure' procedures. Nevertheless things had changed irrevocably.

Firstly, the stage was set for the host of 'growth movement' therapies which took off from around 1970 (e.g. Gestalt Therapy, Rogerian 'client-centred' therapy, primal therapy, encounter groups, psychodrama, transactional analysis, and psychosynthesis). These mostly derived from different schools of psychotherapy created during the first half of the century but had a different, more positive, agenda. They began surfacing in America in the late 1940s, although their founders were frequently immigrants (e.g. Gestalt Therapy's Fritz Perls). The sane/insane boundary had been permanently breached, *there was now a market for psychotherapy for normal people* – surely a development of huge, if still not fully appreciated, cultural significance. The aim was no longer 'cure' but personal growth, while everybody had some degree of psychopathology or psychological damage. It is against this background that the huge expansion of counselling has taken place. The genuine insights of the anti-psychiatry movement, into family dynamics for example, were not lost either. The idea that therapy might need to move beyond a single 'sick' individual and consider the complex social dynamics of their life became well established.

For Psychology this has meant that since about 1970 Clinical Psychology has expanded from being primarily a servicing auxiliary for psychiatrists (providing diagnostic tests and what psychiatrists – if not practitioners – saw as mere morale boosting activities like occupational and art therapy), to a subdiscipline therapeutically engaged in dealing with what are seen as psychogenic problems. The central core of 'mad' syndromes – psychoticism and what is problematically termed 'schizophrenia' (see M. Boyle, 2002) – nevertheless remain in the psychiatric realm, as do conditions with a clear physical basis (although psychologists may be involved with these in research contexts).

To pull all this together: 'madness' is not a fixed entity. Definitions, meanings and treatment have been in constant flux in western culture since the Renaissance. While ostensibly a medical matter medicine's boundaries cannot contain it. The thrust of Psychiatry (a medical specialism only established in the United Kingdom around 1840 and generally a nineteenth-century innovation) has always been to explain insanity in physical terms, either, as in the late 1800s, as due to inherited neurological degeneration or, more recently, genetics, brain damage, neuropathology or some biochemical imbalance. The cultural role of madness as a definer of sanity has, though, always meant that it eludes this kind of neat objectification. Society as a whole, not just doctors, decides on what should count as 'normal' behaviour. And society is forever changing its mind.

For most of its modern history Psychology has been closely involved with the treatment, diagnosis and interpretation of psychopathology. This is evident in the dependence of personality theory on the clinical or 'abnormal' arena, the way in which psychologists have serviced psychiatric diagnosis and assessment, and finally, post-1970, in the way the discipline has established itself as an appropriate professional authority in dealing with a wide assortment of behavioural and psychological problems, no longer considered in stigmatising fashion as madness, but as genuine problems of living requiring some kind of professional involvement for their solution. The aspiration is to render the seeking of psychological help for such problems no odder than seeking medical help for physical ones, though differentiating these is difficult and raises a host of other issues (hence the rise of holistic approaches).

Psychoanalysis and associated schools

Culturally the single most influential point of connection between Psychology and madness has been psychoanalysis and associated schools of psychodynamic thought. Everyday language incorporates concepts and expressions invented or promoted by Freud and his associates to an extraordinary extent: having an inferiority or mother complex, projecting one's anger, regressing, doing something unconsciously, suffering from neurotic anxiety, being repressed or fixated, having a fragile persona or inflated ego and free-associating are but some of them. For academic Psychology, psychoanalytic thought has always presented a problem. While an enormously fecund source of concepts and hypotheses psychoanalysis notoriously resists experimental evaluation. And while their influence on how we think about ourselves is a psychological fact in its own right, as 'scientific theories' the Freudian and allied systems patently failed to meet the criteria of 'good science' being proposed by philosophers of science. As Karl Popper claimed, they are simply unfalsifiable. Engagement with psychoanalytic thought was nevertheless unavoidable, since it seemed to illuminate a vast array of topics beyond psychopathology ranging from child development to personality structure, dreams to race prejudice, subliminal perception to art and religion (G. Richards, 2000).

And behind all this lay the charismatic and enigmatic figure of Freud himself, which rapidly became modernist culture's iconic image of the bearer of Psychological expertise, the reader of our innermost thoughts. Say 'psychologist' and for most people it is still 'Freud' who springs to mind. Freud's personality continues to remain strangely elusive, he curiously maintains his professional role as target of our transferences and successive waves of historical and biographical attention seem only to have reinforced rather than dispelled his mystique.

Rather than again recount the basic tenets of psychoanalytic theory which are available in a thousand books, it will be more useful here to step back a little and consider such questions as the following. Why, as a matter of Psychological interest in its own right, *did* Psychoanalysis have such an impact? Why do numerous schools of thought ultimately stemming from psychoanalysis continue to flourish? What does the phenomenon of psychoanalysis tell us about Psychology's 'place'? These are now more promising issues than the hoary debates about whether psychoanalysis is scientific or the validity of specific Freudian doctrines.

The impact of psychoanalysis

Three main reasons, I suggest, may be given for the cultural and psychological success of psychoanalysis. First and most obvious, although perhaps in the long run least important, it was about sex. The notion that before Freud discussion of sex was taboo has long been dispelled. Numerous late-Victorian psychiatrists and doctors (like Krafft Ebing) penned mighty tomes on the subject, and while a flood of popular publications railed against the evils of masturbation and sexual license, others (like Havelock Ellis and Auguste Forel) were attempting to promote more enlightened attitudes. Late nineteenth-century culture was, in its way, as obsessed with the topic as is ours. Ellis and similar writers aside, what was distinctive was that sexual discourse (other than the frankly pornographic) was seemingly impossible unless infused with official morality or packaged as something else. Writings on sex adopted one of two stances (to oversimplify somewhat). They could espouse an attitude of great squeamishness as if dealing with inherently unpleasant and embarrassing matters, striving to eliminate the slightest hint of 'prurience'. This was common in popular 'advice' genres aimed at adolescents which posed as imparting necessary but delicate knowledge best kept from the immature and irresponsible. Alternatively there were books ostensibly for medical or scientific male professionals, seemingly scientific treatises on anthropology or sexual deviance containing detailed engravings of sexual organs, accounts of 'savage' sexual customs and medical cases, often with the more explicit passages in Latin. The borderline between genuine medical works and pornography posing as medicine or anthropology was in fact rather blurred (see also Chapter 17).

The Freudian move was unique not in openly discussing sex but in identifying it as the motivational force underlying all human behaviour from infancy onwards. In effect it sought to enable people to admit and confront their sexuality, identifying the primary ætiological factor in psychopathology as failure to do this. The centrality of sex, and the apparently reductionist implications of this, undoubtedly fuelled the initial *succès de scandale* which psychoanalysis enjoyed. This effect was heightened by the fact that Freud's position could be read in two ways, as both legitimating greater sexual freedom *and* as reaffirming traditional sexual morality.

The second factor is that the theory incorporated numerous central ideas of turn-of-the-century science, notably the evolutionary perspective (with its stress on instincts) and the energy concept being developed in physics. Coupled with Freud's own brilliance at deploying expositional metaphors, often drawn from contemporary science, this amounted to the first thoroughly *modern* image of human nature. The times were ripe for this. All other areas of scientific knowledge had been revolutionised and now at last this revolution had reached human nature itself. As I once heard Roy Porter say in a lecture, psychoanalysts 'stormed the broadcasting station'. A surprising number of Freud's ideas can be traced to various predecessors, but in integrating them as he did Freud constructed a radically new and modern vision, transcending its clinical origins. It coincided with cultural revolutions on a much wider front in painting, literature and music, of which the turn from 'reason' to emotion and the 'primitive' was a common feature. Freud's scientific self-dethronement *of* reason *by* reason was the arch scientific example of this (although Einstein's Theory of Relativity contributed to the prevailing mood by overthrowing commonsense notions of space and time). However, what was, historically, perhaps the most crucial factor was World War One, in the wake of which almost all traditional wisdoms about human nature seemed inadequate to Europeans suffering what amounted to profound collective post-traumatic stress disorder. Only after 1918 does psychoanalysis begin to make the huge inroads into western popular culture and consciousness to which its fame is due (G. Richards, 2000).

Again though, since other Psychologists were being equally, and more respectably, 'scientific', one may wonder why this image was not soon replaced by even more 'scientifically advanced' ones. The key, I think, lies precisely in its central clinical character. The third factor I would suggest is that Freudian theory was immediately applicable by all who acquainted themselves with it. Adopt this framework and you discover an exciting, enlarged, inner world of primal dramas, significant dreams, and secret motives. It promised lay aficionados and professional therapists alike a route for liberation from the stultifying effects of long-forgotten traumas and for re-evaluating themselves from a fresh standpoint. It was not just a theory *about* human nature, it offered an ostensibly 'modern' and 'scientific' procedure for self-exploration.

The endurance of psychoanalytically rooted theories

Insofar as Freud succeeded in establishing (though he did not create) the new role of 'psychotherapist' he may be said to have originated virtually every contemporary school of psychotherapeutic thought. And while non-Freudian approaches are now widespread, an extremely high proportion are theoretically descended from psychoanalysis. Controversy and disagreement are not necessarily indices of failure; on the contrary, they often signify where the action is. Discord is exciting. And so it was with psychoanalysis. A succession of followers found cause to break with Freud and develop their own variants, most famously Carl Jung and Alfred Adler. Even within the Freudian camp, by the 1930s there were increasing tensions regarding the future direction of Psychoanalysis. In Britain, Melanie Klein and Anna Freud were at each other's throats. In the US a new school of 'ego-psychologists' were formulating a more optimistic version of the theory, and figures like Erik Erikson, Erich Fromm and Karen Horney soon extended, complemented and diverged from the original to varying extents. More radically, French psychoanalytic thought assumed an even more distinct form under Jacques Lacan, while in Californian exile Henri Marcuse sought to integrate it with a version of Marxism. After 1970 several feminists began modifying and reformulating Freudian doctrines in order to expunge their inherent male-centredness (see Chapter 17).

Ironically it is partly because psychoanalysis does *not* conform to the canons of hard scientific theorising that it has been able to take so many different directions. Each generation and culture encountering it can rearrange, reinterpret and modify its conceptual repertoire to meet its own needs.

Now this begins to suggest something very important about the nature of psychoanalytic thought as a whole, which we have already hinted at. It is obviously *not* an orthodox scientific theory, but something both more and less than this, a framework for providing behaviour and experience with *meanings*. (This was in fact L. Wittgenstein's view of it, see J. Bouveresse, 1995.) But unlike traditional religious or philosophical frameworks its scientific *style* rendered it consistent with modernist culture. Any such framework or structure by which we bestow meaning on the psychological is in itself a psychological phenomenon, which leads us to the final question.

What psychoanalysis tells us about the place of Psychology

Understanding the extraordinary success of psychoanalysis can, I believe, help clarify the place Psychology occupied in modernist culture, and as yet continues to occupy in more post-modernist times. To be provocative, all Psychology to date aspires to the condition of psychoanalysis in the sense of aiming eventually to offer a complete scientific account of the psychological by which people will live more satisfactory lives. True, psychoanalysis never entirely succeeded in this, yet for a while it came impressively close. But the lesson of psychoanalysis is actually that such 'totalising' aspirations are vain, since the reason for its success lay, paradoxically, precisely in its fundamentally unscientific (in the hard positivist sense) and ambiguous nature. What psychoanalysis did was *bring about* a psychological change by, as we have said, providing a new system of psychological ideas within which people could construe their lives. It is the scale on which it did so, not the fact itself, which is so remarkable, for we can now begin to see that to a lesser degree this is what Psychology, when successful, always does. Psychology succeeds to the extent that people find it worth their while adopting its ideas in making sense of their lives – which means psychologically *changing* them. This requires that the new ideas must be felt to be an improvement on those already used. Clearly those suffering some form of mental distress will be especially receptive. This is, though, a disturbing perspective for it again raises the question of Psychology's scientific status. If *this* is how Psychology's theories and concepts are ultimately evaluated, if the populace at large is the final court of appeal and arbiter of their value as evidenced by how far 'folk psychology' assimilates them, what price the scientific virtues of rigour, consistency, and amenability to empirical testing? Further discussion of this is best postponed until the Epilogue.

Conclusion

I began by pointing out the universal need to differentiate between sanity and madness. Mad behaviour is, by definition, that to which we can give no meaning (though we may ascribe causes), it is irrational, crazy, deluded. But the situation just sketched is one in which Psychology serves to provide meanings. In relation to madness it seeks, in the case of psychoanalysis quite directly, to ascribe meaning to that which previously lacked it. Sometimes the meanings given may turn out to be physical ones – there has been brain damage or some neurochemical pathology – and 'madness' is clearly bracketed as an effect of physical pathology. When this is not so we seek, as it were, to find routes by which the sufferer can be brought back across the boundary. (And a boundary can only be crossed and recrossed so often before it disappears.) These 'frameworks of meaning' which Psychology supplies are thus, when they pertain to psychopathology, part and parcel of the cultural process by which the boundary is continually revised and the meaning of madness itself constantly reformulated.

Further reading

Alexander, F.G. and Selesnick, S.T. (1966) *A History of Psychiatry*. New York: Harper & Row. Progressivist with a Freudian bias, useful for reference.

Ellenberger, H.F. (1970) *The Discovery of the Unconscious: The History and Evolution of Dynamic Psychiatry*. London: Allen Lane. Monumental and scholarly account of the pre-history and emergence of Psychoanalytic schools.

Foucault, M. (1967) *Madness and Civilization: A History of Insanity*. London: Tavistock. Additional chapter now translated: (1989) 'Experiences of Madness'. *History of Human Sciences* 4(1): 1–25. Key text, although less than half was translated into English.

Shorter, E. (1997) *A History of Psychiatry from the Era of the Asylum to the Age of Prozac*. New York: Wiley. Contains excellent coverage of numerous less-well known therapies, and while the author professes to be anti-social constructionist much of the content hardly confirms this.

Other references

The following are among the more important or useful texts in a vast literature.

Boyle, M. (1990, 2nd edn, 2002) *Schizophrenia: A Scientific Delusion*. London: Routledge. 'Schizophrenia' is an unacceptable category. Nobody now suffers from the original symptoms, which were indistinguishable from those of post-traumatic encephalitis (of which there had just been an epidemic).

Burton, R. (1621, rep. 1896) *The Anatomy of Melancholy*. London: Bell. Under the guise of reviewing its causes, ends up as a polymathic discussion of everything under the sun from the perspective of a chronic sufferer.

Bynum, W.F., Porter, R. and Shepherd, M. (1985) *The Anatomy of Madness: Essays in the History of Psychiatry*, 2 vols. London: Tavistock.

Castel, R. (1988) *The Regulation of Madness: The Origins of Incarceration in France*. Berkeley, CA: University of California Press. An important challenge to Foucault's account.

Cooper, D. (1971) *The Death of the Family*. Harmondsworth: Penguin.

Doerner, K. (1981, 1st German edn, 1969) *Madmen and the Bourgeoisie: A Social History of Insanity and Psychiatry*. Oxford: Blackwell. Particularly good on early German psychiatry.

Drinka, G.F. (1984) *The Birth of Neurosis: Myth, Malady and the Victorians*. New York: Simon and Schuster. Excellent on the American scene and 'neurasthenia'.

Goldstein, J. (1987) *Console and Classify: The French Psychiatric Profession in the Nineteenth Century*. Cambridge: Cambridge University Press.

Hunter, R. and MacAlpine, I. (1963) *Three Hundred Years of Psychiatry, 1535–1866*. Oxford: Oxford University Press. Extracts tracking the 'progress' of psychiatric thought.

Jackson, S.W. (1986) *Melancholia & Depression from Hippocratic Times to Modern Times*. New Haven: Yale University Press. The only substantial monograph on the topic.

Kretschmer, E. (1925) *Physique and Character*. London: Kegan Paul, Trench & Trübner.

Kretschmer, E. (English edn, 1934, 2nd edn, 1952) *A Text-Book of Medical Psychology*. London: Hogarth Press.

Laing, R.D. (1959) *The Divided Self*. London: Tavistock. This effectively launched British anti-psychiatry. He followed up with *The Self and Others, Knots* etc.

Lyons, B.G. (1971) *Voices of Melancholy. Studies of Literary Treatments of Melancholy in Renaissance England*. London: Routledge & Kegan Paul.

MacDonald, M. (1981) *Mystical Bedlam: Madness, Anxiety and Healing in Seventeenth Century England*. Cambridge: Cambridge University Press. Study of a seventeenth-century doctor's notebooks, acclaimed by historians for its new material and methodological innovations.

Micale, M.S. (1989a) 'Hysteria and its Historiography: A Review of Past and Present Writings I.' *History of Science* xxviii : 223–251.

Micale, M.S. (1989b) 'Hysteria and its Historiography: The Future Perspective.' *History of Psychiatry* (1) 33–124. Disputes accounts such as I. Veith's (see below).

Porter, R. (1988) *Mind Forg'd Manacles, A History of Madness from the Restoration to the Regency*. Boston, MA: Harvard University Press. Entertaining and detailed account of the eighteenth-century British story.

Scull, A. (1979) *Museums of Madness: The Social Organization of Insanity in Nineteenth-Century England*. London: Allen Lane (reprinted Penguin 1982).

Skultans, V. (1979) *English Madness: Ideas on Insanity 1580–1890*. London: Routledge & Kegan Paul.

Skultans, V. (1975) *Madness and Morals: Ideas on Insanity in the Nineteenth Century*. London: Routledge & Kegan Paul.

Szasz, T. (1962) *The Myth of Mental Illness*. London: Secker & Warburg.

Szasz, T. (1971) *The Manufacture of Madness: A Comparative Study of the Inquisition and the Mental Health Movement*. London: Routledge & Kegan Paul. Szasz's later works suggest he is more a right-wing libertarian than a spiritual soul-mate of Laing and co.

Tourney, G. (1967) 'A History of Therapeutic Fashions in Psychiatry, 1800–1966'. *American Journal of Psychiatry* 124: 784–796.

Veith, I. (1965) *Hysteria: The History of a Disease*. Chicago: University of Chicago Press.

Wolpert, E.A. (1977) *Manic-Depressive Illness: History of a Syndrome*. New York: International Libraries Press. Only major monograph on the topic.

Zilboorg, G. (1941) *A History of Medical Psychology*. New York: Norton. A classic history of the area and good information resource.

Psychoanalysis

The history of psychoanalysis has become a virtual sub-discipline in itself and the literature is vast. The following are a few, mostly fairly recent, publications relevant to the approach adopted in this chapter.

Appignanesi, L. and Forrester, J. (1993) *Freud's Women*. London: Virago. A fascinating study of the influence on Freud of various women associates, and of his own complex attitude towards women.

Bouveresse, J. (1995) *Wittgenstein Reads Freud: The Myth of the Unconscious*. Princeton: Princeton University Press. An interesting analysis of Wittgenstein's views on psychoanalysis.

Cocks, G. (1985) *Psychotherapy in the Third Reich: the Goring Institute*. New York: Oxford University Press. Fascinating account of how a version of psychoanalysis flourished in Nazi Germany.

Decker, H.S. (1977) *Freud in Germany. Revolution and Reaction in Science, 1893–1907*. New York: International Universities Press. One of the few detailed studies of Freud's initial impact in Germany available in English.

Ellesley, S. (1995) *Psychoanalysis in Early Twentieth-Century England: A Study in the Popularization of Ideas*. Unpublished Ph.D. thesis, University of Essex. Although unpublished this has to be cited since it is the most extensive study so far of this important topic, focusing on the press and popular magazines.

Forrester, J. (1998) *Dispatches from the Freud Wars: Psychoanalysis and its Passions*. Boston: Harvard University Press. A useful survey by one of the leading historians of psychoanalysis.

Hale, N.G. Jr (1971) *Freud and the Americans. The Beginnings of Psychoanalysis in the United States, 1876–1917*. New York: Oxford University Press.

Hale, N.G. Jr (1995) *The Rise and Crisis of Psychoanalysis in the United States: Freud and the Americans, 1917–1985*. New York: Oxford University Press. Hale's two volumes are essential reading for anyone interested in the cultural impact of Psychoanalysis in the US.

Hilgard, E.R., Kubie, L.S. and Pumpian-Mindlin, E. (1952, rep. 1956) *Psychoanalysis as a Science*. New York: Basic Books. A major mainstream critique, though not entirely hostile.

Kerr, J. (1994) *A Most Dangerous Method. The Story of Jung, Freud and Sabina Spielrein*. London: Sinclair-Stevenson. Explores the covert role of the long-forgotten Russian analyst Sabina Spielrein in the lives and thought of both Jung and Freud.

Richards, G. (2000) 'Britain on the Couch: The Popularization of Psychoanalysis in Britain 1918–1940'. *Science in Context* 13(2): 183–230. Complements Ellesley's thesis (see above) and offers some broader conclusions.

Sears, R.R. (1943) *Survey of Objective Studies of Psychoanalytic Concepts. A Report Prepared for the Committee on Social Adjustment*. New York: Social Science Research Council, Bulletin 51. Important early American review of the experimental Psychological evidence related to psychoanalysis.

Webster, R. (1995) *Why Freud was Wrong: Sin, Science and Psychoanalysis*. London: HarperCollins. Controversial and, in the author's view, seriously flawed critique of Freud, but raises some interesting issues and contains much useful information.

Chapter 15

Psychological uses of animals

- Types of use of animals
- Tracing the roots of human behaviour
- Animals as behavioural units
- Animals as sources of insight into social behavioural dynamics
- Tracing the human-animal borderline
- Some general observations on the topic

Animals have been central to human psychology at least since the first cave paintings 30,000 years ago. Their behaviour has been used to encode psychological insights certainly since Aesop's *Fables* and the biblical *Book of Proverbs* while folk-psychological language is rich with animal terms. Physiognomists like the Italian G.B. Della Porta in the sixteenth century and J.C. Lavater in the eighteenth century drew heavily on similarities between human and animal forms as indicators of character. After Charles Darwin the relationship became even closer, if different in kind, and Psychology continued the traditional practice of looking to animal behaviour to provide insight into our own. What I want to do here is consider some of the ways Psychology has used this 'resource'. Although animal behaviour may be studied in its own right, it is invariably, perhaps inevitably, construed as having broader implications relating to human behaviour. There are I think four, infrequently spelled out, uses to which animal behaviour research has been put. Each has been particularly in vogue at different times and places, although none ever entirely absent. One underlying message is that the use being made of animal behaviour evidence will determine the kind of theories being produced, and also to some degree the research methods employed. That is to say, psychologists do not approach animal behaviour in a neutral fashion, but with prior assumptions about why they are doing so. (Before proceeding further I would draw attention to Donna Haraway (1989), a provocative feminist exploration of this line of thinking in regard to primate research.) The four kinds of use which I am provisionally identifying are:

1.　To trace the evolutionary roots of human behaviour.
2.　As 'behavioural units' for studying something called 'behaviour'.
3.　As sources of insight into behavioural dynamics, especially social dynamics.
4.　To trace the borderline of what is distinctively human.

Each of these makes its own demands and has its own requirements. There is one common assumption, of course, namely that animal behaviour is somehow *simpler* than ours, though how precisely this simplicity is conceptualised varies, and sometimes the aim is to show that it is less simple than hitherto assumed.

Tracing the roots of human behaviour

The evolutionary perception of a continuum between human and animal behaviour quickly generated an interest in identifying what we might call 'the animal in the human' – how far human behaviour retains pre-human ancestral features. Entailing the existence of in-built determinants of behaviour, this involved the elaboration of the concept of 'instinct'. Prior to Darwin this typically referred to ways of behaving built into the animal by God, but evolutionists radically changed this by replacing God with inheritance (although this meaning was not novel). Aside from a relatively quiescent period from c. 1915–late 1930s (roughly during the height of behaviourism) 'instinct' theories have maintained a strong presence in Psychology. The lineage runs from Darwin's own followers (such as Romanes) through C. Lloyd Morgan, W. McDougall, and J. Drever to the ethologists

K. Lorenz, N. Tinbergen and I. Eibl-Eibesfeldt down to contemporary sociobiologists and evolutionary psychologists. That hiatus was important, because it ended with a further shift in the concept's meaning. Although Lloyd Morgan was subtler, most earlier theorists viewed instinct in terms of innate goals or drives of a general kind: sex, food, aggression, maternality, etc. Behaviour was construed as driven by such instincts, which might have specific energies allocated to them, and human behaviour was instinctive insofar as it was in the service of these. With behaviourist environmentalism the concept fell from favour, and rightly, since it amounted to little more than listing the necessary conditions for survival – but the fact that all organisms reproduce does not mean they share a common 'sexual instinct'.

The ethologists gave the term a more specific meaning, no longer referring to broad goals but to behavioural patterns of a more-or-less fixed and unlearned kind, often highly species-specific. A new vocabulary of Fixed Action Patterns (FAPs), Innate Releasing Mechanisms (IRMs) and 'imprinting' was developed to deal with this. Far from hampering the application of their findings to humans, it became apparent that much human behaviour had close parallels in other species, suggesting that, for example, territorial marking, postural signalling and mother–child attachment had a high innate component because human behaviour of these kinds had a high *formal* resemblance to behaviour in some other species. Lorenz's *On Aggression* (1966) was a classic example of this logic. As the evidence came crowding in during the 1960s and early 1970s some psychologists such as John Bowlby began incorporating it into their theories of child development (see Chapter 16). This evidence had a twofold effect. First, it had a salutary impact on how behaviour hitherto dignified by traditional political, moral and cultural values was perceived – military emphasis on epaulettes was upgraded bristling of shoulder hair as shown in angry gorillas, the courting male's presentation of food to the female was basically the same whether Black Magic chocolate or the bird's worm, while the boss's vast desk was pure social hierarchy signalling no different essentially from the top stag's behaviour during the mating season. Kneeling at prayer is a typical primate submission posture. The first effect, then, was a fairly direct psychological influence on those reading the literature, changing their way of looking at the world – adverts became territorial markers, political speeches rival bellowings of would-be dominant walruses.

But there was a second effect, somewhat slower to manifest itself: a revival of the nineteenth-century doctrine known somewhat misleadingly as Social Darwinism (Social Spencerism would be more accurate). This held that human, like animal, behaviour was governed by the goal of maximising reproduction and competing for the resources enabling one (or one's closest kin) to do so and was formulated using concepts emerging in evolutionary theory such as 'inclusive fitness' (an idea introduced by a biologist, the late W.D. Hamilton). From this stemmed 'Sociobiology', launched in E.O. Wilson's 1975 book of that title. The lesson of this is generally read as being that various aspects of human behaviour are so deeply rooted genetically that attempts at modification are totally misguided; sex differences in behaviour, certain features of social organisation and human conflict are irremovable. Altruism is but selfishness in disguise. Are these valid conclusions? The attempt to over-ride or modify such 'instinctive' behaviours is also surely a fact of human behaviour. Nor does genetic mean unchangeable – after all evolution is itself a process of genetic change. In G. Richards (1987) I provided a fuller critique of this controversial position, drawing attention to the conceptual incoherence (as I saw it) of R.L. Trivers's key 1971 paper on altruism, possible alternative, and more plausible, evolutionary arguments, the misleading obsession with male self-sacrifice in battle as typical altruism – and much else besides! Over the last decade a specific sub-discipline of Psychology, Evolutionary Psychology, has emerged from this approach. At its best, as in R. Byrne's recent ethologically-rooted work on the evolution of deception and cognitive capacities (Byrne, 1995) this has been highly illuminating, at its worst it is little more than scientistic speculative theorising invoking inclusive fitness scenarios in a way reminiscent of late nineteenth-century invocations of recapitulation (see Chapter 3).

Such questions may be debated at great length. More to the point here: what are the features of this Type 1 usage of animals? First, it is very wide-ranging in the species it studies. Although Tinbergen concentrated primarily on the herring gull and Lorenz on geese and dogs, field research now covers species from gorillas to bats, dingoes to elephants. One consequence of this which we ought to mention in passing is that whatever human behaviour you are dealing with, *somewhere* in the animal kingdom you will find a parallel. This perhaps weakens rather than strengthens the case for human behaviour being instinctive because really such behaviour should be of a species-specific stereotyped character. We ought then to expect human behaviour to resemble one particular lineage – but in fact it seems to resemble them all!

Second, stemming from this, the nature of the inference from animal to human is usually analogical. Except, arguably, when dealing with closely-related primate species we are not really seeing the evolutionary roots of our own behaviour; at best we are seeing what is called 'convergent evolution' – in which unrelated species evolve similar solutions when faced with similar problems. Third, this evidence is basically of a field-study rather than laboratory-based kind, lending the findings themselves an ecological validity lacking in laboratory work. The wider effect, bolstered by heavy media coverage of wild-life and Green concerns, has been to narrow the perceived gap between humans and animals by demonstrating our similarities with other species, however problematic the reasons for these resemblances. While, during the 1980s, sociobiology seemed to be taking things in a politically conservative direction, replaying nineteenth-century arguments that competition and national strife were somehow 'natural', the force of this now appears to have diminished somewhat – although Evolutionary Psychology retains, to a high degree, the fatalism inherent in all strongly 'nativist' theories. I must stress here that interpreting behaviour in ethological terms does not exclude alternative interpretations with different meanings. Saying a particular behaviour is 'territorial', for example, does not actually exclude alternative meanings like 'patriotic', 'projected patricidal wish' or 'result of cognitive calculations regarding reward expectancy'. We are free to choose the 'framework of meanings' that suits us – we cannot prove one 'True' and others 'False'.

Animals as behavioural units

I will say relatively little about this here, having already covered this usage in discussing behaviourism (Chapter 5). From this point of view the animal is interesting not as a unique example of instinctive adaptation patterns but as a convenient learning or behaving machine, suitable for study because it shows learning (or some other) behaviour in a simpler form to that in humans, because it can be experimented on with fewer moral qualms and because it can be easily reared and housed.

As we saw, research of this kind focused on a very small range of species: the Norwegian white rat, the domestic dog (in I. Pavlov's conditioning research), and the pigeon (in much of B.F. Skinner's work). I drew attention in the earlier chapter to the underlying circularity in all this as far as its support for environmentalist theories was concerned. By the 1950s and 1960s primates, particularly rhesus monkeys, were being added to the repertoire, both because they had become available and for face validity reasons – they were closer to humans and so more suited for the study of behaviours present in only rudimentary a form in rats and dogs. This was construed in terms of their being more generally intelligent rather than in terms of differences in 'instinctive' make-up. Thus we find J.V. Brady's experiments on 'executive monkeys' and the massive programme of research on rhesus monkeys undertaken by Harry and Margaret Harlow. In neither case were the researchers interested in monkeys but in a general behaviour category: 'anxiety' in Brady's case and 'attachment behaviour' in the Harlow's.

This usage is not necessarily environmentalist in orientation; it can involve (as with the Harlow's) experimental exploration of ideas originating from ethology. What we need to note is (a) the focus on a category of behaviour rather than on a species of animal; and (b) the assumption of generalisability from animal to human with due allowance for the greater complexity of human behaviour. Since the 1970s the more extreme environmentalist assumptions once common in such research have largely disappeared due to the discovery of apparently innate factors preparing or counterpreparing animals for certain kinds of learning task (see Chapter 5).

Sources of insight into social behavioural dynamics

Associated, though not exclusively, with the ethological and sociobiological work, has been the use of animals to explore the effects of environmental factors on social behaviour. This varies from experimental work on rodent overcrowding to inferences from field studies regarding, for example, the differences between plain-dwelling South African baboons and rocky valley-dwelling North East African ones. This does not claim to be identifying the roots of human behaviour so much as identifying relationships between species' environments and their social organisation. The boundary between this and the first category may at times become blurred, but the basic distinction is that the behaviours studied are not so much 'innate' as logical – or at least 'natural' – consequences for a species of a particular type when having to adapt to the environment in question. The assumption of a human-animal resemblance in salient respects is of course maintained.

Sociobiologists have, however, insisted that the basic explanatory level for even these social dynamics lies in the optimising of 'inclusive fitness' (enhancing the survival of one's genes by promoting the reproductive success either of one-self or one's closest kin, who in part share them). Thus infanticide among langurs, lesbianism among gulls, and food-sharing among vampire bats can all be viewed as logical solutions to the inclusive fitness problem. Theoretically much of this work hinges around the notion of 'reciprocal altruism' introduced by Hamilton and Trivers. (In G. Richards, 1987, I tried to elucidate what I see as the logical incoherence of this position.)

Prior to the rise of Sociobiology, the effect of this kind of work was similar to much of that in the first category, particularly the work on overcrowding in rats which resulted in increased violence, increased abortion, abnormal sexual beha-viour, drop in grooming standards, 'forced mating' (i.e. rape) and so on – though they did not actually throw petrol bombs. Again the change in perception was to see human responses to overcrowding as 'natural' responses to extreme con-ditions and to narrow the human–animal gap.

Tracing the human–animal borderline

Consider first a preoccupation of many people in around 1900: the presence of consciousness in animals (e.g. Margaret Washburn, 1908). This direction of con-cern is the reciprocal of the first of our categories: instead of tracing the animal in humans we are here tracing the human in animals, especially, in recent decades, in higher primates. Best known are studies of the linguistic capacities of chim-panzees, gorillas and pygmy chimpanzees (bonobos). Similar research has been conducted with dolphins (L.M. Herman, 1984) and sea-lions (R.J. Schusterman and K. Krieger, 1984). The ethological work of primatologists such as J. Goodall (1971), C. Boesch and H. Boesch (1981) (both on chimps), the late Diana Fossey (1984), G. Schaller (1963) (both on gorillas) and S.A. Altmann and J. Altmann (1970) (on baboons) – to mention only some of the best known research – derives much of its appeal from demonstrating the presence in other species of such supposedly human behaviours as grief, ornamentation, tool-use, warfare, pathological jealousy and traditions of socially learned behaviour. This has, since N. Kohts' ground-breaking Russian study of 1935, been supplemented by experimental work com-paring primates and humans, e.g. J. Vauclair (1984) on cognitive development and S.D. Suarez and G.G. Gallup (1981) on self-recognition (see Fig. 15.1). This remains a flourishing area, increasingly closely related to human evolution research (see K.R. Gibson and T. Ingold, 1993).

Although such work primarily focuses on higher primates and, to a lesser extent, cetaceans, the species studied may include any of the higher mammals felt to approach us in abilities of one kind or another. Here we are not concerned so much with the roots of human behaviour as with the very nature of human unique-ness, and the trend in recent years has been to continue that whittling away of neat criteria begun by Darwin (1871).

Thus we can utilise animals in various ways, and I must stress that within particular research programmes elements of more than one of these may occur.

Figure 15.1 Comparing the child and the chimpanzee. A plate from N. Kohts (1935) pioneering study. Reproduced by permission of the Centre for the History of Psychology, Staffordshire University.

Table 15.1 Underlying orientations of animal psychology

1. To minimise animal–human differences by animalising humans.
2. To minimise animal–human differences by humanising animals.
3. To deny any essential, 'innate' character altogether, especially to humans but also as far as possible to animals.

The fourth orientation, by definition generating no animal research is:

4. To maximise the animal–human difference by denying the applicability of animal behaviour research to humans.

We can perhaps rearrange our original listing more neatly by identifying three underlying orientations (see Table 15.1).

Of these the first two are now most active, for the third has lost credibility in the light of findings within its own tradition, while the fourth is fighting a losing battle against the sheer intrinsic appeal of animal-behaviour research. I am here ignoring psychophysiological studies (which would most easily fit under (a)). Psychophysiological research, while the most controversial from an animal welfare perspective, is nonetheless assuming a central role in cognitive neuropsychology and related fields (including Evolutionary Psychology to some extent) for which it offers a route for the direct study of brain functioning and the behavioural correlates of biochemical and genetic factors. In a sense we may therefore see it as a continuation of the 'Tracing the Roots of Human Behaviour' strand in a particularly biologically reductionist fashion, but merging into the medical and psychopharmacological fields. For a detailed account of the British side of this story covering such issues see D. Wilson (2001).

I would like to end on a more distanced note: seeing this whole topic as an expression of the intrinsic psychological significance of animals for humans. Since the eighteenth century, anthropologists have utilised the idea that all societies distinguish between culture and nature – the Human and the Natural World. Culture converts Nature into new cultural forms, a process Marxists ascribe to our supposedly unique 'labour' based life-style. Humans identify themselves as somehow apart from nature, however intimate their involvements with it. The psychological uses and meanings of animals are rooted in this cultural processing of animals first into food, clothing and ornament, and then as a psychological resource – as models of how to behave, spiritual symbols, external templates for mapping human diversity of temperament and character, and moral emblems of virtues and vices. The complementary moves of putting the human into the animal and bringing the animal into the human have always, it seems, been present. And notwithstanding the hard strictures of C. Lloyd Morgan and others of his generation against the former, as unscientific 'anthropomorphism', the intertwining of the two subverts the apparent simplicity of such injunctions. The fact that modern Psychology is still involved in this game, at however sophisticated a level, further testifies to the inseparability of Psychology and psychology.

The preferred direction of movement – animalising humans, humanising animals, assertion of separation, denial of distinction – reflects contemporary cultural preoccupations. Although this cannot be explored in depth here, consider the shift from mid-Victorian 'anthropomorphic' humanising of animals to the Darwinian reversal of animalising humans. The former is a kind of psychological imperialism: animals embody all kinds of human virtues, their behaviour is laden with moral lessons for us, their meaning is as exemplars of divine wisdom designed for our edification in a creationist, divinely engineered universe. This image then moves into reverse: evil becomes transformed into the 'beast within' (see Chapter 3), and the animalisation of European humans continues with Sigmund Freud's demotion of the power of reason in favour of that of the sexual instinct, culminating in an orgy of mutual projection in World War One. At this point the Americans opt for a denial of any essential difference between animal and human at all, there is only behaviour and behaving organisms, humans included. World War Two, in its turn, brings a sense of difference from nature: all humans have is consciousness, they define themselves, they are responsible for their own fate, the rest is denial of freedom and responsibility. Optimists plump for A. Maslow and C. Rogers, pessimists for J.-P. Sartre and existential angst. But what of those who cannot grasp the nature of this human freedom? Generals and businessmen, politicians and status-seekers – under the new ethological gaze they suffer a Circean metamorphosis, their behaviours mere unconscious enactments of animal rituals. Ethology thus returns animals to the role of moral emblems, turning the wheel full circle. Psychology participates in and reflects these shifting cultural moods and phases. One is driven to C. Lévi-Strauss's dictum: 'animals are good to think with'. Of all natural phenomena animals are psychologically the most potent – a still unexhausted source of ways of thinking about ourselves. From animal-headed Egyptian gods to Greenpeace our relations towards animals define who and what we think *we* are. But animal behaviour really exists in and of itself, it is not an argument for or against anything. So is it we who supply animal behaviour with its meanings – or is it animal behaviour that supplies the meanings for our own?

Further reading

Boakes, R. (1984) *From Darwinism to Behaviourism*. Cambridge: Cambridge University Press. On Comparative Psychology.

Desmond, A. (1979) *The Ape's Reflexion*. London: Blond & Briggs. Meditation on the psychological relationship between humans and higher primates.

Haraway, D. (1989) *Primate Visions. Gender, Race, and Nature in the World of Modern Science*. London: Routledge. Controversial feminist critique of the entire topic.

Richards, G. (1989) *On Psychological Language and the Physiomorphic Basis of Human Nature*. London: Routledge. Especially Chapters 1 and 3 on 'anthropomorphism' and the natural world sources (including animals) of psychological concepts.

Other references

Altmann, S.A. and Altmann, J. (1970) *Baboon Ecology: African Field Research.* Bibliotheca Primatologica, No.12. Basel: Karger.

Boesch, C. and Boesch, H. (1981) 'Sex Differences in the use of Natural Hammers By Wild Chimpanzees. A Preliminary Report'. *Behaviour* 83: 585–593 (They have produced numerous additional papers since.)

Bowlby, John (1969) *Attachment and Loss. Volume 1: Attachment.* Harmondsworth: Penguin.

Brady, J.V. (1958) 'Ulcers in "executive monkeys"'. *Scientific American* 199: 95–100.

Byrne, R. (1995) *The Thinking Ape: The Evolutionary Origins of Intelligence.* Oxford: Oxford University Press.

Campbell, J. (1984) *The Way of the Animal Powers: Historical Atlas of World Mythology. Volume I.* London: Times Books. Jungian influenced work by a renowned authority on mythology. A resource for exploring the psychological significance of animals for humans.

Cesaresco, Countess E.M. (1909) *The Place of Animals in Human Thought.* London & Leipzig: T. Fisher Unwin. An isolated, early, and neglected foray into the topic. (Incidentally, her husband, the Count, wrote a book on the psychology of the horse.)

Darwin, C. (1871) *The Descent of Man.* London: Murray. Essential primary source.

DeVore, I. (ed.) (1965) *Primate Behavior. Field Studies of Monkeys and Apes.* New York: Holt Rinehart Winston. A collection of pioneering papers.

Drever, J. (1917) *Instinct in Man.* Cambridge: Cambridge University Press. Classic statement of then mainstream British 'instinctivist' position.

Fossey, D. (1984) *Gorillas in the Mist.* New York: Houghton-Mifflin.

Gibson, K.R. and Ingold, T. (eds) (1993) *Tools, Language and Cognition in Human Evolution.* Cambridge: Cambridge University Press. Ingold's last two chapters are especially valuable.

Goodall, J. (1971) *In the Shadow of Man.* London: Collins.

Harlow, H.F. and Harlow, M.K. (1965) 'The Affectional Systems'. In A.M. Schrier, H.F. Harlow and F. Stollnitz (eds) *Behavior of Non-human Primates*, 2nd edn. New York: Academic Press, 287–334.

Herman, L.M., Richards, D.G. and Wolz, J.P. (1984) 'Comprehension of Sentences by Bottle-nosed Dolphins'. *Cognition* 16: 129–219.

Klingender, F. (1971) *Animals in Art and Thought to the End of the Middle Ages.* London: Routledge.

Kohler, W. (1925, rep. 1957) *The Mentality of Apes.* Harmondsworth: Penguin. The ethological aspects have been overshadowed by the learning experiments.

Kohts, N. (1935) *Infant Ape and Human Child* (2 vols). Moscow (publisher unknown).

Lauder Lindsay, W. (1880) *Mind in the Lower Animals* (2 vols). London: Kegan Paul, Trench & Co. Full-blooded anthropomorphism – heroic horses, criminal magpies, canine suicide, etc.

Lorenz, K. (1966) *On Aggression.* London: Methuen.

Richards, G. (1987) *Human Evolution: An Introduction for the Behavioural Sciences*. London: Routledge & Kegan Paul. See especially Chapter 5 on sociobiology and altruism issues.

Romanes, G. (1882) *Animal Intelligence*. London: Kegan Paul, Trench, Trübner.

Schaller, G.B. (1963) *The Mountain Gorilla*. Chicago: Chicago University Press.

Schusterman, R.J. and Krieger, K. (1984) 'California Sea Lions are Capable of Semantic Comprehension'. *Psychological Record* 34: 3–23.

Suarez, S.D. and Gallup, G.G. (1981) 'Self-recognition in Chimpanzees and Orang-utans but not in Gorillas'. *Journal of Human Evolution* 10: 175–188.

Tinbergen, N. (1953) *The Herring Gull's World*. London: Collins.

Trivers, R.L. (1971) 'The Evolution of Reciprocal Altruism'. *Quarterly Review of Biology* 46: 35–57. Canonical, but highly problematic, text on the topic.

Trivers, R.L. (1985) *Social Evolution*. Menlo Park, CA: Benjamin/Cummings. Hard sociobiology position statement.

Vauclair, J. (1984) 'Phylogenetic Approach to Object Manipulation in Human and Ape Infants'. *Human Development* 27: 321–328.

Washburn, M.F. (1908) *Animal Mind*. New York: Macmillan.

Willis, R. (1974) *Man and Beast*. London: Hart-Davis. Interesting anthropological study comparing the cultural significance of specific animals for three African cultures. Illuminates how we use animals to define ourselves.

Wilson, D. (2001) 'A Precipitous *Dégringolade*'? The Uncertain Progress of British Comparative Psychology in the Twentieth Century'. In G.C. Bunn, A.D. Lovie and G.D. Richards (eds) (2000) *Psychology in Britain: Historical Essays and Personal Reflections*. Leicester: British Psychological Society and London: The Science Museum, 243–266.

Wilson, E.O. (1975) *Sociobiology: the New Synthesis*. Harvard: Harvard University Press. The sociobiology 'manifesto'.

Yerkes, R.M. (1943) *Chimpanzees. A Laboratory Colony*. New Haven: Yale University Press. Yerkes' chimp colony was the major site of US primate research from the 1920s until the mid-1940s.

Chapter 16

Psychology and the child

- The diversity of images of the child
- The Romantic image and its legacies
- The Lockean environmentalist image and its legacies
- The Freudian image
- The Ethological image
- Discussion of the issues raised by this diversity

Since ancient times children have been scrutinised by savants, philosophers and (later) scientists, and became one of Psychology's most important subject-groups. Books on education and child-rearing began to appear in the sixteenth century and a modern 'Psychological' approach is discernible in John Locke's *Some Thoughts Concerning Education* (1693). During the latter 1700s a plethora of educational works appeared inspired by Rousseau's *Emile, ou de l'education* (1762). In Britain Richard and Maria Edgeworth, Thomas Day, Elizabeth Hamilton, Erasmus Darwin, Joseph Priestley and Hannah More were among the most important writers, while in mainland Europe J.H. Pestalozzi and J.F. Herbart further developed Rousseau's ideas. During the 1820s Friedrich Froebel, inventor of the 'kindergarten', developed an advanced system of primary education. By the mid-1800s 'subnormal' children were receiving attention from the French educationist Edouard Séguin, the Swiss J.J. Güggenbuhl and the American Gridley Howe. This topic may be dated to J.M.G. Itard's efforts at educating the feral child Victor (see Chapter 2). Later in the century, as explained in Chapter 3, child study acquired a new significance in the light of the evolutionary idea of 'recapitulation'.

In this chapter I will explore the 'images' of the child that have underlain Developmental Psychology. All cultures produce such images to guide and justify child-rearing and educational practices, and in European cultures some have served, often covertly, to underpin Psychological work. It is, I suggest, the presence of such underlying meanings of childhood that accounts in part for the diversity of approaches Developmental Psychology has taken.

To bring some order to this diversity we can identify the following images:

Table 16.1 Major images of the child in western culture

1. *Empiricist* originating with J. Locke.
2. *Romantic* originating with J.-J. Rousseau.
3. *Evolutionary* originating with C. Darwin and E. Hæckel.
4. *Behaviourist* developed most notably by J.B. Watson.
5. *'Christian'* the child as innately sinful, which affected nineteenth-century popular attitudes towards child-rearing.
6. *Psychodynamic* primarily from Freud, but with several variants.
7. *Ethological* later version of the evolutionary image.
8. *Social Constructionist* e.g. L. Vygotsky and social constructionist approaches to gender identity formation.
9. *Existentialist* e.g. in R.D. Laing's account of the origins of schizophrenia.
10. *Cognitive* e.g. J. Piaget, J.S. Bruner.

Two important dimensions of variation underly these. The most obvious is how far innate factors are invoked as opposed to learning and experience – the 'nature-nurture' question. The second may be termed 'optimism vs. pessimism'; optimistic images include both the romantic and behaviourist, pessimistic ones both the Freudian and existentialist (although not in all versions). There is no clear-cut correlation between these two dimensions. Individual psychologists may well of course incorporate elements of more than one image into their thinking.

Of all these, the most deeply influential has been the romantic image. Its central feature as formulated by J.-J. Rousseau, J.H. Pestalozzi and F. Froebel is the notion that the child contains the innate potential for a more-or-less unique fulfilment – an explicit metaphor is frequently that of the seed and the flower with the educator cast as gardener. Given a sufficiently nurturing and insightful developmental regime the essentially good child fulfils this potential, maturing into an integrated and happy adult. The educator must attend to the child's individual needs, identifying their strengths and helping them to overcome weaknesses. This notion of the flowering of an individually unique potential has been a persistent theme in European developmental thought.

The precise terms in which writers developed the romantic image were affected by their broader philosophical and religious allegiances. Thus Froebel's system is structured around a triad of faculties: feeling, doing (the will) and thinking constituting a 'tri-unity' which must be developed in balance with each other. This is fairly typical of contemporary German *Naturphilosophie*, but Froebel gives it a more pious spin by equating these with love, life and light respectively, which in turn signify humanity, nature and God. Notwithstanding its very devout character, Froebel's system was based on intense study of children and implemented in his own pioneering educational practice. He stressed how the three faculties must all be kept involved and placed great emphasis on mother–child interactions. He even identified a very early 'sucking in' phase, adumbrating Freud's 'oral' stage. J.F. Herbart, for his part, more sternly stressed the need to help the child develop a strong will to rein in their unruly instincts.

While the evolutionary image somewhat darkened the picture, the romantic image of childhood was readily incorporated by evolutionary writers like James Sully, for whom infancy remains a golden age, a state of enchanted consciousness with which we have great difficulty in regaining contact. Clearly the doctrines of recapitulation and 'unfolding inner potential' bear some resemblance to one another, detectable in the ongoing predilection of European psychologists for stage theories of development. Nor has the view that childhood provides a route for gaining access to earlier stages of human evolution entirely disappeared. Although no longer pursued in recapitulationist terms, human evolution research has rediscovered a place for the child in comparative studies of child and primate development.

While one could not strictly call Jean Piaget, the single most influential developmental psychologist of the last century, a romantic, his image of a natural dynamic unfolding process of cognitive and moral development clearly descended from the romantic tradition (he also taught in Geneva at the Institut Rousseau – the choice of name being no coincidence). (Jung's concept of individuation, along with that of archetypes, as well as his tendency to quote Goethe at the drop of a hat, clearly place him in this lineage too, though he did not deal extensively with child development.) The German Wilhelm Stern (1924), while attempting to reconcile empiricist and nativist approaches, again stressed the holistic and active nature of development and reiterated the 'gardening' analogy. The Gestalt psychologist K. Koffka (1928) was far less romantic in tenor, but once more expounded a holistic model of the developmental process.

In general, while the recapitulationism of such pioneer child psychologists as W. Preyer, G.S. Hall, E. Claparède, K. Groos, W. Stern and J. Sully is theoretically distinct from romanticism, the enthusiasm with which European writers adopted this approach owed much to its perceived continuity with the traditional romantic 'unfolding' concept of the child. Only perhaps in Freud was this romantic connotation explicitly dismissed; indeed R. Webster (1995) controversially sees his position as fundamentally puritanical. Romantic optimism resurfaced dramatically after World War Two in American Humanistic Psychology and post-Freudianism. Once more the goals of 'self-realisation' and 'individualisation' are held up as 'natural' outcomes of truly healthy development. One should also mention the Adlerian variant of psychodynamic theory with its focus on the striving, power-seeking nature of development (it was A. Adler who coined the term 'inferiority complex'). Such approaches in turn affected American popular views on child-rearing, notably the rise of 'permissive' approaches (famously associated with Dr Benjamin Spock) calculated to avoid creating neuroses and other debilitating hang-ups in the child.

Romantic

The Psychological legacy of this image may be identified therefore in the following: (a) a belief in a realisable innate potential; (b) a holistic concept of development; (c) a tendency towards stage theories and models; (d) a view of the child as actively participating in its development (though emphasis on this varies); and (e) a belief in a qualitative difference between child and adult modes of consciousness.

Except during the heyday of recapitulationism the opposite 'Lockean' camp has also always had powerful advocates. For them development is essentially a process of learning, and adult character a product of developmental experience. Instincts are downplayed, even ignored or, in the case of Watsonian behaviourism, effectively denied. Up until the early 1800s this was most popular in Britain, but in modern Psychology it has taken three major forms: North American behaviourism and two more socially oriented, often ideologically left-wing, European versions derived from Marxism and existentialism. For Watson the child was almost entirely malleable by applying learning-theory principles. His project was to create scientific child-rearing methods that would eliminate the deleterious consequences of irresponsible parenting and excessive 'love-conditioning' (especially by mothers), which rendered children emotional, dependent, undisciplined and unhappy. J.B. Watson (1928) is a rich source of material stating this in terms which now sound quite extraordinary:

> There is a sensible way of treating children. Treat them as though they were young adults. Dress them and bathe them with care and circumspection. Let your behavior always be objective and kindly firm. Never hug and kiss them, never let them sit in your lap. If you must, kiss them once on the forehead when they say good-night. (pp. 81–2)

There is much more in this vein. Watson was extreme even by American standards. His contemporary Arnold Gesell successfully implemented a large-scale empirical investigation of child development norms guided by a more orthodox biological-evolutionary orientation (Fig. 16.1). Nevertheless, the underlying rationale for this was also to provide firm scientific data to inform child guidance clinics and child-rearing advice manuals and retained few traces of romanticism.

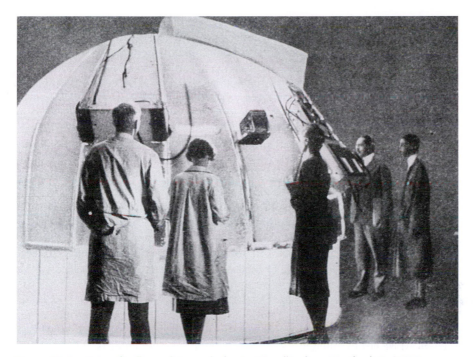

Figure 16.1 Scientifically studying a baby in 'Gesell's dome' in the late 1920s, an image reminiscent of an early science fiction film still (A. Gesell, 1937). Photo: George Singer. Reproduced by permission of the Centre for History of Psychology, Staffordshire University.

The factors behind the emergence of this unromantic view of child-rearing are complex but two may be singled out here. First, the absence of elaborate indigenous folk-wisdoms regarding child-rearing, such as there were originating in the old self-reliant, pioneering rural culture, a culture often infused with fairly extreme Protestant attitudes. Second, there was the future-oriented nature of North American society with its belief in scientific and technological solutions to social problems. The thesis of an entertainingly polemical feminist analysis by B. Ehrenreich and D. English (1979) is that child-rearing practices are determined by economic needs and interests, the behaviourist phase being promoted by fund-giving agencies to produce the kind of work-force required by contemporary American capitalism. Although somewhat overstated their argument contains a number of important insights, but cannot be easily applied to the European context.

Equally environmentalist or 'nurturist', but quite different in tenor, was the Marxist-influenced approach developed in Europe by people like Karl and Charlotte Bühler and Lev Vygotsky in which the social nature of child development was emphasised (in the US G.H. Mead's 'social behaviorism' has some affinities with this, as does the rise of comparative anthropological work by people such as Margaret Mead and Wayne Dennis). This holds that consciousness is a product of social relations and child development is socially managed in a pervasive fashion. The child's concept of its 'self' is learned via its social relationships as are the

223

meanings it gives to its experiences. The Marxists view psychological structure as an internalisation of social structure, hence psychological conflicts and pathologies are created by, and reflect, social conflicts and pathologies.

For social constructionists the very meaning of childhood is socially produced, historical and cross-cultural studies disclosing wide differences in how far children are viewed as autonomous/dependent, good/sinful, adult/infantile, responsible/irresponsible, or sexual/asexual. The central issue of gender identity is similarly seen as culturally determined: what behaviours are considered typically male or female, at what age gender differences become significant, attitudes towards homosexuality, appropriate age for sexual activity to begin, are all matters of cultural, not biological, meaning.

The second European version of environmentalism stems from Existentialism. This ultimately places responsibility back on the individual: we all have to choose what we are to be, there is no 'human nature' analogous to the species natures of other animals. 'Existence precedes essence' as Sartre somewhat enigmatically put it. The implications of this for child development were explored primarily in the psychiatric field. In Britain R.D. Laing in particular traced schizophrenia and other psychopathologies to the social dynamics of the family during childhood (see Chapter 14). According to this thesis, children create their identities from the messages received from those around them; if these are contradictory or confused they are driven to increasingly bizarre lengths in trying to understand what is going on. In addition to the 'double-bind' phenomenon (see Chapter 14) there may also be mystifications about parenthood (e.g. the child is told its grandmother is its mother when in fact it is the child of an older 'sister'), or straightforward denial of the child's experience (e.g. parent insists child has always liked school when child denies it, parent then says it is lying). From these all kinds of 'knots' (as Laing called them) are created, and the meanings of love/hate, dependence/independence, etc. can become distorted. This image of the child is of someone constantly facing the task of self-creation on the basis of available evidence – the child, like everyone else, has to choose what to be in the absence of a clear-cut, genetically given identity.

While behaviourism is, in its own terms, optimistic, European versions of environmentalism are less so. The existentialist view in particular has a basically pessimistic air about it. And while behaviourism guarantees its results by applying the scientific laws of learning, the existentialist child is active, rather than passive; experience remains the raw material, but it makes its own choices, interpretations and decisions. Unlike the optimistic neo-romanticism of American growth movement approaches (which sometimes co-opted existentialist ideas) there is no guarantee of ever finding your 'true self'. Indeed you probably cannot: life does not stand still and you are forever faced with new existential choices, older 'true selves' appearing in retrospect more or less 'inauthentic'. This view later became related to the post-modernist critique of the 'self' concept (see Chapter 11).

The most radically new Psychological image of the child was undoubtedly Freud's, the roots of which are especially tangled. He was certainly working within an evolutionary framework (although not a crude recapitulationist), but the formal structure of his theory (particularly the super ego/ego/id division) was foreshadowed several times in earlier nineteenth-century German psychiatric thought. The primacy of the irrational and unconscious harks back to romanticism, but the entirely negative character Freud ascribes to it clearly conforms to late nineteenth-century perceptions of it as the legacy of a primitive evolutionary past. And then there was the theoretical centrality of sex, which, if not unprecedented, had never before been spelled out so explicitly. In terms of nature vs. nurture psychoanalysis was ambiguous – the stages of psychosexual development, the primacy of the sexual instinct, the structure of the psyche, were all biological givens. On the other hand the interaction of these with the demands of the child's domestic world was crucial in determining each adult's unique constellation of fixations, sublimations and repressions. As a therapeutic procedure it might be thought that it was optimistic – after all therapy seeks to cure and assumes this as a viable possibility. In fact it became rather pessimistic – cures were never complete, and some degree of psychopathology was the price universally paid for our 'civilised' life-style. In the US the 1940's generation of psychoanalysts rejected much of this pessimism, introducing such notions as ego-autonomy, and reverting to a more romantic vision. (See also Chapter 14.)

In the 1950s a revised 'ethological' version of the evolutionary image emerged, adopting a number of concepts initially developed by ethologists studying animal behaviour, notably 'attachment', 'imprinting', and 'innate releasing mechanisms'. From this angle child behaviour appeared to share some typically mammalian features: the mother–child linkage was not due to a simple conditioned association between food and mother in learning theory fashion (this was experimentally refuted by H.F. and M.K. Harlow, see Chapter 15) but represented a complex, innately governed, system which had evolved to ensure successful child-rearing. The child 'imprinted' onto the mother and formed specific 'attachments' to particular adults. Both infant and parent behaviour had evolved to maintain the communicative links between them (hence the notion of maternal 'bonding'). Some Freudians, notably John Bowlby, assimilated much of this, thereby de-emphasising the primacy of essentially 'sexual' instincts. 'Attachment' remains a major focus of developmental research. Among other things, this perspective brought about a radical rethinking of the psychological character of separation and loss in children.

Discussion

At present there is a risk of the wood and the trees becoming indistinguishable. While research on everything from effects of adverse life events to neonate perception, from cognitive development to origins of gender differences, flourishes we should be wary of losing sight of the persisting influence of implicit underlying views of the child. Psychologists have no more reached agreement than anyone else on such fundamental questions as how far children should be controlled, how far they can be trusted (e.g. current controversies over reliability of child witnesses), and how far their personalities are 'learned' or 'innate' (and is this a sensible question?). Even the simple question of how much attention should be paid to them has not really been satisfactorily answered. Children are perfect projective material – adults fantasise about them endlessly – and perhaps it is these fantasies which, for better or worse, children end up realising. And our adult fantasies about children are also fantasies about our own childhoods. What I am suggesting here is that we continue to have a variety of such fantasies about the child: as original sinner, as innocent embodiment of spiritual potential, as primitive adult, as raw material for producing a good citizen, as existential victim of conscious existence, as mirror of society, as an amoral seeker of instinctual gratification, as an amusing and charming example of wild-life, and more recently (though not discussed here) as a self-programming information processor. This plurality generates a constant tension between the ideas of psychologists and those of others such as politicians and religious leaders whose own images may diverge from those currently prevailing in Psychology. At the twenty-first century's more sceptical onset, unlike certain previous periods, no image is culturally dominant, each has its advocates. Developmental Psychology is in fact *less* able than it has occasionally been in the past to authoritatively promote its latest theories under the banner of 'scientific knowledge'.

Even so, Psychology has clearly acquired a role as the site where society's concerns and anxieties regarding children and child-rearing are most systematically and authoritatively debated. In this sense Developmental Psychology constitutes the institutionalisation of a universal social practice: discussing how children should be treated and raised. A particularly significant move in recent years has been the attempts by J.R. Morss (1996) and E. Burman (1995) to abandon the very concept of 'development' on the grounds that it involves viewing the child solely in terms of what it might become and how it compares to the behavioural norms of its contemporaries. Instead, they argue, we should be seeing the child as a person fully functioning in the present, albeit differently from adults.

Despite this plurality of approaches there is, however, one contextually enforced trend which should be noted. During the twentieth century one concern which threatened to over-ride all others was education, and Child Psychology in many respects became an adjunct to Educational Psychology. This reinforced the 'developmentalist' orientation by focusing on monitoring children's performance vis-à-vis their peers within the school. Modernist societies' felt need to certificate and standardise educational performance and practice in turn fuelled the psychometric testing and assessment project. Initially educational tests were implemented to assess the qualities of the child's performance and teaching, but over time the scales turned so that educational practice itself became geared to the assessment technology. This has clearly had an insidious effect on educational practice itself, rendering it tantamount to a coaching exercise in quiz performance. The assessment tail has ended up wagging the educational dog. This is a far cry from the aspirations and insights of Froebel, A.S. Niell and other creative educational pioneers.

My own position, for what it is worth, is an unsatisfactory fusion of romantic and social constructionist. The sheer range of individual differences in temperament, ability and personality from even earliest infancy seems too great to be completely explained in even the subtlest social constructionist terms. I am romantic enough to believe that general rules of good child-rearing are probably an illusion except for that which says you should focus on the specific individual needs of each child. But it is, nevertheless, in the social and cultural arena in which values and meanings originate, where the child has to find the content which can give its existence meaning. And it is certainly in this arena where Developmental Psychology itself does so.

Further reading

Aries, P. (1962) *Centuries of Childhood*. London: Cape. Classic French social historical study.

Burman, E. (1995) *Deconstructing Developmental Psychology*. London: Routledge. Major critique of the concept of 'development'.

Cleverley, J. and Phillips, D. (1988) *Visions of Childhood: Influential Models from Locke to Spock*. London: Allen & Unwin. Very useful, fairly short survey with an orientation similar to that adopted here.

Ehrenreich, B. and English, D. (1979) *For Her Own Good – A Hundred and Fifty Years of the Experts' Advice to Mothers*. New York: Pluto Press. An entertaining feminist reading of the American story.

Morss, J.R. (1990) *The Biologising of Childhood. Developmental Psychology and the Darwinian Myth*. London: Erlbaum. Critique of Developmental Psychology identifying its adoption of a primarily biological orientation as the major flaw.

Morss, J.R. (1996) *Growing Critical. Alternatives to Developmental Psychology*. London: Routledge. A further elaboration of the theme of his earlier book into an attack on the 'development' concept.

Richards, G. (1992) *Mental Machinery Part One: 1600–1850*. London: Athlone Press. See Chapter 4 for the eighteenth century and Chapter 7 for Froebel.

Romantic Image

Romanticism proper

Rousseau, J.-J. (1762) *Emile* (4 vols). Amsterdam: Néaulme.

Day, T. (1789–1793) *Sandford & Merton*. London: A Miller.

Edgeworth, M. and Edgeworth, R.L. (1798) *Practical Education*. London: A. Johnson.

Froebel, F. (1826, English edn 1897) *The Education of Man*. New York & London: Appleton. There is a large literature from c. 1890–1910 due to a revival of interest among educationists. The best accounts are the following: W.H. Herford (rev. edn D.B. and C.H. Hertford, 1916) *The Student's Froebel*, London: Pitman; E.R. Murray (1914) *Froebel as a Pioneer of Modern Psychology*, London: George Philip.

Herbart, J.F. (1901, 1st edn 1835) *Outlines of Educational Doctrine*. New York & London: Macmillan. As with Froebel there was a later revival of interest: see H.B. Dunkel (1970) *Herbart and Herbartianism: An Educational Ghost Story*. Chicago: Chicago University Press. This is the best historical account and F.H. Hayward (1903) *The Critics of Herbartianism*, London: Swan Sonnenschein, also provides useful coverage of much German nineteenth-century educational thought.

Itard, J. (1799, trans. 1972) *The Wild Boy of Aveyron*. London: New Left Books.

Pestalozzi, J.H. (1803) *Buch der Mütter*. Collected Works 1819–1826. English editions of his work seem scarce, but see: Rev. C. and E. Mayo (1873, 3rd edn) *Pestalozzi and his Principles*, London: Home & Colonial School Society; A. Pinloche (1902) *Pestalozzi and the Foundation of the Modern Elementary*

School, London: Heinemann; and K. Silber (1960) *Pestalozzi: The Man and his Work*, London: Routledge & Kegan Paul.

Romantic influence

Boden, M.A. (1979) *Piaget: Outline and Critique of his Theory*. Brighton: Harvester. A sound basic introduction. The Piagetian literature, primary and secondary, is vast and easily accessible, so omitted here. This is a good general introduction.

Koffka, K. (1928) *The Growth of the Mind*. London: Kegan Paul Trench & Trübner.

Montessori, M. (1913) *Pedagogical Anthropology*. London: Heinemann.

Montessori, M. (1936) *The Secret of Childhood*. London: Longmans Green. Montessori, founder of the Montessori movement and Montessori schools, was a prolific writer. It might be noted that her thought was originally also influenced by degenerationist and eugenic concerns (fellow Italian Lombroso, discussed elsewhere, being a major formative figure), although this has been largely forgotten.

Stern, W. (1924) *Psychology of Early Childhood up to the Sixth Year of Age*. London: Allen & Unwin. Based on an observational diary by his wife Clara.

Anti-romantic

More, H. (1799, 12th edn 1818) *Strictures on the Modern System of Female Education* (2 vols). London: Cadell. Also representative of a certain kind of Christian evangelical viewpoint. (Historically, Hannah More is a profoundly significant figure in several respects which we cannot enter into here.)

Empiricist

Classic

Hamilton, E. (1801) *Letters on the Elementary Principles of Education* (2 vols). London: Robinson. She later became a follower of Pestalozzi.

Locke, J. (1693, rep. 1902) *Some Thoughts Concerning Education*. Cambridge: Cambridge University Press.

Spencer, H. (1929, 1st edn 1861) *Education, Intellectual, Moral and Physical*. London: Watts. Spencer's evolutionary associationist perspective.

Behaviourist etc.

Gesell, A. (1925) *The Mental Growth of the Pre-School Child*. New York: Macmillan. First in a series which continued up to the 1940s which included the following:

Gesell, A. (1937) *Infancy & Human Growth*. New York: Macmillan.

Gesell, A. and Ilg, F.L. (1946) *The Child from Five to Ten*. London: Hamish Hamilton.

Watson, J.B. (1928) *Psychological Care of Infant and Child*. New York: Norton. It would be unfair to identify all subsequent behaviourists with the often bizarre sentiments of this landmark text.

Evolutionary

See Further reading in Chapter 3 for evolution-influenced developmental titles.

Psychoanalytic and post-Freudian

Erikson, E. (1950, rev. edn 1965) *Childhood and Society*. Harmondsworth: Penguin.
Freud, A. (1959, 1st German edn 1926) *The Psycho-analytical Treatment of Children*. London: Imago.
Isaacs, S. (1929) *The Nursery Years. The Mind of the Child from Birth to Six Years*. London: George Routledge.
Isaacs, S. (1933) *Social Development in Young Children. A Study of Beginnings*. London: George Routledge. Isaacs was one of the most successful British Kleinians, bringing Kleinian ideas to a wide popular audience.
Klein, M. (1932, rev. edn 1935) *The Psycho-Analysis of Children*. London: Hogarth Press.
Klein, M. (with J. Riviere) (1937) *Love, Hate and Reparation*. London: Hogarth Press.
Rickman, J. (ed.) (1936) *On the Bringing up of Children*. London: Kegan Paul. Collection of popular papers including one by Klein tying herself in knots trying not to say that without breast feeding all is lost.
Webster, R. (1995) *Why Freud was Wrong: Sin, Science and Psychoanalysis*. London: HarperCollins. Seriously flawed in many respects but raises some important issues.
Winnicot, D.W. (1971) *Playing and Reality*. Harmondsworth: Penguin. Leading exponent of Kleinian 'object-relations theory'.

For Freud himself see especially:
Freud, S. (1905, 1970) *Three Essays on the Theory of Sexuality*. London: Hogarth Press. 'One of the two most important books Freud ever wrote' – Ernest Jones.

Marxist and Social Constructionist

Bühler, C. (1935) *From Birth to Maturity*. London: Kegan Paul.
Bühler, K. (1930, rep. 1949) *The Mental Development of the Child*. London: Routledge & Kegan Paul. Although not strictly Marxist, the Bühler's position was infused with their socialist ideals.

There are few Marxist texts explicitly on childhood; for the general Marxist position on psychological issues see:
Sève, L. (1978) *Man in Marxist Theory and the Psychology of Personality*. Brighton: Harvester.

For L.S. Vygotsky see:

Newman, F. and Holzman, L. (1993) *Vygotsky: Revolutionary Scientist*. London: Routledge.

Vygotsky, L.S. (1978) *Mind in Society: The Development of Higher Psychological Processes*. Cambridge MA: Harvard University Press. Most accessible English statement of his, hardly party-line Marxist, views.

Wertsch, J.W. (ed.) (1985) *Culture, Communication and Cognition: Vygotskian Perspectives*. Cambridge: Cambridge University Press. Especially Part III for discussion of Developmental Psychology.

Ethological

Bowlby, John (1969) *Attachment and Loss. Vol. 1: Attachment*. Harmondsworth: Penguin. Combined ethology and psychoanalysis.

There is a vast subsequent literature on attachment and related issues. On Bowlby see:

Holmes, J. (1993) *John Bowlby and Attachment Theory*. London: Routledge.

Rutter, M. (2001) 'The Emergence of Developmental Psychopathology'. In G.C. Bunn, A.D. Lovie and G.D. Richards (eds) *Psychology in Britain: Historical Essays and Personal Reflections*. Leicester: British Psychological Society and London: The Science Museum, 422–431. Autobiographical account with much on the impact of the ethological approach.

Existentialist

Laing, R.D. (1959) *The Divided Self*. London: Tavistock.

Laing, R.D. and Esterson, A. (1964) *Sanity, Madness and the Family*. London: Tavistock.

Other

Dennis, W. (1940) *The Hopi Child*. New York: Appleton-Century.

Gregory, J. (1765, rep. 1798) *A Comparative View of the State and Faculties of Man with those of Animals*. London: Cadell & Davies. Interesting Scottish Enlightenment work in which children are considered as driven by instincts rather than reason, a stage theory is suggested, and later 'eugenics' ideas on breeding foreshadowed.

Maccoby, E.E. (ed.) (1967) *The Development of Sex Differences*. London: Tavistock.

Mead, M. (1928, rep. 1943) *Coming of Age in Samoa*. Harmondsworth: Penguin.

Mead, M. (1930, rep. 1973) *Growing up in New Guinea*. Harmondsworth: Penguin.

Mussen, P.H. (1963) *The Psychological Development of the Child*. Englewood Cliffs: Prentice-Hall. Orthodox US mainstream approach of the post-Second World War period.

Chapter 17

Psychology and gender

- Background and problems of defining the academic genre
- Nineteenth-century images of woman
- Early physiological and psychiatric views of gender differences
- Havelock Ellis's position
- Freud's and Jung's theories on the nature of gender differences
- Orthodox Psychological approaches and the impact of feminism after 1970
- Some observations on the current situation

Few topics are currently more controversial than gender-differences and the 'Psychology of Women'. It is a telling fact that until R. Miles (1991) the idea of an explicit 'Psychology of Men' had never been seriously broached, and has, since then, been but fitfully pursued any further except in some areas of evolutionary Psychology. I cannot do justice here to recent feminist scholarship but hope, in focusing primarily on the earlier period, to provide a complementary historical perspective. Traditionally Psychology saw no need to differentiate between the sexes regarding basic processes such as perception, memory and learning (although the existence of sex-differences in performance was always asserted), otherwise the white male was considered as the norm and primary focus of interest. With a few notable exceptions, attitudes towards women found in mainstream Psychology between 1850 and 1950 are mostly little more than restatements of prevailing stereotypes and assumptions given an authoritative 'scientific' gloss. L.M. Terman and C.C. Miles's (1936) 'M–F' (masculine–feminine) Scale for instance still took stereotypical gender-trait linkages as unproblematic. Gender issues largely remained a side issue until the 1950s but expanded rapidly with the 1960's revival of feminism, also a period when larger numbers of women were entering the discipline. In 1969 the ratio among Psychology students in Britain was c. 60 : 40 in favour of males, today (2001) it is at least 80 : 20 in favour of females. Thus the rise in concern reflects the cultural preoccupation with the position of women and their influx into the discipline – one aspect of their changing position and aspirations associated with that preoccupation.

Psychological work can be hard to differentiate from the wider body of texts published since the late 1960s. Was Germaine Greer's *The Female Eunuch* Psychology? Or Foucault's volumes on the history of sexuality? Or Kate Millet's *Sexual Politics* and Sheila Rowbotham's *Woman's Consciousness, Man's World*? It was in the very nature of their task that those critically rethinking the issue had to move beyond conventional Psychological genres to make their case. Not that there is an absence of readily classifiable 'Psychology' work, Mitchell (1974) being an early example, Morawski (1994) a more recent one. The APA's Psychology of Women Division was established in 1973 and the journal *Psychology of Women Quarterly* followed in the late 1970s, the BPS Psychology of Women Section was founded in 1988, and the British journal *Feminism and Psychology* launched in 1991.

Although prior to the 1960s Psychology paid women relatively little explicit attention, psychoanalytic schools were a major exception, not least because women figured prominently as both practitioners and clients. Neo-Freudian women analysts like Karen Horney also contributed to the beginnings of modern feminism in the late 1940s and early 1950s. Sabina Spielrein's role in C.G. Jung's intellectual development, his relationship with Freud and the dissemination of psychoanalytic thought in the post-revolutionary Soviet Union was only recovered in the 1990s (J. Kerr, 1994).

One difficulty in focusing on 'Psychology and gender' as a specific topic is that discipline and subject matter levels are fused even more than usual. Comprehensive treatment would involve venturing into the realms of social history and the numerous works of writers such as Michel Foucault, Lawrence Stone (1977), P.G. Boucé (ed.) (1982), R. Pearsall (1969) and Marina Warner (1976) on the history of gender relations in European culture. Starting in the mid-nineteenth century is to enter a story which had been running for centuries and seen many vicissitudes. We discover a situation in which the idealisation and infantilisation of women (particularly middle-class women) was at a singularly high pitch, and evolutionary thought soon provided new arguments to reinforce this. Compared to Victorian men Victorian women were weaker, more emotional, less rational, more fickle, more dogmatic, more infantile, more aesthetically sensitive, more prone to hysteria, much less or far more sexual, more suggestible, superficially more spiritual and talked too much. Regarding a woman's place being in the home, here is Mrs Copley probably writing sometime in the 1850s:

> Are married women never to go abroad? are they to be confined to the storeroom, and to the nursery, as to a nunnery or prison? No: this is not required of them; though it will be found that the best and happiest wives and mothers are those who, without any irksome feeling of confinement, are so constantly, and agreeably, and usefully employed at home, that it requires a very clear and imperative call of duty to get them abroad, and a very strenuous effort on their parts to comply with it; and, even then, they can hardly take their hearts with them, but in the midst of society are 'stung with the thought of home'.
>
> (*The Young Wife; or, Hints to Married Daughters* c. 1860: 203)

When nineteenth-century Psychological writers mention women it is generally in passing. Here is Francis Galton, for example, somewhat at odds with prevailing notions of greater female sensitivity:

> I found as a rule that men have more delicate powers of discrimination than women, and ... business experience ... seems to confirm this view. The tuners of pianofortes are men, and so I understand are the tasters of tea and wine, the sorters of wool, and the like. These latter occupations are well salaried, because it is of the first moment to the merchant that he should be rightly advised on the real value of what he is about to purchase or to sell. If the sensitivity of women were superior to that of men the self-interest of merchants would lead to their being always employed; but as the reverse is the case, the opposite supposition is likely to be the true one. // Ladies rarely distinguish the merits of wine at the dinner-table, and though custom allows them to preside at the breakfast-table, men think them on the whole to be far from successful makers of tea and coffee.
>
> (1883: 20–21)

Specifically Psychological texts on women are virtually non-existent before the 1890s. The three major relevant genres were: (a) works arising from the growing feminism controversy, e.g. J.S. Mill's pro-feminist *The Subjection of Women* (1869) and Alexander Walker's less well-known *Woman Physiologically Considered as to Mind, Morals, Marriage, Matrimonial Slavery, Infidelity and Divorce* (c. 1850); (b) pious advice manuals such as Mrs Copley's promoting respectable bourgeois sex-roles; and (c) semi-underground works (see Chapter 8) posing as sex education manuals or pseudo-medical books – one, *Aristotle's Masterpiece* (which had nothing to do with Aristotle), first appeared around 1684 and was continually being reprinted.

In 1901 an extraordinary German work appeared, translated into English as *Sex and Character* (1906). Its author, 21-year-old Otto Weininger, committed suicide two years later aged, we are told Adrian Molishly, '23 and a half'. Though hardly mainstream Psychology it attracted wide acclaim and displayed precocious academic erudition. Weininger belonged in the late nineteenth-century *fin de siècle* Neo-Romantic camp (a reaction against positivism and materialism haunted by visions of decadence and decay) rather than the scientific one. His bizarre thesis is clearly expounded in Chapter IX 'Male and Female Psychology'. Women quite simply have no soul or ego, existing at a totally different level of consciousness to males. Being incapable of genius, logical thought and significant creative achievement, and possessing neither free-will nor genuine morality, when they display such qualities women are merely imitating men. Mother and Prostitute are the two forms to which female character always tends. This is embedded in, and emerges from, a complex metaphysical system into which, mercifully, we need not enter. One quote from among many astonishing passages (p. 191):

> Woman's thought is a sliding and gliding through subjects, a superficial tasting of things that a man, who studies the depths, would scarcely notice; it is an extravagant and dainty method of skimming which has no grasp of accuracy. A woman's thought is superficial, and touch is the most highly developed of the female senses, the most notable characteristic of the woman which she can bring to a high state by her unaided efforts. Touch necessitates a limiting of interest to superficialities ... When a woman 'understands' a man ... she is simply, so to speak tasting ... what he has thought about her.

Weininger's near pathological misogyny was ironically destined to provide Germaine Greer (1970) with a telling target and point of reference. Curiously, he consulted Freud while writing the work and its appearance played a role in the split between Freud and his friend Wilhelm Fleiss. Most significant is surely the very fact that it was not laughed out of court, but hailed as a work of genius, containing the 'ripest wisdom' according to the publisher, William Heinemann's, prefatory note, who continued '... no thoughtful man will lay down this book without deep emotion and admiration; many, indeed, will close it with almost religious reverence' (p. viii).

If Psychological discussion of women was rare, physiological and psychiatric discussion was not. As well as Weininger's book, 1901 saw the publication of the German psychiatrist Moebius's *On the Physiological Imbecility of Woman*, advancing similar doctrines of greater female animality and poor self-control. The exposition of physiological differences, coupled with evolutionary theory, was regularly deployed to reinforce existing stereotypes (as also happened regarding race). Women's brains were, it seemed, smaller with less developed frontal lobes, hence their poorer reasoning and weaker wills. (I am still keen to track down a paper I once encountered called 'The Missing 4 Ounces'.) Women, by being biologically tied to basic instinctual functions, especially reproduction and child-rearing, were simply less neurologically, hence psychologically, evolved than men. Decent male behaviour towards them should thus be patronising, protective, care-taking, tolerant of their irrationality and respectful of the intuitive emotional insights their closer connection with Nature bestowed – coupled with judicious intellectual distancing. Psychiatric evidence endorsed this image, women being especially prone to hysteria, widely believed to reflect a less well-integrated nervous system. H. Ellenberger (1970) discloses, among much else, how psychiatrists like J.C. Charcot could get unwittingly drawn into playing sex typical games with female patients throughout this period.

From a different direction, criminology, came the leading degenerationist C. Lombroso's *The Female Offender* (English edition, 1895) written with fellow Italian William Ferrero. To amplify on the point made in Chapter 13, Lombroso considers that female criminals are hairier, have more warts, less symmetric faces and weightier jaws than their law-abiding sisters, and the work contains many mug-shots to 'prove' it (Fig. 17.1).

This book is valuable on two counts: firstly as illustrating how deeply, yet naively, sexual stereotyping permeated supposedly 'scientific' work; secondly as a source of numerous case histories providing a grim picture of the plights in which women could find themselves. Quite counter to Lombroso's intentions it enables us to redeem some forgotten women from oblivion. As far as stereotyping is concerned here are a couple of quotes illustrating the belief that women are capable of worse immorality than men:

On 'Crimes of Passion':

... often premeditation in the woman is longer than in the man; it is also colder and more cunning, so that the crime is executed with an ability and a gloating which in the deed of pure passion are psychologically impossible. Nor does sincere penitence always follow the offence; on the contrary, there is often exultation; and rarely does the offender commit suicide.

(p. 147)

On habitual criminals:

... there is among them a small proportion whose criminal propensities are more intense and more perverse than those of their male prototypes. // Another terrible point of superiority in the female born criminal over the male lies in the refined, diabolical cruelty with which she accomplishes her crime.

(p. 148)

And one case:

M. the daughter of an eccentric, unpractical mother, received a high literary but incomplete education, crowned by a university degree, which only unfitted her for real life. At twenty-three she found herself an orphan, ruined by family reverses ... After various vain efforts she accepted a post of teacher ... but was dismissed ... on its being discovered she was a Protestant. Then, alone in the world, without means of existence, and haunted by the memory of more happy days, she began buying articles of jewellery in shops, where she obtained credit in virtue of the former position of her family ... A series

Figure 17.1 'Russian women criminals'. A typical plate from C. Lombroso and W. Ferrero (1895) *The Female Offender*. If, to us, these faces speak of tragic abuse, hardship and brutalisation, Lombroso saw only anomalies and asymmetry in cranial morphology: the 'stigmata' of degeneration. Photo: George Singer. Reproduced by permission of the Centre for History of Psychology, Staffordshire University.

of such frauds finally brought her to prison, where she died before her trial, worn out by misery and shame.

(pp. 205–206)

But it is in the setting of the doctor–patient relationship that women first receive intensive Psychological scrutiny around 1900, and nowhere more so than on Freud's couch. The views of psychiatrists, including Freud and Jung, nevertheless remain clearly related to those being expressed in contemporary literature and philosophy. Again Ellenberger summarises this well, demonstrating the close affinities between their ideas on feminine psychology and those of philosophers (especially F. Nietzsche) and Neo-Romantic novelists (many of whom they cited with approval). Not all shared the extreme views of Weininger and Moebius, of course, but there was a common consensus that women were passive, receptive and less rational than men. This sometimes took the semi-mystical 'complementarity' form: male and female are complementary parts of a single whole – an idea underlying Jung's later Anima and Animus archetypes. Fascination with archetypal female roles, especially the Mother, was widespread during this period (J.J. Bachofen's 1861 *Das Mutterrecht* (Mother Right) was widely cited by turn-of-the-century writers). Many males seem, at this time, quite genuinely unable to see women except through the lenses of such images. Sceptics really should read some of the original material. Feminist opposition to this was intense, with egalitarian views also being promoted by many socialist men, and it was this controversy which rendered the issue so highly charged.

Havelock Ellis's *Man and Woman* (1896), revised and reprinted up to 1914, is in this latter camp. This is far more sober than those texts mentioned so far, critically reviewing all the available data on sex differences (including physiology). Regarding brain size he affirms that it is relative, not absolute, brain-size, which is relevant – and finds that when the body-weight/brain-size ratio is used women emerge as having slightly larger brains (a finding which still stands and is typical for higher primates), a fact, he notes, known since 1836. There are, however, further technical and logical difficulties that might serve to further underestimate female brain-size (although nobody, he believes, has arrived at a satisfactory method of settling the question). A similar reversal of the assumption that women have smaller frontal lobes (traditional site of 'lofty intellectual processes') emerges from recent data; again they are equal or slightly superior to men – although there is actually no real reason to ascribe any 'specially exalted functions' to them.

While Ellis (quite erroneously) holds women's sense of smell to be inferior to that of men, their taste-sense, contrary to Galton, is superior. He also finds fault with Lombroso, countering his findings of inferior female sensitivities to touch and pain with those of better designed studies by the American psychologist Jastrow. On intellectual capacity he is, in 1896, somewhat more supportive of traditional views, but aware of how environmental factors and the inferior social position of women might be implicated. By 1914 he has changed tack, insisting that although there may be differences in kind, 'In all the ordinary affairs of life the intelligence of women, whatever sexual differences may exist, proceeds side by side with that of men' (1914, p. 263). Ellis was a leading male supporter of feminism and sometimes curiously anticipates points made more recently:

> Men have had their revenge on Nature and on her protégé. While women have been largely absorbed in that sphere of sexuality which is Nature's, men have roamed the earth, sharpening their aptitudes and energies in perpetual conflict with Nature. It has thus come about that the subjugation of Nature by Man has often practically involved the subjugation, physical and mental, of women by men.
>
> (1896, p. 395)

And he sarcastically observes,

> Women, it is true, remain nearer than men to the infantile state; but, on the other hand, men approach more nearly than women to the ape-like and senile state.
>
> (1896, p. 394)

Even more pertinently he comments:

> So long as maternity under certain conditions is practically counted as a criminal act, it cannot be said that the feminine element in life has yet been restored to due honour.
>
> (1896, p. 396)

Ellis, one of the most important Psychological writers on sex, represented a liberal empirically oriented position, highly critical and cautious regarding prevailing stereotypes. His was, however, rather a lone voice within Psychology during the first half of the century. Much more influential were the new Psychoanalytic and Jungian accounts. Although steeped in late nineteenth-century ideas about women, both Freud and Jung develop more ambiguous and complex theories regarding psychological sex-differences. They may nonetheless be considered traditional insofar as they tend to see these as universal and in some sense innate or inescapable, rather than culturally produced. Both were initially seen by most feminists as embodiments of the patriarchal attitude towards women, but the present picture is far less straightforward than this (see e.g. L. Appignanesi and J. Forrester, 1993). Concepts like 'penis envy' (in Freud's case) or 'Mother Archetype' (in Jung's) are easily taken from the full theoretical contexts providing their technical meanings and ridiculed. Freud departed further from tradition than Jung. The key to female psychology for Freud lies primarily, of course, in the distinctive features of the infant girl's family position, combined with her biology. To grossly oversimplify: unlike the male, the female is not required to shift her primary identification from the mother to the opposite sex parent; for this reason – coupled with her lack of a penis – the Oedipal phase during which the boy resolves incestuous and patricidal wishes and emerges identifying with the father (now internalised as his 'Super Ego'), takes a very different form. Although her incestuous desires for the father have, like a boy's for his mother, to be somehow resolved, this resolution is necessarily less clear-cut given her original identification with the mother and the fact that she does not suffer the boy's intense castration anxiety – a threat emanating primarily (though not exclusively) from the father. This in turn entails failure to acquire a mature Super Ego. The upshot is that within Psychoanalytic thought it was possible to preserve the notion of women as less securely moral and insightful, and more reliant on uncritical conformity to received precepts handed down by male authority. She is also less pressurised to transcend the early stages, in J. Mitchell's summary:

> She can with impunity continue to love her father and hate her mother as a rival, especially as these emotions are 'desexualized' with the latency period. That her mother as rival is stronger than the little girl does not seem to matter much, because she has no absolute strength and the little girl has nothing to lose. But the little boy fears the father who is his rival for his mother's love, because the father is truly powerful and potent and the boy has just that potency to lose. So while the girl can linger secure in this phase of life, the boy must leave it quickly . . .
>
> (Mitchell, 1974: 97)

The Freudian woman remains to a large degree the traditional woman with many of her negative traits (though not less intelligent), but the universality of her plight is due less to biology as such than to the universality of the developmental psychodynamics which ensue from this, involving a particular patterning of family relationships and targeting of the sexual instinct. While the Freudian male continues to see women in terms, particularly, of the Mother role, this is not due to the projection of some archetypal image but to the persistence of an inner *imago* of his own mother as a desired ideal. The woman too sees men through the *imago* of her father. This backtracks markedly from neo-romantic doctrines.

Jung remained more loyal to Romanticism. For him we are all psychologically androgynous, a female anima dominating the male unconscious and a male animus the female one. The great female sex-role archetypes (along with more numerous male equivalents) are universal psychic realities, underlying our individual identities. One task is to avoid becoming, as it were, 'possessed' by any one of them. In Jung's personality typology females are more typically dominated by the 'feeling' and to some extent the 'intuition' functions than men, in whom 'thinking' and 'sensation' tend to prevail. Jung's notion of complementarity precluded overt judgements on the relative merits of the sexes, but he gave a green light to quasi-mystical exaltation of archetypal roles like earth mother, virgin, wise old woman and the like which some feminists have eagerly exploited and revalued. Not perhaps quite what Jung had in mind. One's impression is that he was an unregenerated romantic, in the everyday sense, regarding women. Kerr (1994) argues that Sabina Spielrein (who ironically became a Freudian) was the ultimate source of his anima concept. He had numerous relationships with female clients and colleagues, and surely he flattered them all mightily as avatars of the archetypal Sophia, goddess of wisdom. A woman engineer – with her he would have had trouble.

In the meantime, from c. 1910–1939, mainstream Psychology seems to have paid the psychology of women little attention of any importance, despite the number of women psychologists (see Table 17.1; B. Scarborough and L. Furumoto, 1987). Sex itself, however, was a topic of growing interest; in addition to Ellis there was a pioneering US study of women's sexual behaviour by Katherine Bement Davis

Table 17.1 Some eminent pre-1970 women psychologists

Name	Country of working domicile	Field	Decades of most productive work
Anne Anastasi	USA	Mental testing and psychometrics	1930s–1960s
Magda Arnold	USA	Emotion	1950s–1960s
Ruth Benedict	USA	Anthropologist-psychologist, culture and personality	1930s–1940s
Charlotte Buhler*	Austria, Norway (1940–43) US	Developmental	1920s–1960s
Mary Whiton Calkins	USA	General psychologist-philosopher	1890s–1920s
Mamie Phipps Clarke*	USA (African American)	Developmental	1940s–1950s
Mary Collins	UK	Experimental, text-book writer	1920s–1930s
Helen Deutsch	USA	Psychoanalysis	1930s–1940s
June Etta Downey	USA	Mental testing and expressive behaviour	1910s–1930s
Beatrice Edgell	UK	General Psychology, memory	1920s–1930s
Else Frenkl-Brunswik	Austria, USA	Social psychology	1930s–1950s
Anna Freud	Austria (daughter of Sigmund Freud)	Child psychoanalysis	1930s–1950s
Eleanor J. Gibson*	USA	Perception	1940s–1980s
Florence Goodenough	USA	Mental testing, developmental	1920s–1940s
Ruth Hartley*	USA	Social psychology	1940s–1950s
Edna Heidbreder	USA	General psychology	1930s–1950s
Hilde Himmelweit	UK	Social psychology	1940s–1970s
Leta S. Hollingworth*	USA	Developmental	1910s–1930s
Karen Horney	Germany, USA	Psychoanalysis	1930s–1950s
Barbel Inhelder	Switzerland	Developmental (colleague of J. Piaget)	1930s–1970s
Susan Isaacs (née Brierley)	UK	Developmental psychology, psychoanalysis	1920s–1940s
Marie Jahoda	UK, USA	Social psychology	1940s–1970s
Melanie Klein	Germany, UK	Psychoanalysis	1920s–1960s
Christine Ladd-Franklin	USA	Perception	1910s–1920s

Table 17.1 *(cont'd)*

Name	*Country of working domicile*	*Field*	*Decades of most productive work*
Margaret Lowenfeld	UK	Psychotherapy	1920s–1950s
Eleanor E. Maccoby	USA	Social psychology, cross-cultural psychology	1950s–1980s
Margaret Mead	USA	Anthropology, cross-cultural psychology	1920s–1970s
Maria Montessori	Italy	Pioneer educational theorist	1890s–1940s
Lois Barclay Murphy*	USA	Developmental psychology	1920s–1950s
Sabina Spielrein	Switzerland, Austria, Soviet Union	Associate of Jung, Freud, Piaget, Vygotsky	1910s–1930s
C.W. Valentine	UK	Developmental, experimental, psychometrics, psychoanalysis	1910s–1930s
Margaret D. Vernon	UK	Perception, psychology of reading	1930s–1960s
Mary Floy Washburn	USA	Comparative psychology	1900s–1930s

* collaborated with psychologist husband

(1929), a precursor of the famous Kinsey Report (1953). All the research was conducted by women and the findings helped to begin to erode popular assumptions about the low extent of premarital female sexual activity, masturbation, and such. Another source of relevant literature at this time was the contraception and birth-control campaign (which to some extent took over the energies of the suffragette movement) the leading British figure in which was the redoubtable Dr Marie Stopes.

It is only around the late 1940s and early 1950s that there are signs of a real awakening of Psychological concern with the position of women. Horney counters the notion of 'penis envy' with a corresponding 'womb envy' in males, the existentialist Simone de Beauvoir publishes *The Second Sex*, and Betty Friedan's *The Feminine Mystique* follows soon after. Even so, as late as 1968 such works appeared (to this male at least) to represent feminism's last throes, not a new beginning. Then, during 1970, 'women's lib' stormed the cultural centre-stage, with Germaine Greer's *Female Eunuch* (actually a quite academic work) somehow becoming the eye of the storm. One significant work from this first phase was

Elaine Morgan (1972) which caused a furore in human evolution circles by arguing that women too had played a central role, rather than male hunters making all
the running.

The impact of the new feminism on Psychology was complex. Since the
1930s the US-based anthropological tradition of studying child-rearing had expanded
into a broader investigation of cross-cultural differences in character and sex-roles
(Eleanor Maccoby being most eminent in the latter). The new feminism coincided
with the wider academic dissemination of this information, especially on Social
Psychology courses. The lesson was that there were huge cross-cultural differences
in sex-roles, although a few underlying trends did exist (e.g. women rarely fought
as warriors) and developmental psychologists embarked on intensive research into
the acquisition of sex-roles in relation to child-rearing practices. The topic now under
scrutiny underwent an important shift, paralleling events in the area of 'Race' (see
Chapter 21). Previously, insofar as Psychology considered women it was with
respect to their seemingly distinctive psychological characteristics – 'the psychology
of women'. The new move was to consider the psychological and social sources
of sexism and sex-differences. It being more-or-less axiomatic at this point that
one must assume the sexes were *not* essentially different psychologically to any
significant degree then the agenda had to be to explore how, as a matter of fact,
the *apparent* psychological differences are imposed (by culture, child-rearing,
and social psychological processes) on psychologically neutral biological traits.

A further move rapidly followed: existing modes of research and theorising
are themselves distinctively masculine in character in that they centre on objectification, distancing of scientist from subject-matter and systematic repression of
feelings and emotional responses (see e.g. Sandra Harding, 1986). Something
quite complex is going on here, with ramifications way beyond Psychology. With
a mounting crisis of confidence in humanity's ability to manage its affairs, responsibility for this failure is naturally seen as resting with the most empowered section of the species, i.e. white males. In this context traditional female qualities such
as greater emotionality or closeness to nature, hitherto patronisingly contained or
denigrated, become revalued, while traditionally highly valued male rationality
and objectivity are the very traits implicated in their failure. Philosophers are,
in any case, increasingly questioning the positivist notion of 'objectivity'. For Psychology this problematises orthodox methodologies as *themselves* being one more
arena of expression of male psychology (in the subject-matter sense). But it is
now also an open question how far, if at all, the 'feminine' virtues are necessarily
distributed along biological gender-lines; what is clearer is that their traditional
cultural classification of psychological traits in this way backfires on the males
largely responsible for creating and sustaining it. Instead of Psychology studying
the psychology of women, we have an emerging 'women's Psychology' viewing
Psychology as itself an expression of male psychology.

As an example of this, consider 'The One or the Other? Textual Analysis of
Masculine Power and Feminist Empowerment' by J. Morawski and R.S. Steele
(1991). Among many points in this complex paper is one occurring during a
critique of a 1969 publication by the personality theorist Walter Mischel, who has
already, it is shown, got carried away by a 'valve' metaphor. Having established
the actuality of the mental 'reducing valve' Mischel off-handedly comments:

'When we observe a woman who seems hostile and fiercely independent some of the time but passive, dependent, and feminine on other occasions, our reducing valve usually makes us choose between the two syndromes'. Suddenly introducing women into a previously genderless text in this way produces a number of perturbations. First, and most obviously, it throws the reader's position into question. 'When we observe a woman' is a phrase requiring the reader to join the author in a typical male activity, 'girl watching' (p. 114). A few more quotes reveal how Mischel has imported into his apparently ungendered 'objective' account a whole fantasy about castrating 'ladies' and the superiority of traditional male values, typifying traditional Psychology's adoption of 'the male gaze'. One central lesson to be drawn is that empathising, non-objectifying, 'feminine' modes of enquiry can be just as useful, and often superior, to 'male' ones, especially in the area of psychological knowledge.

The current situation defies easy summarisation. First the notion that there *is* an essentially distinct 'psychology of women' is itself called into question, undermining the whole rationale for a sub-specialism 'the psychology of women'. The issue then becomes a contingent one of how gender differences are produced, by whom, and in whose interests, moving the question into the arena of social power-relations. There is a risk here, however, that denial of essential differences becomes tantamount to saying that (still inferior) women can become like (still superior) men in the right circumstances. This is averted by an ironic return to much of the traditional stereotyping, in which the traditional evaluation of the classic sex-role traits is challenged, along with the notion that they are necessarily gender-exclusive. There can be no return to the older 'Psychology of women' (in which men define a human normality from which women deviate), at least without a corresponding 'Psychology of men'. But also note the continued tension here, as in many other areas, between the needs to positively affirm differences and to deny them. At present we are again in the middle of the story (we were never anywhere else). Numerous outstanding issues remain unresolved. In particular we still, I think, have not fully understood if and how psychology and biological gender are related. Evolutionary psychologists in particular, not all of them men, have been reasserting the biological basis of traditional sex-roles. There are heated debates within women's Psychology, which have not yet reached any clearcut resolution, regarding whether research into sex/gender differences should be further pursued. It is logically possible that there are in some sense 'essential' differences – at least in how psychological traits are distributed. The difficulty is our notorious inability to pay more than lip-service to the slogan 'equal but different'. The solutions are either to deny difference, or to decouple the evaluative connotations of psychological traits from biological gender identity.

Does this mean that all the things written on the topic prior to, say, 1950 are worthless? Certainly not. As Juliet Mitchell argued regarding psychoanalysis, they are themselves evidence, often highly revealing, for how gender relations are constructed and managed. We do not need to read texts on their author's own terms, and this chapter is, I acknowledge, no exception.

Being deliberately provocative, however, a further ironic development should be noted regarding the American 'Psychology of Women' genre, now firmly established in many undergraduate courses (on which women students often predominate). This appears to be at risk of pursuing an agenda increasingly convergent on that of popular women's magazines. While the psychological aspects of menstruation, the menopause, pregnancy and mothering are clearly crucial, will they soon be supplemented by clothes, cosmetics, cooking, shopping and weight-control – a defiant re-immersion in precisely the stereotypical domestic female concerns from which feminism intended to liberate them? There is a disturbing parochialism about this, a 'naturalisation' of the concerns of middle-class middle-American women and uncritical acceptance of the commercial culture of which they are targets. Perhaps the 'mall culture' life-worlds of these women have, psychologically, drifted so far from those whence the mainstream western Psychological and philosophical traditions sprang that they can no longer connect with them and are in the process of creating a virtually autonomous P/psychology of their own. And maybe there is, after all, nothing wrong with this – in some senses it would indeed run counter to the whole orientation of the present work to protest. Even so, it would be a cruel outcome of the struggle for women's liberation if its main impact on Psychology was to reinstate what really amounted to a glossy version of domestic science (with apologies to that over-abused discipline).

Further reading

Appignanesi, L. and Forrester, J. (1993) *Freud's Women*. London: Virago. Encyclopaedic study of the role of women in the history of psychoanalysis.

Chodorow, N. (1992) *Feminism and Psychoanalytic Theory*. London: Yale University Press.

Ellenberger, H.F. (1970) *The Discovery of the Unconscious: The History and Evolution of Dynamic Psychology*. London: Allen Lane. Essential reading for the background to the psychoanalytic approach.

Matlin, M.W. (1993) *The Psychology of Women*, 2nd edn. New York: Harcourt Brace Jovanovich. A major current US textbook.

Mitchell, J. (1974) *Psychoanalysis and Feminism*. London: Allen Lane.

Morawski, J.G. (1994) *Practical Feminisms. Reconstructing Psychology*. Ann Arbor: University of Michigan Press. Major theoretical statement by this important writer.

O'Connell, A.N. and Russo, N.F. (eds) (1990) *Women in Psychology. A Bio-Bibliographic Sourcebook*. New York: Greenwood Press. A good survey, despite some gaps and the US-centred nature of the selection.

Sayers, J. (1986) *Sexual Contradictions: Psychology, Psychoanalysis, and Feminism*. London: Tavistock.

Scarborough, E. and Furumoto, L. (1987) *Untold Lives: The First Generation of American Women Psychologists*. New York: Columbia University Press. A useful review of the contributions of women psychologists, although restricted in coverage to the US.

Weisstein, N. (1993) 'Psychology Constructs the Female or the Fantasy Life of the Male Psychologist' plus commentaries. *Feminism and Psychology* 3(2): 194–245. Revised and expanded version of her 1968 paper: 'Kinder, Kuche, Kirche as Scientific Law: Psychology Constructs the Female'.

Additional references

Aristotle's Masterpiece, usually published without dates or publisher as a small book in red cloth covers.

Bachofen, J.J. (1967) *Myth, Religion and Mother Right: Selected Writings of J.J. Bachofen.* Trans. R. Manheim, introduction by Joseph Campbell, London: Routledge & Kegan Paul. Contains extracts from *Das Mutterrecht*.

Beauvoir, S. de (1960, 1st French edn, 1949) *The Second Sex.* London: Jonathan Cape. One of the founding texts for late twentieth-century feminism.

Bell, T. (1899) *Kalogynomia or the Laws of Female Beauty: Being the Elementary Principles of that Science.* London: Walpole Press ('for subscribers only'). Typical borderline medical/pornography text.

Boucé, P.-G. (ed.) (1982) *Sexuality in Eighteenth Century Britain.* Manchester: Manchester University Press. Provides a useful historical perspective on the broader nature of the issue.

Copley, Mrs (c. 1860) *The Young Wife; or, Hints to Married Daughters.* London: The Religious Tract Society.

Davis, K.B. (1929) *Factors in the Sex Life of Twenty-Two Hundred Women.* London: Harper. An interesting harbinger of what was to come in the Kinsey report (see below).

Ellis, H. (1896, 5th rev. edn 1914) *Man and Woman: A Study of Human Secondary Sexual Characters.* London: Walter Scott.

Ellis, H. (1936) *Studies in the Psychology of Sex* (4 vols). New York: Random House. Ellis was the major English-language writer on sexual behaviour and sex differences and raised many issues that were only pursued further in the post-1970 period.

Foucault, M. (1979) *The History of Sexuality, Vol. 1.* London: Allen Lane (further volumes followed this). Foucault's key contribution on the topic.

Friedan, B. (1963, rep. 1965) *The Feminine Mystique.* Harmondsworth: Penguin. A founding text for modern feminism.

Galton, F. (1883, rep. 1919) *Inquiries into Human Faculty and its Development.* London: Dent.

Greer, G. (1970) *The Female Eunuch.* London: MacGibbon & Kee. Still Germaine Greer's most famous book; while not the only radical feminist text appearing at this time it was one of the first and rapidly became the iconic focus of public controversy.

Harding, S. (1986) *The Science Question in Feminism.* Milton Keynes: Open University Press. A penetrating feminist analysis of the nature of science.

Kerr, J. (1994) *A Most Dangerous Method: The Story of Jung, Freud, and Sabina Spielrein.* London: Sinclair Stevenson. Revealed Sabina Spielrein's hitherto almost unknown role in the lives and intellectual development of Jung and Freud.

Kinsey, A.C., Pomeroy, W.B., Martin, C.E. and Gebhard, P.H. (1953) *Sexual Behavior in the Human Female.* Philadelphia: Lippincott, London: Saunders. Report of a survey of women's sexual behaviour in the US which caused widespread uproar and controversy. (A companion study of the 'human male' was also published.)

Lombroso, C. and Ferrero, W. (1895) *The Female Offender*. London: Fisher Unwin. Illuminates the mysogynistic side of Lombroso's degenerationist position.

Maccoby, E.E. (ed.) (1967) *The Development of Sex Differences*. London: Tavistock.

Maccoby, E.E. and Jacklin, C.N. (1974) *The Psychology of Sex Differences*. Stanford: Stanford University Press. Maccoby's work played a major role in providing the basis for subsequent, more explicitly feminist, approaches within Psychology.

Miles, R. (1991) *The Rites of Man. Love, Sex and Death in the Making of the Male*. London: Grafton Books. One of the few books on 'the psychology of men'.

Mill, J.S. (1869) *The Subjection of Women*. London: Longmans Green, Reader & Dyer.

Moebius, P.J. (1901) *Über den physiologischen Schwachsinn des Weibes* (On the physiological imbecility of woman). Halle: Marhold.

Morawski, J.G. (ed.) (1988) *The Rise of Experimentation in American Psychology*. New Haven: Yale University Press. See especially her own 'Impossible Experiments and Practical Constructions: The Social Bases of Psychologists' Work', 72–93.

Morawski, J.G. (1990) 'Toward the Unimagined: Feminism and Epistemology in Psychology'. In R.T. Hare-Mustin and J. Maracek (eds) *Making a Difference*. New Haven: Yale University Press, 150–183.

Morawski, J.G. and Steele, R.S. (1991) 'The One or the Other? Textual Analysis of Masculine Power and Feminist Empowerment'. *Theory & Psychology* 1(1): 107–131.

Morgan, E. (1972, rev. edn 1985) *The Descent of Woman*. London: Souvenir Press. This re-reading of the human evolution evidence from a feminist, woman-centred, perspective caused considerable upset among professionals in the field, but many of her arguments have since become orthodox.

Pearsall, R. (1969, rep. 1971 Penguin) *The Worm in the Bud: The World of Victorian Sexuality*. London: Weidenfeld & Nicolson. A good overview of the Victorian cultural situation.

Rowbotham, S. (1973) *Woman's Consciousness, Man's World*. Harmondsworth: Penguin. Adopts a more rigorously neo-Marxist approach than most other feminist texts of this date.

Stone, L. (1977) *The Family, Sex and Marriage in England 1500–1800*. London: Weidenfeld & Nicolson. A primary work on the topic, essential for the deeper historical background.

Stopes, M. (1918) *Married Love. A New Contribution to the Solution of Sexual Difficulties*. London: Putnam's. By 1931 this was into its 20th edition.

Stopes, M. (1928) *Enduring Passion. Further New Contributions to the Solution of Sex Difficulties being the Continuation of Married Love*. London: Putnam's. Stopes was the leading figure in promoting birth control and sexual openness, although her attitudes towards sexual equality and feminist issues are extremely ambiguous.

Terman, L.M. and Miles, C.C. (1936) *Sex and Personality, Studies in Masculinity and Femininity*. New York: McGraw-Hill. An important early mainstream Psychological work.

Walker, A. (c. 1850, rep. 1898) *Woman Physiologically Considered as to Mind, Morals, Marriage, Matrimonial Slavery, Infidelity and Divorce*. Birmingham: Edward Baker. A lesser known nineteenth-century pro-feminist book.

Warner, M. (1976, rep. 1985 Picador) *Alone of All Her Sex The Myth and the Cult of the Virgin Mary*. London: Weidenfeld & Nicolson.

Weininger, O. (1906) *Sex and Character*. London: Helnemann. Perhaps the most extreme and bizarre anti-woman work published in the twentieth century.

Two earlier texts not discussed in the main text were:

Patrick, G.T.W. (1895) 'The Psychology of Women'. *Popular Science Monthly* 47: 209–225.

Woolley, H.T. (1910) 'Psychological Literature: A Review of the Recent Literature on the Psychology of Sex'. *Psychological Bulletin* 7: 335–342. A fierce attack on prevailing attitudes.

See also the journal *Signs* and among many other writers, Erica Burman, Donna Haraway, Evelyn F. Keller, Wendy Hollway, Celia Kitzinger, Carolyn Merchant, Paula Nicholson, Ann Oakley, Janet Radcliffe Richards and S.A. Shields. In recent years the Psychology of Lesbianism has emerged as a distinct field, and after much controversy within the British Psychological Society a 'Gay and Lesbian Psychology' section was recently founded.

Part four

TWO GENERAL
ISSUES

We now turn to two general issues which cut across the various sub-disciplines and research topics within Psychology. The first is measurement, in which some often unacknowledged issues are discussed relating to the problematic nature of trying to quantify psychological phenomena. This is not an attack on quantification *per se* but a plea for caution in taking it at face value and assuming its sufficiency as a scientific research strategy. The second is language. This chapter is slightly longer than usual due to the sheer range of material it covers but, even so, is highly selective. The intention is to indicate both how complex, and indeed enigmatic, a phenomenon language is, and how multi-faceted Psychology's own approaches to it have been. Their positions on these two issues largely determine how psychologists understand the intellectual character of the Psychology they are practising, and yet all too often they remain implicit or uncritically reflect positions taught them during their undergraduate years.

TWO: GENERAL ISSUES

Chapter 18

Some problems with measurement

- Centrality of measurement for science and the problem of measuring psychological phenomena
- Measuring intelligence and the effects of this on the concept of intelligence itself
- Measuring attitudes: the example of authoritarianism
- Measuring what does not exist
- Measuring personality
- Some general problems and issues

Measurement has always been central to experimental science, and the data with which scientists are happiest are numbers produced by measuring instruments like rulers, voltmeters, thermometers and chronometers. For Psychology, quantifying the phenomena it studies has been a perennial problem. For many thinkers, such as Immanuel Kant, it was the apparent impossibility of doing so which excluded Psychology from natural science. Furthermore, while, as the American psychologist E.L. Thorndike said, 'everything which exists must exist in some quantity and can therefore be measured', the converse is not necessarily true, everything which can be measured does not necessarily exist. This paradox will become clearer later. There is, moreover, the question of the relationship between the measurement as such and what is being measured. How do you measure something without changing it? This riddle arose first in physics (where the answer is an unambiguous 'you can't'), but we are coming to realise that it arises in Psychology too. It must be stressed then that the nature of measurement raises deep philosophical questions and present-day historians and philosophers of science have revealed it to be a less straightforward and logical matter than one might initially assume. Only some of the more immediately accessible of these questions can be touched on here.

The task facing Psychology once it moves beyond simple phenomena like reaction times (RTs) has been identifying overt, publicly 'measurable', indices of the essentially inaccessible phenomena it seeks to study such as memory, motivation, thinking, imagery, the structure of personality and intelligence. We saw how the behaviourists tried to solve this by eschewing such topics altogether and concentrating on overt behaviour alone. However, even they (excepting Skinner) were eventually driven to postulating sundry 'intervening variables'. If we wish to measure, say, intelligence, we have first to select a set of behaviours which we believe displays this. Initially we will be guided by 'common sense' – the notion of intelligence is already well-established in 'folk psychology' and its meaningful use presents no great difficulty. Thus ability to do sums is part of its meaning while food preferences are usually not (though eating at certain popular fast food chains might well be!). The things we select as relevant must have 'face validity' – they must bear some obvious relationship to this ordinary meaning.

But remaining content with this is to uncritically accept existing folk-wisdom, abandoning the hope of finding out anything more; we will simply be elaborating on current beliefs, unpacking the 'folk-meaning' of a term without challenging it. Psychological measurement is a vast and often highly technical subject, and in this chapter I will be noting only some of the difficulties that strike me as particularly relevant to the theme of this book. Given the cultural salience of IQ testing the history of this topic is a particularly instructive case and warrants examination in a little more depth, not least because what was discovered early in the history of intelligence testing was that some of the things people assumed were good indices of intelligence barely correlated with others.

Measuring intelligence

Although a few anticipations have been spotted, the history of psychometrics really began with Francis Galton's use of Cambridge Tripos Examination results to measure ability but it was obviously necessary to devise other procedures if the project was to progress any further. One major challenge facing him was to devise some way of measuring the variations between people in psychological character- istics in the wake of Darwin's theory of evolution (see Chapter 3). The mathemat- ical basis of this had been laid by L.A. Quetelet in the early years of the nineteenth century and was developed further by Galton and Karl Pearson to provide the now familiar parametric techniques for calculating standard deviations and correlation (see Chapter 3). This approach assumed that variations were distributed on the bell-shaped normal distribution curve; thus it became possible to generate scales in terms of either 'decans' or, later, 'standard deviations', the problem now being what to actually measure and how to measure it. Using the techniques for measur- ing RTs and similar psychophysical phenomena developed in Germany, Galton assembled a sizeable battery of measures which he administered to a large sample of visitors to the Natural History Museum in South Kensington in the 1880s – who paid a penny for the honour. This data provided a basic index of population norms over a number of psychophysical and physical measures.

In the United States J. McKeen Cattell, sharing Galton's assumptions that intelligence and higher-level functions would correlate with such lower level phenomena as RTs and memory-span, embarked on a programme at Columbia University in which all freshmen were measured. Their final degree results were eagerly awaited. When, four years later, they alas proved to correlate poorly with the measures obtained, Cattell's hopes of devising a diagnostic or selection instru- ment on the basis of such data were dashed. Meanwhile in France, against a back- ground of growing eugenic concern, the Paris educational authorities commissioned Alfred Binet, already renowned for his proto-cognitive work, to devise a way of identifying subnormal and backward children. With an associate, T. Simon, he pro- duced the first intelligence test in 1905, comprising a series of tasks of increasing difficulty through which the child had to work its way. The average level attained at each age was identified and on this basis a child could be graded according to its mental age (i.e. the age for which the score it had obtained was the average). A mental age : chronological age ratio was thus obtainable, later multiplied by 100 (by the German Wilhelm Stern) to provide the now familiar IQ score in which 100 is the average (i.e. MA=CA). In the United States the Binet–Simon scale was rapidly adopted, first by H.H. Goddard in the context of his work with 'subnormal' children, and then by L.M. Terman at Stanford University (who produced the 'Stanford–Binet' test), while Cyril Burt pioneered it in the United Kingdom. Mean- while another British psychologist, C. Spearman, was doing similar investigations into children's intellectual abilities and devising statistical techniques for analysing them, resulting in the first version of Factor Analysis. From his research he con- cluded that there was a general factor of intelligence 'g' plus a number of specific abilities, 'g' nevertheless correlating with these and accounting for much of their variance.

At this point IQ measuring was still based on the MA:CA ratio and used almost exclusively on children, who were assessed individually. During the First World War, in 1917, the United States Army was faced with the task of evaluating thousands of conscripts and several leading Psychologists (headed by R.M. Yerkes) rapidly responded, producing Army Tests Alpha and Beta (for illiterates), 'group tests' designed for mass administration. The MA:CA ratio was, it was realised, meaningless for adults since about the highest achievable MA was 18. IQ was now calculated in terms of deviation from the mean adult score (still scored 100). From then on the devising of tests of mental abilities, both general and specific, took off in a big way, though even by 1914–15 it took G.M. Whipple two volumes to review all the Psychological tests available. This burgeoning of the assessment industry was related to America's socio-economic needs, providing techniques for large-scale assessment and evaluation of people in relation to occupational choice, educational level and, in the US, the quality of European immigrants (see Chapter 21). Galton's eugenic concerns indeed underlay the whole movement and anglophone psychometricians espoused strong hereditarian positions (not entirely shared by Binet). A theoretical controversy over the nature of intelligence then erupted, pitting Thurstone and Kelley – two leading American experts – against Spearman and L.M. Terman, namely whether it was multi-factor (L.L. Thurstone, T.L. Kelley) or 'two-factor' ('g' + specific) as Spearman and Terman claimed. The grounds for this were a mixture of statistical theory and interpretation of experimental findings on transfer of learning, which Thurstone argued showed abilities to be highly specific – learning poetry off by heart in one language left the ability to do so in another unimproved. Statistically, the controversy hinged around theoretical points relating to extraction of factors using factor analysis. In the intelligence-measuring psychometric tradition nobody, for a while, seemed to be studying intelligence anymore, only wrangling about statistics! In a sense the methodology became the theory. The work by Jean Piaget on child cognitive development, Gestalt studies of thinking, and the later rise of cognitive Psychology yielded numerous new theoretical models of intelligence but these were long ignored by the single-factor IQ testers whose only interest was in the data yielded by IQ tests consisting of batteries of items chosen in a more-or-less atheoretical, intuitive fashion. Although the controversy has never been fully resolved the single-factor view is undoubtedly theoretically weaker, but the sheer simplicity and appeal of a single number has largely over-ridden conceptual objections. In the 1930s a new, rigorously standardised, intelligence test was introduced, the Weschler–Bellevue, which came in two versions (plus retest ones); the adult WAIS and the child WISC. These soon established themselves as the most widely-used IQ tests, the scaling being in terms of standard deviations (each SD = 15 IQ points).

From Galton onwards the Psychological meaning of 'intelligence' was continually redefined and rethought, a process marked by considerable controversy. Notably, as we have just seen, was there such a general factor as intelligence at all? Or only specific abilities not necessarily related to one another? If so, how many? More profoundly, is the psychometric approach really the most appropriate method for tackling the issue? And how justified are the hereditarian assumptions of the single-factor school?

One odd consequence of this was that Psychology ended up with two different research areas: cognition or thinking on the one hand and intelligence on the other. More detailed study of the history of this area would, I believe, shed more light on how, in Psychology, methodology and theory can get inextricably entangled. There is a risk that the very existence of a measuring technique will mislead us into ascribing an unwarrantedly concrete or objective status to the thing being measured (an error sometimes called 'reification'). This is very evident in Social Psychology's efforts at attitude measurement, which overlaps with the study of personality. Again a look at the history of this area is rewarding.

Measuring attitudes

In the 1920s social psychologists and personality theorists began exploring ways of measuring attitudes and personality. For Social Psychology, in which attitude measurement was a leading theme (see Chapter 12), questionnaire design assumed great prominence, with R. Likert and Thurstone introducing their eponymous scaling techniques. A primitive rating scale was used by some phrenologists in the 1840s, and questionnaires are known from even earlier, but major technical issues remained to be tackled if questionnaires were to serve as measuring instruments. The outcome has been a plethora of questionnaire designs ranging from forced choice to seven-point scale and open-ended, as well as statistical procedures for item selection and standardisation. Designing questionnaires is, of course, not simply a matter of thinking up twenty ostensibly relevant questions and counting up the 'yeses'. I have no immediate quarrel with these procedures. What is of more concern is the status of the things they purport to measure.

Consider the concept of 'authoritarianism' developed immediately after World War Two as part of a widespread American effort, involving many different kinds of psychologists, to understand Nazi anti-Semitism. Some of these came to believe that a particular syndrome or combination of traits was implicated, known as the 'authoritarian personality': authoritarians were rigid and closed minded, intolerant of ambiguity, happiest in hierarchical organisations, held obedience to authority in high esteem, disliked modern art and so forth. One curious point, which immediately alerts us to the problem of how 'objective' such labelling is, was that in the 1930s a Nazi psychologist, E.R. Jaensch, arrived at a very similar notion, but his version had the evaluative loading in the reverse direction: his 'authoritarian', the 'J' type, was strong willed, disciplined, had clear unmuddled ideas, etc., whereas the opposite 'S' type – or *Gegentypus* ('antitype', the good 'democratic' type according to authoritarianism theorists) – was undisciplined, dreamy, changeable, unwilling to respect authority and so on.

But is authoritarianism really a permanent feature of the human condition? Will some people always display this pattern of traits? And how would we find out? This last question brings us back to measurement. We would have to continue administering authoritarianism questionnaires to successive generations over a long period of time, analysing responses to individual items to see whether they continued to correlate. But how would we select the items? The problem is that of all psychological phenomena the accepted indices of such attitudes are perhaps the most obviously historically and culturally embedded.

Here are some items selected from the original 1950 'F (for 'fascism') scale' of Authoritarianism (all scoring positive):

1   After the war, we may expect a crime wave; the control of gangsters and ruffians will become a major social problem.

2   Reports of atrocities in Europe have been greatly exaggerated for propaganda purposes.
3   Homosexuality is a particularly rotten form of delinquency and ought to be severely punished.
4   Although many people may scoff, it may yet be shown that astrology can explain a lot of things.

Here are some others from H.J. Eysenck's 1957 'Social Attitude Inventory' scale (in which he differentiated radicalism–conservatism from tough–tender mindedness in order to incorporate the existence of left wing authoritarianism – 'tough-minded and radical' – now required by the Cold War):

1   Divorce laws should be altered to make divorce easier.
2   Birth control, except when recommended by a doctor, should be made illegal.
3   European refugees should be left to fend for themselves.
4   It would be best to keep coloured people in their own districts and schools, in order to prevent too much contact with whites.

A number of difficulties are immediately apparent: some items have changed their connotations (e.g. belief in astrology) or their context (e.g. – divorce laws *have* since become easier so the very meaning of the item has changed), some are simply obsolete ('after the war . . .'), some, though perhaps still relevant in principle, are couched in obsolete terms (the anti-homosexual item), others have largely faded from public concern (e.g. the birth control issue). The 'coloured people' item assumes all respondents are white – in fact, none of these 1950's questionnaires could be used to measure either non-white or (somewhat strangely in fact) Jewish authoritarianism. Obviously, if you were now starting from scratch at the beginning of the twenty-first century, you would also include topics absent from the original scales (environmental issues, privatisation, feminism and drugs, for example). But then comes the crunch: *if you have changed the items how can you be said to be measuring the same thing?* And with a little historical imagination we can envisage that the typical middle-class Victorian Englishman would probably appear to us as highly authoritarian – even if he was a Liberal or socialist. Returning to the seventeenth century the notions of authoritarianism and radical/conservative would be highly suspect. A seventeenth-century Eysenck would much more likely have devised a 'popery' or 'heresy' scale depending on his religious allegiance.

Now I am not denying that the authoritarianism concept has any validity – at least at present – nor am I denying that these scales in a sense measured it in the 1950s (the creators of the concept actually saw it as a historical development resulting from changes in the nature of the family (M. Jay, 1973)). What I am suggesting is: (a) that the permanent existence of this syndrome is by no means guaranteed; and (b) that keeping our questionnaires up-to-date would actually reflect a drift in meaning of the concept itself. Moreover, as Jaensch's case demonstrates, in this area it is impossible to eliminate the evaluative connotations of the factor and deal with it in a 'neutral and objective' manner. We all 'know' that authoritarianism is supposed to be bad and being 'democratic' good. And curiously, soon after the Korean War, during which there was an upsurge of concern about alleged Chinese 'brainwashing' of American POWs, psychologists came up with another dimension: 'resistant to persuasion' vs. 'easily persuasible'. While it was, implicitly, good to be 'open-minded' it was also implicitly bad to be 'easily persuaded' (and vice-versa for dogmatic vs. resistant to persuasion). In effect the same dimension was available in two versions, depending on which end you wanted to approve! Finally, though, as K. Danziger (1997) has shown, the very concept of 'attitude' as used in Social Psychology was an innovation – 'attitudes' were, in a sense, *created* by psychologists, the term previously referring primarily to physical posture.

Measuring what does not exist

Let us return to a point made at the start: not everything which can be measured necessarily exists. This may sound puzzling, but is actually not so self-contradictory as it seems. The argument is best made using a hypothetical example: were we living in the Middle Ages we might be very concerned about how devout people were. To measure this we devise a questionnaire containing such items as 'I prefer reading a holy book to attending a tournament', 'A strange feeling of Grace sometimes descends upon me', 'I enjoy attending High Mass' or to counterbalance the direction 'I often find sermons boring'. ('I have never been tempted by lust' could serve as a lie item.) It is surely feasible that at the end of the day our 'sanctity scale' would appear to provide a handy way of measuring how holy people were. But no psychologist proposes that there is a measurable 'sanctity' dimension to personality, and not even the most devout psychologists have attempted to devise such a measure. Nor is this as far fetched as you might imagine; among the earliest pioneers of scientific measurement were the fourteenth-century French scholars Jean Buridan and Nicolas D'Oresme whose efforts were spurred by the desire to quantify the amount of Grace in communion wafers.

Measuring personality

In personality measurement one major pioneer in the 1930s was Henry Murray whose intensive research programme at Harvard generated the projective Thematic Apperception Test (TAT). This inspired a number of successors such as Blum's Children's Apperception Test (CAT) and Shneidemann's Make A Picture Story (or MAPS) test, plus the more well-known Blacky test (featuring a cartoon dog and used primarily for assessing aggression). These were all based on the Freudian concept of 'projection' (see Chapter 11). More statistically-oriented psychologists also turned to personality, believing that factor analytic techniques could unravel the dimensions of personality variation, thus the actual devising of such tests became a research method in its own right. Eysenck had opted for the two-factor extraversion/neuroticism model by the end of the 1940s, producing a forced choice questionnaire, the EPI (Eysenck Personality Inventory, later revised as the MPI – Maudsley Personality Inventory), to measure these dimensions.

R.B. Cattell a little later, using a different factor analysis technique identified sixteen personality factors (to which more have been added) measurable by his '16PF' questionnaire. Another popular American test produced in the 1940s was the Minnesota Multiphasic Personality Inventory (MMPI) which became a standard clinical diagnostic instrument. The famous Rorschach 'Inkblot' test dates back as far as 1911, but rater reliability of its interpretation has proved notoriously low. The Draw-a-Man test was devised by Florence Goodenough (1926) for use with children, first as an alternative way of measuring intelligence, but this too came to be seen as having some of the properties of a projective test and thus usable for personality assessment. While psychologists have continued to identify new personality traits such as 'level of aspiration', 'field-dependency', and 'locus of control', the underlying conceptual difficulties already mentioned persist: how 'real' are they? How far are they an artefact of the procedures used to 'discover' them? How far are they permeated by culturally contingent evaluative connotations? (Regarding personality tests, see also Chapter 11.)

More general issues

From the start, the over-riding task of psychometrics has been to develop techniques for measuring psychological processes by identifying reliable operational expressions of these. Notwithstanding its superficial simplicity this has, though, proved difficult because part of Psychology's aim is to discover what these psychological processes are in the first place. It is easy to devise procedures yielding numbers that can be treated as scores and submitted to elaborate statistical procedures from which a pattern of some sort emerges – say a set of factors – which we have to make sense of. The temptation, as we saw, is to treat this as representing some objectively existing reality. It is commonly recognised that behaviours everyday language identifies by a single classification (intelligent, aggressive, etc.) may not in fact be manifestations of single psychological processes, but may variously lump together more than one such process or only partially overlap. The task of identifying the underlying processes has gone hand-in-hand with the project of measuring them, and in factor analysis in particular it was, as earlier indicated, felt that psychometrics was concerned with discovery as well as measurement. The problem with this is its circularity, especially when tackling personality, since there is a difficulty in giving the resultant factors or dimensions a meaning at all unless they can be translated back into everyday psychological language, thus they are either not new or incomprehensible.

It is hard to see how psychometrics alone can actually generate new psychological concepts. However, when we have a non-psychometrically based theory the situation is different, for this may propose genuinely novel Psychological concepts or hypotheses that can be psychometrically tested. We should, for example, be able to derive from psychoanalytic theory a series of statements identifying behavioural traits typifying 'oral aggression' and then see if they do in fact correlate. If we succeed we then pride ourselves on having measured oral aggressivity or our ability to identify 'oral aggressive types'. Similarly, a theory of cognitive development like Piaget's may provide the basis for an intelligence test of more profundity than a purely statistically-derived test, measuring specific 'operations' theoretically identified as significant indices of intellectual attainment. *Even so, those with different theoretical preferences, different 'frameworks of meaning', will reject the concepts of 'oral aggression' and 'operations' as mythical in the first place and, if the scores technically prove robust and reliable, will strive to substitute quite different labels.* Again – because you have measured oral aggressivity it doesn't mean it exists.

Attempts at substituting psychometrics for theory construction have, I feel, not been too successful, notwithstanding the eminence of some of those involved; at best they have a practical function enabling the rapid classification of the respondent. Psychodynamics also tend to elude such models. The 'semantic differential' of C.E. Osgood *et al* (1957) is an interesting case, since it apparently identified three dimensions of meaning that had not been teased out before: evaluative, potency and activity. Yet close examination of this, particularly the 'evaluative' dimension, suggests that some linguistic illusion might underlie the results. The key evaluative term 'good', for example, is highly polysemic, and its apparent dominance does not signify that a single 'meaning' is pervasive ('good' can mean ethically good, functionally good, unbroken or sound, matching a criterion, etc.), only that it can sensibly be applied to almost anything in one sense or another, while other adjectives have less range. Where psychometrics has been successful is in (a) measuring specific abilities where the face-validity of equating the ability to everyday classifications is unproblematic and (b) in theory-related contexts, such as many of the personality and cognitive style measures developed from the 1950s to the 1970s, though as already indicated the reification problem remains.

The final point to be noted is the close intimacy between measurement and technology. The availability of new instruments immediately stimulates us to think of ways of exploiting them. But instruments are not theoretically neutral for they encourage those using them to theorise about their subject matter in the way most consistent with it being amenable to investigation by such instruments. Thus using mazes encourages 'trial and error' theories of learning. Prominent in pre-1914 Psychology textbooks is the 'kymograph' or 'ergograph' (as A. Mosso called his version), ancestor of the modern recording drum. A role of lampblacked graph paper is wrapped round a cylinder and a pointer scores a line as the cylinder rotates. Psychologists of the time were quite carried away, using this to investigate such things as fatigue, amplitude of finger movements, muscular reactions and the like. At the end of the day they could see this behaviour translated into a nice wobbly line. Such research yielded many interesting findings, the data were 'objective', readily quantifiable and so on. Similar techniques are still in our repertoire. But at the same time the ergograph's availability led researchers to prioritise those topics most amenable to it, and to try and think of ways of rendering them so. I once encountered a saying applicable here: 'When the only tool you have is a hammer everything begins to look like a nail'. It is worth wondering whether the currently popular brain imaging techniques will prove to be another instance of this.

The most insidious effect of this is perhaps that of statistics itself. The use of statistics requires that you design your experiments to fit the particular statistical procedure you will be employing. But these procedures themselves contain numerous assumptions about the properties of the data they are being applied to. To some degree they shape the experiments, the kinds of hypotheses that can be tested and the kinds of theory or model the researcher produces. This is too complex an issue to explore at length here, but work by Gerd Gigerenzer (1996; Gigerenzer *et al*, 1989) has started unmasking some curious problems; in particular – and most tellingly – he shows how the use of statistical methods, which is centrally about calculating probabilities, led psychologists to produce theories that viewed psychological processes themselves as involving quasi-statistical calculations of probabilities (for instance in H.H. Kelley's 1967 version of attribution theory in Social Psychology). Since their method led *them* to think in this way, they began to believe that *all* thinking was essentially similar.

The growth of psychometrics has of course not occurred in a vacuum but may be interpreted in contextual as well as internalist terms. Much of the impetus for devising tests between the wars lay in the needs of American culture generally, and the role of eugenics in the promotion of IQ testing is well-known. For psychologists the production of testing instruments was a way of acquiring some expert input into industrial society with its attendant needs for personnel evaluation, certification of expertise, etc. In the United Kingdom, meanwhile, the National Institute of Industrial Psychology was flourishing under C.S. Myers and psychologists were being employed by numerous companies to study factors ranging from fatigue to training, devising many tests on an *ad hoc* basis for particular studies (see Chapter 13). The market research area has, however, been the greatest commercial beneficiary of psychometrics, exploiting expertise in questionnaire design and administration to produce highly-focused evaluations of new products. This may provide us with our closing observations. While market research superficially appears to be about measuring attitudes to consumer products it more covertly serves to *create* such attitudes where they previously did not exist, thereby producing a cultural climate in which 'consumers' (all of us) become psychologically adjusted to the requirements of the economic system itself. We tend to assume that the questions we are asked are sensible. Asked whether we prefer jellies to be round or angular we usually produce an answer – the very question conjures the attitude into existence. More sinisterly, though, it helps create a population for whom issues such as jelly-shape are psychologically important. This brings us back to Danziger's point mentioned earlier and a profounder doubt as to whether 'attitudes' even exist as a 'natural' psychological phenomenon at all, perhaps they are purely a product of 'attitude measurement' technology. At any rate, the act of Psychological measuring has changed that which is being measured, 'psychology'.

Further reading

Gigerenzer, G. (1996) 'From Tools to Theories: Discovery in Cognitive Psychology'. In C.F. Graumann and K.J. Gergen (eds) *Historical Dimensions of Psychological Discourse*, 36–59. Cambridge: Cambridge University Press. A concise statement of the argument that statistical methods become theories in their own right.

Gigerenzer, G., Swijtink, Z., Porter, T., Daston, L., Beatty, J. and Krüger, L. (1989) *The Empire of Chance. How Probability Changed Science and Everyday Life*. Cambridge: Cambridge University Press. See Chapter 6 on statistical methods becoming theories.

Hornstein, G.A. (1989) 'Quantifying Psychological Phenomena: Debates, Dilemmas, and Implications'. In J.G. Morawski (ed.) *The Rise of Experimentation in American Psychology*. New Haven: Yale University Press, 1–34.

Richards, G. (1997) *'Race', Racism and Psychology: Towards a Reflexive History*. London: Routledge. See Chapter 8 for problems in assessing 'Negro' personality in the post-Second World War period and Chapter 9 for the 'race differences in intelligence' issue. These illustrate some of the problems discussed above.

Sokal, M.M. (1987) *Psychological Testing and American Society, 1890–1930*. New Brunswick: Rutgers University Press. Explores the cultural dimension of psychological testing and has good coverage of the World War One United States Army tests.

Sternberg, R. (1990) *Metaphors of Mind: Conceptions of the Nature of Intelligence*. Cambridge: Cambridge University Press. Excellent overview of concepts of intelligence.

Zenderland, L. (1998) *Measuring Minds. Herbert Henry Goddard and the Origins of American Intelligence Testing*. Cambridge: Cambridge University Press. Provides an in-depth account of the introduction of intelligence testing into the United States and the effect this had on Psychology's place within American culture.

Additional references

For English and American versions of the Binet–Simon test:

Burt, C. (1921) *London County Council Mental and Scholastic Tests*. London: P.S. King.

Terman, L.M. (1919) *The Measurement of Intelligence: An Explanation of and Complete Guide for the use of the Stanford Revision and Extension of the Binet–Simon Intelligence Scale*. London: Harrap.

On the Spearman vs. Thurstone debate and a proposed resolution invoking 'group factors' see:

Vernon, P.E. (1961) *The Structure of Human Abilities*, 2nd edn. London: Methuen.

The 'Likert Scale' method of attitude measurement uses a statement with a 5-point scale from 'strongly agree' to 'strongly disagree':

Likert, R. (1932) 'A Technique for the Measurement of Attitudes'. *Archives of Psychology*, Monograph No.140.

The 'Thurstone Scale' offers the alternatives agree/disagree:

Thurstone, L.L. and Chave, E.J. (1929) *The Measurement of Attitudes*. Chicago: University of Chicago Press.

Both of these preceded the fully developed factor analytic methods used by R.B. Cattell and H.J. Eysenck:

Adorno, T.W., Frenkl-Brunswik, E., Levinson, G.J. and Sanford, R.J. (1950) *The Authoritarian Personality* (2 vols). New York: Science Editions. Introduced the 'authoritarian personality' concept to a wider audience, although it had been in circulation for some years previously.

Cattell, R.B. (1965) *The Scientific Understanding of Personality*. Harmondsworth: Pelican. Contains an accessible account of his 16PF personality inventory, which he subsequently elaborated further.

Eysenck, H.J. (1957) *Sense and Nonsense in Psychology*. Harmondsworth: Pelican. This contains his 'Social Attitude Inventory'.

Jaensch, E.R. (1938) *Der Gegentypus*. Leipzig: Barth. Proposed a pro-Nazi equivalent of the authoritarian personality with the evaluative meanings reversed.

Jay, M. (1973) *The Dialectical Imagination. A History of the Frankfurt School and the Institute of Social Research 1923–1950*. London: Heinemann.

Kelley, H.H. (1967) 'Attribution Theory in Social Psychology'. In D. Levine (ed.) *Nebraska Symposium on Motivation Vol. 15*. Lincoln, NE: University of Nebraska Press, 192–238.

Oppenheim, A.N. (1966) *Questionnaire Design and Attitude Measurement*. London: Heinemann. A useful introduction to the issues as understood up to c. 1970.

Osgood, C.E., Suci, G.C. and Tannenbaum, P.H. (1957) *The Measurement of Meaning*. Urbana: University of Illinois Press.

For the 'ergograph':

Mosso, A. (1906) *Fatigue*, 2nd edn. London: Swan Sonnenschein.

Schulze, R. (1912) *Experimental Psychology and Pedagogy*. London: George Allen.

For critiques of the whole IQ business see:

Block, N. and Dworkin, G. (1977) 'IQ, Heritability, and Inequality'. In N. Block and G. Dworkin (eds) *The IQ Controversy: Critical Readings*. NY: Pantheon (rep. London: Quartet). This is quite penetrating conceptually and really should be read by anyone interested in the issue.

Gould, S.J. (1992) *The Mismeasure of Man*, 2nd edn. London: Penguin. A good critique of intelligence testing but historically misleading on H.H. Goddard.

Chapter 19

Psychology and language

Language is the hardest of Psychological topics on which to write a coherent brief account. Language researchers approach it with varied agendas and assumptions, while it often forces its attention on psychologists concerned with other topics. It is, moreover, the most multi-disciplinary of subjects; linguistics itself, philosophy, anthropology, sociology, literary criticism, neurology and psychiatry, for instance, all have their legitimate interests (see Table 19.1).

Concern with language transcends academic specialisms, partly no doubt because it is the primary medium in which we live and understand both ourselves and our worlds. Naturally, therefore, a disciplinary stance from which to appraise it 'objectively' proves elusive. Psychological work on language is thus enmeshed in work drawn from elsewhere.

One current intellectual challenge (raised in the Introduction) is to establish how far language simply labels that to which it refers and how far it actually constitutes the world we experience. Regarding the language used for naming and explaining psychological phenomena the reader will recall my espousal of a basically 'constructionist' position. Language is not all there is, but however 'natural' or 'universal' some human psychological phenomena may be it is only via its mediation that we can refer to them, reflexively affecting such phenomena themselves in doing so. Exploring that particular point is not the task here, but it cannot be entirely evaded.

In contrast to topics like perception, or sub-disciplines like Developmental Psychology, chronologically plotting the development of 'Psychology and language' is difficult. Imagining a continuum from theoretical to applied themes, the most significant and enduring include the following: 'meaning' and the language-thought relationship, language origins and evolution, linguistic memory (see Chapter 7), language acquisition in children, language functions in everyday life ('sociolinguistics'), linguistic capacities of non-human species, language simulation in the context of Artificial Intelligence (AI), and language pathologies (e.g. dyslexia, aphasia and stammering). In practice, these can inter-relate in quite complex ways. If few are Psychology's monopoly, it has had a place in addressing them all. Even this list ignores issues like the nature of metaphor, second-language learning, reading, and use of linguistic stimulus material in psychological research. All

Table 19.1 Principal disciplines concerned with language

Cultural and literary history
Linguistics, including such subdisciplines as:
     psycholinguistics, sociolinguistics, ethnolinguistics, phonetics, semiotics
Literary criticism
Media and cultural studies
Neurology
Philosophy
Psychology, especially the following fields:
     memory, developmental, psychopathology, social, physiological,
     evolutionary, artificial intelligence (AI)
Rhetoric

I offer here are a few observations concerning Psychology's engagements with a handful of them. But to set the scene let us consider first the views of that now neglected doyen of American Mental and Moral Philosophy in the 1860s and 1870s, Noah Porter, President of Yale and editor of *Webster's Dictionary*.

Noah Porter's view of language

The necessary derivation of psychological language from that used for referring to the public world has long been known (G. Richards, 1989, 1992, see also the Introduction). John Locke spelled this out in his *Essay Concerning Human Understanding* (1690) and it was generally accepted by mid-nineteenth-century linguists as varied in their views as Dwight Whitney and Max Müller. Yet the 'constructionist' implications of this fell from view after 1880 as Psychology, in establishing itself as a 'Natural Science', began accepting the orthodox scientific assumption that its technical language referred unambiguously to naturally-occurring phenomena, reflecting an 'objective' reality. Porter's *The Human Intellect* (1868) (until the 1880s the most widely-used American academic textbook in the field) and *The Science of Man and the Sciences of Nature* (1871), provide an interesting glimpse of the turning-point. While highly sensitive to the language problem, Porter argued himself into a position from which it is hard to see how Psychological knowledge could be further advanced.

To summarise his various statements on the matter, this position was as follows:

(a) All psychological concepts are expressed in analogies drawn from external world phenomena. This is basically correct (although an over-simple description of the relationship – see G. Lakoff and M. Johnson, 1980; G. Richards, 1989).

(b) Words basically label 'ideas' existing independently of words themselves. This is now almost universally rejected.

(c) The collective tribunal of human experience has so shaped everyday language that its psychological concepts and classifications are basically accurate. Any innovations must thus be tested *against* existing psychological language, which, as it were, retains a right of veto – which is correct, but not in the way Porter thought (see G. Richards, 1996).

(d) The new 'cerebral philosophers' – Alexander Bain, W.B. Carpenter and evolutionary thinkers – are falling into a fundamental error by explaining the mind with analogies drawn from specific scientific fields. This is to explain the greater by the lesser, for it is this mind which produces scientific knowledge in the first place. For Porter Psychology, the science of the 'mind' which creates all other knowledge, is *the* foundational discipline. In principle this last point is perhaps correct.

This is all oddly frustrating because, despite his insights, (c) seems to signify almost a loss of nerve by insisting on ultimate submission to traditional wisdoms, while (b) ignores the possibility that language plays any active role in determining our ideas about the psychological or – which follows – the character of psychological phenomena themselves. Porter does not really treat language as a psychological phenomenon at all, only a medium for rendering such phenomena publicly knowable. His rejection of the 'cerebral philosophers' now looks like a pre-emptive strike against further enrichment and elaboration of psychological language by drawing 'analogies' from novel scientific phenomena, although the everyday psychological language he praises so highly was created in just this way. Porter's account is in fact rooted in his firm religious conviction (as a Congregationalist minister) that the existing Protestant Christian view of human nature was eternally valid, needing only refinement and rigorous exposition. He ardently, and honestly, seeks to promote Psychology's fortunes but in the final analysis his theology trumps, or paralyses, Psychology.

Porter is usually overlooked in orthodox disciplinary histories. But daunting as *The Human Intellect* is, it is a crucial transitional text in which numerous theoretical riddles besides this one are aired in a way which faded as Psychology grew in self-confidence and natural scientific commitment. Most significantly for us, after Porter Psychology discreetly ignored the 'constructionist' role of language until the 1960s. In consequence, its attitude to language became remarkably complacent. Eschewing reflexive investigation of the nature of Psychological language entailed in its turn a wider inattention to language in general, tacit acceptance of a crude 'picture theory' of meaning and the assumption that language was simply, as Porter thought, a vehicle for communicating pre-existing thoughts (see, e.g., W.B. Pillsbury and C.L. Meader, 1928). From the 1920s, though not within Psychology, this doctrine began to be challenged.

Language, thought and meaning

Leaving C.S. Peirce's groundbreaking work on 'semiotics' aside, alas, the modern phase might be dated from C.K. Ogden and I.A. Richards' landmark book *The Meaning of Meaning. A Study in the Influence of Language upon Thought and the Science of Symbolism* (1923). (L. Vygotsky's and A.R. Luria's contemporary work in the Soviet Union long remained virtually unknown elsewhere.) In the US the 'general semantics' of Polish exile Alfred Korzybski (1921, 1933) was an analogous, although more totalistically ambitious, development which sought to cure all human problems via a 'non-Aristotelian' rethinking of the nature of meaning. Within mainstream anglophone Psychology the topic only assumed its current character when the 'Sapir–Whorf' hypothesis, promulgated in the 1930s by Benjamin Lee Whorf and anthropologist Edward Sapir, became widely known during the 1950s (Sapir, 1949; Whorf, 1956). Whorf argued from studies of Hopi and Zuñi native American languages that language itself determined the nature of thinking. This was not a matter of vocabulary alone but, more fundamentally, of grammar. Many languages, especially non-Indo-European ones, differed radically from English in the number and kind of tenses they employed and, for instance, in how verb/noun distinctions were drawn. Languages thus determined how speakers thought and, conversely, rendered them unable to think in ways which speakers of other tongues routinely managed.

This argument reinforced the 'cultural relativism' associated with Columbia University's 'Culture and Personality School', and with people like Margaret Mead, Clyde Kluckhohn and Abram Kardiner, and the 1950s and 1960s saw a new flurry of interest in the language–thought relationship. Yet it soon became evident that it was extremely difficult to prove, especially as Noam Chomsky was now arguing for a universal 'deep grammar'. Its limited validity at the lexical level was conceded, but were grammar's effects on thinkability as penetrating as Whorf claimed? Certainly, even European languages varied grammatically in how, for example, agency for events was ascribed, and the longstanding borrowing of terms between them demonstrated how speakers of one often discovered ideas only expressed in another. But this also indicated that the limits on thinkability were not insuperable if speakers of different languages were in contact. More seriously, since the Sapir–Whorf hypothesis was in English, English at least was presumably capable of transcending the limits on thinkability – how else could it refer to and discuss cases where it seemed to occur? (J.N. Hattiangadi (1987) has a fuller analysis of this point.) This implies either that the hypothesis is fundamentally flawed or that English (and any other tongue into which texts expounding it can be translated) are exceptions, rendering it self-negating. Even so, we might still accept that *at any given time* our language to some degree constrains how we think. Such constraints are, however, impermanent, for language is in constant flux and these constraints are forever shifting. The hypothesis depended on a view of languages as isolated and virtually static, but such languages have almost vanished in today's global community. But whatever its flaws, nobody henceforth could assume, as a (possibly apocryphal) nineteenth-century French general did, that French was the world's best language because the words exactly followed the sequence of one's thoughts.

The Psychological debate shifted to addressing the language–thought relationship in rather wider terms, a particularly influential review of the issues being American social psychologist Roger Brown's *Words and Things* (1958). While the influence of Korzybski's 'general semantics' remained strong during the 1950s (e.g. S.I. Hayakawa (ed.), 1954), briefly assuming almost cult status, by the early 1960s the scene was becoming dominated by Noam Chomsky, B.F. Skinner and British linguistic philosophy, although the work of C.W. Morris (1938, 1946) was also influential. A 'nativist' position identified with the linguist Chomsky was seen as pitted against Skinner's behaviourist position, although other behaviourists, often in the Hullian tradition, also tackled the issue (see C.N. Cofer (ed.) (1961); C.N. Cofer and B.S. Musgrave (eds) (1963)), C.E. Osgood *et al* (1957) (see Chapter 18) being a more cognitivist-cum-psychometric variant of this. Meanwhile the cognitivists, although co-opting Chomsky into their camp, began developing a distinct tradition of their own (F. Smith and G.A. Miller, 1966).

Ludwig Wittgenstein's *Philosophical Investigations* (1953) and, more accessibly, Gilbert Ryle's *The Concept of Mind* (1949) and John Austin's amusing *How to do Things with Words* (1962) were initially read as philosophically legitimating behaviourism (especially Ryle), but from their perspective explaining meaning by some paired associate conditioning of words to referents looked crude and invalid. An understanding of this 'pointing game' of teaching word-meanings was a necessary pre-condition for being able to play it (Wittgenstein, 1953) hence the 'meaning of meaning' could not itself be so taught. Worse, meanings shifted according to the 'language game' being played (praying, seducing, instructing, ordering, etc.) and the relationship between the parties. Wittgenstein's main achievement was perhaps to bring home quite how systematically pervasive language is for us, being, he said, 'a form of life', an insight complemented by Austin's notion of 'illocutionary force' (we are always *doing* something beyond making simple referential utterances – adjudicating, promising, confessing, etc.).

As these ideas percolated into Psychology during the late 1960s and 1970s the effect was ambiguous. While the logical irreducibility of 'meaning' to 'paired association' might reinforce the credibility of Chomsky's universal, innately determined, 'deep grammar', they otherwise reinforced a constructionist view of meanings emerging within the innumerable linguistic 'games' of which human life largely consists. Capacity for language may be a genetically-based human universal, but in practice its functions and use were infinitely varied. Entailing a dynamic image of language as constantly changing and adapting, this could not rescue the original Sapir–Whorf hypothesis.

Something odd now happens during the late 1960s: the rising, optimistic, cognitivist psycholinguistic and AI school (see Chapter 7) chooses virtually to ignore contemporary philosophical developments. Cognitivists such as J.A. Fodor, although conceding the importance of 'context' in principle, now adopt highly individual-centred approaches to the topic characterised by formalised modelling of the internal mechanisms involved in 'language processing'. The language and thought issue became one of whether or not the language and thought 'systems' were independent or not (most, departing from Chomsky, felt they probably were not). For British sociolinguist M.A.K. Halliday (1978) their 'object of study was the idealized sentence of an equally idealized speaker' (p. 4). Only somewhat belatedly did some AI researchers begin to see the light (e.g. T. Winograd, 1980).

The 'language and thought' and 'meaning of meaning' issues initially developed largely beyond Psychology's boundaries in philosophy, linguistics and anthropology, and philosophy remains central (e.g. J.N. Hattiangadi, 1987; P. Suppes, 1991). While philosophers and linguists made the major theoretical break-throughs, it fell to psychologists to consider their real implications by applying and empirically exploring them (although much of the philosophical debate might be classified as Philosophical Psychology). Yet while many in Social and Developmental Psychology rose to this challenge, the dominant late twentieth-century school, cognitivism, ironically failed to do so, pursuing an independent approach *ab initio* and having to relearn the same lessons all over again. It is the incompletion of this relearning process, the chronic gulf between their conceptions of language, which largely underpins the continuing split between contemporary cognitive science and the various 'constructionist' schools within Psychology.

Evolution and origins of language

The origin of language has fascinated people since antiquity. Judaeo-Christian cultures believed in an original divine 'Adamic' language, lost as punishment for building the Tower of Babel. Secular speculations began appearing during the

Enlightenment, assuming such a Babel-like diversity themselves that in 1866 the Société de Linguistique de Paris banned further communications on the matter. This did not lay the topic to rest. The main theories were subsequently (by whom, I know not) jocularly labelled, according to a proposed source, as the 'bow-wow' (imitation of natural sounds), 'pooh-pooh' (emotionally expressive exclamations), 'ding dong' (noises made by struck objects), 'yo heave ho' (sounds emitted during collective effort) and 'sing-song' (vocal play) theories (H. Aarsleff, 1976; J.H. Stam, 1976). R. Paget's (1930) 'pantomime' theory proposed mimicking of objects with the vocal apparatus. (A gestural theory was later developed by G.W. Hewes (1973) and recently revived by the late U.T. Place (2000)). Serious scientific interest in the topic declined after 1900 because it seemed impossible to investigate empirically. The late 1960s saw renewed interest, culminating in 1976 in a major New York Academy of Sciences conference (S.R. Harnad, H.D. Steklis and J. Lancaster (eds) 1976; see also G. Richards, 1987, 246–264 for an overview of the debate as it then stood).

Informed by the new insights into the nature of language itself, those addressing the topic (now a province of the subdiscipline Evolutionary Psychology) have, since 1980, sought a scientific grip on it by integrating advances in brain-neurology, linguistics, evolutionary theory and primate language research. One important forum for debate is the Netherlands-based Language Origins Society. Has all the recent effort clarified anything? The answer must be a qualified yes, although controversy remains rife. Two points emerging from the hubbub are that (a) modern human language is highly 'laminated' in character, densely integrating features of widely varying evolutionary depth (e.g. intonation, lexicality, grammar); and (b) although the earliest functions of language remain obscure, on balance they more likely relate to emotional expression and social control than to conveying factual information. The topic may also, many now argue, help answer more central theoretical questions about the very nature of human consciousness (D. Bickerton, 1990; J.N. Hattiangadi, 1987; S. Pinker, 1994).

But what is the psychological significance of this debate itself? Its antiquity surely signifies that it exerts some deep-rooted fascination. Language is the principal medium by which we acquire conscious self-knowledge and mediate our social existence, but also exists separately from us as individuals. Sensing its power over us it is perhaps unsurprising that discovering its origins should be so appealing. The notion of an original divinely endowed 'Adamic' tongue reflected what C.K. Ogden and I.A. Richards (1929) called a 'magical' view of language which saw words and their referents as essentially connected. The Adamic language portrayed the world as it truly was, the names it gave things were their 'real' ones. At one level we are now more sophisticated, seeing language as an arbitrary system in which the 'signifier'–'signified' relationship is merely (bar theoretically trivial onomatopoeia) a matter of convention. Yet actual experience suggests that this sophistication is skin deep; song lyrics can still send shivers down our spines, personal proper names *feel* fundamentally connected to the person named (especially our own) and, even if unbelievers, the ritual 'magical' language of hymns, prayers and religious ceremonies can still move us. The very sounds of words sometimes seem to have a direct psychological impact. While its fascination as an intellectual or theoretical scientific riddle more than justifies its investigation, the deeper sources of the language origins debate may, I suggest, rest barely consciously in the enchantment which such experiences of its power creates. Perhaps language-origins researchers are in a sense pursuing, on our behalf, a perennial quest of a very profound kind for the source of that 'magical' power which we actually experience language as possessing?

Sociolinguistics

Surveying the whole field of sociolinguistics being impossible, we will focus on one instructive episode: the late Basil Bernstein's work and the responses to it. Basil Bernstein continued to develop his ideas over a long career, but we consider only his core theory as formulated by 1971. The disciplinary context of his research was Sociology of Education and, initially, primarily concerned the role of linguistic factors in determining school performance. Assimilating ideas from numerous directions (including the Sapir–Whorf hypothesis, L. Vygotsky and A.R. Luria's studies of speech as 'an orientating and regulative system', D.H. Hymes' ethno-linguistics, M.A.K. Halliday's analysis of language functions and Mary Douglas's social anthropology) Bernstein synthesised a quite complex theory of his own. Its most famous feature was a distinction between 'restricted' (R) and 'elaborated' (E) 'codes'. R code language requires knowledge of the context in order to be understood, is relatively simple grammatically and uses a limited vocabulary; E code language is context-independent, grammatically complex and deploys a large vocabulary.

A much more extensive model gradually evolved from this. By 1971 this incorporated taxonomies of family types, their distinctive socialising regimes, and the 'primary socialising contexts' (regulative, instructional, interpersonal and imaginative), plus a clearly formulated differentiation between the 'surface level' of modes of real speech use ('speech variants') and the deeper level where the 'codes' themselves as regulative principles are located. Linking mode of language use with child-socialisation, this supplied a framework for addressing the source of differences in school performance, especially the underperformance of working-class as opposed to middle-class children. It appeared that, for various reasons, working-class families chose R 'speech-variants' more than the middle class, placing working-class children at a disadvantage in educational settings where the premium was on E ones.

This theory was soon simplistically condensed into 'working-class children use R codes, middle-class children use E codes, so working-class children are intellectually inferior'. Bernstein wrily noted four ideological reactions, all radically misrepresenting his position: the old left saw a powerful indictment of the class system, the new left saw patronising middle-class stereotyping, the right felt he had demonstrated working-class unfitness for high culture and liberals saw a route for assimilating the working class into the middle class. All, erroneously, viewed Bernstein's account as a 'deficit model' – working-class language-use was somehow 'deficient'. (In America his theory was even, somewhat Americo-centredly, read as insulting black working-class use of variant 'Black American English', a topic which his British work naturally never addressed.) This was far from Bernstein's intentions. Everyone can use both 'codes', and restricted speech variants are frequently perfectly appropriate. What was important was that schools operated a linguistic culture divergent from that in which working-class children lived, thereby disadvantaging them in the classroom.

One can, however, see why Bernstein's protests were condemned to failure – the polarity Restricted vs. Elaborated is inescapably evaluative. Whatever theoretical moves are made to neutralise the evaluative connotations, at the end of the day the claim remains that somehow one class of children is linguistically handicapped in educational settings, and nobody would argue for establishing an 'R variant' socialisation ethos in schools. Nonetheless, Bernstein's work remains one of the most impressive efforts at integrating linguistic, philosophical and anthropological theoretical approaches with practical research on real, even urgent, sociological and social psychological issues.

Bernstein's associate, M.A.K. Halliday, further extended his own sociolinguistic work during the 1970s, producing the impressive *Language as Social Semiotic: The Social Interpretation of Language and Meaning* (1978). This cannot be discussed here, but he incidentally raises an interesting problem regarding what counts as Psychological in the study of language, stating 'I would have to say that for me linguistics is a branch of sociology. Language is a part of the social system, and there is no need to interpose a psychological level of interpretation' (pp. 38–39). Certainly his target here is the individualist cognitivist orientation of people like D. Katz and J.A. Fodor, but I cannot help reading his own work as a social psychological analysis. This again indicates the serious boundary problems arising in connection with the study of language.

The Turing Test and the Chinese Room

This section is perhaps an indulgence, but both Alan Turing's 'Turing Test' (Turing, 1950) and John Searle's 'Chinese Room' argument (1980) are canonical reference points for debates around computer simulation of language and AI, and each, in my view, rests on fatally flawed assumptions about language. Although it is a divergence from the generally historical character of this book, I need to explain why (see G. Richards, 1994, 1996 for a more extensive but earlier version of the argument). This section may also stand in lieu of a critique of much of the broader cognitivist tradition of language research.

The Turing Test proposed an operational criterion for the presence of consciousness in a machine. An individual is faced with two interactive termini, one linked to a machine, the other to a human. If, after communicating with each, the individual cannot differentiate between their responses then the machine can legitimately be considered conscious. Ever since, the AI project's goal has widely been couched as designing a system that 'passes the Turing Test'.

Searle's 'Chinese Room argument' is more complicated, purporting, by means of a scenario demonstrating how non-'intentional' simulation of human language use is logically possible, to prove that 'intentionality'[1] is something which *cannot*

---

[1] 'Intentionality' and 'personhood' have widely replaced 'consciousness' as technical terms in this context, partly to sidestep the morass of the 'mind–body' problem.

be programmed into a computer, thus refuting the Turing Test. An English-speaker ignorant of Chinese is placed in a sealed box into which a Chinese-reader passes written messages. Consulting a rule-book the person selects an appropriate reply, knowing nothing of what either message means. The Chinese-reader nonetheless experiences themselves as engaged in as equally meaningful an exchange as a literate English-speaker communicating with the occupant in written English. The 'system', when using Chinese, operates according to purely formal rules but apparently passes the Turing Test. This too has been controversial ever since first publication.

Although opposed these arguments share an affinity of approach which is itself, I believe, in error. My objections pertain (a) to the nature of thought-experiments, (b) to how we ascribe 'intentionality' or 'personhood' and (c) to the location of 'agency'.

Thought-experiments

Each is a 'thought-experiment' involving imagining a situation and its possible outcomes or implications. Several major scientific discoveries originated this way: Galileo's pondering on motion in a vacuum produced the concept of inertia for instance, while Einstein's theory of relativity was allegedly sparked when he wondered what happens to clocks when they are moving at the speed of light. In a different mode of usage Wittgenstein frequently used quasi-anthropological thought-experiments to demonstrate philosophical points. But rather than raising hitherto unrecognised riddles requiring solutions, or clarifying conceptual points, these current cases supposedly carry the whole burden of an argument. We are being asked, in effect, to replicate the writer's thought-experiment to confirm his 'results'. Yet taking this literally, the information in the texts is surely insufficient, we want more details of precisely what we are to imagine, e.g. how the human role is played in the Turing Test; how, in the Chinese Room, the rule-book can include responses to all possible inputs. The upshot is that either the experiment's coherence collapses under such interrogation or one uncritically colludes with the original account, in which case the 'result' becomes uncontestable. One obviously cannot, as with real experiments, actually conduct such kinds of thought-experiment and arrive at independent results. They are not replicable in the ordinary sense but more like literary fictions – if we start picking holes in the plot their credibility evaporates. This will become clearer in due course.

The grounds for ascribing personhood

Both assume that we ascribe personhood to something on the grounds that it can use language (albeit Searle's point is that this is insufficient). This is completely the wrong way round. We ascribe a linguistic character to something's behaviour because we believe it is a person, and ascribe 'personhood' to that with which we *choose* to live (or experience ourselves as living) in a reciprocal social relationship of some kind – which might include pet budgerigars or statues of the Blessed Virgin (G. Richards, 1989). Only in the twentieth century did scientists 'scientifically' reject choices other than 'all fellow humans' as irrational. It would be its ability to converse about its experiences as a computer (involving a reciprocal social relationship and some degree of apparent spontaneity and unpredictability), not falsely persuading me it was human (as in the Turing Test), that would convince *me* a computer possessed 'intentionality'. In the case of the Chinese Room, in which the user is convinced that they are dealing with a 'person', we have a converse query – if this is not the person in the room, who is it? The answer must be the genius who compiled that inconceivably thorough rule-book including their personal responses to every possible 'input'.

Location of agency

The nub of the issue is really where we locate agency within a system. The Chinese Room argument obscures this by excluding the rule-book writer from consideration. There are, however, no logical grounds for this. Agency is not in fact an empirical property at all, but refers to where within a system we locate the origin or responsibility for its operations – but the boundaries of knowable systems are never impervious. We frequently ascribe all or part of the agency to a higher-level 'system' in which the one in question is embedded. The delinquent is responsible for stealing the car but the social system in which he dwells and which in part produced him is *not* his responsibility – government agencies in quite a literal sense have perhaps failed him. Where we locate agency is a moral decision, settled, when problematic, by a complex social process of negotiation.

With sundry qualifications contemporary social life and individual sanity require us to consider individuals as autonomous moral agents, whereas we treat technological systems as means via which human agency is exercised. The 'Strong AI' school, however, maintains that it is at least logically possible to create a system (an android perhaps) which itself possesses agency and is thus morally autonomous, its creators being no more (but no less?) responsible for its actions than parents are for those of adult offspring. But this assumes that possession of agency *is* some kind of empirical property. Now there is a tenuous sense in which the Turing Test is valid – such a technologically engineered entity might indeed so successfully display the features of autonomous personhood that we feel we have no choice but to consider it a responsible moral agent. *But this would not be because 'agency' or 'intentionality' had been programmed into it as distinct properties, it would be a collective psychological response to its total ensemble of behaviours.* Searle rightly denies that 'intentionality' is programmable, but errs in assuming its absence from his Chinese Room scenario.

Further problems arise with the conceivability of the Turing Test: e.g. the criteria required for passing it (fooling 90% of 100 people?), how the role of 'human' is to be played (are they competing against the machine? naive 'subjects' of the experiment?), and whether change over time (analogous to our ability to spot fake photographs) might mean it 'passes' the test at one time but later fails. Unlike litmus paper turning red as a test for acidity, 'passing the Turing Test' is more like keeping people puzzled about a conjuring trick. The Turing Test is not actually a test of the machine but of the ability of those taking the test to realise that it is one. One final point – however convincing a simulation of human behaviour, the effect normally dissipates when the mechanisms achieving it are disclosed. This is not, cannot be, the case with humans. Humans are the criterion by which simulations are judged, they cannot themselves (as is often apparently implied) somehow be reduced to the status of simulations simply by enhanced understanding of 'how they work'.

The preceding digression illustrates how a field marked by extremely hard-headed and technical theorising can be radically misled in its understanding of what it is doing by failing to grasp the nature of language (although T. Winograd, 1980, was an exception). These now-canonical reference points continue to be taken seriously. Those in the field contesting them rarely challenge the legitimacy of the original game, typically counterposing alternative (but similarly problematic) thought-experiments. The present argument is that they are interesting – indeed valuable – case-studies of how bad thinking can succeed under favourable cultural and intellectual circumstances, but fundamentally fallacious, shedding no light in their own terms on the matters they purport to address.

Comments and conclusion

As indicated previously, language is an intellectual free-fire zone. Since we can all talk we are entitled to talk about how we do so, suggesting perhaps a condition of 'meta-Babel'. This is misleading. A century's rumination of diverse professional kinds (in which psychologists have increasingly participated) has genuinely enhanced our understanding of the social character, pervasiveness, complexity, functions, neurological basis and pathologies of language. But why has language become such a bone of contention, the target of so many sorts of inquiry? Returning to a running theme of the present work, I suggest that it again relates to the chronic psychological crisis accompanying the rapid and unceasing changes of the last century and a half. This centres on the need for new ways of defining our identities, new 'modes of subjectivity' (see Chapter 11) and, deriving from this, new terms in which to communicate, heightened by the advents of radio, film, TV, the telephone, and most recently email and text-messaging. Globalisation, meanwhile, extends the range of people with whom we may have to communicate or seek to understand. Power considerations loom large, as politicians, entertainers and industry seek to use mass media to control, and sell to, mass audiences. The message is not lost on the less empowered. Language is a public battleground on which ideological contests are fought. Sometimes quite useful terms become unusable as their opponents succeed in rendering them unfashionable or impose negative connotations (e.g. much Marxist language), sometimes change is implemented successfully (e.g. loss of the gender-inclusive 'he' and in relation to racist language) only to elicit a subsequent backlash. ('Political correctness' is an intriguingly involuted instance of this latter, since those to whom belief in the doctrine is ascribed rarely use the term themselves except ironically.) The often violent reactions to linguistic change testify to the psychological profundity of language, both for individuals and society at large. Each psychological constituency seeks to create and maintain a language expressing its own psychology, 'naturalising' it in so doing. This is neither good nor bad, covering both politicians describing environmental despoliation as 'development' and replacement of 'idiocy' with 'learning difficulties'. It is how we are – each of us engages in this process as effectively as we can.

That such circumstances should heighten concern with language from a multitude of directions is unsurprising. Among other things this affects how such linguistic struggles are conducted, the 'rules of the game'. One 'place' of Psychology (particularly perhaps Social Psychology) is to heighten general awareness of this highly fraught process and reach a finer-grained understanding of its nature. But psychologists, themselves representing diverse psychological constituencies, cannot rise entirely above the linguistic fray.

Some clear gains have nonetheless been made. Traditional 'picture' theories of meaning have disappeared, few (consciously anyway) imagine words are 'magically' connected with their referents, or argue that language can refer in a theoretically or ethically neutral fashion to the world as it 'really is'. We increasingly appreciate how our language is inextricably involved with who we think we are and how we view the world. More practically we are beginning to get a handle on problems such as dyslexia, aphasia, how children acquire language and language teaching. All these gains owe much to Psychology. But some theoretical issues are too deeply rooted both in ideological differences and in the profounder, less conscious, dimensions of the power of language itself, to be quickly resolved either within or beyond Psychology. The talk continues. . . .

Further reading

To keep this manageable I have excluded Linguistics proper – hence no F. de Saussure etc. If not rendering the bibliography entirely analogous to *Hamlet* without the Prince of Denmark, *Waiting for Godot* without Lucky might hit the mark. I have also omitted language pathology as too large and distinct a subject. Even so, canonical entries aside, this is, I concede, a ludicrously selective list. Length considerations have also restricted the level of annotation.

History

Aarsleff, H. (1976) 'An Outline of Language Origins Theory since the Renaissance'. In S.R. Harnad, H.D. Steklis and J. Lancaster (eds) *Origins and Evolution of Language and Speech*. New York: New York Academy of Sciences, issued as *Annals of the New York Academy of Sciences*, vol. 20, 4–13.

Richards, G. (1992) *Mental Machinery: The Origins and Consequences of Psychological Ideas. Part One 1600–1850*. London: Athlone Press.

Rieber, R.W. (ed.) (1980) *Psychology of Language and Thought: Essays in the Theory and History of Psycholinguistics*. New York and London: Plenum Press.

Stam, J.H. (1980) 'An Historical Perspective on "Linguistic Relativity"'. In R.W. Rieber (ed.) *Psychology of Language and Thought: Essays in the Theory and History of Psycholinguistics*. New York and London: Plenum Press, 239–262.

Psychological language

Danziger, K. (1997) *Naming the Mind. How Psychology Discovered its Language*. London: Sage.

Graumann, C.F. and Gergen, K.J. (eds) (1996) *Historical Dimensions of Psychological Discourse*. Cambridge: Cambridge University Press.

Lakoff, G. (1987) *Women, Fire, and Dangerous Things. What Categories Reveal about the Mind*. Chicago and London: Chicago University Press.

Lakoff, G. and Johnson, M. (1980) *Metaphors We Live By*. Chicago: Chicago University Press. Essential reading.

Leary, D.E. (ed.) (1990) *Metaphors in the History of Psychology*. Cambridge: Cambridge University Press.

Richards, G.D. (1989) *On Psychological Language and the Physiomorphic Basis of Human Nature*. London: Routledge.

Richards, G.D. (1996) 'On the Necessary Persistence of Folk Psychology'. In W. O'Donohue and R. Kitchener (eds) *The Philosophy of Psychology*. London: Sage, 270–275.

Language and thought, and the Sapir–Whorf hypothesis

Early texts

Buchler, J. (ed.) (1940) *The Philosophy of Peirce. Selected Writings*. London: Kegan Paul, Trench & Trübner.

Goudge, T.A. (ed.) (1950) *The Thought of C.S. Peirce*. New York: Norton. Peirce was the leading exponent of American 'pragmatism' at the turn of the century and his writings on language and semiotics frequently anticipate later developments. His contemporary impact was, however, limited beyond an immediate circle of intellectual associates such as William James.

Locke, J. (1894, 1st edn 1690) *An Essay Concerning Human Understanding*, collated etc.: A.C. Fraser, Oxford: Clarendon Press.

Müller, M. (1887) *The Science of Thought*. London: Longmans Green.

Ogden, C.K. and Richards, I.A. (1923, 4th edn 1936) *The Meaning of Meaning. A Study in the Influence of Language upon Thought and the Science of Symbolism*. London: Kegan Paul, Trench & Trübner.

Porter, N. (1868, rep. 1872) *The Human Intellect with an Introduction upon Psychology and the Soul*. London: Strahan.

Porter, N. (1871) *The Science of Man and the Sciences of Nature*. New York: Dodd-Mead.

Whitney, W. (1875) *The Life and Growth of Language*. London: Henry S. King.

Whorf and after

Asch, S.E. (1952) *Social Psychology*. Englewood Cliffs: Prentice-Hall.

Brown, R. (1958) *Words and Things*. New York: Free Press; London: Collier-Macmillan.

Carroll, J.B. (ed.) (1956) *Language, Thought and Reality*. Cambridge, MA: MIT Press. A collection of papers by B.L. Whorf.

Chomsky, N. (1957) *Syntactic Structures*. The Hague and Paris: Mouton & Co.

Hattiangadi, J.N. (1987) *How is Language Possible? Philosophical Reflections of the Evolution of Language and Knowledge*. La Salle: Open Court.

Mandelbaum, D.G. (ed.) (1949) *Selected Writings of Edward Sapir in Language, Culture and Personality*. Berkeley & Los Angeles: University of California Press; London: Cambridge University Press.

Morris, C.W. (1938) *Foundations of the Theory of Signs*. Chicago: Chicago University Press.

Morris, C.W. (1946) *Signs, Language and Behavior*. New York: Prentice-Hall.

Ortony, A. (ed.) (1979) *Metaphor and Thought*. Cambridge: Cambridge University Press.

Osgood, C.E., Suci, G.C. and Tannenbaum, P.H. (1957) *The Measurement of Meaning*. Urbana: University of Illinois Press.

Sebeok, T.A., Hayes, A.S. and Bateson, M.C. (eds) (1964) *Approaches to Semiotics*. The Hague: Mouton.

Suppes, P. (1991) *Language for Humans and Robots*. Oxford: Blackwell.

Vygotsky, L.S. (1962) *Thought and Language*. Cambridge, MA: MIT Press.

General semantics

Hayakawa, S.I. (ed.) (1954) *Language, Meaning and Maturity. Selections from ETC: A Review of General Semantics 1943–1953*. New York: Harper.

Korzybski, A. (1921) *Manhood of Humanity*. Lakeville, CT: The International Non-Aristotelian Library.

Korzybski, A. (1933) *Science and Sanity*. New York: The International Non-Aristotelian Library.

The linguistic philosophy perspective

Austin, J.L. (1962, 2nd edn 1975) *How to do Things with Words*. Oxford: Clarendon Press.

Hacking, I. (1975) *Why Does Language Matter to Philosophy?* Cambridge: Cambridge University Press.

Ryle, G. (1949, rep. 1963) *The Concept of Mind*. Harmondsworth: Peregrine.

Searle, J.R. (ed.) (1971) *The Philosophy of Language*. London: Oxford University Press.

Wittgenstein, L. (1953) *Philosophical Investigations*. Oxford: Blackwell.

The behaviourist perspective

Cofer, C.N. (ed.) (1961) *Verbal Learning and Verbal Behavior*. New York: McGraw-Hill.

Cofer, C.N. and Musgrave, B.S. (eds) (1963) *Verbal Behavior and Verbal Learning*. New York: McGraw-Hill.

Place, U.T. (1992) 'Eliminative Connectionism: Its Implications for a Return to an Empiricist/Behaviorist Linguistics'. *Behaviour and Philosophy* 20(1): 21–35.

Rush, J. (1827, 7th edn 1879) *The Philosophy of the Human Voice*. Philadelphia: Lippincott. This is often noted as distantly anticipating the behaviourist position, indeed Rush has been called J.B. Watson's John the Baptist.

Skinner, B.F. (1957) *Verbal Behavior*. New York: Appleton-Century-Crofts.

The cognitivist perspective

Anderson, J.R. (1980) *Cognitive Psychology and its Implications*. San Francisco: W.H. Freeman. Part V provides an overview of cognitivist psycholinguistics at the end of its initial phase.

Fodor, J.A., Bever, T.G. and Garrett, M.F. (1974) *The Psychology of Language*. New York: McGraw-Hill.

Johnson-Laird, P.N. (1977) 'Procedural Semantics'. *Cognition* 5: 189–214.

Miller, G.A. and McNeill, D. (1969) 'Psycholinguistics'. In G. Lindzey and E. Aronson (eds) *The Handbook of Social Psychology. Volume III*, 666–794. Reading, MA: Addison-Wesley.

Smith, F. and Miller, G.A. (eds) (1966) *The Genesis of Language. A Psycholinguistic Approach*. Cambridge, MA: MIT Press.

Winograd, T. (1980) 'What Does it Mean to Understand Language?' *Cognitive Science* 4: 209–241.

Origins and evolution of language

Anon (1848) *The Origin and Progress of Language*. London: The Religious Tract Society.

Bickerton, D. (1990) *Language and Species*. Chicago and London: University of Chicago Press.

Harnad, S.R., Steklis, H.D. and Lancaster, J. (eds) (1976) *Origins and Evolution of Language and Speech*. New York: New York Academy of Sciences, issued as *Annals of the New York Academy of Sciences*, vol. 20.

Hattiangadi, J.N. (1987) *How Is Language Possible? Philosophical Reflections of the Evolution of Language and Knowledge*. La Salle: Open Court. Chapters 10 and 11.

Hewes, G.W. (1973) 'An Explicit Formulation of the Relationship between Tool-using, Tool-making, and the Emergence of Language'. *Visible Language* 7(2): 101–127.

Hockett, C.F. (1960) 'The Origin of Speech'. *Scientific American* 203: 89–96. Famous for proposing a list of 'design features' of language, all of which are only present in human language.

Lieberman, P. (1984) *The Biology and Evolution of Language*. Cambridge, MA: Harvard University Press.

Paget, R. (1930) *Human Speech. Some Observations, Experiments, and Conclusions as to the Nature, Origin, Purpose and Possible Improvement of Human Speech*. London: Kegan Paul, Trench & Trübner.

Pinker, S. (1994) *The Language Instinct*. New York: Morrow.

Place, U.T. (2000) 'The Role of the Hand in the Evolution of Language'. *Psycoloquy* 00.11.007. (This is an APA-sponsored online refereed journal run from Princeton University.)

Richards, G. (1987) *Human Evolution. An Introduction for the Behavioural Sciences*. London: Routledge, 246–273.

Stam, J.H. (1976) *Inquiries into the Origin of Language: The Fate of a Question*. New York: Harper & Row.

General psycholinguistics

Carroll, D.W. (1986) *Psychology of Language*. Pacific Grove, CA: Brooks/Cole.

Carroll, J.B. (1953) *The Study of Language: A Survey of Linguistics and other Disciplines*. Cambridge, MA: Harvard University Press.

Pillsbury, W.B. and Meader, C.L. (1928) *The Psychology of Language*. New York & London: D. Appleton.

Sociolinguistics and Social Psychological approaches

Atkinson, P. (1985) *Language, Structure and Reproduction: An Introduction to the Sociology of Basil Bernstein*. London: Methuen.

Bernstein, B. (1971) *Class, Codes and Social Control*. London: Paladin.

Billig, M. (1987) *Arguing and Thinking: A Rhetorical Approach to Social Psychology*. Cambridge: Cambridge University Press.

Garfinkel, H. (1967) *Studies in Ethnomethodology*. New York: Prentice Hall.

Halliday, M.A.K. (1978) *Language as Social Semiotic: The Social Interpretation of Language and Meaning*. London: Arnold.

Hymes, D.H. (1977) *Foundations of Sociolinguistics: An Ethnographic Approach*. London: Tavistock.

Labov, W. (1966) *The Social Stratification of English in New York City*. Washington DC: Centre for Applied Linguistics.

Shotter, J. (1993) *Conversational Realities: Constructing Life through Language*. London: Sage.

The Turing Test and Chinese Room arguments

Richards, G. (1994) 'The Chinese Room Revisited'. *B.P.S. History & Philosophy of Psychology Section Newsletter* 18: 22–28.

Richards, G. (1996) 'The Chinese Room Re-Vacated?' *B.P.S. History & Philosophy of Psychology Section Newsletter* 20: 5–8.

Searle, J.R. (1980) 'Minds, Brains, and Programs'. *The Behavioral and Brain Sciences* 3: 417–457. This includes extensive Peer Commentary and Searle's reply. As is usual with this journal the debate is further pursued in some subsequent issues.

Turing, A.M. (1950) 'Computing Machinery and Intelligence'. *Mind* 49: 433–460.

Child acquisition of language

(Selected foundational texts only)

Bellugi, U. and Brown, R. (eds) (1964) *The Acquisition of Language*. Lafayette, IN: Child Development Publications, *Monographs of the Society for Research in Child Development* 92.

Bruner, J.S., Olver, R.H. and Greenfield, P.M. (1966) *Studies in Cognitive Growth*. New York: John Wiley & Sons.

Lewis, M.M. (1936, 2nd edn 1951) *Infant Speech. A Study of the Beginnings of Language*. London: Routledge & Kegan Paul.

Luria, A.R. (1961) *The Role of Speech in the Regulation of Normal and Abnormal Behaviour*. New York: Pergamon Press.

Luria, A.R. and Yudovich, F. Ia. (1959) *Speech and the Development of Mental Processes in the Child*. London: Staples Press.

Piaget, J. (1926, rev. and enlarged 1959) *The Language and Thought of the Child*. London: Routledge & Kegan Paul.

Part five

THREE CULTURAL ENTANGLEMENTS

In this final part we look at three issues that have preoccupied Psychology's host societies throughout most of the discipline's twentieth-century history: religion, 'race', and war. These have provided the deeper background context within which Psychology has so far been practised. A full understanding of how Psychology has engaged with these would, potentially, shed more light on its overall character and 'place' in the world than any in-depth scrutiny of specific theories or research topics. While no claims for having reached such an understanding are being made here, the following discussions may hopefully provide a starting point towards doing so.

Chapter 20

Psychology meets religion

- Importance of the topic
- The relationship between Psychology and religion before the Second World War: the US
- The relationship between Psychology and religion before the Second World War: Protestant mainland Europe
- The relationship between Psychology and religion before the Second World War: Britain
- The relationship between Psychology and religion before the Second World War: Catholic mainland Europe
- The relationships between Psychology and religion since 1945
- The problematic meanings of religious concepts
- Psychology's role in the present situation

The heated late nineteenth-century confrontation between religion and evolutionary thought, and the prominent role of evolutionary thought in Psychology's creation (see Chapter 3), might lead one to expect an even more intense conflict between religion and Psychology. After all, conceding understanding of the physical world to science left religion's central claims to expertise on human nature and the 'soul' more-or-less intact, but with Psychology science now presumed to invade even this hallowed territory. What is curious, therefore, is such a conflict's failure to materialise, as even a relatively cursory historical exploration of the topic bears out. Some contemporary psychologists appear unaware of this; K.M. Loewenthal (2000) for example, opening a section on 'A Short History of the Uneasy Relationship between Psychology and Religion', states quite baldly that 'Each domain has been seen as exclusive: if you are a psychologist you cannot take religion seriously, and if you are religious you cannot take psychology seriously' (p. 6). This is calamitously wrong. While many psychologists have indeed been hostile or indifferent to religion, the discipline itself has never achieved, or even sought, an anti-religion consensus comparable to geology's rejection of the Genesis creation myth, and many canonically eminent psychologists have, as we will see, taken religion extremely seriously (while the first Psychology laboratory in Belgium was founded by the Catholic Cardinal Mercier in 1891!). It has become a cliché to say that the psychologist (or psychotherapist) usurped the role of priest or church minister, but the reality is rather more complex. One could even argue that many twentieth-century clergy sought to redefine their role in terms of being psychologists or psychotherapists. Psychology's place in modernist cultures did, even so, have to be established alongside, and to some degree in competition with, that of religion. We may begin, therefore, with examining why the two camps appear, against the odds, to have co-existed relatively amicably.

Before the Second World War

One reason concerns Psychology's late nineteenth-century founding phase in the United States. As we saw in Chapter 4, the 'New Psychology' of the 1880s and 1890s emerged from the pre-existing American university and college tradition of 'Mental and Moral Philosophy' led by Yale's Noah Porter and Princeton's James McCosh, both typically devout. The majority of institutions in which it was taught had denominational affiliations, usually Presbyterian, Methodist or Congregationalist (the only Catholic college being the University of Notre Dame founded in 1842). Most of America's first psychologists were deeply imbued with the values of this school, several turning to Psychology after initially intending to pursue ministerial careers (G. Richards, 1995). One assumption they typically retained from the Mental and Moral Philosophy school's Psychology was that religious belief was the normal outcome of successful child-rearing (as spelled out in detail in Porter, 1868). G. Stanley Hall, James M. Baldwin and G. Trumball Ladd were all among these early Christian psychologists, while William James, no Christian, was still deeply fascinated by religion, his most popularly successful work being *The Varieties of Religious Experience* (1902). Overthrowing Christianity (especially Protestantism) was very definitely not on their agenda. Hall founded *The American*

Journal of Religious Psychology and Education in 1904, retitled *Journal of Religious Psychology* in 1909 (which folded in 1915), and later wrote a 2-volume work, *Jesus the Christ in the Light of Psychology* (1921) (see H. Vande Kemp, 1992 on the Hall school of Psychology of Religion) – although this was hardly orthodox in approach. Unsurprisingly then, a sub-discipline 'Psychology of Religion' soon emerged, continuing as a recognised, if somewhat minor, branch of Psychology down to the 1950s, reviving again, though far less conspicuously, after the mid-1970s. This may be dated from E.D. Starbuck's *The Psychology of Religion. An Empirical Study of the Growth of Religious Consciousness* (1899), largely written under Hall's aegis.

The tenor of this genre was not uncritical of religion, and some of its findings (e.g. about the transience of many conversions, and their association with phases of adolescent stress) were not entirely comfortable. Nonetheless this had a benefit, facilitating a distinction between 'healthy' and 'pathological' forms of religion which enabled respectable mainstream denominations to police their boundaries against embarrassing fanaticism and evangelical excesses. As far as psychotherapy was concerned, an early collaboration was the Boston Emmanuel Movement which briefly flourished between 1906 and 1910 (E. Caplan, 1998). James Leuba (1909, 1925), the major, and most controversial, figure in anglophone Psychology of Religion during the early twentieth century, strongly criticised organised religion, but primarily because it was now failing as an authentic and satisfactory vehicle of spirituality (see D.M. Wulff, 2000, on Leuba's quite complex position). Another figure to note is H.H. Goddard, famous for introducing IQ testing to North America and notorious (somewhat unjustly) for his hereditarian and eugenic views of 'subnormality' – he, too, it transpires, was profoundly affected by a passionately Quaker childhood environment (see L. Zenderland, 1998).

This fundamental sympathy towards religion continued in many of the next generation of American psychologists; Gardner Murphy and Gordon Allport, for example, were deeply affected by the religious values of their early upbringing. Allport gave several lectures relating religion to Psychology and psychiatry plus sermons at Harvard University's Appleton Chapel, eventually publishing a book entitled *The Individual and His Religion. A Psychological Interpretation* (1950) (see H. Vande Kemp, 2000, for Allport's work on Psychology of religion up to this point, also I. Nicholson, 1997). During the 1920s and 1930s the proportion of major American psychologists expressing overt religious sympathies did indeed decline, and occasionally, as in the case of J.B. Watson, some were explicitly hostile. Nonetheless, inter-war American Psychology usually remained non-confrontational, explicit religious sympathy being more typically replaced by seeming indifference, as Allport complained in a 1948 review of the content of college textbooks over the 1928–1945 period. Religion had little relevance to prevailing interests in learning, psychological assessment technology and applied psychologists' increasing involvements with social problems. In the psychotherapy field religion also becomes less visible (unlike the British situation, as discussed later). While it is difficult to be sure, one suspects that religion's relatively low profile in applied Psychology and psychotherapy at this time may relate to American culture's combination of religious tolerance with religion's high profile in everyday life. These would, paradoxically perhaps, render religion out of bounds as a topic for psychologists working within the community as a whole. Espousing explicit religious adherence in one's professional role would risk alienating clients, and might even be unconstitutional. Psychology and psychotherapy were now secular, pragmatic, problem-solving disciplines, and had no business intruding on people's religious beliefs. Even so, *within* religious pastoral care organisations, colleges and seminaries Psychological ideas did have an impact and a distinct, Psychologically-informed tradition of pastoral counselling subsequently took off in the 1950s (see H.J. Clinebell Jr, 1966, H. Vande Kemp, 1996), along with a more concerted effort among the religious to bridge the gap between Psychology and theology (F. Künkel, 1954, marking the onset of this).

In Germany Külpe (leader of the 'Würzburg School') and Estonian psychologist Karl Girgensohn (of Dorpat) jointly founded a society of Psychology of Religion (*Die internationale Gesellschaft für Religionspsychologie*) in 1914, launching a journal still in existence (*Archiv für Religionspsychologie*). Girgensohn undertook extensive research on the nature of religious experience, published in a 'magnum opus' in 1921. In 1927 the society came under the direction of his protegé Werner Gruehn, a role he maintained until the late 1950s (D.M. Wulff, 1985; T. Nørager, 2000). Gruehn continued to pursue a variant of the Würzberg School's version of 'experimental introspectionism' espoused by Girgensohn, eliciting extensive 'protocols' from subjects regarding their responses to religious stimuli. The other school in German-language Psychology of religion was the psychoanalytic one led from Zurich by the pastor and educationist Oscar Pfister, one of Freud's more important correspondents (E. Nase, 2000). (In 1930 Pfister rejected a chair in the topic at the University of Chicago.) Until the 1930s Pfister and Gruehn were virtually at one another's throats over the respective merits of their methods until a shared concern with pastoral care and education provided the occasion for a more civil rapprochement between them. This Gruehn–Pfister axis clearly dominated inter-war German-speaking Psychology of Religion. Martin Kusch (1999) has also identified an earlier religious dimension to the differences within German Psychology between the Catholic Würzburg School and Protestant Wundtians in the early twentieth century, but this pertains more to the style and orientation of their Psychological research than to its content. Among Dutch Calvinists there was considerably heated controversy about the acceptability of the topic. J.A. Belzen (2000, 2001), examining the situation, finds it getting perennially bogged down in institutional and theological wrangles, but achieving a relatively stable and enduring, if modest, Dutch presence for the field until 1960, after which, untypically, it expanded considerably.

In Britain events took a rather different course. Psychology's British nineteenth-century founders (far fewer than in America) were mostly evolutionists indifferent, or even hostile, to established religion. His religious apostasy hindered Alexander Bain's academic career for many years and his new journal *Mind* (see Chapter 3) studiously rejected religious writers such as James Martineau. It was a topic on which few entered into print. One exception was Francis Galton's hilarious trio of papers which included 'Statistical Inquiries into the Efficacy of Prayer' (1872). With ostensibly deadpan seriousness this investigated, among other approaches, whether monarchs, for whom vast numbers of prayers for long life were said, actually did have longer than average life-expectancy. Of course they did not, falling if anything slightly below average. (Galton solemnly conceded that it remained possible that without the prayers they might have fallen even further

below.) He also established that insurance premiums for ships carrying mission-
aries (prayers for whose safe passage were always enthusiastically offered up on
embarkation) were no less than those for other vessels – thus such prayers apparently did not affect the odds of ships sinking. After this little exercise in statistical
satire religion barely recurs in British Psychology until after the First World War.
However, a caveat must be promptly entered. if religion does not figure, psychical
research certainly does. Concern with spiritualist and kindred phenomena led
to the founding of the Society for Psychical Research (SPR) in 1882, and this
engaged in quite serious research into the psychological phenomena involved
(see I. Grattan-Guinness, 1982; G. Richards, 2001). E. Gurney, F.W.H. Myers and
F. Podmore's *Phantasms of the Living* (1886) and F.W.H. Myers' *Human Personality
and its Survival of Bodily Death* (1903) were both serious, well-researched works.
Myers' interest in the psychological nature of such phenomena led him to propose
the existence of a 'subliminal personality', and he was the first in Britain to cite
Freud in print (F.W.H. Myers, 1893). Later British psychologists interested in this
topic include such major names as Cyril Burt, William McDougall, R.H. Thouless,
C. Spearman and H.J. Eysenck, some (such as Thouless) being SPR members
(see also J. Hazelgrove, 2000, on popular spiritualism between the world wars).
William James had been similarly involved in psychic research in the US. Such
concerns at least signify a preoccupation with the basic religious issues of the
'soul's' survival of death and the existence of a 'spiritual' realm. Thus, even in
evolutionism's heyday, British Psychology was not entirely indifferent to religious
questions, Galton himself attending a few séances in the 1870s.

After 1918, however, in contrast to North America and mainland Europe, the
two parties suddenly become closely and openly involved with each other, particularly in the field of psychotherapy, R.H. Thouless publishing the first British-
authored book on the Psychology of religion in 1923. This episode is discussed in
more detail in G. Richards (2000). The interpretation offered there is that after
1918 mainstream British churches urgently needed to re-establish their credibility
as sources of psychological, or 'spiritual', comfort and pastoral care in a climate of
widespread mental distress. For many, the war had undermined the adequacy of
traditional religious wisdoms about human nature, and often they turned to cults
and non-Christian religions, or secular and materialist doctrines like Marxism and
psychoanalysis. The major churches, if sympathetic, could not throw their energies
wholeheartedly into overtly political social reform, which would have required
alliance with revolutionary communists. But successfully to play their alternative
role of source of 'spiritual', psychological comfort required updating their ideas
and image in an increasingly science-oriented, sceptical, secularised world. This
meant reaching a settlement with what was being called 'The New Psychology'. It
would be less confusing had it been called 'The New New Psychology', since it
was actually a reaction against 1880–1890's American 'New Psychology' which
typically focused on experimental psychophysics. This 'New Psychology', by contrast, tackled more obviously relevant issues regarding the roots of human emotions, feelings and behaviour. The term covered, for example, William McDougall's
work on instincts and emotions (McDougall, 1908), William Trotter's *Instincts of
the Herd in Peace and War* (1916), the 'autosuggestion therapy' of the Frenchman
Émile Coué and, above all, Freud's psychoanalysis.

As it happened (why, though an interesting question, we cannot explore here) several prominent British psychologists and psychotherapists at this point were also devout Christians; besides Thouless the most prominent were H. Crichton-Miller (founder of the Tavistock clinic), William Brown (Wilde Reader in Mental Philosophy at University College London, leading psychometrician and prominent psychotherapist), Francis Aveling (an ex-Catholic priest and professor at King's College London) and J.C. Hadfield (also lecturer at King's College London). A professorship in the Psychology of Religion was also established at Manchester University during this period. But equally significant were numerous Christian academics and ministers keen to incorporate 'New Psychological' insights into their pastoral practice and reconcile them with Christian doctrine. Some, like Eric Waterhouse, Professor of Psychology and Philosophy at Richmond College (part of the University of London), straddled both camps. Most prominent was Leslie Weatherhead, a highly popular Methodist writer who established the (now defunct) City Temple Psychological Clinic in London. Despite psychoanalysis being the most antagonistic to religion of all the New Psychology schools (particularly in the hands of Ernest Jones), many such Christian writers eagerly adopted its central concepts (especially 'sublimation'), charitably dismissing psychoanalysts' anti-religious sentiments as an unfortunate blind spot, a failure to realise that the final 'transference' had to be onto God. No one in Britain, however, matched O. Pfister's sophisticated in-depth synthesis of psychoanalysis and religious belief.

For various contextual reasons there was, in short, little to be gained, and much to be lost, by a confrontation. Neither camp wanted mainstream medicine to monopolise treatment of the mentally distressed while religious believers were a major market for Psychological expertise as well as an important source of recruits for the discipline. Given that the two camps overlapped anyway, what amounted to an informal alliance emerged. Most sceptical or indifferent psychologists contentedly kept their heads below the parapet, adopting the simple line that, as a science, Psychology was only about 'facts', while religion was about 'values'. Neither Cyril Burt nor C.S. Myers were believers, but each happily stated, for popular audiences, that religion was a positive force in human affairs and that prayer could, for whatever reason, be psychologically efficacious. Perhaps we no longer appreciate quite how psychologically disturbed the British cultural climate was in the aftermath of the Great War, and how anxious were otherwise disparate professional groups to find common cause in re-establishing and maintaining some civilised order against the destructive forces so evidently at large. Mainland European chaos during the same years is, retrospectively, far more visible.

In the 1930s another voice became audible, apparently offering an inspiring reconciliation of ancient religious with modern Psychological wisdom – that of Carl Jung. His *Modern Man in Search of a Soul* (1933) provided a seemingly profound analysis of the modern world's spiritual plight and religious attention began shifting from Freud to his erstwhile colleague. (Freud's own *Civilisation and its Discontents*, appearing in English in 1930, struck a far more dour, cold and pessimistic note, yet one which I at least feel was far more courageous and genuinely penetrating.) Jung's metamorphosis in popular perception from 'follower of Freud' to 'spiritual sage' signalled the end of British Psychology's initial intimacy with mainstream British Christianity. Christians would now play out their reconciliation with 'scientific Psychology' vis-à-vis Jung, failing to observe that 'scientific Psychology' was largely dismissing him as an embarrassment. While Freud too was falling from favour as scientifically flawed, Jung, it was widely felt, had abandoned science altogether.

In France, southern Europe and various other regions of Europe, Psychology's encounter was with Catholicism rather than Protestantism, and Catholic theology since Thomas Aquinas had developed a doctrinal image of human psychology which was far more clearcut, yet also more elaborated, than any Protestantism could now offer. If, from the outset, some Catholic psychologists took up the challenge of what they perhaps saw as a Protestant Psychology (hence such works as N. Joly's *The Psychology of the Saints*, 1898), the explicitly Catholic strand in Psychology has never been especially prominent. The exceptions are mainly mainland Europeans. The Italian S. De Sanctis (author of a 1927 book on religious conversion), for example, was a contemporary of the US 'founding fathers' of the 1890s. Three other prominent early Catholic psychologists were: Cardinal D.F.J.J. Mercier aforementioned founder of a laboratory at Louvain (Belgium) in 1891 and whose 2-volume *Psychologie* (1892) became one of the most influential mainland European textbooks (an 11th edition appearing in 1923); the Franciscan Father Agostino Gemelli who dominated Italian Psychology from 1907 into the 1940s; and Thomas V. Moore (who finally became a Carthusian monk in 1947), the most prominent US Catholic psychologist from the 1920s to 1940s, who was particularly concerned with mental illness as well as more mainstream topics. While, in these cases, their Catholicism infused their Psychologies, other Catholic psychologists such as Henri Michotte, Eric Wasmann (a pioneer comparative psychologist), J. Lindoworsky and the German Father Joseph Fröbes kept their religious and Psychological work distinct. The fullest survey of the Catholic role in early twentieth-century Psychology is H. Misiak and V.M. Staudt (1954). To generalise, it would appear that while numerous Catholic psychologists played major roles in the development of experimental and applied Psychology, when venturing into theory they tended to fall back on the sophisticated Thomist scholastic tradition – a notable work from this direction being R.E. Brennan's *The History of Psychology, from the standpoint of a Thomist* (1946). In France the encounter between psychoanalysis and Catholicism came to a head only after the Second World War as J. Lacan, P. Ricoeur and others became involved in intense debate over the Catholic doctrine of guilt. Lacan (in vain) even sought a personal audience with the pope (P. Vandermeersch, 2000).

Until 1939 any direct collision between Psychology and the main Christian churches was, for various reasons, averted. In America, the majority of the discipline's founders and early followers being believers, major 'science' versus 'religion' tensions were easily held in check. In Britain, where Psychology and religion shared too many common interests, as well as actual members, for outright confrontation to arise, a patronising tolerance was the worst that most psychologists, aside from the psychoanalysts, were prepared to express. In more Catholic locations co-existence was achieved by a combination of (a) differentiation between scientific Psychology proper and theology and (b) using updated Thomist scholastic Psychology to provide theoretical gravitas.

Since 1945

'Since 1945' is a long time, but precisely how it should be chronologically analysed in relation to the present topic is unclear. While a number of rather complicated developments – both Psychological and psychological – have undoubtedly occurred, they have yielded few clearcut outcomes. H. Vande Kemp (1996), in a densely referenced review of the relationship between religion and Clinical Psychology in the US, argues for the largely post-1945 emergence and maturation of what is in effect a distinct discipline (with its own journals, professional organisations and undergraduate training programmes, etc.) integrating Psychology, theology and religion. This is seen as rooted in dissatisfaction (such as Allport's, cited earlier) with orthodox Psychology's failure to recognise or admit the psychological centrality of 'spiritual' integration and religious values in ordinary people's lives. Her view of what this covers is, however, extremely broad extending across the whole range of more-or-less exotic growth movement and alternative therapies, Jungian traditions and non-Christian religious-based approaches such as Sufism and Zen Buddhism.

Obviously the new millennium finds the expectations of religion's impending demise, widespread among 'progressive' scientists and materialist thinkers in 1900, unrealised. That these expectations were unrealistic was already evident by 1950, however, since when, in Britain at least, Psychology and religion appear to have warily circled each other unsure if they are engaged in a dance or a boxing match. In the US, due partly to the higher incidence of religious belief and in part to the sheer size of the country, a religiously-oriented clinical tradition has been able to grow and flourish in parallel with orthodox Clinical Psychology, both camps, however, acknowledging certain key figures such as A. Maslow. A group called 'Psychologists Interested in Religious Issues' (PIRI) acquired APA Divisional status in 1976, this Division (36) being retitled Psychology of Religion in 1993.

In Britain, as the intensity of the relationship between the parties waned during the 1950s Psychology of Religion as a sub-discipline followed suit, only beginning to revive in the 1990s (see K.M. Loewenthal, 2000, for some data on this), rather later than in the US. Psychology's angle of interest in religion typically became a fairly straightforward social Psychological one (e.g. M. Argyle, 1958), with an admixture of psychometric-style personality theory. Psychology rarely treated religion as a rival authority on human nature, choosing instead to study (sometimes collaboratively) such topics as the social psychology of deviant religious cults, superstition (G. Jahoda, 1969), or personality and social class correlates of religious belief. Psychotherapies, by contrast, were becoming increasingly quasi-religious, reviving the concept of 'spirituality' for example, and engaging in therapeutic practices formally akin to religious ones (e.g. the parallels between events in primal therapy and the 'possession' frenzies associated with some classical cults and Christian exorcism rites). G. Murphy and J.K. Kovach (1972) were already seeing the then new 'growth movement' approaches as religious in character. The present menu of therapies spans an extraordinarily broad spectrum from the frankly materialist pharmaceutical via the rationally 'scientific' (e.g. cognitive behavioural therapy) to the neo-shamanistic (consider also the role of the Westminster Pastoral Foundation in British counselling). But if individual practitioners at various points on this spectrum often regard each other with contempt, no obvious line of confrontation is discernible. Despite H. Vande Kemp's view of the religiously oriented therapies representing a shared project, the reigning impression of an atmosphere of mutual toleration, respect and universal complementarity (in which all critical faculties are suspended aside from random outbreaks of internecine bickering) is surely somewhat false. (And it must be admitted that the few anti-religion voices now prominent in popular culture, such as Richard Dawkins', have hardly advanced their arguments beyond Thomas Huxley's.) It is at least possible that post-Hiroshima and the Holocaust European and North American societies have, psychologically, been in a condition of weightless suspension as far as religion is concerned, and that Psychology's involvements with it have reflected this. Nonetheless, there was, as already noted, something of a revival of Psychology of Religion and Christian interest in Psychology after the mid-1970s (later in Britain), and a *Journal for the Scientific Study of Religion* had already been founded in 1961 with much Psychological content. In Britain the real problem was that few people now actually cared about the topic anyway, unlike the pre-1939 period when books like Leslie Weatherhead's *Psychology in the Service of the Soul* (1929) were best-sellers. Psychology of Religion was now a distinctively minority interest. As in the US, the application of Psychological ideas to religious and pastoral concerns within Christian churches has continued to develop; for example, the Psychology and Christianity Project established under the aegis of the Centre for Advanced Religious and Theological Studies in Cambridge in 1996 headed by ex-British Psychological Society president and applied psychologist Rev. Fraser Watts (see e.g. F. Watts, R. Nye and S. Savage, 2001). But the visibility of such projects remains, as yet, confined within religious circles.

Reflexively viewed, this prolonged stand-off between Psychology and religion signifies a genuine lack of resolution, a chronic uncertainty shading into indifference, regarding religion within the psychology of the 'developed' world, the borderline in any case blurring as far as psychotherapy is concerned. Since the British, American and mainland European situations have obviously diverged in various ways, instead of imposing some historical plot-line on the late twentieth century it will be more useful to try and appraise the nature of the problem. The remainder of this chapter thus shifts from a historical treatment to a more speculative diagnosis of the present situation.

The problem of religion concepts

While Psychology and religion, whatever their past intimacies, represent fundamentally different approaches to the task of reflexive understanding, it would generally be acknowledged that neither is an entirely satisfactory alternative to the other. Religion does address widely-felt psychological needs and aspirations or serve certain psychological functions, which the 'scientific' orientation of Psychology cannot, by its very nature, tackle. Not everyone experiences such needs, but this does not mean they are pathological or illegitimate. Nor can religions be reduced to sets of empirically refutable beliefs, they constitute overarching frameworks of meaning within which individual adherents and adherent communities live. Religion's (particularly Christianity's) current central problem is, I suggest, the declining meaningfulness of its basic concepts. In a predominantly secular world the very meanings of such terms as 'worship', 'grace', 'prayer', 'holiness' and – most obviously – 'God', have become peculiarly elusive. What, for example, does it mean to 'worship' something? Unpacking this it appears to reduce to a combination of two, rather unreligious, things: (a) the kind of incessant praise and admiration bestowed upon, and demanded of their subjects by, traditional absolute rulers, and (b) personal infatuation, a near synonym for 'love' – as in the secular usage 'I worship and adore you'. A God requiring incessant grateful praise from 'His' own creations hardly strikes us nowadays as in any way admirable. Similarly it is hard to understand the extension of 'love' to an abstract, invisible divine entity as more than a generalisation beyond their legitimate range of normal human emotions of familial or sexual love. None of the other concepts listed is any easier.

This is meant not as a criticism of such concepts, only as a statement of the current linguistic situation. They refer not to 'natural' psychological experiences, behaviours or emotions, but are fully meaningful only within the framework of a total religious system. Unless you are living and interpreting your life within such a system they are enigmatic, incomprehensible or, at best, trivialised into secular metaphors. In that respect they are, however, no different from Psychological concepts within secular theories, as has been argued elsewhere regarding e.g. psychoanalysis. Philosophical exploration of this issue was initiated in A. Flew and A. MacIntyre's 1955 edited collection *New Essays in Philosophical Theology* in which a number of British philosophers, both believers and sceptics, strove to articulate the problem from the standpoint of the, then new, linguistic philosophy. But this fell upon stony ground, and was too technically intellectual to have much impact beyond academia.

Few twentieth-century thinkers from either camp succeeded in reaching a position which transcended the dichotomy. For unsympathetic psychologists religious behaviour and experience were explicable as quasi-pathological aberrations in, or naive prescientific interpretations of, the operation of whatever psychological processes their theories proposed, be they behaviourist, psychoanalytic, cognitive, socio-biological or whatever. For the religious, such psychologists were merely suffering from a blind-spot or ignorance. In the author's opinion the person coming closest to a resolution was Paul Tillich in his 1953 book *The Courage to Be*. An associate of the Frankfurt School, familiar with contemporary existentialism and having, despite being a minister, a strong bohemian streak, Tillich does seem to have cut through to a universal core issue – where the source of our courage to live meaningfully actually lies, and the consequences of failures in that courage. In character it is more an existentialist 'Psychological' analysis than a theological one. Aside from its somewhat opaque and technical first chapter it is one of the few books I would unreservedly recommend to everybody! Even so, the price Tillich paid was heavy from a religious point of view, for he virtually abandons all doctrinal specificity, leaving only a kind of general existentialist affirmation standing. The defence is that he was seeking to reconnect with the starting point, a basis for doctrinal reconstruction. Again though, beyond a restricted, if enduring, circle Tillich's impact has so far been minimal.

Some additional comment is required on the concept of 'spirituality', a term currently recklessly bandied about in phrases like 'spiritual values', 'spiritual side of life' and 'spiritual hunger'. There is, purportedly, a 'spiritual' gap in our lives which science cannot address. But like the concepts listed earlier, its meaning is now obscure. We no longer accept the underlying 'breath' metaphor, the notion of some non-material, quasi-gaseous, thing-like 'soul' made of a divine substance, or an alternative parallel realm of the same kind. In practice it increasingly denotes such things as concern with ethical and aesthetic issues, moral striving, taking one's moral condition seriously, rejecting the notion that 'science' has achieved a 'materialistic' closure of our knowledge of the universe, or – in psychotherapeutic contexts – seeking holistic self-fulfilment. Any feeling of awe and wonder, or of cosmic unity, is dignified as a 'spiritual experience'. All these may be admirable aspirations or highly valuable, cherishable, experiences, but they are not essentially 'spiritual' in the traditional religious sense of signifying contact with, and participation in, a 'purer' 'divine' realm, the eternal dwelling place of a superhuman intelligence (or intelligences). Equating 'spirituality' to concern with self-fulfilment and integration, ethical issues, the beauty of nature, or transient psychedelic raptures, is to give a religious gloss to concerns and experiences which even the most atheistic may well share, and amounts to a secularisation of the notion, rather than signifying a return to religion itself. From a traditional religious perspective the films about angels, the devil, anti-Christ, etc., now so in vogue, would appear as peculiarly sacriligious, religion degenerating into ghost story and fairy-tale.

Psychology's role

The preceding remarks are suggestive regarding Psychology's possible future role in the situation. In the past its relationship with religion took several forms. During its founding phase, North American Psychology often explicitly engaged in providing a Psychological rationale for orthodox religious belief, legitimating it as 'natural'. In the early twentieth century it, ironically, provided Christianity with the intellectual resources to maintain its credibility as an authority in pastoral care in modernist societies. It also helped mainstream churches keep quasi-pathological fanaticism and religious hysteria at bay, and differentiate genuine 'spiritual' problems from 'mental illness' within their own congregations (Weatherhead likened the minister's relationship with the psychotherapist to that between general practitioner and specialist in medicine). In addition, Psychology provided much data on the social psychological and personality factors involved in religious belief, information which, if at one level subversive, could also be co-opted by religious authorities attempting to promote their doctrines.

In the present 'stand off' situation, however, we might see Psychology playing a rather different role. While its remit is neither to refute nor affirm religion it might at least start diagnosing the present state of affairs more systematically and rigorously than hitherto. Psychology's 'critical' wing, with its social constructionist orientation and sensitivity to language, might turn some of its sights from reflexive critiques of the discipline to treating religion in a similar fashion. In doing so it might also engage some of the ideas of the linguistic philosophers mentioned earlier, and later work by the leading student of comparative religion, Ninian Smart, in which the functions of religion are explored and analysed in detail (a start in this direction was attempted by K. Dunlap, 1946). We might then begin to develop a better, but not necessarily hostile, understanding of what kind of psychological phenomenon religion actually *is*. (And how far Psychology itself is a religious phenomenon?) What religions in their turn might make of this is another matter.

I would like to close by observing that we no longer live in a world where totalistic claims to unique religious certainty are sustainable (though most religions continue to claim it). The deepest irony is perhaps that westernised societies are now largely immune to internecine religious conflict (despite obvious exceptions) only because the various religions all see themselves as beleaguered islands in a sea of rampant secular materialism. They are thus, deep doctrinal commitments to their own unique validity notwithstanding, inclined to find common 'ecumenical' cause as representatives of core moral and 'spiritual' values. (For believers beyond this pale we have now been tragically reminded that such a strategy can appear as the deepest betrayal.) Somewhat wickedly, therefore, I suggest that our best hope for the foreseeable future is a continuation of the dampening effects of secular religious indifference, at least until religion, with a little help from its Psychological friends and enemies, reaches a new understanding of what it is really all about.

Notes

1. Historical analysis of the Psychology–religion relationship is as yet patchy and what is said here represents only a preliminary view. In particular it almost certainly fails to reflect the levels of controversy among the, usually believing, exponents of Psychology of Religion itself. Perhaps this also reflects the author's own irenic temperament.

2. I am acutely aware of considering only Psychology's relationships with Christianity. This is partly justified by the fact that Psychology's history has lain primarily in cultures defining themselves as Christian (an exception is Japan, where Psychology also took off around 1900, but it would require a Japanese scholar to tackle this). Many psychologists have been Jewish, but while the rich cultural legacies of Kabbalistic and rabbinical Talmudic thought have undoubtedly played a part in determining the character of their Psychological thought (see D. Bakan, 1958, on Freud for example), they have rarely, to my uncertain knowledge, engaged in relating Psychology to Judaism as American pioneers and inter-war British psychologists did vis-à-vis Christianity. (One exception is the Canada-based *Journal of Psychology and Judaism* founded in 1976.) Buddhist Psychological thought is a separate tradition which western Psychology only recently began to engage seriously. Jung, of course, tried to absorb everything, but L.A. Govinda (1961) was an early attempt to introduce it to the English-speaking world on its own terms; however, this was too technical and full of Sanskrit terminology to have a wide appeal (see also R.E.A. Johansson, 1969, for a relatively early Psychological engagement with Buddhism). Hinduism has received even less Psychological attention, although Akhilananda (1948) might be mentioned, this having an

introduction by G.W. Allport. Psychology's more recent encounter with Islam cannot yet be evaluated, although Sufism (like Zen Buddhism, with which there is some evidence of a historical connection) has had an impact within some branches of psychotherapy since the early 1970s (notably, despite its awesomely positivistic name, neuro-linguistic programming).

Further reading

Allport, G.W. (1950) *The Individual and His Religion: A Psychological Interpretation*. New York: Macmillan. A sympathetic examination of the topic by one of the most eminent mid-twentieth-century American psychologists.

Belzen, J.A. (ed.) (2000) *Aspects in Contexts – Studies in the History of Psychology of Religion*. Amsterdam-Atlanta GA: Rodopi. Primarily concerned with mainland European developments, on which it is one of the few English-language sources readily available.

Caplan, E. (1998) 'Popularizing American Psychotherapy: The Emmanuel Movement, 1906–1910'. *History of Psychology* 1(4): 289–314.

Dunlap, K. (1946) *Religion. Its Functions in Human Life*. New York: McGraw-Hill. A somewhat isolated attempt at getting to grips with the full scale of the issue.

Flew, A. and MacIntyre, A. (eds) (1955) *New Essays in Philosophical Theology*. London: S.C.M. Press. Pioneering exploration of the meaningfulness of religious concepts from a linguistic philosophy perspective.

James, W. (1902, rep. 1960) *The Varieties of Religious Experience*. London: Fontana. This classic text was James's most popularly successful book.

Loewenthal, K.M. (2000) *The Psychology of Religion: A Short Introduction*. Oxford: Oneworld Publications. A useful overview of the current agenda of Psychology of Religion.

Misiak, H. and Staudt, V.M. (1954) *Catholics in Psychology. A Historical Survey*. New York: McGraw-Hill. An invaluable resource, albeit more celebratory than analytical in its approach and oddly coy about the 1930's and 1940's activities of some of the German and Italian figures.

Richards, G. (2000) 'Psychology and the Churches in Britain 1919–1939: Symptoms of Conversion'. *History of the Human Sciences* 13(3): 57–84.

Smart, N. (1973) *The Phenomenon of Religion*. Oxford: Clarendon Press. An important book by the leading scholar of comparative religion.

Tillich, P. (1953, rep. 1973) *The Courage to Be*. London: Collins. Tillich's most accessible position statement, fusing theology, Psychology and existentialist philosophy.

Vande Kemp, H. (1992) 'G. Stanley Hall and the Clark School of Religious Psychology'. *American Psychologist* 47(2): 290–298.

Vande Kemp, H. (1996) 'Historical Perspective: Religion and Clinical Psychology in America'. In E.P. Shafranske (ed.) *Religion and the Clinical Practice of Psychology*. Washington DC: American Psychological Association, 71–112. Extremely informative and an obvious starting point for anyone attempting to get their bearings on the topic.

Wulff, D.M. (1985) *Psychology of Religion: Classic and Contemporary*, 2nd edn. New York: Wiley. Currently the major general text.

Other cited, and some additional, references

Akhilananda, S. (1948, rep. 1953) *Hindu Psychology. Its Meaning for the West.* Introduction by Gordon W. Allport. London: Routledge & Kegan Paul.

Allport, G.W. (1948) 'Psychology'. In *College Reading and Religion: A Survey of College Reading Materials.* New Haven, CT: Yale University Press, 80–114.

Argyle, M. (1958) *Religious Behaviour.* London: Routledge & Kegan Paul.

Bakan, D. (1958) *Sigmund Freud and the Jewish Mystical Tradition.* Princeton: Van Nostrand.

Belzen, J.A. (2000) 'Tremendum et Fascinans: On the Early Reception and Nondevelopment of the Psychology of Religion among Orthodox Dutch Calvinists'. In J.A. Belzen (ed.) (2000) (see Further reading above), 91–128.

Belzen, J.A. (2001) 'The Introduction of the Psychology of Religion to the Netherlands: Ambivalent Reception, Epistemological Concerns, and Persistent Patterns'. *Journal of the History of the Behavioral Sciences* 37 (1): 45–68.

Brennan, R.E. (1946) *The History of Psychology, from the Standpoint of a Thomist.* New York: Macmillan.

Burt, C. (1935) 'The Psychology of Religion'. In C. Burt (ed.) *How the Mind Works.* London: Allen & Unwin, 311–333. Originally a series of BBC radio talks.

Clinebell, H.J. Jr (1966) *Basic Types of Pastoral Counselling. New Resources for Ministering to the Troubled.* Nashville: Abingdon Press.

Coster, G. (1934) *Yoga and Western Psychology: A Comparison.* London: Oxford University Press and Humphrey Milford. An isolated early exploration of the topic.

De Sanctis, S. (1927) *Religious Conversion. A Bio-psychological Study.* London: Kegan Paul, Trench & Trübner. A Catholic perspective on the phenomenon.

Freud, S. (1930) *Civilization and its Discontents.* London: Hogarth Press.

Galton, F. (1872, 1883, 1883, rep. 1951) *Three Memoirs: Statistical Inquiries into the Efficacy of Prayer, Enthusiasm, Possibilities of Theocratic Intervention.* London: Eugenics Society.

Govinda, L.A. (1961, rep. 1969) *The Psychological Attitude of Early Buddhist Philosophy and its Systematic Representation according to Abhidhamma Tradition.* London: Rider & Co.

Grattan-Guinness, I. (ed.) (1982) *Psychic Research. A Guide to its History, Principles & Practices in Celebration of 100 Years of the Society for Psychical Research.* Wellingborough: Aquarian Press.

Gurney, E., Myers, F.W.H. and Podmore, F. (1886) *Phantasms of the Living.* London: Society for Psychical Rsearch.

Hall, G.S. (1921) *Jesus the Christ in the Light of Psychology.* London: Allen & Unwin.

Hazelgrove, J. (2000) *Spiritualism and British Society between the Wars.* Manchester & New York: Manchester University Press.

Jahoda, G. (1969) *The Psychology of Superstition.* London: Allen Lane.

Johansson, R.E.A. (1969) *The Psychology of Nirvana.* London: Allen & Unwin.

Joly, H. (1898) *The Psychology of the Saints*. London: Duckworth.

Jung, C.G. (1933) *Modern Man in Search of a Soul*. London: Kegan Paul.

Künkel, F. (1954) 'The Integration of Religion and Psychology'. *Journal of Psychotherapy as a Religious Process* 1: 1–11.

Kusch, M. (1999) *Psychological Knowledge: A Social History and Philosophy*. London: Routledge.

Leuba, J.H. (1909) *The Psychological Origin and Nature of Religion*. London: Constable.

Leuba, J.H. (1925) *The Psychology of Religious Mysticism*. London: Kegan Paul, Trench & Trübner.

McDougall, W. (1908) *An Introduction to Social Psychology*. London: Methuen.

Mercier, Cardinal, D.J. (1982) *Psychologie*. Louvain: Institut Superieur de Philosophie.

Murphy, G. and Kovach, J.K. (1972) *Historical Introduction to Modern Psychology*. London: Routledge & Kegan Paul.

Myers, C.S. (1933) *A Psychologists' Point of View*. London: Heinemann.

Myers, F.W.H. (1893) 'The Subliminal Consciousness'. *Proceedings of the Society for Psychical Research* 9: 14–15.

Myers, F.W.H. (1903) *Human Personality and its Survival of Bodily Death* (2 vols). London: Longmans.

Nase, E. (2000) 'The Psychology of Religion at the Crossroads. Oskar Pfister's Challenge to Psychology of Religion in the Twenties'. In J.A. Belzen (ed.) (2000) (see Further reading above), 45–90.

Nicholson, I.A.M. (1997) 'Gordon Allport, Character, and the "Culture of Personality", 1897–1937'. *History of Psychology* 1(1): 52–68.

Nørager, T. (2000) 'Villiam Grønbaek and the Dorpat School. Elements of a "History" based on the Correspondence between Villiam Grønbaek and Werner Gruehn'. In J.A. Belzen (ed.) (2000) (see Further reading above), 173–234.

Pandora, K. (1997) *Rebels within the Ranks: Psychologists' Critique of Scientific Authority and Democratic Realities in New Deal America*. Cambridge: Cambridge University Press.

Porter, N. (1868, rep. 1872) *The Human Intellect, with an Introduction upon Psychology and the Soul*. London: Strahan.

Richards, G. (1995) '"To know our fellow men to do them good": American Psychology's continuing Moral Project'. *History of the Human Sciences* 8(3): 1–24.

Richards, G. (2001) 'Edward Cox, the Psychological Society of Great Britain (1875–1879) and the meanings of an institutional failure'. In G.C. Bunn, A.D. Lovie and G.D. Richards (eds) *Psychology in Britain. Historical Essays and Personal Reflections*. Leicester: British Psychological Society & London: The Science Museum, 33–53.

Starbuck, E.D. (1899, rep. 1901) *The Psychology of Religion. An Empirical Study of the Growth of Religious Consciousness*. London: Walter Scott.

Thouless, R.H. (1923) *An Introduction to the Psychology of Religion*. Cambridge: Cambridge University Press.

Trotter, W. (1916) *Instincts of the Herd in Peace and War*. London: Fisher Unwin.

Vande Kemp, H. (2000) 'Gordon Allport's pre-1950 Writings on Religion. The Archival Record'. In J.A. Belzen (ed.) (2000) (see Further reading above), 129–172.

Vandermeersch, P. (2000) 'The Failure of the Second Naiveté. Some Landmarks in the History of French Psychology of Religion'. In J.A. Belzen (ed.) (see Further reading above), 235–280.

Waterhouse, E.S. (1927) *An ABC of Psychology for Sunday School Teachers and Bible Students*. London: Epworth Press, J. Alfred Sharp.

Waterhouse, E.S. (1930) *Psychology and Religion: A Series of Broadcast Talks*. London: Elkins, Matthews & Marrot.

Watts, F., Nye, R. and Savage, S. (2001) *Psychology for Ministry*. London: Routledge.

Weatherhead, L.D. (1929) *Psychology in the Service of the Soul*. London: Epworth Press.

Weatherhead, L.D. (1934) *Psychology and Life*. London: Hodder & Stoughton. Weatherhead, a leading Methodist thinker, was in the forefront of the British churches' efforts to find a rapprochement with Psychology in the 1920s and 1930s, particularly in relation to psychotherapy.

Weatherhead, L.D. (1951) *Pychology, Religion and Healing*. London: Hodder & Stoughton. The fullest statement of Weatherhead's position, this went through several subsequent revised and enlarged editions.

Worcester, E., McComb, S. and Coriat, I. (1908) *Religion and Medicine. The Moral Control of Nervous Disorders*. London: Kegan Paul, Trench & Trübner. (Reprinted 1920 as *The Subconscious Mind*.)

Wulff, D.M. (2000), 'James Henry Leuba. A Reassessment of a Swiss-American Pioneer'. In J.A. Belzen (ed.) (2000) (see Further reading above), 25–44.

Zenderland, L. (1998) *Measuring Minds. Herbert Henry Goddard and the Origins of American Intelligence Testing*. Cambridge: Cambridge University Press.

Reference

Vande Kemp, H. (1984) *Psychology and Theology in Western Thought 1672–1965. A Historical and Annotated Bibliography*. White Plains, NY: Kraus. Absolutely invaluable for anyone seeking to investigate the topic further.

Chapter 21

Psychology and 'race'

- Author's position and focus of chapter
- Nineteenth-century 'scientific racism'
- US 'Race Psychology' c. 1910–mid-1930s
- Emergence of 'race prejudice' and 'culture and personality' research, and the demise of Race Psychology
- Summary of anti-race differences arguments and responses to them
- Post-Second World War developments in the US and the mergence of Black Psychology
- The Jensen (1969) controversy and its aftermath
- The current agenda and some observations

There is a vast historical, philosophical, political, sociological, and anthropological literature on 'Race', perhaps the most sensitive issue currently perturbing our culture (notoriously, in Psychology, in the 'Race and IQ' debate). Here we consider only Psychology's involvements, the present chapter being essentially a distillation of some of the major points covered in G. Richards (1997), which provides a more detailed and comprehensive account. Though (unlike 'racism') 'race' is not a psychological concept it has always been seen as having a psychological dimension. Psychology, we will see, has both promoted and opposed racism. Before pursuing this I should make my position clear: I do not believe the notion of innate psychological racial differences is meaningful. Current genetic understanding of human diversity is roughly as follows: there is a single human 'gene pool' containing numerous alleles for each genetically-determined trait. Within this, sub-pools may, for mainly geographic reasons, become relatively isolated from the remainder for longer or shorter periods. These are less genetically diverse than the total pool, containing only a sample of the total number of alleles. During isolation some new mutations may occur adding unique alleles to a group's repertoire – but these will never be *universal* within it. Circumstances may exert their own selection pressures on the frequency of distribution (e.g. hairiness genes may be favoured in cold climates) thereby rendering them more-or-less frequent than elsewhere. The upshot is that isolated groups may acquire a distinctive typical physical appearance (although not all group members will conform to this). If, however, we map the frequency of different alleles globally we find they vary enormously. Blood groups provide one pattern, hair-type another, ear-wax type a third and so on – in other words the world population is carved up differently for different genes. This must presumably also apply to any genes determining psychological traits (if such there be) – *there is no reason to assume they would correlate with those physical traits traditionally used to identify 'races'*. Moreover, we never encounter genetic traits which are both unique to *and* universal within a particular group, while no group is ever 100% isolated – there is always some genetic exchange with outside. Gene-pool composition constantly shifts in any case, both by chance and as conditions of life change.

'Races' as distinct biological entities with some essential character therefore do not exist. Shifting from physical to psychological the situation becomes even more obscure since the linkage between the two is highly convoluted, involving the cultural meanings given to physical traits or genetically-rooted behaviours. It is at the cultural level that genetic traits with no essential psychological meaning of their own are given psychological significance. To explore this here would take us too far afield, but one implication must be spelled out: the very concept of 'race' itself and the psychological meanings which have accreted to racial classifications and their associated physical traits are *themselves* products of modern European culture.

Concerning 'racism', D.T. Goldberg (1993) argues that we should avoid the trap of imagining this as a single, unitary phenomenon. Rather we must approach it pragmatically since it varies in character over time, culture and circumstance. He offers a definition which I find acceptable, namely that 'racism' should be used for any practice which has as its effect, intended *or unintended*, the exclusion of a group from full access to the rights, responsibilities and opportunities enjoyed by the majority population. This needs qualifying somewhat to differentiate it from sexism, 'ablism' or homophobia but is broadly adequate. What is especially interesting for us, however, is that the concept of 'racism' as, by definition, a 'bad thing' and a psychological phenomenon – a psychological property some people possess – was largely created by psychologists. This is ironic because over time the adequacy of seeing it as a purely psychological phenomenon has been increasingly challenged.

What follows is only a sketch of the main features of a story beginning in the mid-nineteenth century when evolutionary theory provided an apparently scientific rationale for racial inequality, a doctrine now called 'Scientific Racism'. 'Races' formed an evolutionary hierarchy with Europeans at the top and e.g. indigenous Australians, South African 'Bushmen' and South American Indians at the bottom. Intermediate rankings varied but Africans were always low, while Chinese and Indians as it were jostled for silver and bronze medal placings. Much could be said about this but a few points must suffice. (a) Physically the human evolutionary process was widely held to have finished and Europeans to have effectively won. (b) 'Civilisation' was seen as a sort of natural phenomenon, the pinnacle of evolutionary development. European culture's superiority was not therefore seen as *cultural* but as *natural*. The white European was, by virtue of his (definitely!) evolutionary superiority, the vehicle by which this essentially *natural* progression had been accomplished. (c) 'Lower races' were thus in diverse states of 'arrested development', in evolutionary dead-ends from which escape was impossible without white aid, if at all (levels of optimism differed). (d) Though fervently promoting this image, anthropologists and biologists were actually unable to discover clear-cut criteria for identifying racial groups. Skin colour, skull shape, hair-type and complicated physical anthropometric ratios all proved inadequate. (e) Victorian interest in race was as much devoted to identifying the different European races as nonwhite ones. History itself being widely seen as driven by racial competition, European nations were cast as representing different racial groups. While resulting in the most extraordinary muddle, this political dimension to the race issue persisted in Europe with eventually catastrophic results.

Psychology's involvement begins with Francis Galton. Galton acquired his contempt for non-Europeans during an expedition in his twenties to South West Africa (Namibia). Only later did he give this a scientific gloss. He is, up to a point, optimistic in the long term; some lower races are capable, under white guidance, at least of improvement – if not full equality with whites. He also attempted to quantify levels of racial intelligence, estimating the percentage in each race likely, on a 13-point scale, to be geniuses, or equivalent to the European average, and so on. While writing relatively little on the issue as such, Galton's Scientific Racism was fundamental to his evolutionary viewpoint, and though more immediate matters of domestic degeneration and eugenics dominated his work, sooner or later Psychology would, he foresaw, have to attend to nurturing and controlling the 'lower races'. Galton, one must stress, was a major player in the mid-nineteenth century scene, not merely a follower of 'Scientific Racism' but among its leading architects. Theoretically, however, Herbert Spencer had more impact, especially in the US. Of most importance was what we might call the 'Spencer hypothesis' that the amount of energy allocated to higher functions of reason and will was much greater in whites than in 'primitives'. Conversely the latter allocated proportionately more to basic psychophysical and instinctive functions, thereby *excelling* whites on things like reaction time (RT), perceptual and auditory discrimination, rote memory and mimicry, while being more dominated by instincts, less capable of self-control and long-term planning. This idea suggested some kinds of Psychological research. Two papers claiming to confirm Spencer appeared in the *Psychological Review* during the 1890s, one on RT and one on memory, comparing white, 'Negro' and (in the RT case) American Indian performance. It was obviously a no-win situation for non-whites: superior performance confirmed the Spencer hypothesis, while inferior performance 'proved' them inferior anyway.

Psychologist's positions were not entirely uniform, Scientific Racism providing some latitude for interpretation. At one extreme is G. Le Bon (1899) for whom heredity is the most important factor in human life: every race has its distinct soul, and the major races are virtually different species (harking back to the pre-evolutionary doctrine of 'polygenism', especially popular in France). By contrast, G.S. Hall (1904) argued that 'lower races' were not in a state of arrested development but of adolescence, and would eventually reach maturity. He roundly attacked European treatment of other 'races', lamenting the destruction of peoples and cultures in terms befitting the anti-Columbus literature which greeted the 1992 Quincentenary. We should respect native cultures, the white civilising and Christianising mission should be based on understanding and building upon existing beliefs and customs. Translated into practice this apparently more enlightened, if extremely paternalistic, view nonetheless provided a rationale for segregation, separate education for blacks and American Indians, and black disenfranchisement.

The turn of the twentieth century saw two events of major importance for the study of 'race differences': the 1898 Cambridge Anthropological Expedition to the Torres Strait (between Australia and New Guinea) and research carried out at the 1904 St Louis Exposition by R.S. Woodworth and F.G. Bruner. The Cambridge expedition included three subsequent leaders of British Psychology: W.H.R. Rivers, C.S. Myers and William McDougall, all experienced in the new experimental Psychology (Fig. 21.1). Their wide-ranging studies of psychophysical performance, including visual perception (Rivers), hearing (Myers) and RTs (McDougall), disclosed *no* systematic superiority among Torres Strait islanders (1901). Inspired by this, Woodworth took advantage of the presence of large numbers of foreigners at the St Louis Exposition to further study differences in perception and hearing (Bruner doing the latter) as well as some other phenomena. Although not published until 1908 (Bruner) and 1910 (Woodworth) the general thrust of the results was soon widely known: the Spencer hypothesis again found no confirmation. These two sets of findings largely laid the notion of primitive superiority in basic functions to rest (at least in scientific circles) and little further research was undertaken on the question. Attention now turned to the higher functions, especially intelligence, but these had to await appropriate research techniques. By 1910 several of these were available, including the Binet intelligence test, and 'Race and IQ' research proper started with Alice Strong (1913).

After this 'Race Psychology' remained a strand in US Psychology until the mid-1930s. The context of the earliest work was the issue of 'Negro education' and

Figure 21.1 W.H.R. Rivers demonstrating the colour wheel to Tom, Mabuiag, Torres Strait, 1898. Reproduced by permission of Cambridge University Museum of Archaeology and Anthropology. (Accession number: Haddon Colln. T.Straits 69.)

typically compared white and African American children's performance. Although Northern black children performed better than those in the South they neverthe-less always underperformed the white groups. In the South such results helped justify continued educational segregation and restriction of black curricula to practical subjects like woodwork and gardening (e.g. Ferguson, 1916). This phase culminated with the 1917–1918 Army group intelligence test data (see Chapter 18). While not directly contributing much themselves, many leading psychologists such as L.M. Terman, R.M. Yerkes and E.L. Thorndike initially supported Race Psychology.

Another topic had now arisen upon which the Army tests were also seen as bearing – the poor quality of southern European immigrants. This was bolstered by the rise of Eugenics and what was then called 'Nordicism' – belief in north European superiority – promoted in particular by Madison Grant's best-seller *The*

Passing of the Great Race (1916). The Army results revealed both dramatic African American, and to a lesser but still considerable extent, southern European, under-performance and received their most influential evaluation in C.C. Brigham (1923), which accepted Grant's Nordicism and was adamantly racialist in tone. Along with smaller-scale studies of European 'race differences' this fuelled the immigration control campaign, and helped ensure the passing of an Immigration Restriction Law (1924). As far as African Americans were concerned it was spotted fairly quickly that some northern 'Negroes' actually outperformed whites from some southern states, triggering a controversy which persisted until the 1940s (and was still rumbling on in the 1990s, see for example F.J. Galloway, 1994). Until the early 1920s Scientific Racism, minus the 'Spencer hypothesis', provided the main the-oretical framework for race difference research.

The Army tests have received most historical attention, but Race Psychology's concerns extended far beyond this. While African Americans remained the largest single group studied, by 1930 they constituted only about 20% of non-native white American subjects, alongside Japanese, Italians, Zulus, Jews and native Americans, etc. And although intelligence was the main topic studied, research also con-sidered, for example, colour preferences, 'will-temperament', fatigue-proneness, 'social efficiency' and mental illness. Two psychologists in particular adopted this field as their speciality: T.R. Garth who mostly studied American Indians and Mexicans and S.D. Porteus, a Honolulu-based Australian immigrant who studied Hawaii's several 'racial' groups (Japanese, Chinese, native Hawaiian, Portuguese, Filipino, and various 'mixed race' permutations). Numerous one-off studies sup-plemented their work and several other psychologists devoted much effort to race difference research. J. Peterson, for example, undertook several large-scale pieces of research, becoming the principal expert on 'Negro intelligence'.

Opposition and criticism, never entirely absent, escalated during the 1920s, firstly in the popular liberal press and black magazines, but increasingly within the Psychological literature. By 1930 Race Psychology was under extreme pres-sure. Firstly, those studying the topic shared contemporary US Psychology's aspirations towards scientific credibility and were thus very sensitive to methodo-logical criticisms. As a result many became increasingly conscious of the difficul-ties in unambiguously establishing the existence of innate racial differences. Some, like Brigham himself, totally recanted their earlier positions, while others became more qualified and cautious in interpreting their results. Only a small handful (such as Porteus) held firm beyond the mid-1930s. Internally, its own scientific rigour was sapping the race-differences project at the heart of Race Psychology. Externally, however, the assault also intensified on several fronts after 1928. Thoroughgoing attacks on its methods and interpretations achieve more promin-ence, a major figure being the social psychologist Otto Klineberg. On the Sociology/ Psychology borderline there was growing interest in race prejudice and attitudes. This in effect reversed the logic of the entire problem: instead of the distinct psy-chological character of different races, it is the need to see races as psychologically distinct in the first place which has to be explained. On the anthropology border-line (incorporating some psychoanalytic thinkers) the 'Culture & Personality School' is crystallising. M. Mead (1928) may perhaps be taken as its starting point although it really originates at the beginning of the century when Franz Boas, Mead's teacher and leading US anthropologist, abandoned race in favour of culture. Meanwhile, growing numbers of Psychology graduates (including some non-whites) were working in the field as social workers, educationalists, clinicians and the like. The race differences issue simply had no relevance to the practical issues they faced, and after c. 1930 we find a steep rise in the number of atheoretical applied papers being published (often intra racial) on such topics as dealing with clients from ethnic minorities, factors affecting children's self-esteem and so on (there is some overlap here with the prejudice studies). With Klineberg's *Race Differences* (1935) constituting its funeral service, Race Psychology was to all intents and purposes dead, while the contemporary political and ideological climate was increasingly hostile in view of the rise of Nazi anti-Semitism. Most tellingly Garth, Race Psychology's leading advocate, unequivocally changed sides (G. Richards, 1998).

The Race Psychology phase served a curious function for Psychology and the wider understanding of 'race'. Usually considered a simple manifestation of racism, it would be more accurate to see it as a process in which the debates between supporters and critics collectively emancipated the discipline from theoretical commitment to racism, enabling Psychology, in effect, to *create* the concept of 'racism' (a word first used in the 1930s). While not the only factor, Psychology's scientific failure to find race differences enabled it to *discover* 'racism'. Before about 1930 'racialist' doctrines and theories were acceptable intellectual positions, controversial perhaps but not seen as necessarily having ethical implications. Scientific Racism's legacy of respectability took some time to dispel. The controversy within Psychology, in which most participants acted in good faith, finally enabled most psychologists, including erstwhile Race Psychologists, to see that (a) race differences were proving extraordinarily elusive and were possibly an illusion and (b) given this, fervent belief in such differences must (as they saw it) be irrational and, *ipso facto*, a form of psychopathology (and by the late 1930s the discipline had a number of conceptual resources for elaborating on this, including psychoanalysis). While not intended as such, Race Psychology served as a self-emancipatory exercise via which the unconscious racism initially motivating it was forced into consciousness.

This process saw the first formulation of numerous criticisms of race differences research which have largely persisted to the present (although more have been added). I will now outline these and suggest why the pro-differences responses to them were inadequate. The arguments were both methodological and theoretical (or conceptual).

- Differences may be accounted for by non-hereditary factors. Typical responses: (a) psychological race-differences must be the default assumption in the light of evolutionary theory and by analogy with physical differences; (b) current socio-economic status itself reflects ability; (c) environmental factors can be controlled for in designing research. The first of these arguments had a high *prima facie* plausibility – surely major physical differences would be accompanied by covert psychological ones? Technically, the key fallacy here is that, as explained earlier, the assumption that distribution of psychological traits systematically maps onto the physical traits traditionally defining racial identity is mistaken. This was seen somewhat hazily from fairly early on, but only became clear with advances in genetics from the mid-1930s. For Klineberg (1935) the fallacy lay more simply in the assumption (which he denied) that physical traits were of some, albeit covert, psychological significance. The 'status reflects intelligence' argument tended to be dropped as time went on, its flaws being fairly glaring (especially during the Depression), though it re-emerged in C. Herrnstein and R.J. Murray (1994). Finally, optimism about the possibility of eliminating environmental factors in research design progressively faded, this being in any case environmentalist behaviourism's heyday. Although some persisted in thinking it was logically feasible, most came to suspect that insoluble methodological paradoxes were involved.

- Tests may be culturally biased. Usual response: bias can be offset by adopting non-verbal and performance-type tests. In the late 1920s doubts also arose about the value of group tests; individual tests (on which 'race differences' were generally smaller) might, it was felt, be more appropriate. There was, though, a poorly-developed appreciation of the profundity of this problem among experimentalists before the mid-1930s. Conversely, for social anthropologist critics it appeared patently obvious, and as their views gained wider airing after 1930 the problem of 'culture-fair' tests became more acute. It is still not entirely resolved and involves a paradox: you can only know you have succeeded in designing a culture-fair test if it shows no differences, if it does show differences there is no way of knowing whether these are innate or culturally determined.

- Overlap in distribution of scores demonstrates that there is no essential connection between 'race' and ability (or any other trait). Typical responses to this were: (a) the frequency of exceptional individuals determines a race's character and fortunes; (b) non-white high performers are those with some white 'blood' (the 'mulatto hypothesis'). The first was an old Galtonian Scientific Racist tenet which faded during the early 1920s. The latter was empirically falsified – performance did not correlate with amount of white ancestry. The modern response is that significant mean differences between racial groups are scientific 'facts' and, notwithstanding overlap, they have socio-economic policy implications for attempts at enabling underperforming groups to achieve equality. This, however, still hinges on the false assumption that racial groups have an objective existence, with a fixed genetic character, in the first place.

- The tester's own 'race' will have an 'experimenter effect' (as we now say) on performance. 'Experimenter effects' were largely ignored, though occasionally noted as a possible minor factor distorting the magnitude of differences in specific cases. They were not considered of fundamental importance. Klineberg included 'rapport' as a factor affecting credibility of race differences research but full appreciation of experimenter effects did not dawn on Psychology until the 1960s.

- Sampling of non-white subjects may be unrepresentative. Some data, such as the US Army findings, were seen as overcoming this by sheer weight of numbers. Sampling was a perennial headache for Race Psychologists, however the cumulative impact of repeated findings of differences similar in direction, if not degree, reassured them. In retrospect the variations in degree of difference may themselves be seen as weakening the nativist hypothesis. Since large *within* race differences were, it was usually agreed, environmentally caused, invoking heredity to account for sometimes minimal *between* race differences would appear superfluous. This argument was not, however, clearly developed prior to Klineberg (1935). One should add that if races are mythical entities anyway the notion of fair sampling becomes irrelevant – there is nothing to be sampled.

- The concept of 'race' has no clear scientific biological meaning. The usual response was that 'race' might be theoretically problematic, but this did not affect the current reality of the existence of identifiably distinct peoples possessing unique and ineradicable innate traits resulting from millennia of reproductive isolation. This partly reflected an exaggerated view of the extent and duration of episodes of reproductive isolation and partly an old-fashioned awe of big numbers when applied to years. For relatively slow-breeding species like humans even a few thousand years reproductive isolation (rare anyway, and probably never complete) amounts to little against a species history now estimated at c. 150,000 years (for anatomically modern *Homo sapiens*).

- 'Racial' levels of performance can change over time therefore current under-performance may be transient (Garth called this 'Race Mobility'). This was often simply rejected; evidence for 'race mobility' really reflected genetic changes resulting from out-breeding and racial contact, hence the 'decline' of Greek civilisation following the classic age. Even if it did occur it was on a timescale too long realistically to take into account. It is perhaps necessary to differentiate this issue from the previous one. 'Race mobility' (an obsolete expression) really referred to the possibility of rapid (and reversible) changes to a gene-pool's composition when new environmental circumstances alter the selection vectors. The previous issue, however, relates to an irreversible process of quasi-speciation involving mutation events and long-sustained idiosyncratic selection pressures. Acceptance of the former as a source of fluctuations in 'racial' performance does not entail acceptance of the latter as a source of racial sub-species. The deeper implication that this 'race mobility' subverts the heredity/environment distinction itself does not seem to have been drawn (and often remains unacknowledged to this day): in a nutshell, it means that heredity is itself environmentally determined.

- The entire project was racist in motivation. People like Porteus responded that as scientists they were interested in finding the objective facts. Sentimentally philanthropic 'race-levelling' and racially biased 'race dogmatism' represented the poles between which they had to steer to find the truth. Versions of this are still used by the pro-differences camp. Credibility of this evaporates when funding sources are identified (see below).

The baton now passed to those studying race prejudice. With the rise of Nazism, anti-Semitism naturally became the primary focus of concern. Throughout the 1940s various publications on this appeared, sometimes psychoanalytic in character, but the best known and most influential was *The Authoritarian Personality* (1950) (see Chapters 12 and 18). The pathologising of 'racism' now reached its apotheosis: it symptomatised a particular 'Authoritarian' personality type, driven to project its Oedipal fantasies onto outgroups as a result of distorted psychological development. As the 1950s progressed US concerns shifted from anti-Semitism towards a domestic agenda increasingly dominated by the Civil Rights issue. Psychodynamic arguments persisted, but were clearly insufficient. Racism took more than one form. For those raised in racist cultures like South Africa or the Deep South, it was no more than conformity to the values they had been reared into, not a personal pathology (at least no more so than conformity itself). Racism, like apparent race differences, was culturally determined. As observed previously, Social Psychology's studies of prejudice were part of the intellectual wing of the Civil Rights movement itself. Black US psychologists like Kenneth and Mamie Clark had also (though not without predecessors) begun to develop an African American strand within the discipline, rooted in the earlier applied genre mentioned above. By the mid-late 1960s President Johnson had enacted the appropriate legislation. One innovation for redressing African American deprivation was the educational programme 'Head Start' aimed at boosting the educational performance of deprived children. This coincided with the emergence of a self-consciously radical 'Black Psychology' movement within the discipline, signalled by the creation in San Francisco of the Association of Black Psychologists in 1968. This was followed by R.L. Jones (ed.) *Black Psychology* (1972) and further boosted by R.V. Guthrie's *Even the Rat was White: A Historical View of Psychology* (1976, 2nd edn, 1998), the work of W.E. Cross on the development of African American identity (see W.E. Cross, 1991) and the founding of the *Journal of Black Psychology* in 1974. (Hispanic, Asian American and Native American psychologists have since followed this lead and there is now an A.P.A. Division 45: Society for the Psychological Study of Ethnic Minority Issues.)

But quite suddenly, after three decades of relative quiescence, bar a few die-hards like Columbia University's Henry Garrett, the race differences issue re-erupted with Arthur Jensen's 1969 report (in the prestigious *Harvard Educational Review*) on the success of the Head Start programme: 'How much can we boost IQ and Scholastic Achievement?' Jensen argued that Head Start had failed and that, notwithstanding the historical effect of environmental factors, African American underperformance had a genetic basis. In the UK H.J. Eysenck took up the cudgels on his behalf, although how far Eysenck himself accepted race differences in any essentialist sense remains ambiguous. A replay of the 1930s match ensued, but with a much narrower focus: only intelligence was discussed and the debate was virtually restricted to US white vs African American performance. While some geneticists tightened up the counter-arguments, in some ways the controversy suffered by conflating issues of different kinds: theoretical (heritability of IQ being the principal red herring), methodological, political and moral arguments became inextricable. By the end of the 1970s it had simmered down only to receive further airing in the context of the sociobiology approach emerging in evolutionary biology. Many of the old arguments were still basically unanswered, while eminent geneticists (like R.C. Lewontin) and biologists (like Stephen Jay Gould) produced new ones. Again the issue subsided, but remained undead, J.P. Rushton (1994) and Herrnstein and Murray (1994) briefly resuscitating it in the mid-1990s. Among mainstream journals only *Intelligence* now appears willing to continue giving the topic a sympathetic airing. The publicity the issue receives is grossly disproportionate to its importance within Psychology. It directly involves only a small minority of psychometricians, while for most psychologists it is simply not a meaningful topic of enquiry. A major source of funding for pro-differences research has been the New York-based Pioneer Fund, founded in 1937 by the pro-Nazi Wickliffe Draper, and recipients of their bounty include Rushton ($656,672 from 1982–1992), Richard Lynn ($388,187) and Jensen ($108,994). One is bound to conclude that the persistence of this controversy owes more to domestic US politics than it does to anything else, and it is worth stressing that, despite a small body of research from further afield during the 1920s and 1930s, 'race differences in IQ' began as, and remains, an overwhelmingly North American research genre.

Elsewhere, Psychology continues to be concerned with racism and prejudice, but the terms of engagement have changed. As increasing numbers of non-whites have entered Psychology the running is being made not by white academics but by those on the receiving end, racism and gender studies fusing in this respect (A. Mama, 1995). Attention now typically focuses on such topics as children's perceptions of ethnicity and gender-identity formation in ethnic minority groups rather than 'race prejudice' as once simplistically conceived. We currently face two dilemmas here. Firstly, viewing racism as a psychological issue may divert attention from other levels of analysis which are actually more relevant. Ascribing problems to psychological flaws in human nature rather than economic policies or institutional and social structures can let those responsible off the hook. Psychologists are sometimes too prone to being lured into playing this role. Secondly, 'race' is a myth, but identification with one's ethnic or cultural group (still inescapably racially characterised in western culture whatever the labels) is a central and necessary tactic in achieving liberatory aims. Imposed categories have to be adopted, redefined and revalued by those labelled as belonging to them before they can be transcended. How we resolve this dilemma is not something I can deal with here, even if I knew how (which I do not) but I would observe that the terms used for discussing the issue have become largely obsolete and misleading ('race', 'ethnicity', 'community', 'culture' and 'multicultural' for example). Certainly as far as Britain is concerned they are quite inadequate to capture the complex reality: not all people with some physically obvious non-European ancestry live in identifiable 'ethnic communities' or have life-styles 'culturally' distinct from their white peers, let alone one single identifiable 'racial' identity. This linguistic difficulty clearly needs resolving. Table 21.1 summarises the kinds of involvement Psychology has had with 'race' issues.

To conclude, Psychology has both promoted and opposed racist policies and attitudes, more often, on balance, the latter. In focusing on the US-centred Race Psychology and 'race and IQ' stories the preceding sketch omits some interesting and important facets of the topic, for example the inter-war mainland European fascination with the notion of 'primitive mind' (expounded by L. Lévy-Bruhl) and its relationship to Freudian and especially Jungian theorising about the unconscious. The Nazi version of Race Psychology promulgated by, among others, E.R. Jaensch,

Table 21.1 Major genres in which Psychology has been involved in 'race' issues

- *Race differences* Has received most publicity and generated most controversy, primarily in relation to alleged IQ differences. Actual research has always been centred in the US and, since c. 1940, focused primarily on US white vs African American differences.
- *Anti-race differences* Attacks on the former of numerous kinds.
- *Race prejudice and racism* A major theme in Social Psychology since the 1930s, more widespread than *Race differences* work, including much on anti-Semitism during the mid-20th century.
- *Educational and other applied Psychology work on, with or by ethnic minorities* Initially emerged in the US in fields such as social work, now a major research area in many countries. Generally anti-racist, in aspiration at least.
- *'Culture and Personality' School* Flourished from 1930s to 1950s in work by US anthropologists, often influenced by psychoanalytic theory. Anti-racist in principle but in its later work sometimes somewhat ambiguous.
- *Social Psychological work on group-relations* A major topic in post-World War Two Social Psychology both in the US and Europe.
- *Genetics of colour-blindness, PTC taste-blindess* and Down's syndrome* A minor theme with no clearcut racist connotations.
- *Epidemiology of mental illness* A longstanding theme in the US and also elsewhere since the 1930s. Eventually tended towards anti-racism but often ambiguous in this respect.
- *'Primitive mind' theories* Common in the 19th century and in mainland Europe during the early 20th century, major figures being L. Lévy-Bruhl and C.G. Jung. Now effectively defunct.

* phenyl-thio-carbamide

L.F. Clauss and B. Petermann and British responses to the issue have also been left undiscussed.

Despite the marginalisation of explicitly racist positions the rosiness of the contemporary Psychological garden should not be overstated (see e.g. D. Howitt and J. Owusu-Bempah, 1994; J. Owusu-Bempah and D. Howitt, 1994). As a discipline, Psychology is, for the most part, now clearly opposed to racism, but as far as racism *within* the discipline is concerned the temptation of professional organisations in the US and, to some extent in Britain, has been to deny it rather than confront it. Eliminating racism at the level of organisational and disciplinary practice is indeed a hard task. Insofar as racism continues to operate (wittingly or not) in the institutions and organisations within, and for which, psychologists work the task will remain unfinished. Moreover, white psychologists have still not entirely succeeded in abandoning expressions and assumptions with racist, or at least Eurocentric, connotations. The term 'tribal', for example, is currently causing some difficulty since it is most often used of non-European and primate groups, whereas 'clan' and 'nation' are typically used in European contexts. It would be churlish to deny that a vast sea-change has occurred since 1960, but even in the new post-millennial cultural climate the 'race differences' issue remains unburied, for all the efforts of most professional psychologists.

Additional points

1. There is a notion abroad that 'ethnic' is related to 'heathen', leading some to object to its use in phrases such as 'ethnic minority'. The 2nd edition of the *Oxford English Dictionary* notes this belief and rejects it.
2. The ethics of race-differences research is, it is now recognised, quite problematic. While proponents invoke the 'academic freedom' argument, this may be countered by the argument that the rights of ethnic minority colleagues and, more importantly, the subjects in such research are of equal weight (e.g. data on ethnic minority children should not be used by researchers concerned to demonstrate their inferiority).

Further reading

Barkan, E. (1992) *The Retreat of Scientific Racism: Changing Concepts of Race in Britain and the United States between the World Wars.* Cambridge: Cambridge University Press. Helpful, but deals primarily with biology and anthropology.

Biddis, M.D. (ed.) (1979) *Images of Race.* Leicester: Leicester University Press. Extracts from British writers (including Herbert Spencer), 1864–1880.

Goldberg, D.T. (1993) *Racist Culture: Philosophy and the Politics of Meaning.* Oxford: Blackwell. Crucial reading, but stylistically difficult.

Guthrie, R.V. (1976, 2nd edn 1998) *Even the Rat Was White. A Historical View of Psychology.* Boston: Allyn & Bacon. Written from an African American standpoint this was a landmark text when it first appeared. The second edition has been considerably expanded and includes a survey of the careers of eminent African American psychologists.

Howitt, D. and Owusu-Bempah, J. (1994) *The Racism of Psychology: Time for a Change.* New York: Harvester-Wheatsheaf. A scathing survey of the various racist tendencies within the discipline although the tension between scholarly subtlety and polemical Manicheism is not really resolved.

Kovel, J. (1970, new edn 1988) *White Racism: A Psychohistory.* London: Allen Lane. A challenging psychoanalytic interpretation of the issue.

Mama, A. (1995) *Beyond the Masks: Race, Gender and Subjectivity.* London: Routledge.

Richards, G. (1997) *'Race', Racism and Psychology: Towards a Reflexive History.* London: Routledge. An attempt at a systematic historical appraisal.

Samelson, F. (1978) 'From Race Psychology to Studies in Prejudice'. *Journal of the History of the Behavioral Sciences* 14: 265–278.

Stepan, N. (1982) *The Idea of Race in Science: Great Britain 1800–1960.* Hamden, CT: Archon Books.

Tucker, W.H. (1994) *The Science and Politics of Racial Research.* Urbana & Chicago: University of Illinois Press. An invaluable investigation into the political and ideological linkages of race differences research in the US.

Scientific racism and nineteenth-century background

Beddoe, J. (1885, rep. 1971) *The Races of Britain. A Contribution to the Anthropology of Western Europe*. London: Hutchinson.

Galton, F. (1869, rep. 1962) *Hereditary Genius*. London: Collins Fontana.

Hunt, J. (1865) 'On the Negro's Place in Nature'. In *Memoirs Read before the Anthropological Society of London 1863–4*. London: Trübner, 1–64. A key 'scientific racism' text.

Le Bon, G. (1899) *The Psychology of Peoples*. London: Fisher Unwin.

Prichard, J.C. (1813, 3rd edn 1836) *Researches into the Physical History of Mankind* (2 vols). London: Sherwood, Gilbert & Piper.

Spencer, H. (1876) 'The Comparative Psychology of Man'. Rep. in M.D. Biddis (ed.) (1979) *Images of Race*. Leicester: Leicester University Press, 187–204.

Race Psychology and its critics

Benedict, Ruth (1943) *Race and Racism*. London: Scientific Book Club.

Brigham, C.C. (1923) *A Study of American Intelligence*. Princeton: Princeton University Press.

Bruner, F.G. (1908) 'The Hearing of Primitive Peoples'. *Archives of Psychology* 11, New York: Science Press.

Ferguson, George Oscar Jr (1916) 'The Psychology of the Negro. An Experimental Study'. *Archives of Psychology* 36, New York: Science Press.

Garth, T.R. (1931) *Race Psychology*. New York: Whittlesey.

Hall, G.S. (1904) *Adolescence* (2 vols). New York: Appleton. See the last chapter of vol. 2.

Klineberg, O. (1935) *Race Differences*. New York: Harper.

Mayo, M.J. (1913) 'The Mental Capacity of the American Negro'. *Archives of Psychology*, Monograph 28.

McDougall, W. (1921) *Is America Safe for Democracy?* (Published in the UK as *National Welfare and National Decay*). London: Methuen.

Mead, M., Dobzhansky, T., Tobach, E. and Light, R.E. (eds) (1968) *Science and the Concept of Race*. New York: Columbia University Press.

Montagu, M.A.F. (1942, 5th edn 1974) *Man's Most Dangerous Myth: The Fallacy of Race*. Oxford: Oxford University Press.

Odum, H.W. (1910) *Social and Mental Traits of the Negro: Research into the Conditions of the Negro in Southern Towns*. New York: Columbia University Press.

Porteus, S.D. (with M.E. Babcock) (1926) *Race and Temperament*. Boston: Badger.

Richards, G. (1998) 'Rethinking Race Psychology: Thomas Russell Garth 1872–1939. The Race Psychologist who Changed his Mind'. *Journal of the History of the Behavioral Sciences* 34(1): 15–32.

Rivers, W.H.R., Myers, C.S. and McDougall, W. (1901, 1903) *Reports of the Cambridge Anthropological Expedition to Torres Straits. Volume 2: Physiology and Psychology*. Cambridge: Cambridge University Press. (Generally catalogued as edited by A.C. Haddon.)

Strong, A.M. (1913) 'Three Hundred and Fifty White and Colored Children Measured by the Binet–Simon Measuring Scale'. *Pedagogical Seminary* 20: 485–512.

Woodworth, R.S. (1910) 'Racial Differences in Mental Traits'. *Science* N.S. 31: 171–186.

Prejudice

A vast topic, these are some founding texts only.

Ackermann, N.W. and Jahoda, M. (1950) *Anti-Semitism and Emotional Disorder: A Psychoanalytic Interpretation*. New York: Harper.

Adorno, T.W., Frenkl-Brunswik, E., Levinson, D.J. and Sanford, R.N. (1950) *The Authoritarian Personality* (2 vols). New York: Science Editions.

Allport, G.W. (1954) *The Nature of Prejudice*. Reading, MA: Addison-Wesley.

Benedict, R. (1943) *Race and Racism*. London: Labour Book Service.

Bettelheim, B. and Janowitz, M. (1950) *Dynamics of Prejudice: A Psychological and Sociological Study of Veterans*. New York: Harper & Brothers.

Dollard, N. (1937, rep. 1957) *Caste and Class in a Southern Town*. New York: Doubleday Anchor.

Fenichel, O. (1940) 'Psychoanalysis of Antisemitism'. *American Imago* 1(2): 24–39.

'Culture & Personality' school

Benedict, R. (1935, rep. 1966) *Patterns of Culture*. London: Routledge & Kegan Paul.

Dennis, W. (1940) *The Hopi Child*. New York: Appleton-Century.

Erikson, E.H. (1950, rev. edn 1965) *Childhood and Society*. Harmondsworth: Penguin.

Kluckhohn, C. and Murray, H.A. (eds) (1948, rep. 1949) *Personality in Nature, Society and Culture*. London: Cape.

Mead, M. (1928) *Coming of Age in Samoa*. New York: Morrow.

Mead, M. (1930) *Growing Up in New Guinea*. New York: Morrow.

Post-1969 'race' and IQ controversy

There is a vast amount on this, the following is a basic list only.

Pro-differences

Jensen, A. (1969) 'How Much can we Boost IQ and Scholastic Achievement?' *Harvard Educational Review* Reprint Series 2. This reprint includes Jensen's paper and responses.

Herrnstein, C. and Murray, R.J. (1994) *The Bell Curve: Intelligence and Class Structure in American Life*. New York: Free Press.
Rushton, J.P. (1994) *Race, Evolution and Behavior*. New York: Transaction.

Anti-differences

Block, N. and Dworkin, G. (eds) (1977) *The IQ Controversy: Critical Readings*. New York: Pantheon. Contains several major theoretical critiques of race-differences theories.
Fraser, S. (ed.) (1995) *The Bell Curve Wars: Race, Intelligence, and the Future of America*. New York: Basic Books.
Gould, S.J. (1981, rep. 1984) *The Mismeasure of Man*. London: Penguin.
Kamin, L.J. (1974) *The Science and Politics of I.Q.* New York: Erlbaum.
Richards, G.D. (1984) 'Getting the Intelligence Controversy Knotted'. *Bulletin of the British Psychological Society* 37: 77–79.
Rose, S., Kamin, L.J. and Lewontin, R.C. (1984) *Not in Our Genes*. Harmondsworth: Penguin.

Black Psychology

Cross, W.E. (1991) *Shades of Black: Diversity in African American Identity*. Madison WI: Wisconsin University Press.
Jones, R.L. (ed.) (1972, 2nd edn 1980) *Black Psychology*. New York: Harper.

Other

Banton, M. (1967) *Race Relations*. London: Tavistock.
Banton, M. and Harwood, J. (1975) *The Race Concept*. Newton Abbot: David & Charles.
Bolt, C. (1971) *Victorian Attitudes to Race*. London: Routledge & Kegan Paul.
Curtin, P.D. (1964) *The Image of Africa. British Ideas and Action, 1780–1850*. Madison WI: The University of Wisconsin Press.
Galloway, F.J. (1994) 'Inferential Fragility and the Army Alpha: A New Look at the Robustness of Educational Quality Indices as Determinants of Inter-state Black–white Score Differentials'. *Journal of Negro Education* 63(2): 251–266.
Grant, M. (1916) *The Passing of the Great Race*. New York: Scribner.
Haller, J.S. Jr (1971) *Outcasts of Evolution. Scientific Attitudes of Racial Inferiority 1859–1900*. Urbana: University of Illinois Press. See especially Chapter 5 on Spencer's influence.
Jordan, W.D. (1974) *The White Man's Burden: Historical Origins of Racism in the United States*. London: Oxford University Press.
Lorimer, D.A. (1978) *Colour, Class and the Victorians' English attitudes to the Negro in the Mid-nineteenth Century*. Leicester: Leicester University Press.

Owusu-Bempah, J. and Howitt, D. (1994) 'Racism and the Psychological Textbook'. *The Psychologist* 7(4): 163–167. See also the correspondence in subsequent issues.

Shyllon, F.O. (1977) *Black People in Britain 1555–1833*. London: Oxford University Press.

Stocking, G.W. Jr (1968) *Race, Culture and Evolution: Essays in the History of Anthropology*. New York: Free Press.

Winston, A. (1996) '"As his name indicates": R.S. Woodworth's Letters of Reference and Employment for Jewish Psychologists in the 1930s'. *Journal of the History of the Behavioral Sciences* 32: 30–43.

Chapter 22

Psychology and war

- Pervasiveness of war as a contextual factor affecting Psychology
- The two kinds of engagement of Psychology with war and military issues
- Significance of the Second World War for Psychology: N. Rose's argument
- General discussion of issues raised

Since 1914 Psychology has generally been practised in contexts dominated by war, either as a current, recent or prospective reality. Unsurprisingly then this has left a deep imprint on the discipline. War presents Psychology with a dilemma. The majority, if not quite all, modern psychologists accept that war is an evil pathology (particularly in its current forms). This being so their task should, presumably, be to diagnose its psychological roots. Such principled opposition to war is nevertheless offset by the fact that most (if again not quite all) psychologists, no less than anyone else, usually feel bound to support the war efforts of their host societies. Psychologists have been called upon increasingly to deploy their professional skills in such tasks as selection and training, propaganda and designing military technology. Perennially status-conscious, they have often welcomed the opportunities war offers for forging links with other, 'harder', disciplines. Wartime provides abundant scientific funding and research opportunities, and Psychology, like other disciplines, has had few inhibitions in exploiting these. This does not imply cynicism; in the final analysis the psychologist's own fundamental identification is generally with national war aims. If the roots of the conflict appear to lie in the psychological character of the enemy, then the implicit dilemma between cure and combat is easily evaded. Since the First World War psychologists have also become clinically involved in the treatment of those suffering war-related mental disturbances of various kinds, primarily though not exclusively military personnel traumatised by combat, victims of 'shell-shock' or 'combat fatigue' (categories which were of course created by psychologists undertaking this work, although an ancestral condition, 'cannon-ball wind', was known from the early nineteenth century).

The involvements of Psychology with war can, therefore, initially be seen as of two basic kinds.

1. Disciplinary cooperation with war aims and military tasks in general. This would include treating 'shell-shock' (in the United Kingdom) and the United States Army intelligence tests during the First World War; continuing studies during the Second World War of 'combat fatigue'; research on perception, instrument design and other psychological aspects of aviation in the context of air warfare (which has continued ever since); involvements with training and selection; a long-standing interest in propaganda, and post-Second World War social Psychological studies of leadership and group dynamics. By the Second World War a subdiscipline called 'Military Psychology' had emerged in the United States (e.g. N.C. Meier, 1943), applying Psychology for military purposes. As U. Geuter (1992) shows, the demands of *Wehrmachtpsychologie* in the 1930s were crucial in professionalising German Psychology (see Chapter 13), as were the 1917–1918 Army tests for United States Psychology (F. Samelson, 1979). During the early Cold War phase a vast amount of Psychological research was funded by various defence agencies into such topics as the psychological aspects of aviation (e.g. radar research at the Johns Hopkins Psychological Laboratory and numerous defence-related studies at the Applied Psychology Research Unit in Cambridge, UK). This extensive and well-financed corpus of research has remained largely invisible as far as Psychology's public face is concerned

and is rarely mentioned in texbooks, the results often appearing only in classified or restricted research report form (Fig. 22.1). And yet Psychology's martial face is hardly a secret – the APA's Section 19 Military Psychology website provides a proud history of its achievements and also notes that the military sector is the largest single employer of psychologists.

2. Attempts at diagnosing the psychological roots of war, accepting this as in some sense pathological. These have taken several approaches including traditional instinct theory (Wilfred Trotter, 1916), Freudian (Ernest Glover, 1933), Jungian (Anthony Stevens, 1990), behaviourist (E.C. Tolman, 1942) and ethological (Konrad Lorenz, 1966). T.H. Pear (ed.) (1950) also presents further viewpoints, while the research on various psychological aspects of the effects of nuclear weapon deployment during the mid-1980's Cold War crisis can perhaps be included here. Two points about these should be made immediately. First, it may well be that seeking psychological explanations for war is inappropriate or at least inadequate, but psychologists have invariably concurred with John F. Kennedy's view that 'war begins in the hearts of men'. As we saw in the 'racism' case, Psychology risks being used to divert attention from economic or social-structural level causes. If war arises from a tragic flaw in human nature 'we are all guilty', which translates in practice as into 'nobody is really responsible'. Second, we are concerned here only with twentieth-century warfare, which clearly differs from earlier forms by its hi-tech genocidal and ecocidal character and increasing lack of demarcation between combatants and non-combatants in terms of risk exposure. How far this is explicable in terms appropriate for understanding earlier and simpler modes of violent inter-social conflict is very much a point at issue. R.J. Lifton and N. Humphrey's anthology *In a Dark Time* (1984), though not itself Psychological, is a clear expression by two psychologists of the anti-war values of many psychologists, produced at the height of the 1980's nuclear crisis.

An important work fitting uneasily into either of these broad categories is Norman Dixon's *Psychology of Military Incompetence* (1976), although in spirit it is nearer the second.

Simply classifying war's significance for Psychology in this way is nevertheless insufficient to elucidate its more pervasive influence on the discipline. It suggests that war operates as a contextual 'boosting' factor for certain discrete areas of research, as against other areas where it plays no part. This is seriously to misrepresent the true situation; as N. Rose (1990) argues, war has deeply affected the role of Psychology in twentieth-century western culture. War, both real and prospective, provides a hot-house environment in which virtually the entire range of Psychology's interests are both co-opted in the service of the national interest and, in the process, given specific orientations and social functions. These range from the needs to monitor and manage public and military morale through personality and ability assessment to the more technical applications of expertise on perception, vigilance, human-machine interaction and the like involved in developing hi-tech military equipment. P. Galison (1994) has, controversially, argued that the character of American cognitive Psychology, the underlying way in which it conceptualised people, was profoundly affected by the military context in which it initially emerged, humans being viewed as expendable pieces of equipment or dehumanised targets (see also R. Hayward, 2001). Industrial Psychology has been deployed in managing and organising munitions and military equipment production, psychiatrists and psychologists alike may find themselves engaged in psychological warfare, propaganda and morale-related tasks, while the treatment of psychologically traumatised service personnel has promoted exploration of new therapeutic techniques. Even Developmental Psychology became involved in British psychoanalytic work on nurseries, evacuation and child mental health issues in London during the Second World War (S. Isaacs, 1942; D. Burlingham and A. Freud, 1943).

In fact Psychology's Second World War entanglements in particular largely determined its post-war character in areas as apparently distinct as the emergence of group psychotherapy, the rise of Cognitive Psychology, the flourishing of the 'culture and personality' school and the salience of attachment theory in Developmental Psychology. Since virtually all psychologists were drafted into war-related work in some way or another it is not surprising that this played a large role in their professional careers. For younger psychologists it tended to determine their

Figure 22.1 Military Psychology in the Cold War: unidentified USAF subject in a late 1940's study of the effects of gravitational stress on visual functions. Reproduced by permission of the Centre for History of Psychology, Staffordshire University.

initial research interests and areas of professional expertise, for older ones it provided new, well-funded opportunities for expanding their existing ones. To give but two examples: J.J. Gibson's war-time perception research with the Army Air Force was a major factor in leading him to rethink the nature of space-perception, while it was at the Mill Hill Emergency Hospital, in the context of psychiatric treatment of soldiers, that H.J. Eysenck began formulating his two-factor personality theory and extending factor analysis beyond intelligence to personality.

In Rose's view the Second World War was crucial in Psychology's full emergence as a discipline centrally concerned with what he calls 'technologies of subjectivity' – that is, with devising technologies enabling the subjective realm to be rendered visible and quantifiable, 'inscribable and calculable', in the forms of graphs, scores, statistics and charts. While on this route already (the First World War Army Intelligence tests and less well-known US Army work by W. Dill Scott on assessment of specific abilities had marked the start of the process) it was the Second World War which brought it to fruition, exploiting and advancing the still relatively novel techniques of attitude-scaling, factor analysis and personality measurement.

We may then need to go beyond seeing the issue in terms of specific fields of interest and consider the more general character of the discipline. During the 1945–1970 period virtually every American university Psychology department was at some point engaged on research contracted by the Office of Naval Research (ONR) or some other official defence agency. This would surely have had considerable impact on Psychology's status within the university and its image among students, it might also (echoing Galison's argument) affect the whole style of laboratory-based experimental Psychology's 'culture', the traditional demands for unemotional 'scientific objectivity' neatly fusing with the hierarchically organised macho military culture. This is something as yet unexplored but the historical data clearly suggest some interesting lines of inquiry regarding precisely how far US Psychology, in particular, was affected in a very general fashion by its close relationship with the military during the early Cold War.

From these perspectives the opening dilemma begins to blur, or at least shifts to the intra-psychic level. Even while being at war psychologists (or many of them), are driven to ponder more intensely its psychological roots. This may express itself, as in psychodynamic approaches, by offering explanations in terms drawn from personality theory: the Nazi 'authoritarian' personality projecting or displacing unresolved Oedipal aggression, or, in the Jungian scheme of things, a collective projection of the 'Shadow' archetype (e.g. by each of the Cold War blocs). Ethologists, on the other hand, have tended to view war as the activation of instinctive mechanisms such as 'territoriality'. At a different level there has been a whole sub-area in Social Psychology concerned with 'conflict resolution', drawing on empirical research into group dynamics, attitude formation and various mainstream theories of aggression like the 'frustration–aggression' hypothesis. The British social psychologist Henri Tajfel's life-long commitment to studying the nature of groups and group-relations was clearly rooted in his having lost many of his relatives in the Holocaust. Much of this does, however, beg the question:

perhaps wars, modern ones at any rate, are *not* rooted in individual psychological processes but in socio-economic ones. While 'the hearts of men' may be involved, the purses of arms manufacturers cannot be ignored. This is not to deny that individual psychological factors can be utilised to motivate the 'national will'. Appropriate propaganda can easily trigger what are probably in some sense 'instinctive' reactions to defend the nation's womanhood etc. ('What would you do if you saw a German raping your sister?' was the classic First World War question to conscientious objectors.) This, of course, returns us to the Gustav Le Bon territory discussed in Chapter 12.

The technology of modern warfare curiously requires the very opposite of normal aggressive behaviour for its success: a bomber crew behaves almost identically to an airline flight crew except for some additional button-pressing. Can we really gain insight into, say, the development of the atom bomb from studying the territorial behaviour of robins? Does this approach itself not seem a bit like a 'displacement' activity? Pub-brawl type aggression is actually physiologically limited, the adrenalin-loaded, high arousal state involved is necessarily short-lived. By contrast, firing artillery shells could be just like any other manual job. Can the one really shed light on the other? Cognitive factors are also involved: if the probability of being shot for desertion is perceived as higher than that of being killed in battle then continued fighting becomes the rational choice. Second World War research also highlighted the importance of small-group dynamics in facilitating fighting 'morale', identification with comrades and group pressures to conform playing perhaps the major role in sustaining the 'fighting spirit' of combatants.

Sometime during the Second World War Kenneth Craik wrote 'War is a normal part of life; it has been in the past; those who say it ought to be unnecessary cannot prove their case from history' (1966, p. 176). As such it pervades all aspects of psychological life, and hence all areas of Psychology become relevant. But this does not mean that psychological factors are sufficient to explain why such a way of life is embarked upon. To answer this we must turn to more detailed examination of specific historical circumstances. Nevertheless, it is hard to escape the feeling that there *was* some deeper collective psychological dynamic involved in the origins of each of the twentieth century's World Wars. The First World War *does* in retrospect seem to be linked to the nineteenth century's 'beast within' model and the growing psychological insecurity of ruling class 'reason' touched on in previous chapters, while Nazism was clearly in some way rooted in the deeper psychological condition of the German people. In an attempt to get to grips with this latter some psychologists have sought to identify widely-shared pathogenic features of the 1900–1920 German generations from a psychodynamic angle. As far as more recent wars are concerned, such as the Vietnam and Gulf Wars, the psychological roots would seem more typically to lie not in human nature as a whole but in the specific psychologies of policy-makers and politicians; it is *their* perceptions of the global geopolitical situation and ideological assumptions that (via the power they enjoy to promote them) create the 'realities' in which war seems logical. In short, each war – whether international or civil – presents us with a unique blend of psychological (both individual and collective), economic and ideological or religious factors. When the latter are the more heavily weighted, the adequacy of Psychological explanations is at best limited.

Since the first edition of this book our attention has been increasingly drawn to civil war, ethnic conflict and 'terrorism' – the Balkans, central Africa, Columbia, Indonesia, Algeria, Sierra Leone, Chechnya, the Israel–Palestinian conflict and, as this text goes to press, the destruction of the World Trade Center, all being cases in point. Any insights psychologists may have into the roots of such events are effectively impotent when it comes to curbing them – such insights perhaps only giving psychologists' despair an additionally painful edge. But while overtly the pressure is on Psychology to play its part in helping us find ways of ending such conflicts and ensuring they do not recur, more covertly Psychology is still used to enable us to engage in them more effectively when they affect our own national interests.

To conclude, war has been the most far-reaching and insidious of all 'contextual' factors in its effects on Psychology, reflecting the fact that war has, after all, been the most universal psychological preoccupation (apart, I suppose, from sex) of modern culture. War, real or prospective, has impinged directly or indirectly on all our biographies, and saturates our cultural lives from films to literature, poetry to technology. Any attempt to 'put Psychology in its place' must at some point confront the reality that whatever this 'place' is, it has hitherto been located somewhere within the bloodiest century on record – a location which must in turn have reflexively affected the character of Psychology itself. And (without minimising the heroic efforts of those who have tried) it is hard to believe that without Psychology the bloodshed could have been significantly worse. That Psychology may do better in the century now beginning is perhaps only a pious hope, but pious hopes are, in the end, wiser than cynical despair.

Further reading

Bramson, L. and Goethals, G.W. (eds) (1968) *War: Studies from Psychology, Sociology, Anthropology*, 2nd edn. Chicago: Chicago University Press. A useful anthology.

Dixon, N.F. (1976, rep. 1994) *The Psychology of Military Incompetence*. London: Pimlico. An entertaining and now classic examination of the psychological dynamics involved in military disasters, definitely essential reading.

Geuter, U. (1992) *The Professionalization of Psychology in Nazi Germany*. Cambridge: Cambridge University Press. A fascinating exposé of the participation of mainstream German psychologists in the German war effort.

Gilgen, A.R., Gilgen, C.K., Koltsova, V.A. and Oleinik, Y.N. (1997) *Soviet and American Psychology during World War II*. Westport, CT and London: Greenwood Press. A rare US–Russian cooperation and the most thorough historical work on the topic to date of which I am aware.

Rose, N. (1990) *Governing the Soul*. London: Routledge. Contains one of the best analyses of the topic currently available.

Additional references

The following is a small sample from a substantial literature.

Bartlett, F.C. (1927) *Psychology and the Soldier*. Cambridge: Cambridge University Press. A relatively low key and brief exposition of the role Psychology might play in training and understanding combat behaviour.

Boring, E.G. (ed.) (1945) *Psychology for the Armed Forces*. Washington DC: The Infantry Journal. An interesting compendium aimed at both education and promoting the use of Psychology in military contexts.

Bourke, J. (2001) 'Psychology at War, 1914–1945'. In G. Bunn, A.D. Lovie and G.D. Richards (eds) *Psychology in Britain. Historical Essays and Personal Reflections*. Leicester: British Psychological Society/London: The Science Museum, 133–149. Particularly good on the ways in which psychologists became involved in military training.

Burlingham, D. and Freud, A. (1943) *Infants without Families. The Case For and Against Residential Nurseries*. London: Allen & Unwin. Arose from the British wartime situation in which large numbers of orphaned children and children with mothers engaged in war work needed to be cared for.

Cantril, H. (ed.) (1950) *Tensions that Cause Wars*. Urbana: University of Illinois Press. Classic mainstream American Social Psychological account.

Craik, K. (ed. S.L. Sherwood) (1966) *The Nature of Psychology. A Selection of Papers, Essays and Other Writings*. Cambridge: Cambridge University Press. See the Bibliography by Mrs S.J. Macpherson for titles like 'A note on windscreen design and visibility from fighter aircraft' (1941).

Durbin, E.F.M. and Bowlby, J. (1939) *Personal Aggressiveness and War*. London: Kegan Paul. A psychoanalytically pitched analysis of the issue published on the eve of hostilities.

Galison, P. (1994) 'The Ontology of the Enemy: Norbert Wiener and the Cybernetic Vision'. *Critical Inquiry* 21: 228–266. A highly critical reading of the psychological effects of doing Psychology in wartime.

Glover, E. (1933) *War, Sadism and Pacifism*. London: Allen & Unwin. A brief psychoanalytic exploration.

Grinker, R.R. and Spiegel, J.P. (1945) *Men Under Stress*. Philadelphia: Blakiston. With often quite moving case histories, this report on the treatment of 'combat fatigue' in the US Air Force during World War Two may be read as providing the background for Heller's *Catch-22*.

Hayward, R. (2001) '"Our Friends Electric": Mechanical Models of Mind in Post-war Britain'. In G. Bunn, A.D. Lovie and G.D. Richards (eds) *Psychology in Britain. Historical Essays and Personal Reflections*. Leicester: British Psychological Society/London: The Science Museum, 290–308. Discusses Galison's position in relation to the British situation.

Isaacs, S. (1942) 'Children of Great Britain in Wartime'. In S.M. Gruenberg (ed.) *The Family in a World at War*. New York: Harper. Discussed effects of evacuation on children.

Lasswell, H.D. (1938) *Propaganda Technique in the World War*. New York: Peter Smith. Important early study of World War One propaganda.

Lifton, R.J. (1974) *Home from the War. Vietnam Veterans: Neither Victims nor Executioners*. London: Wildwood House. One of the first, and best, studies of the unique psychological problems of American Vietnam War veterans.

Lifton, R.J. and Humphrey, N. (eds) (1984) *In a Dark Time*. London: Faber & Faber. An anti-war anthology compiled by two ardently anti-war psychologists.

Lorenz, K. (1966) *On Aggression*. London: Methuen. Influential ethological analysis of the nature of aggression.

McDougall, W. (c. 1925) *Janus or The Conquest of War*. London: Kegan, Paul, Trench & Trübner. A curious little monograph. McDougall recommends establishing an international air-borne police force.

Meier, N.C. (1943) *Military Psychology*. New York: Harper. Cited as an example of an important textbook for this sub-discipline.

Myers, C.S. (1940) *Shell-Shock in France 1914–1918*. Cambridge: Cambridge University Press. A laconic synopsis by Myers of his 'shell-shock' work, based on his war-time journal in which he rues his adoption of the term (which had come into use among front-line soldiers).

Pear, T.H. (ed.) (1950) *Psychological Aspects of Peace and War*. London: Hutchinson on behalf of the United Nations Association. Includes papers by Gordon Allport, H.J. Eysenck, J.C. Flugel and Hilde Himmelweit among others.

Samelson, F. (1979) 'Putting Psychology on the Map: Ideology and Intelligence Testing'. In A.R. Buss (ed.) *Psychology in Social Context*, 103–168. New York: Irvington.

Stevens, A. (1990) *The Roots of War: A Jungian Perspective*. New York: Paragon House. War as a result of projection of the 'Shadow' archetype.

Stone, M. (1985) 'Shell-shock and the Psychologists'. In W.F. Bynum, R. Porter and M. Shepherd (eds) *The Anatomy of Madness: Essays in the History of Psychiatry* (2 vols). London: Tavistock. Volume 1. Good historical account of the 'shell-shock' episode.

Stouffer, S.A. *et al* (1949–1950) *The American Soldier* (4 vols). Princeton, NJ: Princeton University Press. A monumental semi-official report on all aspects of the American soldier's psychology during the Second World War.

Tolman, E.C. (1942) *Drives towards War*. New York & London: Appleton-Century. Attempt at a neo-behaviourist diagnosis.

Trotter, W. (1916) *Instincts of the Herd in Peace and War*. London: Fisher Unwin. The most influential early English-language work on the topic.

Watson, P. (1978) *War on the Mind*. London: Hutchinson.

Epilogue

In this book I have snaked back and forth over a variety of issues, throwing the odd opportunistic coil around some of them. In these final pages I wish to try and pull things together and see if a verdict on 'Psychology's place' can be reached.

A recurrent theme has been that Psychology eludes neat categorisation as an orthodox scientific discipline. Psychology indisputably adopts scientific research methods and derives theories from them, but a problem arises from the very nature of its subject matter: does the psychological realm exist as an objective 'natural' phenomenon amenable to the same kind of scientific enquiry that characterises astronomy, chemistry and biology? Moreover Psychology's goals, though often said to be 'the prediction and control of behaviour', patently extend beyond, and in some cases conflict with, this. In the orthodox sciences, however, prediction and (where feasible) control of their subject matters is of the essence. These difficulties largely arise from the reflexive nature of Psychology as a direct, unmediated, expression of its own subject matter. Put another way, Psychology consists of Psychological discourse, but such discourse in itself represents 'the psychological' insofar as it is knowable and meaningful (a text on geology, by contrast, is not itself a specimen of rock). When Psychology describes or explains psychology in novel ways it is actually engaged in a process of psychological change. As previously observed, to talk about oneself in a new way is to have changed oneself. One aspect of this 'status' issue was raised at the end of Chapter 14: the success or otherwise of Psychological theories and models is not determined by the court of strictly 'scientific' evaluation alone, but ultimately by the court of public opinion. Do we *like* or find useful the ways of talking about ourselves that Psychologists propose? Naturally this is rarely a straight thumbs up or thumbs down verdict, as our responses will depend on which psychological 'constituencies' we belong to or identify with. And some are better placed to fund the promotion of those they favour than others.

But this is not the end of the story; modern culture has set as a general condition for all knowledge claims that they be 'scientific'. In this context, to be acceptable, Psychological work must be conducted in a scientific style, involving experiments and generating theories. That is, it must reflect the *scientific psychology* of the 'modernist' humans who created it. In other words such 'modernist' humans really have tended to think and operate in a 'scientific' way – construing their failures to do so as evidence of 'irrationality'. Thus the pressure is always to bring the psychological under the ægis of reason, including our emotions, feelings, and perceptions. This dominance of 'scientific reason' is not uncontested, of course, and is increasingly under pressure as we enter the new millennium. But much of this criticism is, interestingly, couched not as a critique of reason but of a too-limited concept of reason, seeking not science's overthrow but its extension and loosening. Such tensions are much in evidence within Psychology itself, ranging as it does from highly positivist hard-line approaches to more intuitive non-experimental ones. That chronic pluralism of the discipline identified at the beginning of the book may indeed be understood as reflecting (though not fully representing) the psychological diversity of the population at large. In psychoanalysis, as we saw, Freud's apparent dethronement *of* reason *by* scientific reason presented a challenge still with us.

The 'reflexivity' concept may offer us a way forward. Humans, collectively and individually, always face the challenge of making sense of their lives and experience. Unlike other creatures we have no 'essential', distinctively 'human' nature (though we may have genetic legacies of ancestral pre-human natures) – a cat, walrus or sheep has no worries about its identity, it just *is* a cat, walrus or sheep. This challenge was traditionally met at various levels from religious and cosmological systems via bodies of 'folk-wisdom' in the form of stories and proverbs, down to the meanings embodied in everyday psychological language. When circumstances changed, so these systems of meaning adjusted. 'Human nature' is thus something we have continually to recreate and rediscover, each generation in turn testing received wisdoms against its own experience. Since around 1800 the pace of historical change has meant that the gulf between each successive generation's experience has widened (this perhaps reached a peak in the mid-twentieth century). The rise of science and technology being a central feature of this flux, traditional wisdoms were seen as increasingly obsolete by those confronted with worlds radically different from those in response to which they were formulated.

This process of constant recreation of our 'human nature' (also known as being alive) is at the heart of the whole issue. How does it operate? To verge on tautology, we deploy the world of lived experience as a source of ideas for making sense of, giving meaning to, our individual lives. In doing this we to varying degrees supplement and/or replace traditional ideas which no longer seem relevant. What then is Psychology? The broadest answer is that *it is an institutionalisation of this process*. Why did it get institutionalised in this way? The answer is twofold. Firstly, insofar as the 'raw material' for the process came increasingly from the realms of science and technology (as against the commonly accessible realms of nature and folk-crafts for example) expertise in such realms became necessary for the process to continue. Thus a discipline oriented to scientific and technological develop ments emerged, the goal of which was to explore their psychological meanings. This discipline is thus concerned with reflexively applying scientific discoveries about the external world (including the technologies which these yield) and novel social phenomena to human nature itself, to 'the psychological'. While never mono-polising the process, inventing a discipline of Psychology was perhaps the only route by which it could be continued vis-à-vis the increasingly sophisticated and arcane phenomena discovered and created by modern science and technology and the alterations they wrought in our socio-economic world. And as we saw, the event around which Psychology finally cohered as a unified discipline was the scientific acceptance of an evolutionary cosmology.

The second part of the answer is more specifically contextual. The mid-nineteenth-century expansion of urban industrial culture moulded the form which this reflexive process took. From the mid-eighteenth century 'human nature' was assuming a new social significance in the face of growing needs to manage such things as crime, madness and education. A century later this managerial need to understand human nature had greatly intensified. The new, city-centred, incipiently hi-tech and heavily industrialised cultures of Europe and North America required management on an unprecedented scale. A multitude of new governmental agencies fed on statistical data and information on policy implementation. One aspect of this was a need to classify people for various purposes, and for this to be possible they had to be *rendered* classifiable. For example, whereas traditional village society could handle one or two people with severe learning difficulties within its informal community structure, in urban settings 'subnormality' or 'idiocy' became a major issue; as education spread so did the needs for its bureaucratic monitoring and standardisation and concern with the education process itself, and so on. The world vis-à-vis which society's rulers and managers were recreating human nature was the world of their own managerial and policy-making lives. (Further ramifications of this were discussed in Chapter 3.) It was not their own 'human nature' they were consciously having to make sense of so much as that of everybody below them – but indirectly they were also making sense of their own by so doing. In this context the reflexivity of the enterprise, hitherto acknowledged by several philosophical writers, rapidly faded from view. The process became institutionalised in a form reflecting the psychological position and character of those institutionalis-ing it. Such 'top down' forces were not the only factors in play, however, for the pressures for improved social governance to which they were a response emanated from the bottom up also, while psychological confusion itself knew few social boundaries (see Chapter 11). Nearly everybody was seeking new ways of under-standing themselves.

We can thus see that while Psychology's place is the institutionalisation of something the human race has always done, interpreting human nature in the light of its lived experience, its agendas, priorities and approaches have also been deeply affected by the historically specific managerial and social power interests of those implementing this institutionalisation, in a word, their own 'psychologies'. The discipline has, though, always included some for whom this was an insufficient response to the deeper task of sustaining meaning in human life. In Germany, for example, a variety of anti-Wundtian thinkers such as W. Dilthey and E. von Hartmann strove during the late nineteenth century to forge a new *Lebensphilosophie* ('philosophy of life') more satisfying than mainstream Psychology could offer, while Gestalt Psychology's desire to preserve meaning against reductionism was a central goal of their labours as we saw in Chapter 6. (*Lebensphilosophie* was unfortunately co-opted by Nazi-era psychologists such as P. Lersch.) The twists and turns in the discipline's history may be partly understood as reflecting the various, somewhat erratic, steps by which that initial hegemony was weakened and the range of 'lived experience' being fed into the process broadened. Thus in the last three decades the influx of women, non-whites and uncloseted gays into Psychology has wreaked havoc with many assumptions, both theoretical and methodological, previously largely unquestioned (as discussed in Chapter 17 for example). One could say the discipline has become more 'democratised' – something both the cognitivist George Miller and the social constructionist Kenneth Gergen were advocating around 1970. Even so, while it may have extended beyond those original 'managerial' interests it has not abandoned them.

So, we now live in a world where, thanks to Psychology, our intelligences can be measured, our personalities 'tested', assessed and graphically profiled, our mental distresses variously diagnosed as anxiety states, neuroses and stress disorders, our attitudes quantified, the steepnesses of our learning curves praised, and our cognitive styles ascertained. In Nikolas Rose's terms, our 'subjectivities' have become 'inscribable and calculable'. It takes a leap of historical imagination to appreciate quite how bizarre all this would have seemed in, say, 1840, when at most one might have preened oneself on the size of one's phrenological 'organ of benevolence'.

If the 'place' of Psychology is to play the role outlined here, we are bound to reflect on the implications of this for our understanding of ourselves as psychologists. For a start there is the moral implication, alluded to in Chapter 1, that what we say about human nature really matters. If we are participating in this collective social process of maintaining and creating psychological meaning we cannot shrug our shoulders, disclaiming responsibility for how society 'misuses' our 'scientific' expertise. Authoritatively promoting the notion that humans are a kind of computer, for example, will make us see ourselves as such. This may be fine up to a point, but if we claim they are *only* a kind of computer and that this claim has the status of a final scientific truth we are unethically exceeding our authority (as well as being wrong!). In some circumstances it might well enrich our self-understanding to reflexively utilise the computer image, but this should be as an expansion of our repertoire of psychological ideas, not as its wholesale replacement.

Finally, reinforcing this, it means we are basically making the very odd claim that we are, in effect, professional human beings. Usually of course we delimit this – we are professional experts on dyslexia or perception or post-traumatic stress disorder or management training – but this does not dispel the oddness, if anything it heightens it. We are claiming livelihoods, salaries and careers as experts not even on the human condition as a whole (as a priest arguably does) but on one segment of it, as experts on talking, seeing, or suffering. If we wish to continue enjoying such roles we have to persuade our fellow humans it is worth their while funding us. I suggest we would, in the long run, be wiser to try and articulate the reflexive situation we are in than continue the arch pretence that we are but simple humble scientists. I should observe here that this account raises certain difficulties for the feasibility of implementing successfully some currently widely-voiced aspirations for disciplinary unity and visions of psychologists working happily in harmony to benefit human well-being. It is not that most psychologists do not want to do this which is the problem, but that they *necessarily* reflect the diversity views in the population at large, *of which they are a sample*, on how this moral imperative should be interpreted. Their reaching an agreement would ultimately be conditional upon everyone else's having done so. If such aspirations and visions (which I in principle share) are to be realised we need more fine-grained historically informed analyses of what Psychology's places in the social world have really been, and the kinds of dynamics (many themselves psychological) which govern these. The present book may be read as a contribution to this.

So what are my aspirations for Psychology? It should, for a start, feed into everyday psychology a heightened critical awareness of the complexities of human behaviour and experience, of the deceptiveness of much 'common sense', and of the folly of assuming that what happens to be familiar to us is the 'normal' and 'natural' state of affairs from which all deviance is to be viewed as pathological and threatening – or, at the very least, peculiar. But more broadly than that, for me, Psychology should aspire to wisdom as well as to knowledge; it should be about expanding, not reducing, possibilities, about enriching not removing meanings, about liberation not finalisation. It should be a contribution to an active process of collective consciousness-expansion, not a supposedly purely 'objective' process of expert mind-control and behavioural management. If this sounds grandiose, I would suggest this is no more than what, without knowing it, it has *always* been, despite its attempts at being something else. 'Human nature' is something we constantly live and recreate, achieving some kind of 'scientific closure' would be fatal, but fortunately the quest for it is futile.

Glossary

This glossary provides definitions and explanations of various words, expressions and acronyms that may be unfamiliar to the non-psychologist or first-year student. It is not intended as a comprehensive 'dictionary of Psychology'.

Agnosia   Literally 'state of not-knowing', this is used to refer to a group of conditions in which there is typically a loss of the ability to recognise familiar objects or people, or inability to name them.

Ames Room   The 'Ames Room' creates the illusion of a normal-sized person and a giant-sized person standing in the far corners of a square room. In fact the room plan is trapezoid rather than square and the ceiling slopes downwards towards the 'giant's' corner.

APA   American Psychological Association (founded in 1892).

APU   Applied Psychology Unit (see Chapter 13).

aphasia   The aphasias are a group of conditions in which language competence has been impaired, usually due to brain damage.

associationism   The philosophical doctrine that the contents of consciousness are created by associations of elementary sensations according to a few basic 'laws of association' (typically 'contiguity', 'contrast', 'cause and effect', although the last major associationist, James Mill, reduced all to 'contiguity'). In the late nineteenth and early twentieth centuries this mutated into the learning-theory approach within Psychology. The classic 'bottom up' theoretical orientation.

autokinetic movement   The apparent movement of a stationary spot of light against an otherwise dark background.

Baconian   In the early seventeenth century the English philosopher, essayist (and corrupt politician!) Francis Bacon (to whom authorship of Shakespeare's works is also sometimes ascribed) published his *Novum Organum* and *The Advancement of Learning*, effectively the first 'philosophy of science' texts. His approach was resolutely empirical: knowledge was advanced by accumulating facts in a cataloguing fashion. The term 'Baconian' now refers to this conception of scientific research, although during the seventeenth century 'Baconian', along with 'Natural Philosopher', was used in roughly the sense that 'scientist' is now (there are however some subtle differences).

blind-sight A phenomenon in which, while consciously unaware of having seen something, it is clear from other indices that the person has in fact done so, e.g. when asked to guess what they have seen having been fleetingly presented with an image of an orange they might say 'lemon'. Particularly characteristic of some forms of **aphasia** as well as occurring in normal everyday life.

BPS British Psychological Society (founded in 1901 as The Psychological Society).

cognitive dissonance Term introduced by social psychologist L. Festinger (see Chapter 12) to refer to a situation where two cognitive elements are contradictory, e.g. 'I have spent a fortune on this holiday' and 'I am having a lousy time'. Festinger explored the strategies by which we attempt to reduce, explain away or come to terms with such dissonance.

critical history Although this shades into **revisionism** it is less concerned with radical rewriting of history and more concerned with detailed teasing out and reappraisal bearing social constructionist insights in mind. Within Psychology critical history is loosely allied with critical approaches in fields such as Social and Developmental Psychology. The focus is more on grasping the often convoluted, covert, ironic, paradoxical and reflexive aspects of Psychology's history and less on proposing grand new revised readings – although these may sometimes result.

critical realism Identified with the philosopher Roy Bhaskar this attempts to recoup the implications of social constructionism by accepting that the objects of knowledge are objectively real, but conceding that the terms in which they are known or knowable are in some sense socially determined.

empiricism The doctrine that all knowledge ultimately derives from experience. Methods of research and inquiry based on the accumulation of publicly observable 'factual' data.

epistemology The branch of philosophy concerned with the nature of knowledge: how it is acquired, evaluated, and communicated.

Ethology The study of animal behaviour in its natural setting, usually using observational rather than experimental methods. Not to be confused with Ecology, the study of the inter-relatedness of life-forms in 'ecosystems' (though the latter might involve the former).

existentialism Tracing its roots to the early nineteenth century Danish theologian-philosopher Søren Kierkegaard, the existentialist school of philosophy rose to prominence in France after the Second World War in the work of J.-P. Sartre, G. Marcel and M. Merleau-Ponty, emerging from the pre-war work of the German phenomenologists K. Jaspers, M. Heidegger and E. Husserl. Its concerns centred on the nature of existence or 'Being' itself (**ontology**), and the quest for personal 'authenticity'. There is a distinctively dark and pessimistic flavour to much of the work of this school, with its insistence on inescapable and total personal responsibility combined with a feeling that this existential 'freedom' is nonetheless doomed to ultimate failure. It had a great influence on the various 'Growth Movement' schools of psychotherapy of the 1950s and 1960s, most of which tended to give it a far more optimistic spin. The relations between existentialist, psychoanalytic and Marxist thought during this period are highly complex.

Foucaultian The French cultural historian and sociologist of knowledge Michel Foucault is generally considered to have launched a radically innovative approach to history during the 1960s. This is centrally concerned with the history of consciousness itself and the ways in which this is determined by, and determines, the dominant systems of knowledge (or 'epistemes'), issues of sexuality, social power and management becoming especially prominent. The term 'Foucaultian' refers to those continuing this project or highly influenced by his work.

Frankfurt School A group of social science scholars based at Frankfurt University during the 1920s and early 1930s who, while strongly influenced by Marxism, also became interested in psychoanalysis. Gradually becoming distanced from the Communist party line they pioneered research into the complex inter-relations between economics, culture and psychology with great theoretical originality. Exiled in the US from the mid 1930s they contributed greatly to sociology and social psychology (the latter notably in the work of Erich Fromm and Theodore Adorno). The tradition was revitalised in post-war Germany by H.J. Habermas, transmuting into 'critical theory'. The major figure in the Frankfurt School was Max Horkheimer. The Gestalt psychologists and theologian Paul Tillich had close relationships with the group at various points.

functional/functionalist/functionalism This clutch of terms can be confusing. They usually refer in some way to the notion that social, psychological and biological phenomena can be explained in terms of their use or 'function' for the organism (typically 'survival value' in evolutionary thought, or contribution to social effectiveness and cohesion in anthropology). In mathematics, however, a variable X can be said to be a function of variable Y insofar as their values co-vary. These two senses are not always as entirely distinct as one might assume, coming together in behaviourist learning theory, for example, where a response (R) is considered to be a function of a stimulus (S) (i.e. mathematical sense) because R has been positively or negatively reinforced (see **reinforcement**) in some way (i.e. the first sense). It must be noted, though, that even within the first meaning there are numerous variations in theoretical connotation – for example the 'functionalist' Psychology of early twentieth-century American psychologists and the 'functionalist' school of British anthropology are quite different beasts.

Growth Movement Generic name given to a variety of new psychotherapeutic and personal development schools which began appearing around 1960 (and, if less prolifically, continue to do so). These included Gestalt Therapy, Psychosynthesis, Transactional Analysis, Viktor Frankl's Logotherapy, Primal Therapy and many others. A key early figure was Abraham Maslow. Many, if not all, had roots in psychoanalysis. By the late 1970s the borderline between these and wider quasi-religious, 'New Age' approaches had become very blurred. One outcome, however, has been the rise of counselling and the destigmatisation of receiving Psychological help (see Chapter 14). Some critics consider the whole development to have diverted attention from socio-economic sources of distress to inner psychological flaws.

idealism The philosophical doctrine that the world exists in the mind. This has been formulated in a variety of different ways since Bishop Berkeley's classic exposition of the doctrine in his 1710 *The Principles of Human Knowledge*. Although an idealist strand persists in philosophy (and it can be very plausibly argued) it is perhaps fair to say that, on various grounds, the majority of modern philosophers believe it to be fallacious.

intentionality Related to but not synonymous with having intentions in the everyday sense, this term has been adopted by many philosophers as an alternative to 'consciousness'. It implies possession of understanding and grasp of meaning. (See Chapter 19 pp. 271–274.)

internalism An approach to history of science which concentrates exclusively on the internal history of scientific disciplines, ignoring or marginalising social contextual factors and usually (if not always) treating the topic in progressivist terms as a purely intellectual story. While there is clearly a place for such histories they are now generally felt to be insufficient.

Lamarckian/Lamarckism This term almost always refers to the idea that acquired characteristics can be passed on to offspring, i.e. they become hereditary. (The late eighteenth-century French naturalist Lamarck from whom the term derives actually held a somewhat more complex position than this.) This was rejected (though not

completely) by Charles Darwin who argued that natural selection from spontane-
ously occurring variants (or mutations as we would now call them) was the over-
riding mechanism by which evolution occurred (thus e.g. giraffes did *not* acquire
long necks as a result of constantly straining after higher and higher leaves). It is
now accepted that Lamarckism is false, although it was not until the 1920s that the
issue was resolved to the satisfaction of most geneticists.

linguistic philosophy   British school of philosophy (sometimes termed the Oxford School),
largely inspired by L. Wittgenstein, which emerged in the 1940s. This reconceptualised
the task of philosophy as being the analysis and unravelling of the conceptual errors
into which we are led by language. This had an ambiguous impact: on the one hand
it vastly improved our understanding of the nature of language, on the other it could
lead to sterile conceptual hair-splitting of little apparent relevance. The leading figures
were Gilbert Ryle, John Austin and John Wisdom. Most late twentieth-century philosophers have been influenced by linguistic philosophy to some degree.

logical positivism   An immensely influential modernist school of philosophy originating
in Vienna during the 1920s among a group known as the Vienna Circle (*Vienna Kreiss*).
Too complex to summarise here, its key features were its doctrine that only falsifiable
propositions (and tautologies) were meaningful and a highly formalised, rigorously
logical, approach to the nature of valid scientific theories. The first of these sought to
eliminate what it saw as meaningless metaphysical abstractions and pseudo-science.
Ironically, by the 1950s, it had become apparent that certain conceptual contradictions
and paradoxes were unresolvable within the logical positivist framework (particularly
with regard to its view of meaning). It nonetheless left an enduring conceptual legacy
and permanently altered the ways in which numerous philosophical questions were
addressed. The leading figures were M. Schlick, R. Carnap, F. Waismann, E. Nagel,
O. Neurath and later A.J. Ayer, with Ludwig Wittgenstein being an important associate of the Vienna Circle group in its early days.

LTM   long term memory.

McLuhanish   Marshall McLuhan's works such as *Understanding Media* (1968) and *The
Gutenberg Galaxy* (1962) had an enormous, if in the end somewhat short-lived, influence during the 1960s and early 1970s, focusing attention on the nature of communications media from a quite novel direction. Among his ideas was that we could view
media as extensions of the human nervous system. His best-remembered phrase is
'the medium is the message'.

mind–body problem   Now sometimes abbreviated to **MBP**, this refers to the perennial
and central philosophical conundrum of how consciousness and the material body
are related. Numerous solutions have been suggested since the seventeenth century
but none have proved entirely satisfactory as yet. Most psychologists from the 1890s
to the 1970s chose to sidestep the issue or reject it as meaningless, but it has revived
as a focus of interest since the 1980s.

mutualism   Originating in Gibson's 'ecological' theory of perception, the more general
approach of 'mutualism' has been developed by some British psychologists to refer to
the idea that organisms and their environments are engaged in a continuous process
of mutual construction or creation, undermining any clearcut differentiation between
organism and environment (the environment in any case including other organisms).
Leading figures in this group include Alan Costall, James Good, Arthur Still and the
anthropologist Tim Ingold.

naturalising   One important sense of this term for Psychology is to refer to cases where
a phenomenon is treated as normal and natural when it is actually a product of
specific cultural or historical circumstances: an obvious example would be in relation
to nineteenth-century Victorian views of gender-difference and sex-roles which were
accepted at the time as 'natural'. Other cases might include arguments that competitive capitalism, hostility to foreigners, belief in God, and the nuclear family are
'natural'.

Neo-Freudian, Post-Freudian   The 'Neo-Freudians' are those who, while introducing changes into psychoanalytic theory, have retained its fundamental character, pursuing certain issues further than Freud himself did. These would include the 'object relations school' of Melanie Klein and D.W. Winnicott and, more arguably, the French Lacanian school. 'Post-Freudian' refers to those, mainly in the US during the 1940s and 1950s, who, while working in the psychoanalytic framework, introduced amendments which significantly altered the nature and implications of the doctrine, e.g. by introducing notions of 'ego-autonomy' (which more optimistically broke with Freud's basic argument that all ego-functioning was rooted in unconscious wishes) and post-childhood developmental stages (as in E.H. Erikson's 8-stage theory). Leading figures include Karen Horney, E.H. Erikson and E. Fromm.

NIIP   National Institute of Industrial Psychology (see Chapter 13).

ontology   Branch of philosophy concerned with the nature of existence or 'being'. This has been a more salient concern of mainland European philosophy than English-speaking philosophy, leading figures including G.W.F. Hegel, E. Husserl, M. Heidegger and the existentialist school generally. While this may seem to be an intolerably abstract and intangible theme to wrestle with, it has led to profound engagements with big questions about 'the meaning of life' and, for Psychology, resulted in important contributions to our understandings of children, mental distress and personality.

operationism   Sometimes called 'operationalism', this concept is related to, but developed independently of, the logical positivist concept of meaning. The American philosopher P. Bridgeman proposed, in effect, that the meaning of a proposition was how one tested it. This idea greatly influenced American behaviourist psychologists and experimental Psychology generally. An 'operational definition' is thus a definition of a phenomenon in terms of the procedures by which it is measured or accessed: thus 'intelligence' might be operationally defined as 'that which intelligence tests measure'. While pragmatically useful for certain purposes this approach has not proved the panacea for conceptual confusion which its initial advocates believed it would be.

positivism   This term entered the philosophical vocabulary with the French savant Auguste Comte's 'Positive Philosophy' in the early nineteenth century. For Comte it meant an evangelical scientific ideology which would supplant religion and traditional philosophy. Subsequently, as adopted by thinkers such as Ernst Mach for example, it acquired more explicit meanings, denoting, for Mach, a philosophy of science which was resolutely empirical in approach and viewed theories as parsimonious, preferably mathematical, summaries of empirical data, with no meanings beyond this. This laid the basis for subsequent **logical positivism**. It is now widely used more loosely to mean a commitment to rigorous experimental methods accompanied by progressivist optimism and belief in the ahistorical nature of scientific findings, often in fact being conflated with **Realism** to which, in the strict sense, it is fundamentally opposed. Scientific claims can, it is held, only be falsified or challenged by findings obtained in the same way.

Post-Freudian   See **Neo-Freudian**.

rationalism   The opposite of **empiricism**: the philosophical doctrine that there are certain innate principles which determine our knowledge and that knowledge can be acquired by pure reasoning according to objectively existing but innately known (or knowable) principles of logic. Like empiricism this has actually come in a variety of forms. Few, if any, contemporary philosophers would espouse rationalism in anything like its original eighteenth-century senses, and the polarity is to a large extent obsolete in the wake of twentieth-century **logical positivism**, **linguistic philosophy** and **social constructionist** epistemologies.

Realism   A complex notion but in traditional philosophy of science it refers essentially to the view that the truth of a theory is determined by the accuracy or fidelity with which it reflects an objectively existing 'real world'. There are serious difficulties with this, notably that there is no independent criterion for knowing what the 'real world' is beyond theories themselves. **Positivism** and **logical positivism** were thus radically opposed to it. More recently, however, the term has been used more loosely to refer to those opposed to **social constructionism**, thus, ironically, making realists and positivists bed-fellows.

reductionism   Explaining phenomena in terms of lower order or lower level processes. In Psychology this may take such forms as 'physiological reductionism' or 'reducing' social psychological phenomena to individual-level ones. While reductionism has its place it also has its limits such as that certain phenomena only 'emerge' at more complex levels of organisation and, even more seriously perhaps, it implies that nature has an unambiguous hierarchical structure such that 'higher' and 'lower' levels are self-evident. (See Chapter 6 for the Gestalt School's opposition to reductionism in Psychology.)

reflexivity   In essence this simply means the phenomenon of self-reference, but it has acquired increasing importance within the human sciences over the last few decades. This is because it has become clearer that these disciplines are 'reflexive' in the sense that they are part of their own subject matters (Psychology is itself a psychological phenomenon and a product of psychology, Sociology is itself a sociological phenomenon etc). They are also reflexive in the sense that their practitioners' findings and theories apply to these practitioners themselves. There are in fact numerous kinds of reflexivity operating within Psychology, which cannot be enumerated further here, although some surface at various points in the main text.

reinforcement   The presentation of stimuli ('reinforcers') which increase or maintain (in the case of 'positive reinforcement') or decrease ('negative reinforcement') the probability of a particular response. Introduced by behaviourists to eliminate the mentalistic terms 'reward' and 'punishment'.

reliability   In statistics this term refers to the degree to which the same results are obtained from a test or measurement when administered on successive occasions. 'Split-half' reliability refers to the correlation between scores obtained on alternate or first- and second-half items on a questionnaire. Not to be confused with **validity**.

revisionism   While essentially this means only the radical revision of received historical wisdom, it has acquired a number of connotations. On the positive side it may involve solid fundamental reinterpretations of historical events based on new research or approaching history from new angles of interest which cast events in a different light (as many feminist and non-European historians have done since the 1960s, and left-wing historians did somewhat earlier). This may result in casting canonical heroes in a darker light, or stressing the downside of events previously considered progressive. More negatively it may take the form of rewriting and even falsifying history with the intent of promoting a particular ideology or regime (e.g. under Stalin Soviet revisionist historians claimed that it was a Russian who invented manned flight etc.); most recently 'Holocaust denial' emanating from some extreme right-wing and pro-Nazi historians has attracted attention.

scientism   A pejorative term used to describe theories and ideas that are couched as being scientific and invoke scientific findings but which are seen by the person so describing them as purely speculative, baseless or otherwise devoid of the scientific virtues. More broadly, the allegedly spurious justification of an ideological or ethical position by invoking science.

semiotics (or **semiology**)   The science or study of the nature of signs, centrally concerned with the relationships between language and speech and between signs or 'signifiers' and what they signify. This is at heart a facet of linguistics but views linguistics as but one aspect of a general science of signs, and involves broader philosophical and psychological issues regarding the nature of meaning and human communication. Although the American C.S. Peirce is usually considered to have originated this tradition, its strong European influence is due to the French structural linguist F. de Saussure's independent pioneering work prior to the First World War.

sensationalism   The philosophical doctrine that all knowledge originates in sensations. This is a radical **reductionist** form of **empiricism** which was espoused both by the early British **associationists** and the **logical positivists**.

social constructionism   This has become an umbrella term for all those who argue that knowledge and perhaps psychological phenomena generally are produced or constituted by social processes. This idea emerged during the early 1970s at the confluence of a wide range of intellectual traditions which cannot be detailed here. The epistemological question of whether all knowledge is socially constructed (as some philosophers of science claim) is in principle separable from the more specific issue of how far particular psychological phenomena originate in this way (although since 'knowledge' is itself a psychological phenomenon they cannot be entirely disentangled). Opponents see social constructionism entailing an unacceptable degree of radical relativism and even a new variety of **idealism**, incompatible with science. Defendants argue that this misconstrues their claims and that they are only reflexively applying science to science itself. There are numerous varieties and shades of social constructionism, however, and heated debates among the schools so labelled. Some argue from the opposite direction that the construction metaphor is too crude and propose a more thoroughgoing **mutualism**.

STM   Short term memory. Since the 1970s this has been refined somewhat with the notion of a distinct 'working memory', while 'echoic memory' (the shortlived 'echoing' of speech or music) is considered to be a distinct phenomenon. The traditional **LTM/ STM** distinction is now considered a somewhat crude oversimplification.

structuralism   This is an especially problematic term, having been used in several different ways. 'Structuralism' was used by E.B. Titchener to label his version of Wundtian Psychology, in which he claimed the aim was to identify the structure of consciousness in a fashion comparable to that of anatomy. This was opposed to **functionalism**. In linguistics it refers to the French tradition since F. de Saussure (see **semiotics**) in which attention shifted from such things as etymology and the relationships between different languages to the way language operated as an autonomous system in the present (distinct from specific speech acts or '*parole*'). Anthropologists then adopted the term to denote a shift in attention from cataloguing customs and trying to trace people's roots to analysing how societies were structured in the present (e.g. by genealogical classification systems) – for many this complemented rather than opposed **functionalism**. When, during the 1950s, the French anthropologist Lévi-Strauss turned to studying classification systems and ways of thinking he again explicitly adopted the label 'structuralism' and drew on the Saussurean linguistics sense. In Psychology Jean Piaget was explicitly identifying his developmentalist approach and theoretical orientation as 'structuralist' by the 1960s, seeing the Gestalt psychologists as earlier fellow travellers. For Piaget 'structure' has a quite explicit theoretical meaning, somewhat akin to the cybernetic notion of the self-governing mechanism (see Chapter 7), as a self-sustaining and developing system operating according to certain laws or operations which are reflexively applied to their own products. The meaning and connotations of the term are thus highly dependent on theoretical context.

validity   Basically, whether a test measures what it claims to be measuring. There are, though, a number of sub-varieties of validity such as 'face validity' (e.g. a questionnaire about knowledge of athletics would lack face validity as measuring intelligence) and 'construct validity' (the theoretical credibility of the phenomenon which a test claims to measure, e.g. 'oral aggression'). The fact that a test is technically **reliable** does not mean it has validity. Heated controversy often pertains to issues of validity (e.g. in intelligence testing). (See Chapter 18.)

Würzburg School   A group of anti-Wundtian (see Chapter 3) introspectionist psychologists based at the University of Würzburg prior to the First World War who argued for the existence of 'imageless thought' and against various tenets of Wundt's theory. The leading figure was O. Külpe, others being N. Ach, K. Marbe and K. Bühler.

Name index

Note: 'r' = bibliographic reference, 't' = table reference.

345

Subject index

Timeline 1855–1981

Significant events within psychology are provided in the context of world events and landmarks. Most specific cultural events in the arts, entertainment and literature are excluded, although media (and some medical) technology has been noted. Only a few key books are included, usually from the early period. Ending with the creation of the first computer network seemed appropriate. Subsequent developments within psychology are as yet difficult to date or define clearly.

Herbert Spencer's *Principles of Psychology* and Alexander Bain's *The Senses and the Intellect* published.	**1855**	Crimean war ends.
New journal: *Mental Science* (previously *The Asylum Journal of Mental Science*, founded in 1843, and in 1963 finally becoming the *British Journal of Psychiatry*).		
		Indian Mutiny quashed. Charles Blondin walks tightrope across Niagara Falls.
Charles Darwin's epochal *The Origin of Species* and Bain's *The Emotions and the Will* published. New journal: *Zeitschrift für Völkerpsychologie und Sprechwissenschaft*.		
In Germany Gustav Fechner's *Elemente der Psychophysik* appears, providing the methodological basis for experimental psychology. Paul Broca identifies the 'speech area' of the brain.	**1860**	American Civil War begins.
In Russia Sechenov publishes *Reflexes of the Brain*.		
John Lubbock establishes the modern concept of human prehistory in *Prehistoric Times*. The Association of Medical Officers of Asylums and Hospitals for the Insane renamed as The Medico-Psychological Association of Great Britain and Ireland.	**1865**	American Civil War ends. Elizabeth Garrett Anderson becomes first woman doctor in Britain.
		Alfred Nobel invents dynamite.
Noah Porter's *The Human Intellect* published. Galton's *Hereditary Genius* published.		Suez Canal opened.
	1870	Franco-Prussian War begins. End of Franco-Prussian War.
Wundt's *Grundzüge der physiologischen Psychologie* published. W.B. Carpenter's influential *Principles of Mental Physiology* published (UK).		
Edward Cox founds The Psychological Society of Great Britain.	**1875**	Alexander Graham Bell invents telephone.
The first issue of *Mind: A Quarterly Journal of Psychology and Philosophy* appears, produced by Bain and Robertson. William James sets up a small laboratory at Harvard.		
Darwin's 'Biographical Sketch of an Infant' appears in *Mind*. Lightner Witmer coins phrase 'clinical psychology'.		Alvar Edison makes first recording of the human voice.
New journal: *Brain*.		
Wilhelm Wundt opens first Psychological Laboratory at Leipzig University, Germany.		

The Psychological Society of Great Britain winds up on Cox's death.		
Galton introduces use of questionnaires.	**1880**	The gunfight at the OK Corral.
Wundt founds the journal *Philosophische Studien*, widely viewed as the first modern psychology journal.		
Society for Psychical Research founded in Britain and starts publishing its *Proceedings*.		
Francis Galton's *Inquiries into Human Faculty* published.		
James Sully's *Outlines of Psychology* provides the first English-language textbook embodying the new approaches.		
G.S. Hall sets up an experimental Psychology Laboratory at Johns Hopkins University, the first in the US.		
	1885	Death of General Gordon at Khartoum.
John Dewey's *Psychology* published, often considered to be the first US 'New Psychology' textbook.		Statue of Liberty unveiled.
Bekhterev establishes first Psychology Laboratory in Russia.		
American Journal of Psychology launched by G.S. Hall.		Earliest film footage taken by Louis Le Prince in Leeds, UK.
1st International Congress of Psychology, Paris.		
William James's *Principles of Psychology* published.	**1890**	
G.S. Hall founds the American Psychological Association.		
2nd International Congress of Psychology, London.		
Freud and Breuer's report on the Anna 'O' case.		Henry Ford produces his first car.
The *Psychological Review* launched by J.M. Baldwin and J. McK. Cattell as an alternative to Hall's *American Journal of Psychology*.		Marconi invents the radio transmitter.
Freud and Breuer publish *Studies in Hysteria*. New monograph series: *Psychological Monographs* launched by J.M. Baldwin and J. McK. Cattell.	**1895**	
In France Gustav Le Bon's *The Crowd* is published, generally considered the first 'Social Psychology' text.		Becquerel discovers radio-activity.
3rd International Congress of Psychology, Munich.		
First Psychology Laboratories established in the UK (London, Cambridge), both supervised by W.H.R. Rivers.		Queen Victoria's Diamond Jubilee celebrated, marking the high point of the British Empire.
E.B. Thorndike's *Animal Intelligence* published.		Boer War begins.

Psychology	Year	World Events
4th International Congress of Psychology, Paris. Founding of the British Psychological Society. Freud publishes *The Interpretation of Dreams*. *Philosophische Studien* ceases publication, being replaced by the *Archiv für die gesamte Psychologie*. New journals: *Psychological Bulletin, British Journal of Psychology, Journal de Psychologie*. C. Spearman proposes 'general intelligence' notion.	**1900**	Death of Queen Victoria. Marconi transmits first transatlantic radio signals. End of Boer War. Wright brothers fly first heavier-than-air machine. Mme Curie announces discovery of radium. Russo-Japanese War begins.
5th International Congress of Psychology, Rome. First journal of applied psychology (*Zeitschrift für angewandte Psychologie*). I. Pavlov's conditioning experiments first published. New journal: *Journal of Abnormal Psychology* (from 1921: *Journal of Abnormal and Social Psychology*). A. Binet and H. Simon develop first intelligence tests. W. McDougall's *Introduction to Social Psychology* is published, to become one of the most successful psychology textbooks of all time. Clark University Lectures by Freud, Jung and other psychoanalysts, hosted by G.S. Hall, and subsequently appearing in the *American Journal of Psychology*. 6th International Congress of Psychology, Geneva.	**1905**	Russo-Japanese War ends with defeat of Russia. Emmeline Pankhurst founds Women's Social and Political Union (the suffragettes) in UK. Cornflakes invented in US (by J.H. and W.K. Kellogg). King Leopold's personal rule over the Belgian Congo ends; since the 1880s this had caused the loss of an estimated 10 million African lives.
New journal: *Journal of Educational Psychology* (in US). F.W. Taylor's *Principles of Scientific Management* effectively launches Industrial Psychology in the US. Jean Jacques Rousseau Institute established in Geneva by E. Claparède, later becoming J. Piaget's base. J.B. Watson's paper 'Psychology as the Behaviorist Views It' formally initiates 'Behaviorism'. Jung breaks from Freud. *Archiv für Religionspsychologie* launched by Estonian Karl Girgensohn.	**1910**	Sinking of Titanic. Edison admits defeat as discs finally triumph over cylinders after a long phase of competition. Outbreak of First World War or 'Great War'. Gandhi becomes leader of the Indian National Congress.
First Psychology Department in India (Calcutta). *Journal of Religious Psychology* ceases publication. New journal: *Journal of Experimental Psychology* (in US). New journal: *Journal of Applied Psychology* (in US). British Psycho-Analytical Association founded.	**1915**	Easter Uprising in Dublin against British rule. Russian Revolution, and US joins First World War. Treaty of Versailles signed concluding First World War. 18th Amendment to the US constitution initiates prohibition.

J.B. Watson quits academia following a divorce scandal. Foundation of Tavistock Clinic by H. Crichton-Miller. First Psychology Department established in China (Nanjing). *Psychologische Forschung* launched as Gestalt School journal. New journal: *Journal of the National Institute of Industrial Psychology* (*Occupational Psychology* from 1938). 7th International Congress of Psychology, Oxford.	**1920**	Benito Mussolini establishes a fascist regime in Italy. W.T. Cosgrave first president of the Irish Free State. Death of Lenin, Stalin gradually assumes supreme power.
8th International Congress of Psychology, Groningen. The 'Hawthorne Experiments' start, lasting until 1932 (published in 1939). New journal: *Journal of General Psychology*. E.G. Boring's *History of Experimental Psychology* published. 9th International Congress of Psychology, Yale. German Hans Berger publishes first human electro-encephalograph (EEG) reports.	**1925**	Hitler publishes *Mein Kampf*. First 'talking pictures' inaugurate sound cinema. In UK the General Strike raises fears of revolution. Blind Willie Johnson records 'Dark was the Night'. Inventions of television (UK) and tape-recording (Germany). Discovery of penicillin. Wall Street Crash in New York initiates 'The Great Depression'. Stalin now in undisputed control of the Soviet Union.
Berger identifies the Alpha and Beta waves. New journal: *Journal of Social Psychology*. New journal: *Journal of Negro Education* (providing the first journal platform for African American psychologists). 10th International Congress of Psychology, Copenhagen. Berger's EEG work confirmed by E. Adrian and B.H.C. Matthews at Cambridge, UK, who report findings in *Brain*. H.J. Eysenck leaves Germany and settles in UK.	**1930**	In India Gandhi leads a 2 million strong 'salt march' in protest against salt tax and is arrested with 60,000 others. Planet Pluto discovered. Hitler becomes Chancellor of Germany. 21st Amendment to US constitution repeals prohibition.
Prefrontal lobotomy (leucotomy) first performed in Santa Marta Hospital, Lisbon by Egas Moniz and Almeida Lima. Radical American psychologists form the Society for the Psychological Study of Scientific Issues (SPSSI) in reaction to the APA's disengaged stance. 11th International Congress of Psychology, Paris. New journal: *Journal of Parapsychology*.	**1935**	Spanish Civil War begins. Japanese invade China. Sino-Japanese War lasts until 1945.

American applied psychologists split from the APA to form the AAPA (American Applied Psychologists Association). Ugo Cerletti (Rome) first uses electro-convulsion therapy (ECT). Death of Sigmund Freud in London.		End of Spanish Civil War. Outbreak of Second World War. Commencement of Nazi extermination of Jews.
Hans Berger, pioneer of the EEG technique, commits suicide under Nazi persecution.	**1940**	Germany invades Russia. Japanese attack on Pearl Harbor. ENIAC (in the US) and 'Colossus' (in the UK at Bletchley Park) are considered to be the first electronic computers.
Reunification of the APA. AAPA disbanded. Society for Psychological Study of Social Issues (SPSSI) becomes Division 9 of the APA.		
New journal: *The Psychoanalytic Study of the Child*.	**1945**	End of Second World War. Atomic bombs used on Japan.
Benjamin Spock publishes *Common Sense Book of Baby and Child Care*. New journal: *American Psychologist*.		
H.J. Eysenck joins the new Maudsley Institute of Psychiatry. New journal: *British Journal of Statistical Psychology* (as British Journal of Psychology supplement).		India gains independence and is partitioned into India and Pakistan. Invention of the transistor revolutionises electronic technology.
Hixon Symposium: founding event for Cognitive Psychology. 12th International Congress of Psychology, Edinburgh. New journal: *British Psychological Society Bulletin* (*The Psychologist* after 1988).		Apartheid policy established in South Africa. State of Israel founded. First long-playing records marketed.
New journals: *EEG Journal*, *Australian Journal for Psychology*.		NATO formed. Mao Tse Tung establishes communist regime in China.
New journal: *Annual Review of Psychology*. 13th International Congress of Psychology, Stockholm.	**1950**	Korean War starts. First computers sold commercially (the UNIVAC). Ghana (hitherto Gold Coast) becomes independent.
New journal: *British Journal of Animal Behaviour* (*Animal Behaviour* after 1957). 14th International Congress of Psychology, Montreal.		Armistice declared in Korean War. Death of Stalin. Discovery of DNA structure revolutionises genetics. Bill Haley releases 'Rock Around the Clock'.
	1955	
15th International Congress of Psychology, Brussels. New Journal: *Ergonomics*.		Hungarian uprising and Suez Crisis. Elvis Presley releases 'Heartbreak Hotel'. Sputnik, the first orbital satellite. Treaty of Rome establishes the European Economic Union.

'Mechanisation of Thought Processes' Conference in UK. New journals: *Human Factors, Journal of Experimental Analysis of Behavior* (Skinnerian behaviorist forum).		Invention of the printed circuit.
Harvard Center for Cognitive Studies founded. Chlordiazepoxide first marketed by Roche as Librium 16th International Congress of Psychology, Cologne.	**1960**	World's first woman prime minister – S. Bandaranaike of Sri Lanka.
New Journal: *Soviet Psychology and Psychiatry*		US involvement in Vietnam inaugurates the Vietnam War. Yuri Gagarin becomes first man in space. Cuban Missile Crisis.
17th International Congress of Psychology, Washington, DC. Diazepam first marketed by Roche as Valium. New journal: *Neuropsychologia*.		Assassination of President J.F. Kennedy. Nelson Mandela imprisoned in South Africa (released 1990).
New journals: *Advances in Experimental Psychology, Journal of Personality and Social Psychology*.	**1965**	
18th International Congress of Psychology, Moscow. *Journal of the History of the Behavioral Sciences* founded, the first journal devoted to the history of psychology.		Mao Tse Tung initiates the 'Cultural Revolution' in China.
		The author graduates from the University of Newcastle-upon-Tyne with an Upper Second in Philosophy and Psychology.
Association of Black Psychologists founded in USA. New journals: *Developmental Psychology, Journal of Applied Behavior Analysis*.		Student unrest sweeps North America and Europe. Martin Luther King and Robert Kennedy assassinated.
A. Jensen's paper triggers furore over return of race-differences to US psychology agenda. 19th International Congress of Psychology, London.		First moon landing. Formation of Gay Liberation Front in the US.
New journal: *Journal of Cross-cultural Psychology*.	**1970**	Germaine Greer's *The Female Eunuch* inaugurates a new phase of feminism.
Death of Cyril Burt. New journal: *European Journal of Social Psychology*.		Intel introduce first microprocessor.
Leon Kamin claims Burt's data on inheritance of intelligence in twins was fraudulent – the 'Burt Affair'. Computer Axial Tomography (CAT-scanning) invented, earning its UK inventor Godfrey Hounsfield a Nobel Prize. 20th International Congress of Psychology, Tokyo. New journals: *Cognition, Perception*.		
American Psychiatric Association decides, by a vote, that homosexuality is not a mental disorder.		US withdraws troops from Vietnam. UK, Ireland and Denmark join EEC.
Magnetic Resonance Imagery scan invented by Raymond Damalian building on earlier work by Paul Lautebur.		

	1975	Vietnam War ends.
21st International Congress of Psychology, Paris. New journal: *Cognitive Science.* New journal: *Behavioral and Brain Sciences.*		Home computers introduced and Microsoft created. Margaret Thatcher becomes UK prime minister. Soviet Union invades Afghanistan.
22nd International Congress of Psychology, Leipzig.	1980	Iran–Iraq War begins. Zimbabwe becomes independent under Robert Mugabe. BITNET created – the first computer network.